# The Divine CEO

## Creating a Divine Covenant

# The Divine CEO

## Creating a Divine Covenant

### Geoff Thompson

BOOKS

Winchester, UK
Washington, USA

JOHN HUNT PUBLISHING

First published by O-Books, 2020
O-Books is an imprint of John Hunt Publishing Ltd., 3 East St., Alresford,
Hampshire SO24 9EE, UK
office@jhpbooks.com
www.johnhuntpublishing.com
www.o-books.com

For distributor details and how to order please visit the 'Ordering' section on our website.

Text copyright: Geoff Thompson 2019

ISBN: 978 1 78904 424 9
978 1 78904 425 6 (ebook)
Library of Congress Control Number: 2019943743

A CIP catalogue record for this book is available from the British Library.

Design: Stuart Davies

UK: Printed and bound by CPI Group (UK) Ltd, Croydon, CR0 4YY
US: Printed and bound by Thomson-Shore, 7300 West Joy Road, Dexter, MI 48130

We operate a distinctive and ethical publishing philosophy in
all areas of our business, from our global network of authors to
production and worldwide distribution.

# Contents

Acknowledgements                                           x
About the Author                                          xi
Introduction                                               1

Chapter 1: Divine Eschatology                             11
Chapter 2: The Divine Economy                             49
Chapter 3: The Divine Fall                                72
Chapter 4: The Divine Ego                                102
Chapter 5: The Divine Covenant                           138
Chapter 6: The Divine Sword                              166
Chapter 7: The Divine Plan                               208
Chapter 8: The Divine Gifts – The Siddhas                231
Chapter 9: The Divine Work                               332
Chapter 10: The Divine Exchange                          342
Chapter 11: Divine Teachers                              355
Chapter 12: The Divine Shock                             373
Chapter 13: The Divine Pipeline                          396
Chapter 14: The Divine Secret                            406
Chapter 15: Divine Visitors                              413

Conclusion                                               441
Bibliography                                             445

I would like to dedicate this book to all the people out there who are suffering: these words are specifically for you.

To my beautiful wife Sharon.

## I Am That

I am the O in your obscuration
I am inside in the crease of your enemy's palm
I am the face of your prosecution
I am the strength in your jailer's arm

I am the L in your lovers Love
And the beat of the beat of your beauty's heart
I am the fingers in your sweetheart's glove
And the skip when you meet and the ache when you part

I am the fear when it cuts like glass
And the suffering on every cross
I am the reaper at the reaping pass
And the sorrow the sorrow of every loss

I am the blood on the crowning thorn
And the wood and the nails on the broken hill
I am the lance when the heart is torn
And the weight of forsake that breaks your will

I am the L in your hellish lament
And the forces of ill advance
I am the fire when your back breaks bent
And the eyes of the killer with his killing glance

I am the gash that leaves you bled
And the balm that heals your wound
I am the death on your dying bed
And the ruin in the ruin of the things you ruined

I am the king that bestows your grace
And the beggar you turned away

I am the laurels when you end your race
And the fingers the fingers in steepled pray

I am the tally and the sleepless fret
And the guesthouse emptied when you fail to pay
I am the patron who meets your debt
And the kindness in the words that kindness say

I am the kingdom inside your heart
I am below you and before and above
I am your ending I am your start
I am love I am love I am love I am love

Geoff Thompson

# Acknowledgements

This book would not exist without Christ. Thank you, my Lord.

Thank you to my lovely daughter Kerry for doing the first edit on *CEO*.

Thank you to all the wonderful staff at O-Books for their hard work in publishing this book.

Thank you to my good friend Klaus Herold at Watkins Bookshop, London, for his friendship and advice.

Thanks very much to Robert Kirby for early encouragement with this book.

# About the Author

## Geoff Thompson is a BAFTA Winning Writer.

Geoff's first book, *Watch My Back*, detailing his experiences as a doorman in Coventry for over a decade, became a *Sunday Times* Best-selling autobiography. In 2008 it was adapted into a screenplay by Geoff and filmed as a major motion picture, *Clubbed*. Geoff has written over forty books, and has been published in 21 languages. He has appeared three times on the *Sunday Times* Bestsellers List. He is also the author of myriad articles appearing in national magazines and broadsheets, including *The Times*, *GQ* and *FHM*.

## Theatre

Geoff started his theatrical career when he was invited to join the Royal Court Young Writers' Group, in London.

His produced work as a playwright includes· *Doorman* (Liverpool Everyman, Plymouth Theatre Royal and National Tour); *Fragile* (Coventry Belgrade, Edinburgh Festival, King's Head Theatre London, Frankfurt, Berlin and a limited tour), *Three Sacks Full of Hats* (Finborough Theatre London, English Touring Theatre – rehearsed and private readings) and *The Pyramid Texts* (Birmingham Rep. and Soho Theatre, London).

In 2015 Geoff workshopped his play, *Food Order*, at the National Theatre Studio.

Geoff's first musical for stage, *We'll Live and Die in These Towns* (dir. Hamish Glenn/music and songs by Tom Clarke), premiered September 2018 at the Belgrade Theatre, Coventry.

## Screenwriter

His work as a screenwriter includes:

## Short films

*Bouncer* (dir. Michael Baig-Clifford) starring Ray Winstone and

Paddy Considine, which was accepted into 32 international festivals and nominated for a BAFTA. *Brown Paper Bag* (dir. Michael Baig-Clifford) for which he was awarded a BAFTA. *Pink* (dir. Michael Baig-Clifford). *Romans 12:20* (dir. The Shammasian Brothers) which won Best Short at the Arpa International Film Festival, Best International Short Film New York International Independent Film & Video Festival, the Grand Prize at the Rhode Island International Film Festival, and the Long Form Award at Rushes Soho Shorts Festival. *Counting Backwards* (dir. Sean de Sparengo) won Best Narrative Short at the Great Lakes Film Festival 2015, won Best Short Film category at the River Bend International Film Festival 2016 and was in Official Selection for Hamilton Film Festival 2015, Bronx International Film Festival 2016 and San Luis Obispo Film Festival 2016. *Shadow* (2017), Official Selection: Hamilton Film Festival, Maryland International Film Festival, Fastnet Film Festival, Merit Award Winner Awareness Film Festival, Marbella International Film Festival (2018). *The 20 Minute Film Pitch* (dir. Steven Reynolds/ Geoff Thompson) and *Three Sacks Full of Hats* (dir. Debbie Anzalone), starring Alison Steadman and Warren Brown: in competition at the Aesthetica Short Film Festival 2018, official selection at the Underwire Festival 2018, Maryland International Film Festival 2019, Middlebury New Filmmakers Festival 2019 and nominated for Best Short, Best Director (Debbie Anzalone), Best Score (Anne Nikitin) and winner of Best Screenplay (Geoff Thompson) at the Chelmsford Film Festival 2019.

## Feature films

*Clubbed* (dir. Neil Thompson) premiered in London's West End, Birmingham and Paris and was nominated for a BIFFA award for Best Film. *The Pyramid Texts* (dir. The Shammasian Brothers) had its world premiere at the Edinburgh International Film Festival, 2015, and was nominated for The Michael Powell Award for Best

British Film and won The Michael Powell Award for Best Actor in a British Film (James Cosmo). *Romans* (dir. The Shammasian Brothers) held its world premiere at the Edinburgh International Film Festival in 2017 and was nominated for The Michael Powell Award for Best British Film and won The Michael Powell Award for Best Actor in a British Film (Anne Reid). Geoff's fourth feature-film script for cinema, *Animal Day (dir.* The Shammasian Brothers) is currently optioned with producer Ado Yoshizaki (NDF International) and the adaptation of his musical play, *We'll Live and Die in These Towns*, has been optioned, and is in development with producer Lee Thomas (Prodigal Films)

# Introduction

It's 6:30 in the morning.

What a privilege it is to sit here, at home and record my certainties, lessons from the bardo, teachings from my sojourn on this beautiful, wondrous, existential territory we call Earth.

Briefly about myself: my name is Geoff Thompson. I am 59 years old, at the writing of this book. I live in the three-spired city of Coventry in the West Midlands of England.

I spent the first 32 years of my life working in menial jobs – the factory-floor, shops, restaurants, bars, before having a breakdown/breakthrough and deciding to expand the boundaries of my perception and reach for something different, something constant. Certainly I was stretching for a place that, prior to my personal crisis, seemed temptingly within my reach, but frustratingly beyond my grasp.

I was a man with a sensitive sympathetic nervous system.

Let's start with that shall we.

It feels important, and it is relative to this writing; my journey to this book started because, back then, I was disproportionately afraid.

I was (what is known in psychology as) *sympathetic sensitive*. My adrenal-glands were hyperactive; they were trigger-happy, and easily aroused.

Consequently, I suffered more than my fair measure of adrenalin, which is intrinsically attached to the concept of fear.

I always felt afraid.

With no coping strategy in place to deal with the effects on my delicate physiological infrastructure, I struggled uneasily through adolescence and young adulthood. When the lion of fear reared its ugly head (as it frequently did), I was devoured by it. The subsequent feelings were overwhelming. They frequently overpowered me, they consumed and exhausted my seminal

1

energies.

As a consequence I descended rapidly to the ninth circle of depression. I felt like the legendary climber Reinhold Messner, stranded in a tent mid-ascent on the inhospitable mountain Nanga Parbat; I was too scared to go up, I was too scared to go down, I was too scared to stay where I was – at times I felt afraid to be alive.

I realised after suffering a particularly testing depression in my mid-twenties that fear was my only enemy.

Fear was the anxiety-line chalked on the floor, a terror barrier, the fire-and-thorns that stood between me and my nirvana.

It seemed only logical that, if I was to ever transcend the badlands of fear-conditioning and pioneer the new world of my potential, fear needed to be understood and managed. Like a feral horse it had to be broken, so that it could be utilised and manoeuvred and captained.

In the *Tao Te Ching*, Lau Tzu advises us (when confounded by a seemingly unsolvable enigma) to locate the children; once we have located the children, trace the children back to their mother, when we have found the mother we have found the cure.

In other words, if we trace our fears back to their cause, we will find the solution.

If you strike the shepherd, the sheep will scatter.

Viewed from this perspective, fear can be a good thing, fear can be our friend; if our life is a map, then fear is the cross that marks treasure.

My greatest fear (it seemed at the time) was a debilitating terror of violent confrontation. So, amongst myriad other personal, confrontational challenges that I later set myself, I took a job as a nightclub bouncer in a bid to overcome this causal angst, or at least develop a little desensitisation to the feelings it elicited.

The new world can be entered directly through the heart of fear, if you dare turn into it, instead of turning away.

*Blessed is the lion whom the man devours,* St. Thomas forewarns us in his non canonical gospel, *for that lion shall become man. But cursed is the man whom the lion devours, for that man shall become a lion.*

The Christ dealt a coup de grace to his passion in the garden of Gethsemane, when he turned into his blinding terror and said to God, *thy will not mine.*

St. Francis entered his freedom when he embraced the *Leper of fear* on the roads outside Assisi.

And the Holy Prophet found Truth when he returned to the mountain from which he'd run in fear, and stood bravely before the delivering Angel Gabriel.

I devoured my own personal lion by standing in front of fear every night, for a long decade, in the pubs and clubs of Coventry, the city of my birth.

The kingdom lies through, and just beyond the fear horizon.

In human terms, what does this mean, what did it mean to me, what was my fear, and what was this new world I was seeking?

In short, I wanted to be free.

Freedom was my ultimate desire, but it also represented my greatest fear.

There are probably as many definitions of freedom as there are people walking this spinning planet. Some want individual freedom, others crave financial independence: political autonomy – freedom of movement, freedom of speech, the right to vote; democracy is still being fought for today on blood-red streets across the world. People have been striving for emancipation from one form of slavery or another ever since Moses demanded of the Egyptian Pharaoh, *let my people go!*

But Freedom, I have learned, is not to be found in the external life, and if I was to reduce the whole of this book to one concept, it would be exactly this.

You won't find freedom in the world, because it does not exist in the world.

This planet can offer neither sanctuary nor safety; there can be no lasting security in anything material, although there are clues in the world as to its whereabouts.

The gates of heaven are everywhere, for those that seek them.

Freedom is not about working-out, it is all about looking in.

Freedom – the kingdom – exists within, and of course every inner life demands an inner Self.

Until we identify this hidden Self – who we really are – we can never truly be free.

Equally, when you know who you are, you can never be imprisoned.

But you will never know who you are, until you first identify who you are not.

Once you reveal and live in your authentic Self, the real you, and in the process subjugate the imposters, those sub-personalities that masquerade as you, no political, or cultural or financial chains will be able to bind you.

When the internal life is revealed and developed, and the authentic Self invested as sovereign, the outer life will automatically mirror the inner.

*Thy kingdom come, on earth as it is in heaven.*

Hindsight is a gift, one of the modern miracles.

Back then I hadn't yet earned this level of certainty so it couldn't help me. I knew nothing of this elusive Self, and I didn't know what freedom was either, or what it actually entailed.

I had a strong, excited sense that it existed, yes, and that it was available to all, definitely, but I also nursed a quiet dread that, as Rumi had told me in a meditation, *the door there is devastation.* I would have to fall in order *to make great sky circles of my freedom;* in falling (I was promised) I would be given wings.

In a classic Maslovian oxymoron, I was thrilled and at the same time terrified by the potential of being free. Inspired as I was by the idea of my godlike possibilities, I was also rigidly afraid of the godlike responsibilities that came with them.

I wanted to be a writer, I yearned to write, this much I knew.

At the time, this was as close as I could get to what freedom might look like for me.

The concept of finding the true Self didn't come till much later, and even then only as a *happy accident*, a rare gemstone that I discovered whilst looking for something else.

Freedom was the exponential effect of facing down my fears.

I will expand on all this, in the appropriate chapters.

For now, all I really understood was that I had always wanted to write, ever since I was in junior school. When other kids were scribbling five lines in their textbooks, I was spilling out 15 pages and filling in the margins.

Later, as a young man, a menial labourer on the job market, I dreamed of giving up paid employment and working for the joy of the words and the sound of the words and the rhythm of the words on a page.

As much as I respected the pound and the dollar and the fiscal exchange, I knew that I did not want to work *just* for money.

I had been conditioned all my life to put in a shift just for the paycheque, and it depressed me immensely; it held me somewhere I didn't want to be. It kept me in servitude to the 40-hour week, the minimum wage, with a name badge, a company car, the promise of promotion and the distant hope of a gold watch and a pensioned retirement.

Ironically, or abstractly, facing the threat of death working as a club bouncer – a real possibility, four of my friends were murdered – did indeed bring me the desensitisation to fear that I was looking for. It also gave me a wide and a healthy perspective. The mundane fears of ordinary everyday life paled into insignificance when compared to the death threats, and the knife-wielding maniacs that I faced on an astonishingly regular basis.

*The door* taught me to face fear. It schooled me in the art of managing adrenalin. I learned how to absorb and to transform fear. It also gave me the transferable modalities I needed to find the free life that I craved as a writer.

After great efforts, and as many years, I eventually made the transition from the working-wage, to my current life as a professional author, poet, playwright, screenwriter and general all-round buccaneer.

This book is one of the many proofs of a successful and continuing journey.

To anyone out there harbouring doubts about potential, I hope these words act as a *certainty* to the fact that anything is possible; a certainty that you can believe, one you can rely upon.

I know how difficult it can be in the beginning to believe in impossible things.

I do believe in impossible things.

They exist. I am the proof.

They are already there, in situ. It is simply a matter of removing the veils of perception that stand between you and them, as I have done so many times before and as I am still doing now in the practice of making or revealing new realities.

You may be surprised to know that all places you currently think *do not* exist, are fully existent and peopled, somewhere just beyond your own borderlands, in a different density to the one you currently inhabit.

When I started out on my path, I worked largely from a selfish place.

I suppose this is the way with most of us in the beginning.

It's all about *our* life, *our* wishes, *our* desires and the sating of our small but voracious appetites. When I finally became exasperated by this vacuous, hand-to-mouth way of existing, when I realised that lust for all *the usual suspects* – money, approval, fame, accolades, power, *things* – was actually feeding the glut I was struggling to sate, I started to look for more from my life, I started to search for meaning.

This exploration ultimately took me inwards.

It took me into the mystical: self-study, meditation, and some deeply challenging internal dialectics which ultimately triggered a stark moment of divine revelation. It happened during a structured visualisation, where I was shown an undeniable, beautiful but ultimately confusing truth.

I could have anything.

I could literally have anything in the world I wanted, it was available, all of it.

I came out of the meditation and fell almost immediately into a cognitive dissonance. A period of depression followed. I knew in this one, single, clear vision that whilst I could acquire everything the material world had to offer, and realise every physical desire, it would still not slake my thirst. Not in a million years. In my heart I knew this to be true. So (I asked myself) what's the point in having *anything* if it didn't deliver on the happiness it promised, if it was all a lie, a delicious illusion? Even if I owned the whole world and everything in it, I would never truly be happy because happiness does not reside in material things, or in fact in the material world.

I had (knowingly or unconsciously) created/inherited a covenant with the world but knew unequivocally that the world, as I now perceived it, would not and could not reciprocate. The world was not playing its part.

It couldn't play its part; how could it?

It promises security and comfort and control but can offer none of these things, because everything in the world is temporal, none of it is lasting, it is not real. All material things come into being, they are maintained for a short time, and then they dissolve.

Realising this – once I overcame my dissonance – I decided to end my agreement with the world *out there*, and sought instead a new partnership; one that could be relied upon, one that would always and eternally keep its vow.

Through my Christian upbringing, I'd been weaned on the

belief that a true kingdom existed. It was undeniable, it was real, and it was as close as the neck-vein, but it could only be found inside; it was not existent in the world at large. I decided, like the pioneer I had become, to find out for myself if this was actually true or just a remnant of some archaic scriptural dogma. And if it was true, if I did discover *the house with its many mansions,* I would prostrate myself before the Master of the house, and forge a new alliance, but not one that totally eschewed the world of men; rather, one that included and enjoyed and celebrated it as the exponential adjunct to true Reality.

After the poet Dante Alighieri died whilst in exile, he returned in a vision to his mourning brother.

*"Are you really dead?"* his sibling asked.

*"I am dead to this world,"* Dante replied, *"but not dead to the Real world."*

Whilst I was not looking to die in the conventional sense (I was not being called to that yet – things still to do!), I *was* looking to die to the perception of this earthly bardo; the fluid, malleable, illusory, beautiful, magical, perception-built world I was currently living in.

Along the yellow-brick road to my Emerald City, I learned a few truths. More so when I made mistakes than when I got things right, which is a painful if not uncommon method of learning.

I would like to share my findings with you in these pages.

I hope that my *living and dying* will confirm some of the truths you have already unveiled for yourself. Perhaps it will clarify any outstanding confusion you might carry; those free-floating, hard to lock-down abstractions looking for crystallisation. I pray at least that my words will act as an intercession, a *nudge* in the direction of your next learning station in this hard school of life.

I already know before I even begin, that my sharing can only ever be partial. What is experienced can never be fully articulated. As Saint-Exupéry reminds me, *it is only with the heart that one can see rightly; what is essential is invisible to the eye.*

8

If these writings simply inspire you, that will be enough for me.

Inspiration is manna – spiritual sustenance – it is a nourishing alignment that places us on the carpet of proximity. From here we will each get our own personal taste of the Essential, which is within experience, but ever beyond expression.

The true truth can never be articulated, it can only be experienced.

I must also confess that there is a lot of resistance rising in me as I write these words. Energies are trying to persuade me, convince me, coerce me, trick me, bully me, frighten me, seduce me, depress me into aborting this book. They are telling me that my endeavour here is folly, that it is a waste of time, that I am attempting to write about things that are beyond my current knowing; that I am deluded, a foolish dreamer proffering illusion to other foolish dreamers when I should be digging holes and mixing cement still on the building sites of my youth.

Opposition is to be expected.

You know it's a righteous path when you meet opposition.

And when the opposition is strong, you know that your path must be true.

I have no complaints. I am grateful.

Virtue can only be proven and extended in the face of its opposite.

Opposition is the whetstone to every virtue.

In this sense, the enemies that assail me sharpen me.

The Lion that rises in me is ordained; it rises in order to claim or be claimed.

There is always resistance when you approach the essential.

Resistance is a standard house-ghost, it holds sentry at the gateless-gate; it keeps the unworthy out, it lets the worthy in.

Resistance is a sign that what you approach *is* essential and, as uncomfortable as these energies are, their presence is confirmation for me. They are a necessary ingredient in the creative mix.

I am also aware that (an esoteric secret) ascent is entirely commensurate with descent. I can only go as high as I am prepared to go low. If I want to build a high-rise tower, I can't do so from the foundation of a bungalow. If I want to go up, I must be prepared to dig wide and deep and go down. And the higher I am determined to scale, the deeper and wider I must be prepared to excavate. You can't reach the heavens (as the old idiom says) without first negotiating the hell regions. This is a metaphysical precedent, it is the principal reason why so few people do the manual work, and turn their inspiration into perspiration; they desire and chase the highs but they detest and avoid the lows. I have made the same mistakes many times, how else would I learn the folly of it. Even now I get tempted to collect race-ribbons without running the miles, so these words are a reminder to me as much as they are a direction to you. You can't have one without the other. People quietly know they will have to dig through the hell-realms in order to prepare the ground for the kingdom on high, and that's what stops them.

If I am alert – and I intend to remain highly vigilant – I will do the spade work, and when the excavated pain-bodies rise, they will be claimed and processed and individuated and reconfigured into the bricks-and-mortar of my higher reality.

From factory floor to BAFTA Piccadilly, from scarcity to abundant freedom, from imitation to the unique, and from limitation to infinite potential, these are my notes, my revelations about the Divine Economy and the Divine CEO who directs me through the labyrinth that is the human condition.

Geoff Thompson

# Chapter 1

# Divine Eschatology

*Your reality is one room in a house of 100 rooms,* the Mexican shaman Don Juan Matus tells his apprentice, Carlos Castaneda, *if you train with me, I will teach you how to access the other 99 rooms.*

To this idiom I would add: *if you do the work, you can get out of the house all together.*

Before I explore the biblical interpretation of eschatology and why it is important in the context of this book, I thought it might be appropriate to start with this beautiful quote from Matus, inspired I am sure by Jesus telling his disciples that *in my father's house there are many mansions.*

It is important because it explains succinctly what eschatology is: the pre-existence of the Soul and the constant of Potential.

They are at the same time eternally present, and subtly concealed.

Canonical eschatology also presents as a pragmatic methodology for revealing both.

All the myriad faiths, every religion I've studied, have their own version of eschatology. Broadly speaking it is concerned with death, the intermediate state that occurs after death – purgatory, the bardo, heaven and hell – the return of Christ (in Christian and Judaic traditions) and the resurrection of the dead.

It all sounds pretty dark and dogmatic doesn't it?

Not at all accessible to the man and woman on the street.

And depressing!

All this talk of death and perdition sounds very dispiriting, when all most of us want is a practical, working philosophy; something that helps us in our everyday life, with the bills, with our health, and in our relationships.

But this would be to read religious text in a very literal way;

11

it's all about facts and linear causality. Jesus refused to heal a woman, saying he would not *cast pearls before swine* or *give what is holy to the dogs.* Arjuna Pandava fought and killed and decapitated enemy soldiers on a real battlefield to win back a stolen kingdom. Psalms promises that *he who seizes your infants and dashes them against the rocks, will be blessed.*

At this basic entry-level, the bibles read as horrific and bestial; they present as rule-books for daily living, which leaves little tolerance of ambiguity.

At deeper levels of reading (known in monastic tradition as *the four stages of Scripture* – literal, Christological, tropological – pertaining to metaphor – and unitive) when we delve below the surface, we see that Jesus is not comparing the woman to dogs or swine, he is using a parable to explain that pearls of wisdom are wasted on those unable to receive them. Arjuna is not fighting and killing real enemy soldiers on a worldly battlefield, he is warring against the false ego and the twisted perceptions that have usurped his inner throne. And Psalms is encouraging us to bless those of our tutors (and our inner tutor) who *seize* and *dash* our fears against the rocks (not our children) whilst they are still infantile, in order to arrest and destroy them before they become mature and dangerous. It is saying: devour the lion of untruth, whilst it is still a harmless cub.

All the bibles, at the unitive level, lead us, in parable, in metaphor and in allegory, towards True religion; the realigning of man to man, and man to his Source.

When I studied Eschatology, I did so at the most advanced level available to me. Eschatology, I discovered, is not a dark foretelling, it is not a bleak prophecy of worldly and other-worldly judgment and doom; rather, in its truest sense, it reads as an inner map, a divine schematic that can direct us to our own personal potential. And it offers instruction, too, on how to negotiate the way.

The introductory interpretation – death of the body, right

through to the resurrection of the dead at the second coming of the Christ element – when read at the unitive level, tells not the story of birth, life, death and the bardo states in-between; rather, it is the literal story of me and you, it tracks the arc of our lives.

For me, eschatology at its most immediate, at its most obvious reads like a detailed testament of how I have personally advanced and matriculated from one field of understanding to another throughout my whole life. It was my personal methodology of dying to old ideas, old selves, old lives, and being born again into new potentials; reuniting with the Christ force at the centre of the human mandala, our ground of being.

Eschatology revealed to me the house with its many mansions; it gave me access to the other 99 rooms and a doorway out of the house.

Most people never question their one-room-reality.

It is real to them. It's all there is, no questions asked.

But, just because most people are unaware of the other 99 rooms, that doesn't mean they are not there, it certainly doesn't mean they don't exist, any more that a forest doesn't exist, just because an ant crawling up the bark of a giant oak is not immediately aware of it.

Eschatology promises us that *everything* exists. It is just waiting to be discovered, it is just waiting to be revealed.

Potential is always and already here, it is our divine backboard, the Source of everything.

The kingdom is real, it has always been real and it always will be. It is waiting to be occupied; by you, by me, by anyone who can traverse the landscape between here and there.

If we fall into the trap of looking at eschatology too literally, we miss the truth, which is hidden in plain sight, and we fail to discover the arcana that is undeniably right in front of us, hidden from eyes that only see through the conditioned or obscured lens.

I have lived, I have died, and I have experienced the bardo, the purgatory-state between lives, on so many occasions within this one life arc, that I have lost count.

Understanding the unitive interpretation of eschatology will give rise to the growth of consciousness; it will reveal the diamonds of human evolvement that lie right below our feet.

Fundamental eschatology tells us that the Christ figure will return again, and humanity will be saved.

Unitive Eschatology suggests that the *second coming* is experientially individual. The Christ of scripture is not the divine redeemer Jesus who will return to save us, rather It represents in parable the resurrection, or the return of human consciousness.

It is consciousness – where human nature and God nature exist together in one body – that will save humanity.

From this perspective, the *second coming* is quietly developing in countless people every minute of every hour of every day *somewhere in the world*. When people act courageously or selflessly their consciousness ascends, and their awareness expands.

Sometimes consciousness blossoms all at once, fully matured, after a spiritual epiphany or a Kundalini awakening, or a moment of divine clarity, or even after a crisis.

More often I have found it occurs slowly, and over time, by piecemeal.

The phrase *expanded consciousness* can sound pretentious, I know. A pithy, new-age aphorism banded around by spiritual pilgrims without qualification or explanation.

But consciousness can qualify itself easily enough if we demystify it.

First of all it helps to understand that consciousness is all there is. It is the constant. It is the holy grail of scripture, the treasure that every man is secretly searching for. An infinite jewel-studded net that connects and holds everything in the universe together. Except that, searching will not reveal it. Consciousness (the holy contentment) is not something we aim for. It does not exist in a destination that we can head towards.

Rather, it is the quality that we reveal, by dissociating ourselves from (or removing) all the things that hold us back or obscure our view.

Consciousness permeates and nurtures and nourishes every animate and inanimate object and subject in the universe. It is All. Consciousness is always and ever there. Our clear view of it is obscured by our conditioned habits and beliefs. These blocks are what the Christians call the seven deadly sins, or the *hindrances* of Buddhism. If the doors of perception were cleaned (to paraphrase Huxley) we would see reality (or consciousness) in all of its splendid glory

Once we acknowledge that consciousness is the constant, only temporarily hidden from view, we can start working on revealing it, bit by bit.

To understand something today that was an enigma yesterday is an expansion of (your perspective of) consciousness.

To reveal a single new truth is an act of expanded awareness.

If I buy an old house and discover after the purchase that it has a hidden basement room or a secret garden this, in the simplest terms possible, is an expansion of consciousness.

Before I bought the house I was not conscious of the basement room or the garden.

After buying the house, I became conscious of it.

The basement and garden were always there, it was only conscious-knowing that was lacking.

Eschatology, lest we forget, is the revelation of what is already there, but hidden from the eye.

Like the sun, concealed behind clouds, Reality is hidden by obscuration, or what the Buddha called *the obscured view*.

We illuminate what is concealed by widening our span of conscious awareness, thus giving us a clear (or progressively clearer) view.

In analogy: the world could be likened to an inky-black storehouse full of treasure. The bounty remains hidden and unclaimed, until we turn on the light to reveal and claim what was always there, what was always ours.

This, in esoteric parlance, is called **enlightenment** – we are cleaning away dark-ignorance with the light of expanded understanding.

This is how we evolve as soul-saturated human beings.

Those who are spiritually asleep are blind to this reassure-trove-inheritance.

Those who are awake, see the treasure, claim it, and then do their best to help others awaken from their slumbering, so that they too can enjoy the view.

The opening of doors to new rooms can be as literal as discovering a basement in the house you purchased. It also means that we can expand our awareness of what is possible in the world, leave our scarcity behind, and access the opportunities that are available to us all.

I have done this many times. I closed the factory door when I was 28 years old. I opened the doors to business, and art and higher education. I have opened lucrative doors all over the world, and entered rooms that I did not know existed until I expanded my eye.

Eschatology ultimately promotes metaphysical expansion.

Stepping outside of the manifest world, we are gifted access to the mysteries, the miracles that consciousness reveals: the Siddhas, synchronicity, serendipity, shared fields of consciousness, the divine covenant (a direct personal partnership with our Source), the Akashic library or the noosphere (unbounded and intuitive knowledge), the divine sword (spiritual discernment) and the entry to pre-existent freedom.

At this level, accessing the other 99 rooms implies exploring the full human potential, in the hidden doorways of the body, the mind and their projections in the material world. It also promises the potential of getting out of the house completely; the immaterial soul entering and leaving the material body-house at will, and exploring other densities, different worlds. Much more on all of this later.

(In concept) consciousness – realised eschatology – is so easily and readily available it is almost insulting.

People study their whole lives, they devour every bible and pore over the exegesis written by Sufi, shaman and priest alike looking for the answer to the hard question of consciousness, but it is not so complicated, it really isn't. It is simplistically and immediately available to those who have the courage and insight to go straight to it, and see with their heart instead their eyes.

Yaqeen (meaning *certainty* and recognised as one of the 99 names of Allah) says that the Truth is undeniably right in front of us.

I proved this certainty for myself, many years ago, as a burgeoning but insecure student of the fighting arts searching for martial efficacy. Rather than go around the houses, looking for truth in a place where the truth did not exist (a befuddled martial arts community that was mired in denial and obscuration), I went straight to the source. I discovered the secret to physical self-defence by placing myself in a mortally-threatening environment, one that tolerated nothing but the truth. Either your techniques worked on this unforgiving, pavement arena, or you went to the A&E at your local hospital, or worse. In this place, theory, dogma, intellect and martial-hierarchy meant nothing at all. Either you had the truth, or you got a beating.

Encouraged and empowered by this undeniable certainty, this experiential reference point, I did the same on-the-coalface acid-test with consciousness. I didn't take anyone else's word for anything. I knew from experience that theory and scripture and lore and science would not help. In fact the opposite was true; they proved a hindrance and created a confusing logjam of unearned beliefs, each vying for a platform. So again I went straight to the source, and I found out for myself. I placed myself again in challenging situations, I gave myself experiences that encouraged, nay forced my awareness to expand.

You might be surprised to learn that it was not the large ostentations and the grand life experiences – challenging my conditioning (the mores), fighting against institutionalised perceptions, embracing fear – that widened my perspective the most. My consciousness was expanded exponentially through the small hardly recognised acts of loving kindness, those selfless actions that people casually dismiss in pursuit of complication and secrets.

To enact *or* simply witness a selfless act can be enough to turn on the light and reveal consciousness at its most expanded, at its most unconditional.

When the pupil of your inner eye is dilated, you do not doubt eschatological potential, because in that one moment you witness heavenly glory.

I once experienced pure expanded consciousness, a moment of divine love, when I witnessed a homeless man hunting for food in a concrete rubbish bin in Leicester Square, London. This was an absolute light-bulb moment for me. It was instant testament to truths that I did not even know existed before. As I watched him rummage silently and hardly noticed through the rubbish, surrounded on all sides by myriad restaurants and eateries and cafés, I felt such a spontaneous and overwhelming compassion for him, that I abandoned my seat (and my wife), outside a restaurant, and ran over to him.

*"Are you hungry?"* I asked.

He nodded that he was hungry, but didn't speak.

There was such a vacuum created by his silence that it overwhelmed me. I urgently wanted to take off my shoes and offer them to him.

I remember losing myself. It was such an immersive experience that I – Geoff Thompson the personality – was no longer there. There was just this beatific, hungry man, and my absolute desire to feed him.

I became aware afterwards, too, that I was no longer feeding a rough-sleeper in a busy London square, I was directly accessing something raw and profound, something divine, perhaps I was feeding consciousness itself. I am still not entirely sure if he was a divine visitor (more on this in the appropriate chapter) or if I was simply accessing consciousness through him; either way I felt the presence of God.

I gave him my pizza.

He accepted, in mute gratitude, he left a silence in the air that still affects me to this day.

I have to tell you, I categorically knew at this point that it was not me serving this man. I was the one being served. I was the one being honoured when he accepted my gift, and took the food from my hand.

It was him feeding me, and not the other way around.

I offered him finite physical sustenance, he reciprocated with the infinite: divine manna.

When I sat back down with my wife, I don't think either of us realised the full extent of her words when she said, *"Geoff; it will never get bigger than that."*

Mine was an impulsive act of love for a stranger. Through the stranger I was shown that there are many manifestations in the world, but there is only one consciousness, and it works through them all.

Who would have thought; the world is looking to buy their entry to paradise with public displays of charity, and large announced donations to this cause or that, and I felt the full force of Grace, I entered *the garden* with one tiny slice of pizza.

It does not get bigger than this – my wife was right.

On another occasion, outside St. James's Church in Piccadilly, London, on my way to a meeting, I stopped to chat with a young girl – also a rough-sleeper. She was a bag-of-bones teenager, cocooned beneath a filthy quilt, holding a stained and bent paper coffee cup, begging for change. It was December, and she was blue-cold. I felt the ever-so-familiar and yet completely disproportionate overwhelm of love and compassion for her; it swept through my bones. Spontaneously, I offered her my gloves. Her fingers were so stiff with the cold that she was unable to put them on herself. I took each hand in turn, and one by one I gloved her hands. As I peeled the wool over her fingers, I talked to her, and as I talked to her I looked into her eyes. When I'd finally secured the gloves, she smiled at me beatifically. **Bang!** And there it was: full on, full-fat consciousness. An expansion of who I was. A connection to an infinite something that I cannot adequately articulate. Then, I experienced the most startling and emotionally shattering vision; this sweet kid was no longer an anonymous rough-sleeper on a Piccadilly pavement, she was my own child, literally. In fact, she was each one of my own three daughters. I could see all of them in her face; each of my girls was looking at me through her eyes. She was also my son. She was all of my children, wrapped up in one dirty army coat. I was suddenly swept by a sickening realisation, a dread: how am I ever going to be able to leave this kid, and go to my stupid, stupid meeting.

That's how it felt.

That's how everything felt in comparison to the suffering of this one kid; stupid and meaningless. I wanted to gather her up, this child, I wanted to gather her in my arms and take her home with me and watch over her.

I stood for an age, looking at her, holding her hand. How could I possible leave my own child, sleeping rough on a London street to go to a meeting?

Through the eyes of love I was being given a glimpse of consciousness, Reality. I was gifted a momentary peep into the connected universe. Again there was no sense of self there. Geoff Thompson was no longer in the room, just this frail child and an expanded awareness of her, and through her a connection to everyone, everything. This young girl was my own blood, she was my own child, my family – and I could see that this was so with every sentient being, they were all my family, and I theirs. I found it almost impossible to leave her and go to work. I felt emotionally glued to the pavement.

These experiences of entering consciousness are not relegated to just human encounters; I have entered through nature, through animals. I once sat in Leicester Square, London, after a gruelling day of mentoring and entered consciousness simply by looking at the evening sun as it rose in the sky. I was mesmerised by this glowing orange orb that I realised was not the sun. *The sun was not the sun.* It was not separate. It was a part of me, and me a part of it. It was as though I was witnessing a glowing ball of living sustenance that resided in my own mind. It was a familial energy that filled me with a powerful contentment.

On another occasion I experienced consciousness through a bird, a sparrow, or perhaps it would be more accurate to say that I experienced myself in the bird and as the bird. The connection was made, again, when I observed the bird through concentrated attention, through love. I'll try and explain how it occurred, and maybe in the process of elucidation, I will be able to make the experience clearer, to you and to me.

We have sparrows nesting in our roof space, at my home in Coventry. One of my favourite pastimes is to watch them as they develop from chicks in the nest, right through to fledglings, learning to use their wings and negotiate the world in my back garden. I have a fully equipped gym at the back of my house, and on this particular day I was training in there, with the door open. It was summer; the room was stifling so I let in some fresh air. As I was training I suddenly heard a bang on the gym window, then a wild flutter of wings followed by stark silence. I looked across to the source of the noise, and realised that one of the baby sparrows had accidentally flown in through the open door, hit the window (presumably thinking that the clear glass was an open exit back into the garden), stunned itself, and then fell to the floor at the back of my dumbbell rack. When I picked the panicking bird up and felt its life-beat throbbing in my palm, I felt an instant love for this creature; I experienced a familiarity and devotional care beyond rational reasoning. I cradled it gently and carefully out into the garden and sat it down on a safe patch of leaves, close to the bird feeders we had installed in the corner of the garden. I watched over the bird from a distance, until it eventually found its equilibrium, and took to the air again.

It was the next day that my experience proper occurred.

I was sitting in the same spot, watching the same family of sparrows flying back and forward from our house-roof to the garden fence, then to the birdhouse that we had stacked with food. My attention was on them completely, and I disappeared into the moment. Gradually – it literally crept up on me – I became aware that I was no longer watching the birds fly, I was flying with them. I was one of them. I was in the air, I could feel the thrill of flight and the freedom of the wide-open sky; I experienced what it felt like to be a bird, learning to fly. I could feel the very real excitement of actually being alive in the world, and I felt an awareness of the other beings, the ones that fed the birds (us). The experience felt so normal, so usual and natural that it was not until later when I was back in the house that I understood what had occurred. I said to my wife Sharon, *I was a bird today. I felt what it was like, learning to fly.*

She smiled, she seemed to understand.

The connectivity in all of these experiences is an obvious truth. I am sure that at some level we all know it, but perhaps not consciously.

I think I understood why.

Revelation-by-piecemeal is for our own protection. If we were made immediately and instantly aware of our universal connectivity; if we saw all at once that everything-is-everything, and that even when a bird lands in a tree, the whole world changes. If we were shown this all at once, the whole plan, we would blow like a 100-watt light bulb submitted to a 1,000-watt charge.

Even encounters like this, a liaison with unconditional love – and love definitely was the entry point for me – is enough to convert anyone to a lifetime of service.

A philanthropist I knew dedicated his whole existence to selfless service, and it was all triggered by one single experience. He was driving through a toll-gate one evening on his way home from the office, a couple of days before Christmas. Feeling the spirit of the season, he offered the young girl behind the kiosk-glass a $20 tip. She was so overwhelmed by his spontaneous act of kindness that she burst into tears of gratitude. Her state of complete emotional abandon so moved him, that he made philanthropy the purpose not only of his business, but of his entire life. He had no idea that something as simple as a $20 bill could create such joy.

But of course, it was not the money that opened the doors to Love, it was the unconditional intent behind the gift that greased the bolts.

We access love with love.

Love is both the gift and the reward.

We exchange Love for Love, we exchange God for God.

This is why, at the highest level, service is its own reward.

My philanthropic friend recognised this, and said that all he wanted to do after that night was replicate the feeling again and again. He intended to live perpetually in the bliss he felt on that night.

By listening to his intuition, and not his business-brain, he didn't just open a door to a new reality; in one fell swoop he experienced the full and complete force of consciousness.

To experience Love at the unconditional level is not just to expand consciousness, it is to become unified with consciousness.

To challenge and abandon an old belief, and all its associations, to open yourself up to the possibility of a new truth, even and perhaps especially if it radically opposes or grossly offends your old belief, is to open a new door in the house of 100 rooms.

Entering even one new room creates a paradigm shift, and I'll tell you why.

If you believe that your reality is the only reality, and you are able to disprove that belief by opening the door to a new space, it begs a life-changing question: how many more rooms that I am currently unaware of might there be in this house?

What am I saying?

I am reiterating and underlining that everything already exists. It is already there. It is hidden behind veils of obscuration. And love, unconditional selfless service, will pierce the veils and reveal light; over time, with work it can remove those veils completely, and place you eternally in the light.

These obscurations are myriad and varied.

They may be emotional or cognitive – our conditioned beliefs and perceptions – they may be habitual – if we always do what we've always done, we will always get what we always got. It might be karmic obscuration – negative actions block our view like clouds covering the sun; it could be caused by the infringement of the vows we make and fail to keep. A broken promise is like mud smeared on a glass window, you can't see out, you can't see in. These include our vows to abandon all negative actions that harm others, our promise to practise all types of virtue that will benefit others and the commitment we make to tame the unruly mind, so that we can use it to cleanse our obfuscations.

I'll look at this in more detail, in the relative chapters. It is enough to say at this juncture, that realising eschatology involves work.

The path to enlightenment is there, it is just below the muck-and-grime, but it needs to be cleaned before it can be revealed.

As I have said more than once, life, death and purgatory are not just represented by the initiations and punctuations of a human life cycle.

They are just as evident in the hundreds of small deaths we experience every day of our lives, the myriad unnoticed and unannounced births, and the purgatorial bardo that we all experience when we are in those between states – an hour of trembling terror, a day of severe doubt, or a year of debilitating depression.

Every time we challenge an old belief, every time we replace or upgrade or deny a tired perception, each time we very bravely dismantle a redundant cognition to make room for the new (because *the new wine will split the old wineskins*) we experience death, purgatory, and resurrection.

Birth of a new idea kills and replaces an old truth.

When we die to an old truth, a new truth is born.

In-between these two truths (or worlds), we experience the intermediary state, a processing period where the old recedes and the new emerges.

A practical example from my own life: when I first left the factory job to become a full-time, self-employed martial arts instructor, a million years ago, a death had to occur. The death of the old me, the factory worker, the decease of the perception that factory work was all I was good for, manual work was all I could do or that menial work was my lot and I should be grateful for it.

After I left the factory I entered an intermediate state.

I can still vividly remember it, that middle place. I experienced many confusing and oxymoronic emotions. I felt stuck somewhere between the heaven of the new and the hell of the old.

Heaven was knowing that I had escaped. I might never have to work for a menial wage and in dirty conditions again. I could leave behind servile employment, under the cosh of prison-guard foremen, on the carpet of lofty factory managers.

In the factory there was fear. No doubt. We were all quietly afraid, though it was rarely conscious, and it was never acknowledged or spoken about openly. We were scared because of the constant and implicit threat of dismissal; it was held over our heads like the sword of Damocles.

It may have been unspoken, but the threat was as shrill as the hundred lathes that dressed the factory floor. If we did not slavishly conform to the mores and the norms and the expectations of our working class culture we would be out on our ear.

A terrifying concept.

I've seen grown men have nervous breakdowns when merely threatened with the sack from one of these factories. I have known men kill themselves when the job they hated was taken from them and replaced with a place-of-shame in the dole queue.

No job meant no food on the table; no rent money. To the reactive reptilian brain, being sacked was the contemporary equivalent of being kicked out of the tribe, and that spoke of death.

Heaven was being free not just from the working wage, but free also from the prevailing culture of class belief that goes with menial employment and all of its associations.

Hell was simple enough. Retreating back to the comfort of the old; it may have been the devil I hated, but at least it was the devil I knew. Sometimes, even to this day, I still have nightmares about being back on the factory floor, corralled by the bars and doors of those limiting perceptions.

In that first year of freedom I fluctuated between the old and the new. I oscillated between inspiration and desperation. The inspiration of having expanded into self-employment and the despairing fear of not being able to make my new reality a constant, and shrinking back into the inferno I'd just climbed out of.

It took me three attempts before I was finally able to maintain my new density as a self-employed martial arts teacher. Twice I found myself slipping back into the comfort of employed work, where the wage was guaranteed and the promise of a pension at 65 (or 70 or 75 who knows these days) kept your nose to a lifetime of grindstone.

When I finally decided that I would not go back to my old life, I chose the new and I secured my new expanded life.

That opportunity was always there. I just didn't know it before. Or if I did know, I either felt unworthy of it, or I simply did not know how to claim it.

In accessing this new freedom for myself, by proving the possibility, my success acted as a bridge for others, those who would follow, the people that might want to evolve like me, out of their current reality.

Similarly, I have a very close friend who is going through a marriage breakdown at the moment. She recognised that her relationship was dysfunctional and after many years of trying to fix it and failing, she made the strong decision to separate and seek divorce.

She realised that the part of her that'd held on *and held on* was needy and insecure. She didn't think she was worthy of a happy relationship. She feared that if she left this relationship – as dysfunctional as it was – she might never find another partner. Her scarcity-mentality was insisting that *any partner is better than no partner*. But her heart was crying out the truth: *if there is no love, there can be no life*. The needy self had to die (or transcend) in order for her to matriculate and exist outside of an unhappy marriage. The new part of her, the self that had emerged from a courageous place, the inspired self that ended the relationship, knew that she was worth more than this uneven marriage was offering her.

It was accessing this courage, an expanded awareness of her authentic self, that enabled her to leave.

After she left, in the intermediary place, that painful post-relationship bardo, she oscillated between the heaven of being free to explore new worlds with new perspectives and possibly new partners, and the hell of wanting to climb back into the cadaver of her dead marriage. She flittered between moments of high elation, anticipating what her new life might hold for her, and periods of sheer terror where she would ring her ex or text him, usually when she was emotional (or drunk), to reprimand him for not trying hard enough, or to try and rekindle embers of their relationship (that she knew) had already been extinguished.

Like a discarnate spirit, she was trying to re-enter the corpse of her old life, knowing already that *this parrot is dead*.

When she finally, consciously, painfully acknowledged the decease of her marriage with absolute certainty, she was able to move forward as the new self into her new life, without looking back.

This is an important and sensitive process.

I have known people spend whole lifetimes ballooning in the netherworld between one perception and another, this self and that self, unable to go back to an old life but equally unable to move forward to the new.

This limbo is painful but not uncommon.

I had one very young friend whose husband died tragically; his passing was as sudden as it was unexpected. Some 20 years later she is still in purgatory, not dead to the world, but not really living in it either.

She just exists.

She exists in a desert-land of mourning, pining over the old, so much so that she is unable to even contemplate anything new.

For those that see the dichotomy and let go of the old, a new self in a brand new world is born and the next incarnation with all of its many exciting opportunities and choices opens up to them.

In eschatological terms, consciously dying to the old and being resurrected into the new represents the expansion of consciousness.

If eschatology is the belief that potential already exists, just waiting to be revealed by an expanded eye, then consciousness is simply the birth of this awareness.

In the esoteric this is known as **waking up**.

Enlightenment (which is possible for all beings), in metaphorical and metaphysical terms, is the second coming, or the resurrection into Christ.

The first coming of Christ was when the prophet known as Jesus appeared in the world some two thousand years ago; he worked his miracles, he overcame his passions, he was crucified, suffered death, was buried, and then experienced resurrection as the Christ (when human nature and God nature reside as one body). He left his prophecy of potential: *whoever believes in me will do the same works as I have done, and even greater works, because I am with the Father* (John 14:12).

And he does come again, but not as a human personality, rather he returns as consciousness, a fully realised awareness of our birthright.

He comes again as the bridge, which leads us from ignorance to light.

We too do the greatest service to our own children, to our friends and to our fellow creatures when we court the improbable or achieve the impossible, when we escape the confines of class or religion or culture and leave our proof as a bridge for them to cross, in pursuit of their own emancipation.

After I left the factory, lots of friends followed my example. A plethora of people who had only heard about or read of my pilgrimage abandoned the old way and set out on their own odyssey.

Post *Watch My Back* (my first published book), people who previously thought writing an unlikely, even impossible, employ wrote and published their own stories.

We all create a living bridge to potential every time we bravely discover a new room.

There are many heated, theological discussions about whether or not Jesus was the son of God. They have been going on now for 1,700 years and no one seems to be able to agree whether he was or not. But if consciousness is our Source, then it should go without saying that we are all the sons and daughters of God. And when we merge with our Source we actually become the Source, we all become as one with God.

I had a moment of clarity in meditation once, where this was shown me in literal terms. I was lying in bed, meditating, and a state of Oneness gradually, quietly, subtly washed over me. I knew in an ordinary instant (and it did feel absolutely ordinary) that I was consciousness (or God). I was not a part of consciousness, or an element of consciousness, or a representation of consciousness, or *in the likeness* of consciousness; I was consciousness. All of it. I looked at my wife lying next to me in bed, asleep, and I realised that she was consciousness too. She was all of it.

We are all a fragment of consciousness, whilst at the same time, we are all of consciousness.

People get so embroiled in the exegeses of scripture that they often miss the message: Jesus, to me, represents the first proof of the Christ potential in all of us.

He is the bridge.

Potential is possible.

He suffered and died at the hands of the ignorant – who greatly feared any threat to the status quo – in order to leave us this proof.

One man's proof acts as another man's bridge.

It offers a crossing point from dark to light, from ignorance into knowing.

Subsequently, our potential to *"do the same works… and even greater works than these"* has been vouchsafed for us, because one exemplary man sacrificed himself, in order to be the proof. Two thousand years later, his words are still speaking to us, they are still encouraging us, not just to intellectually accept what has been shown, but to put the prophecy to work, and be the living proof.

When Arjuna Pandava, the Prince of the world (in Vedanta), alights on the battlefield to win back his stolen kingdom (consciousness) from his corrupt cousins (false perceptions/the ego), he falls into fear and dissonance. The moment he enters the theatre of war, he loses his courage. His charioteer, Lord Krishna (the Godhead/consciousness), delivers a spiritual discourse (known as *the Gita* – magic sound) to realign the young prince back to his purpose: *whatever actions a great man performs,* he tells Arjuna, *common men follow. And whatever standards he sets by exemplary acts, the whole world pursues.*

Those who live exemplary lives act as evidence, a testimony, a living bridge for those who follow.

That is what my whole life is, this is what it has been about. Hear the proof. Be the proof. Live the proof. Offer the proof to others, those who make room for it.

I know that all things are possible because I have experiential proof of it.

Experience places you in ownership of certainty. It is autonomous. It is not affected by slight or opinion. It needs no external validation. The return of Christ-consciousness tells us that if one impossible thing is achieved, then all impossible things must, by proxy, also be achievable.

Consciousness then just becomes a matter of degree.

If your reality is one room in a house of 100 rooms, consciousness is just a process of: 1) becoming aware that there are another 99 rooms to explore, and 2) developing a strategy, a methodology for opening the other doors.

Once you have proven that at least one other reality exists other than your own – me leaving factory life, and becoming a professional martial arts teacher at the age of 32 is an example – the reality of the other 99 automatically becomes at least a possibility.

For me, it was a small step from proving this one new room,

to opening myriad other doors, and eventually realising my lifelong dream of becoming a published author. Believe me, before I left my job in the factory, the idea of (someone like) me ever writing and having a book in print did not exist in the realms of the possible. When I challenged this old belief, when I did the rigour and found it tenuous and groundless, when I removed all the objections and perceptions, the obscurations that stood between subject and object – myself and published works – subject and object became one.

My first book *was* published.

The old I – the one who believed this to be impossible – died, and Geoff Thompson *the published author* was born.

The intermediary state after publishing that first book was again a wobbly balance between the heaven of crystallising and capitalising on my new certainty, my new belief or density, and the hell of falling back into my former realm.

Whilst it is evidently possible to expand our perspective of consciousness, it is also possible to shrink it, if we allow fear or doubt or confusion to enter the heart-space. My beautiful brother lost his life to teach me this lesson. He died violently at the tender age of 42, because he listened to fear. He fell into depression and addiction, and as a consequence his reality shrank from a place of literary ambition (he was a gifted writer) to a wooden stool in a small kitchen in a shitty tower block in a deprived area of Coventry. He rarely left that room for the last 18 months of his life, he was too afraid. He lived and died, my brother, on a daily diet of strong Russian vodka, cheap red wine and unadulterated fear.

In the bardo state, we have the choice: we can make our expansion permanent, or we can fall back into our smaller perception.

This newborn self, inspired by my achievement, could see a bright future as a professional writer. The habitual remnant of the old me, however, the ghost of my past beliefs, believed that the book deal I'd secured was a fluke, a one-off: *you've had a lucky break*, it insisted unkindly, *but don't start getting above yourself.*

Other associates, friends from my factory identity, reflected this inner doubt. I was told many times that no one would be interested in the first book, let alone a sequel, and that I should stop getting above my station.

I was assailed by the voices of fear and warned to stop *thinking you're something* special and *stick to what you know*.

But no amount of negative whisperings could deny my new certainty; I knew *I was positive* that if one published book is possible that means ten published books are possible.

If I can write a book, I can write a film. If I can write a film, I can write ten films; I can win acclaim. I can expand into as many rooms as I am curious enough to explore. If I can muster the courage I might get out of the house altogether.

You can see how consciousness can exponentially grow if you just take the first step, If you can reveal one seemingly impossible thing.

When I was younger I always believed that I had to *create* new things. I created employment. I created wealth, the earnings from my employment. I had to go out and create happiness or relationships. I had to work relentlessly to earn and deserve the finer things in life.

As I expanded my awareness I came to a broader understanding of this process. Now I could see that everything I wanted, every desire I could imagine (material or otherwise) was already available, I was just unaware of it before.

In the world of us-and-them, of rich and poor, the privileged and the deprived and the growing divide between them, there is a debilitating belief in separation. But separation, I have noticed, is not real, it is illusory. There is no separation between anything, other than the projected gap caused by perception or belief.

Belief is so powerful that when it intercourses with our God-given imagination it erects invisible walls in and around us. These self-erected barriers create the illusion of separation. When we try to close the apparent divide by forcing the external world to change or comply, we are doomed to failure because we are trying to fix the illness at the level of the symptom; we are trying to clean the blemish on the camera-lens by wiping the photograph on to which it has been exposed.

The symptom is not the disease, only a projected indicator that an illness exists.

The blemish is not on the photo, it is on the surface of the camera lens.

If all the lights suddenly go off in your house, it would be folly to try and fix the problem bulb by bulb, socket by socket. The problem does not exist at the level of the bulb or socket, it exists in a central place, the fuse box. Locate the box, identify the specific fuse that has blown, replace the faulty part and suddenly every light and every socket in the house is miraculously fixed at the same time.

## The World Territory

When people tell me that they want to fix the world, I always find myself thinking, *which world?*

Just in our dimension alone there are seven and a half billion people, each with their own very personal, very individual world.

Are we to visit them all, fixing each projection one by one?

There is only one world that we can fix, one view that is obscured, one job on our corporeal worksheet and that is to fix the world of us.

And that is a big job, right there, a large job, weighty.

You tilt a lance at windmills, when you labour to fix the world of men, without first fixing the world of you.

Personalities and perceptions are powerful.

Perceptions and personalities are the hands that sculpt the clay of our world.

Un-policed they can create ugly and indiscriminate worlds.

Aligned and righteous, they can reveal a heaven on earth.

At one end of the perception-spectrum you might have the warring, fascist world of a Hitler, and at the other end the loving peaceful view of a Mahatma.

The state of each world depends entirely on the state of each individual belief.

The Buddha tells us in his teachings that there are no problems in the world.

The only problem is believing that there is a problem.

There is not a problem, he insists, but there is a clear view.

I don't see the world as being something we need to fix.

The world does not need fixing. It is perfect as it is.

If there are imperfections in the world, they are our imperfections, the faults we project on to it with our skewed beliefs.

The world as I see it does not need fixing, because it is not a fixed place.

It is a touch-sensitive, living, breathing, malleable, self-levelling, self-healing, shape-shifting multidimensional extension of you, the Real you, the authentic Self.

Therefore, in real terms, it is not a planet that needs to be saved. In fact, when you become fully aware, you realise that the world is no longer even there. It doesn't exist. All that exists is vast awareness, consciousness (or God).

Heaven and hell might be real phenomena, but when we are in God, all phenomena disappear.

It is not a world that needs to be survived or preserved.

Rather it is a projected territory with its own rules and regulations; it has its own natural laws, chief amongst which is the law of causation.

We use this world-school as a teaching station for the ever-evolving soul, a living whetstone for the sharpening of the virtues, on which the Self relies, to connect it to Grace.

This non-reality-world is a reciprocal habitat.

It is a correlative territory that we are called not to change, but to test ourselves in. And the testing will last as long as it takes – one lifetime, one million lifetimes – until, through that testing, we vibrate at the same level as consciousness. At the density of consciousness, as I said, we become consciousness, at which point we graduate from this world-school. To all intents and purposes, the world as we know it is no longer relevant, certainly not for us, any more than primary school is relevant to a professor at university.

Unless of course we are invited to stay around and become a teacher to those who are still on their journey.

Beyond this earth-school, I intuit that there are countless other such worlds or densities where the schooling of the soul continues at a finer level, and in a similar manner, but perhaps without this particular kind of physical body-vehicle.

While we are here the earth gives us our physical body, and it proffers us food and board.

The planet feeds us, it waters us, and it offers transportation across its chameleonic terrain, and it proffers a place to rest and sleep on our journey. If we are able to fathom and work and respect its laws, it is at once a generous benefactor and a courteous host.

Every delight can be created on our journey through this bounteous realm, but the ultimate aim is not to stay here or to fix here, rather it is to transcend here. It is not a place to settle in; it is a terrain where we work to improve the Self, and through individual refinement navigate our way to a place of higher learning.

This delightful holographic-earth is not the end destination in itself, it is a bardo that we have to pass through and pass-out from, in order to matriculate into the next station.

There are lots of learning stations, within this world and beyond this world, but it appears that we are all ultimately heading for the same place.

According to every bible since the dawn of time, this place is an indescribable nirvana called Home or the Omega Point.

We are all heading Home.

If we do not respect the laws of this reality, the very same bounty can become a seductive honeytrap, and our kindly benefactor a devilish jailer, who imprisons the ignorant in the jail of dualistic materialism.

He is both. She is either or neither.

The character that this reality takes is ultimately determined by the character we project on to it.

As I have said somewhere else, we are the potters at the wheel of life, our hands the servants of myriad perceptions, and we sculpt the clay of our world into the shape of our strongest beliefs.

Travelling through our life cycle, from birth to death, we accumulate karma; the credits accumulated from our selflessness, and the debts we carry for all of our unkind and selfish actions. At the end of our allotted lifespan, there will be a tally, a divvying up. The white pebbles of our kind actions are weighed against the black pebbles of our unkindness. If the black outweigh the white, we remain in debt to the territory of the world, we are reborn into it for a further life cycle, where we get the chance to learn from our mistakes, repay our debts by means of atonement, and acts of loving kindness.

Whatever remains unpaid in this life, will be carried forward to the next, and the next, ad infinitum.

We can remember and employ the growing wisdom earned from previous incarnations, to shape our next sojourn, so that in each proceeding life cycle the Self and the life the Self lives will be an improvement on the last.

If we were able to do this, if we could do the work and clean, eventually eschew, our dualistic, contradictory perceptions, and instead place our hands in the service of the Original Perception, our Source, we would sculpt this clay-world into a beatific utopia, our Self would receive the purest refinement possible within the confines of this earthly classroom, and passage through it to our Omega Point would be as instant as it would be painless.

The moment we find ourselves at the top of this class, we will be automatically delivered and enrolled into the bottom of a higher class, for further refinement.

In my martial arts years, I made sure that I was always at the bottom of someone else's class. If I was not at the bottom of someone else's class, how was I ever going to prove or improve myself?

The best way to elevate to the bottom of the next class up is to reach the top of the class you are currently in.

The way to do that is simple in principle, but will demand a complete paradigm shift. You will have to live a life wholly dedicated to loving kindness. To do this we must empty out of us all the revenge, all the anger, and allow Love or Consciousness to come in (which is perfect peace).

More on this process in the coming chapters.

So… we begin each new life cycle at the level we finished in the last.

Just like a conventional school, the work we do and the grades we earn will determine the level we start at when (or if) we enter university. And the grades we earn at university will predict the level of employment we will be offered when we matriculate into the world of work.

What we think, what we say and what we do today in the world is determined by the perceptions we action. The effects of our volition today will wholly determine the level we re-enter the world at when we wake up tomorrow morning.

This is the reason why the Buddha encouraged people to avoid soothsayers and clairvoyants keen to read our future. The future state, he said, is determined only by our present actions.

Reciprocity is the only rule we need to fully comprehend our personal evolvement (or devolvement); it is entirely determined by how wisely we invest in it.

The karmic universe has perfect recall.

Its ledgers and bookkeeping are meticulous.

Nothing is missed, nothing is forgotten, every debt we accrue on our journey through time and space and causation will be recorded and repayment demanded.

Equally, every act of love and kindness will be registered, accounted, and paid back in kind by the master of the scales.

If we want to get through the territory without having to fall back into the cycle of Samsara (karmic-existence) all we have to do is remember this lesson, and only ever deal in love.

Love is the panacea.

Love cures all ills.

Love wipes clean all of our debts.

Love can get us through the bardo of the world refined, and therefore closer to Home in one lifespan if we make love our only employ.

This is not something I think, this is not something I believe, it is something I know.

When you have made as many mistakes as I have, when you have been cruel, and unkind, when you have lived as a greedy and covetous criminal, indulging every vice in your lust for power, when you have lived the life of an *ill-angel*, and then suffered the pain of reciprocity as debtors turned up on your doorstep like bulky-bailiffs looking for repayment, believe me you do not doubt karma, you do not second-guess reciprocity.

When you open your eyes.

When you wake up to eschatology...

When consciousness is *second-coming* and you see that your crimes wound not only yourself, not only those closest to you – your family, your friends, those you love – but also the whole of humanity, when you truly fathom this you become steeped in regret, and you make a personal vow to never dabble in vice again: you court only love, love, love.

When Catherine of Siena had a profound moment of clarity and God spoke directly to her, He told her that the world was in a dire state, and it was all her fault. Everything she thought, everything she said, everything she did, added to the reciprocal mix.

Everything affects everything.

If you drop a pebble into the water, the ripples are received across the whole pool.

If I am even a part of the problem, I am all of the problem.

The world I see through these eyes is the world I have personally helped to sculpt with these hands.

If there are seven and a half billion different versions of the world, then my own personal version with all of its war and famine and crime is my fault.

God was telling Catherine to change herself.

He was telling her to be the change in the world that she wanted to see.

When she changed, everything and everyone else in her world would reflect that change.

To do this he asked her to place her principal affection in virtue, rather than penance. If we concentrate all of our attention on virtue, our karmic debts will be paid by proxy.

When you fully understand the Law, you eschew all vice, of course you do; only a fool would touch a naked electrical cable, once he experientially understood the inherent dangers.

The wise deal only in love.

Love is their daily bread, it is their intercession; it is their working capital.

When you see how easy it is to love, and how many opportunities there are every single day to administer the healing potion of love, it makes you want to dash out of the house right now, and start serving people.

Every act of love affects not only you and every one of the

trillions of conscious beings that infuse your working cells, it also feeds your family and friends, it sates the stranger in the street – in fact the whole of this spinning cosmos falls into the embrace of anyone that deals in love.

When you experience this first-hand, as I have, all you want to do is exist in a cloud of pure love, and all you want to do is starve your body of vice and clean the doors of perception so that you can become a better vessel for love.

They say that no one gets out of this world alive.

I would respectfully disagree.

Those that sculpt with love enter consciousness, they become eternal, they definitely get out of here alive.

Love is your fast passage to refining and evolving the soul, it is the direct route through this world of suffering.

This is not widely recognised, because of the *obscured view* – and this obscuration varies in degree from one person to the next.

Our only job then is to recognise that a *clear view* does exist for everyone; it is our *ground of being*, the seed of knowing, our birthright.

This *clear view* is enlightenment, and enlightenment is the knowledge that there is only Love.

Love is the constant.

Love is the backboard to every living thing.

Love is the roof over our heads, it is our means of transportation through the world – Love is our breakfast, it is our dinner, our afternoon tea and our supper.

Love is the Original Cause.

Love is the First Perception.

Enlightenment occurs when consciousness has expanded to its fullest aperture, where object and subject meld into One.

The *partial* clear view (as we mentioned) is when consciousness awakens us to our true nature. Once we are awake, we work to widen our conscious net so that we can establish ourselves there.

Each time we expand, we experience the same process of death of (the old) the intermediary state (bardo) and promotion into a new area of knowing (rebirth).

If we experience a crisis and fail to transcend it, of course we may regress back to our old state, or even further.

If we are not moving forward, we are moving back.

Post birth or the second coming, the final part of the divine eschatology is known in the bibles as **resurrection from the dead**.

Christianity assures us that Jesus will return again, and when he does, the dead will be resurrected.

It is tempting to read eschatological doctrine as written and imagine that the personality who lived as Jesus will be born again in the world as a man, bringing with him *rapture, great tribulation, the end of the world, the last judgment* followed by *a new heaven and a new earth.*

It reads like the threat of biblical holocaust.

This is the fire and brimstone of 2,000-year-old scriptures, where sinners are dragged from their muddy-hole for a final judgment. It hints of a jealous and spiteful God who will have his vengeance, leaving only those without sin to enjoy the Land of milk and honey.

This is not what I see.

I would argue that it is not the man Jesus who returns, he is merely the model human, who acts as proof of potential for humankind, he is our bridge to possibility. What returns then is not Jesus the personality, rather, what the personhood of Joshua rose to become: Christ. In Christian theology this is known as Communication of the Properties; Christ is not the man Jesus, neither is Christ God (the three are not synonymous), Christ is the communication of the two; the lower human nature and God nature in one body.

If you mix orange concentrate into water, you create a squash or a cordial. You no longer have a glass of plain water, but neither is it a fruit concentrate. You have created something different, a communication between the two properties that shares elements of both.

My own life and my own experience have shown me that if there is a heaven and a hell, it is here, it is now. I know people who this very moment are living in a fire-and-brimstone reality, because of the choices they have made – but perhaps in a more immediate and obvious way.

When my first marriage expired for example, there was an immediate rapture. I left a dysfunctional relationship and felt union with ecstasy, like a man being released from a jail This was followed by great tribulation. Any kind of divorce, whether it is from a spouse, a business partner, a belief-system or physical life itself (divorced from the body at death), goes through a post-separation limbo, a purgatory where the painful details of our former marriage are processed, and the relationship officially *deceased* in a court of law. To me and to my ex-wife it did feel like the end of the world; certainly it was the end of the world that she and I had made together. And *the dead*, those repressed, suppressed, ignored, denied, unprocessed resentments and hurts and ills that we had buried below the soil of ignorance, under the gravestone Freudian defence mechanisms, they were resurrected and judged, of course.

After the *decree absolute* landed on our doorstep and the marriage officially annulled, there was a long period of truth and reconciliation, a time of honest, heart-rending introspection, a *judgment* but not from a disparate entity called God, but a self-judgment of all the things we did wrong, all the hurts we inflicted on each other and by proxy on our children.

And the heaven-on-earth does not arrive, no peace can be secured until all of those errors are dug up and brought before the court of conscience and atoned. This intermediary period can take weeks or months or years according to our capacity to look with honest eyes at our own life-review.

If we don't exit a marriage with this meticulous eye of self-scrutiny, we may well join new relationships, we will surely start new lives, but the unpaid debt from the last life remains; it is carried over.

This is law. No one escapes it.

It will not be cleared, unless, in entering new relationships, we consciously recognise our many wrongs, and – as St. Catherine advised – place all of our principal affection in virtue.

Whilst the bibles of antiquity might seem archaic and dogmatic, to the open eye they are tomes full of pragmatic modalities.

There can be no heaven on earth until there has been a last judgment.

There can be no self-refinement, or safe passage through the bardo of this world, until all karmic debt is paid, and love prevails.

After the final judgment (our own judgment in our own time and of our own volition) the dead are resurrected.

The literal meaning of this phrase is *the standing up again of the dead: coming back to life again after death.*

The old you – the married man, the factory worker, the violent person – is dead.

The new you – providing you have fully processed the old life – the Self resurrected into a heaven on earth.

This process of incarnation and reincarnation is not reserved, as people might imagine, just for the birth and death of the physical body.

We reincarnate many times within a single lifespan, sometimes multiple times within a single day.

According to the Tibetan tradition there is a state of existence between two lives when one's consciousness is no longer connected to the physical body.

This place is called the bardo (literally, *the intermediate state*).

This bardo (I have noticed) also exists when the physical

body is still alive, and walking the earth. It exists in every absent second or minute or hour, it is there in every pregnant pause, it presents in every departure of consciousness, where we are drawn from the eternal *now* into the remembered past or fearfully projected from the reality of the moment, into the illusion of an anticipated future.

Every time we leave the divine now, seduced or fear-herded by the disparate sirens of the mind, we enter a bardo of sorts, a purgatory that can last seconds, minutes, or hours; some people remain lost for whole lifetimes in this *forest of delusion*.

Every time consciousness leaves the body against our will, in wild imagination or idle or fearful reverie, each loss of presence, when we fall into the false personality of ego and engage in anger or greed or lust or judgment and revenge, every time we are seduced or baited or tricked into depression or anxiety, or self-pity, or envy, it can be said that we have taken on a disparate personality, and, at least temporarily, incarnated into a different life. And we will live there for the duration that the vice in question holds us for. Until the fickle mind is untangled and controlled, and steadied, and held in the moment, and consciousness (Self-awareness) is sharpened and established as a constant, and the door to our heart protected, we will continue to be unknowingly invaded by and incarnated into every passing mood we happen to engage.

Engagement with the sirens of passion is a choice.

Be in no doubt, it *is* a choice.

The obscuration is this: most people are not aware that they have a choice.

They are not even aware that the different and disparate ego-personalities that rise in them, that they unconsciously identify with and engage, are not them.

The gear change between one identity and another is so subtle and so smooth and so habitual, and has occurred so many times and over such long a period of time, that they don't see it happening, they do not know it is happening. Subsequently they have no defence against the literal invasion of semi-autonomous, body-snatching thought-forms, vices that cross their threshold every day and supper on them.

How can you *choose* to stop something from happening, if you are not even aware that it is happening in the first place?

Perhaps this book, and others like it, can be a first step in recognition.

It will hopefully enlighten readers to the fact that **reality only exists at the level of engagement**.

When you identify with a rising thought or belief or perception, when you emotionally engage it, it enters your heart-space and you give it reality.

You.

No one else.

Just you.

It has no reality whatsoever unless you allow it one.

It requires your permission before it can cross the doorway of your heart.

Once across, it will alight in you, it will take command of your fleshy spaceship, and volitionally move you from this place to that, usually locations that do not serve you, that do not serve your life or the souls that share your life. The negative thought-form, once engaged, assaults and debases the very fabric of your reality.

It becomes real through you, and in you and from you.

If you think not, peruse the front pages of our popular tabloids, look at the Twitter feeds, the Facebook posts (yours and others), even a basic inventory of your recent internal monologues will betray a litany of proof that people are *not themselves* more often than they would like to believe.

We (of course) might argue that we do not give anger, or lust, or judgment, or murderous intent, or pestilence permission to engage and inhabit us, but we do. We always have a choice. We can refuse to allow the base-elements, our lower concepts to enter us. We can certainly train ourselves to understand their attack-ritual, and spot the approach of unkind thoughts, and learn their ways, and develop strategies to block their path, and sharpen our consciousness so that we can thwart their onset or boot them out manually, by force if they are already squatting in our human-house.

Even if our permission is the result of ignorance, or fear or lust or any strong passion that we feel unable to stop, it is still us that is letting them in. Maybe we do this by habit, or perhaps because of social conditioning or dogma, but this body is our holy vehicle, it is the temporal housing for God, it contains precious cargo, and it is our duty to learn its ways and protect it wares.

If you own a bank, and you don't place doors on the building, if you don't install locks on the vault, if you fail to invest in the highest spec security, don't be surprised when robbers walk in off the street and steal your bullion.

Protection is your responsibility.

And believe me, the treasure that is contained inside this human infrastructure is worth more than every bankroll in the world combined.

It is precious.

It demands the greatest protection we can afford it.

To protect it is to first understand it.

That is the first instruction and the prime intention of this book: information.

The second intention must be yours: put the information into practice.

To sum up this chapter: eschatology is the concept that everything already exists – opportunity, infrastructure, money, health, wealth, technology, other worlds, other beings, different realities – they are already there. They will appear to us miraculously as we expand our awareness. And we expand our awareness when we remove our obscurations.

You need proof of this of course.

But you will have to provide that for yourself.

I already have my proof but, as with all true valuables, it is non-transferable.

My truth has my fingerprint on it.

Yours, when you find it, will have a fingerprint too: your own.

All I can proffer you is my own process, a personal exploration of the divine economy, and what I learned there.

# Chapter 2

# The Divine Economy

I noticed something.

When I was out and about, as I was going about my busy-business in the world of men, I noticed *something*.

I was doing well; I was providing the necessities *and more* for myself and my family. I understood commerce. I understood the money-shape and how to make it in a moral and ethical way. I learned to make my own revenue. I earned it without the conditioned-fear and angst that *working for other people* elicited; specifically the ever-constant threat of unemployment if the economy took an unexpected downturn, or if I lost favour with the factory-powers.

Employment provided a steady wage but it made me lazy. I became over-reliant on other people to provide the work that I was paid to do.

If they didn't find the work, I didn't get to eat.

The good thing about self-employment was that I relied only on myself; I relied on my own ability to locate commerce and deliver a quality product and service.

And the work I did was not really work. *My* self-employment was a series of very enjoyable learning-tasks that I filled my day with. Even though I was being paid for my product and labour (writing and teaching), the wage itself was not the primary goal, it was not my chief incentive.

I loved the work so much that I'd have done it for nothing.

Working for myself as a martial arts teacher, as a personal mentor, as a writer of books and films and stage plays, I learned how to create; I learned how to maintain what I had created, and I developed the knowledge and the skills and courage (and the discernment) to dissolve those created things, when they no longer served their purpose.

In short I learned how to navigate the fiscal economy and enhance my skills and knowledge within it.

Eventually I could earn as much money in one hour as most people earned in one week. I could make as much cash-money in a single afternoon as I used to earn in a month. For this to be sustainable in the world of commerce the exchanges I made in the marketplace had to be proportionate; my customers had to receive back *with profit* what they'd invested. If they didn't, they would not return; certainly they wouldn't recommend me to other people. They had to see profit from my services or product and I had to see *and know* that they were profiting from the exchange for my conscience to be appeased. As it was, customers who purchased from me often received a disproportionate return on their investment.

They were happy. I was happy. My business grew.

However, during my many thousands of business and personal exchanges in the money economy, I noticed *something*.

It was not something I would have spotted had I continued in paid employment. Working a 50-hour week for someone else, I doubt it would ever have revealed itself to me. The life-altering *something* I received was – what is known in esoteric circles as – *a happy accident*: the gift of grace, an expansion of awareness from a benevolent universe that rewards the pioneer, it favours those that strive.

The gift was (I believe) the result of leaving paid employment, taking my autonomy back and seeking my own way.

Looking at it now, with the benefit of hindsight, I'd say that what I found was proof of eschatology. In other words, what I was shown was already there, it had always been there, sitting just outside the periphery of my consciousness.

My awareness expanded and I just sort of bumped into it.

I'm sure I am not the first, there must be myriad people in the world privy to what I witnessed, but they don't seem to be talking about it, or certainly if they are, they are not talking to me.

This is what I noticed: **there are two economies**.

There are two economies working in the world at the same time.

There is the **world economy**, the one that you and I work diligently in every single day.

Then there is the **divine economy**, an invisible, sub-textual marketplace constantly whirring away in the background.

The world economy works according to the savvy of the individual player; some people live hand-to-mouth, and just about manage to exist in a kind of scarcity realm, due to their lack of understanding. Of those who have learned its laws, a small few are kind with their knowing, and try to share their wealth and knowledge with others – they spread their light. Unfortunately, the greater majority manage and manipulate the fiscal realm, they fill their coffers with coin, and bend or break or completely ignore the rules to suit their own ends. Others still, the victims of circumstance, fall out of the economy all together and end up either living off the welfare state or – in countries where welfare has been swallowed by the greedy throat of dictatorship – hardly living at all. Many unfortunates – even in thriving economies – fall through the cracks and end up rough-sleeping in shop doorways and living from the begging bowl.

The divide between the rich and the poor is probably as it has always been – wide.

In the world economy there is of course division and corruption.

There are lots of people cheating the system.

Many people are *working* the system just for themselves.

Others are simply not working at all.

The general consensus (or perception) is that the rich fat-cats are the ones doing all the cheating. It's common for those at the lower end of the pay divide to tilt their lance at the windmills of capitalism, and blame their sorry lot on the *powers that be*.

But blame is lazy and unintelligent.

Blame is the narcotic of contemporary society.

Blame leaks and wastes more energy than Liza's bucket (and her myriad excuses for not fixing the hole).

Blame is a pastime that further disempowers the disempowered.

There is no quicker way to leak essence than to blame others for our lack.

The only defence I can find for people who blame (and I have been one of them) is that they don't understand how quickly blame manacles them and how securely the locks of self-pity and ignorance keep them imprisoned in their scarcity.

It is easy to see the glaring disparities in the world and to empathise with those whose life expectancy is up to 20 years shorter than the national average simply because of their unknowing.

This is not a denial of the atrocities that occur every hour of every day somewhere in the world. People are in pain. I understand that. They are suffering. I have been there myself, many times. I do not doubt or underestimate their position. I deeply empathise. But even in the direst circumstance, perhaps especially in dire times, we all still have power to choose what we engage, what we identify with and how we react to our situation. This is the one power we all have, and by realising it, and exercising it, we will change our reality from the inside out.

We can only change our future position if we alter our present actions.

I am not necessarily talking about seeking an answer to a particular external problem, rather I am suggesting that we go beyond the belief in problems, and look instead for a clear view.

If you want clarity, don't seek it in a dissonant world.

It will only add to your confusion, when you ask the world a question and you are assailed by seven and a half billion different answers.

Turn inwards instead.

Call on the only help you'll ever need, **the divine economy**.

**Note:** the world is a construct out of consciousness. It is not consciousness proper, only a property that is necessary (and useful) because it contains duality rather than unity. The conditions in the world offer perfect resistance-training for the soul.

Seeking balance with everything is the universal constant, a movement towards the One; duality offers a better, faster and more efficient training ground for this than a unity process.

Imagine going into judo class where there was no opposition, you would never grow. If, however, you entered a class at the bottom, where you were surrounded by senior players, your potential to prove and improve would go through the ceiling.

The earth realm is our metaphoric judo class; full of elite players, they are there for our benefit, and will test us at every turn.

The divine economy is the overseer of this process. It keeps score. It awards points and imposes penalties where they are earned and deserved; it is the ordained arbitrator of justice in this temporal realm. Its rule is law.

If we work with it, it will work with and for us. If we work against it, it will check our resistance. Take one step towards consciousness, and it will take ten steps towards us. To try and place our might against it would be disastrous; it would be like trying to take on the whole universe.

The world and the divine economy are not raw consciousness, but consciousness can be accessed by them, and through them.

In the divine economy there is no corruption.

No one is above the law, no one escapes the law, and no one bends the law to their own will. In this immutable marketplace, equanimity, equality, reciprocity is the absolute constant.

People might *and people do* temporarily escape judicial law in the world of men. And of course in escaping the eye of the judiciary they think that they have evaded the rule of the Law, and beaten the system.

They have not. They cannot.

I was gifted a seeing once. It happened at a time when I was wrestling with the concepts of karma, and reciprocity. I understood and believed the concept, but I was struggling to articulate some of its minutia to others; why for instance (that age old question) do bad things happen to good people, and why do bad people seem to get away with doing bad things? In my meditation and prayer I asked for clarity, and I was given a revelation. Some of what I saw, I have already shared with you. I would like to offer the full extent of the vision with you now.

During the meditation, when my awareness was expanded, I was witness to Divine Law in operation.

It left me in possession of certainty.

Actually, more precisely, it left me in awe of the certainty I felt, and I was greatly afraid.

This is what I was shown. In the divine economy, every thought, every word, every intention, every deed, every transaction is recorded in a ledger. When circumstance aligns, every debt will be accounted for, every error atoned and every wrong righted.

We are all intricately and invisibly connected, so an action from one person will raise an invoice for us all and the bill will have to be met. The universe – a self-levelling organism – will assure that it levels the hills and fills the valleys with its divine reciprocity.

This is true, not only for our misbehaviour with people, but also with animals. When we eat an animal (I was shown) we steal its body. We take its flesh and skin and fur and feathers, *its life*, for our own delectation and display, and we take it without permission.

Even though many people in the world still live in ignorance of this fact, and rationalise their actions, the stealing and the killing does not go without register, it is noticed, and in being noticed, it incurs karmic debt. We have no right to complain, I was told, about human tragedy in the world, whilst the tragedy we inflict on animals remains unresolved. And we have even less chance of ending human atrocity whilst animal cruelty gets swept under the carpet of unqualified justification.

I was shown in graphic detail what it would look like and how horrified we would all be if a superior race descended to earth from space, and killed us, killed our children, killed our family and friends and roasted us in an oven or over a spit, or on a Sunday barbecue. If they rationalised – as we so easily rationalise with animals – that eating human flesh and meat is completely acceptable, because by comparison to them, human beings are just dumb animals, I don't think we'd buy it.

There are a million ways that we consciously and unconsciously inflict pain on other beings, and don't even know it.

Nevertheless, the debt will still have to be paid.

Sooner or later, we all have to face and embrace the leper of our own sin.

Also – this was very clear – every credit, too, will be counted and recompensed.

I will return to karmic credit shortly.

I was told that we cannot escape reciprocity, it is folly to believe we can, it is the height of ignorance. Denial is also very dangerous, because in denying Truth, we leave ourselves open to the lie, and that makes us vulnerable, and more likely to commit further errors that in their turn will stockpile our debt.

All debt in the divine economy is compounded.

The interest will bloat in exact proportion to the length of time it remains unpaid.

It is also proportionate; the return will always be in keeping with the investment.

It is not the quantity of our action that determines the quality of return. It is the intent behind what we do that dictates our level of credit or debt.

A small act of aligned, anonymous charity would bring a greater return than a million bigger donations that are not connected to love.

One single glance from a place of hatred or malicious intent will have as much negative impact in the divine economy as a physical assault.

Hateful intent, even without the corresponding action, can cause the most grievous harm.

Because karma is a force that ripples across the whole pool, this makes us part responsible for everything that happens on the delicate planet.

We cannot deny our deeds.

Everything is rerecorded and it is recorded in us, in our soul.

We are our own record keepers.

We are the living, breathing ledger of our own credits and debits.

We carry the records of every internal and external movement in every cell, in every bone, in every muscle and sinew, in each drop of saliva and in each platelet of blood. When the time comes to repay, there will be no denying what is; even our skin will speak a testimony against us.

The moment we initiate a cause – with our thought, word or deed – the effect is immediately born and recorded and stored in us.

All debts will have to be paid.

All credit too will spread and serve everyone and eventually find its way back to its original investor.

Of the two economies, the divine economy is first.

It is first and it is the only one that is real.

The second economy, the world with all of its 10,000 things, is perishable. You don't have to study this temporal reality for very long to see the truth in this. Nothing here will store, our treasures *will rust away*, (Matthew 6:19-21) *moths and vermin will eat them, thieves will break in and steal them.*

The second economy, with all of its specious promises of security and protection and position, is an illusion. It exists for the briefest moment and is then gone. Better to store up treasures for yourself in the first economy, as the Christian bible suggests, where moths and vermin and rust do not destroy, and where thieves cannot break in and steal.

The Hikam proclaims a similar warning; *if you are working for glory that does not perish, do not give esteem to a glory that vanishes.*

This might all sound depressing and nihilistic, but actually it is the opposite; it is a simple, profound and powerful scriptural instruction that tells us that real profit only exists when we work from a place of selflessness and love. Aligned service is registered in the divine economy, which will of course also be reflected and rewarded in the manifest world around you.

It also tells you what to avoid; the selfish-service, working for the self alone, working from a place of greed, labouring from the fake ego, with false belief that security and safety can be found in a world that cannot offer safety and security because there is none.

In the parable of the talents, the prophet Jesus promises his disciples that talents invested in the divine economy (taken to the marketplace) will be returned to them exponentially, but he also warns that talents buried in the ground (invested selfishly, in the ego) will be taken from them, and given to those who used their talents wisely.

This simple understanding of a reciprocal, divine economy is what the Buddhists would call *the clear view*.

There are no problems. But there is obscuration.

There are no problems. But if we remove the obscuration there is a clear view.

When we reveal the clear view, the right path, the right action presents itself.

Once you are in possession of the clear view, once you are certain of it, you are enlightened. You have been given the blueprint to the reality in which you temporarily live. You can use this certainty to work reciprocal law to the benefit of All, including yourself.

It means you can make every transaction, every interchange of energy, every interaction an act of love, or as I like to call it a *pure function*, where you are only ever exchanging Love for Love, God for God, consciousness for consciousness.

This way of living allows you to negotiate your journey through this living university in the speediest fashion and enjoy the best produce that this delightful and exotic station we call Earth has to offer, en route.

Earth always proffers its best produce and its optimal route to those who trade in the inexhaustible commodity of Love.

The Upanishads tell us that *they took Abundance from Abundance, and Abundance still remained.*

The abundance it speaks of is Love.

Despite all beliefs to the contrary, Love is the only Coin of Exchange.

I am not talking about renouncing the world. This is our school. To renounce the world would be to renounce learning, and that is what we are here to do, learn – it nourishes the universe when we educate. We are living in the world, so of course the world has to be accounted for if our philosophy is to hold might:

*From a balanced place* (the Babaji reminds us) *you will understand that liberation is dependent on inner rather than outer renunciation.*

The key is to be able to employ this philosophy in everything you do. Whether you are selling time and labour to an employer, or producing food for the world at large, place the Alpha and Omega of your business and life interactions in Love.

In the divine economy everything in the world economy is observed and recorded and filed.

Nothing goes unnoticed.

Nobody gets more than they give and nobody gives more than they receive.

It has a perfect accounting system.

Those who think they have cheated or indeed believe they can cheat the system are asleep. Those who believe that others get away with dishonesty are either asleep, or they are simply not looking closely or deeply or broadly enough at the world. They are not seeing the end of things, only their interims.

As little as a few hours of hard rigour and clear honest seeing will show you the divine economy at work.

It will show you perfect justice.

It will show you that whilst there *are* interim periods, where the cause has not yet been reunited with its effect and justice appears to be left unserved, there is always an end to things where balance will be resumed.

People generally hold a very narrow human perspective of reciprocity and have almost no access to the dimensions of spirit.

An associate once tried to convince me that the divine economy did not exist and criminals were getting away with crimes both judicially and karmically. He cited one man in particular as a singular example to qualify his belief. The man in question (E) was a drugs dealer, a millionaire and murderer who lived in a mansion. The car on his drive was worth more than the average man's home and the watch on his wrist cost more than the average man's car. If the divine economy is real and it records and repays all energy-exchange, how come this known criminal was literally getting away with murder?

I knew E, the criminal in question, and I was able to see his life from a deeper perspective than my disgruntled friend. The 90 pounds of excess body fat he was carrying was a beast of burden, it was painful and debilitating – his debts were painfully on view; the obesity of his living was hanging over his belt buckle and clear for anyone with an eye to see. His front door was being kicked down by the police in armed raids, during the middle of the night, every two weeks. His wife was so stressed that she was constantly afraid; her fear was only kept at bay by bottles of antidepressants. His children were clinically dysfunctional. His friends – people that once loved and admired him – were all afraid of him. It was very easy for me to see the divine economy at work in every cell of E's body, and in absolutely every aspect of his life. He was a walking, talking, pulsating manifestation of every crime he'd ever committed. His life was painful. His living – whilst it appeared outwardly profitable – was one of deep anxiety.

People – my disgruntled friend only one amongst many – whilst failing to see things at their end, also failed to see things in the immediate as they were being presented in the here and now. E was a man broiling in some form of private hell, and unfortunately his family were roasting there with him. Whilst it was true that he had temporarily evaded the judiciary and avoided prison by threatening, paying off or even killing witnesses to his crimes, within a decade, the accumulation of his karmic debts, called in by the divine economy, caught up with him and he was sentenced to two life terms in prison. He is in still prison at the time of this writing. I am reliably informed that many of the other criminals he violated during his reign of terror share the same landing with him, in the same cell block. E is routinely the target of savage revenge attacks.

It is popular to pretend that some people escape divine reciprocity. Rigour into the validity of this view is rarely done.

There is an explanation for this.

There is a specific reason why people seldom scratch below the surface of things and this was the uncomfortable essence of my revelation.

To discover the truth about anyone is to unearth the truth

about everyone.

To unearth a general truth is to also reveal the specific truth.

To discover the truth means to discover the whole truth.

If karma is real and everything is recorded then *everyone* has to pay their debts, not just the obvious criminals.

One of my friends flat refuses to accept karmic law. Why? Because if he believes in reciprocity he will have to accept his own historical crimes. He will need to atone for the many indiscretions in his own life, and at this moment in time he is too frightened to do that. But denial will not in any way negate law; it will not stop the law from unfolding, any more than the apocryphal King Canute could stop the tide with his earthly command.

Denial is effective, but only in the intermediate; holding back the eventual swell of reciprocity is not a human power.

Reciprocity is not affected by opinion or lies or denial or any other kind of psychological defence mechanism. Neither does it negotiate, or misremember, or deal out injustice. It is like a self-remembering boomerang; it always returns to the hand that threw it.

In the divine economy everything is transparent.

Nothing slips through the net.

No crime goes unpaid.

No service is unrewarded.

The law has divine clarity, it is meticulously discerning.

It knows when a bad deed was enacted out of ignorance and it understands when it is dealt out of hate, and the intent is included in the calculation (although, like common tax law, ignorance is not an excuse).

It also knows when a good deed is performed out of love and when a common barter is masquerading as an act of charity.

I have said all this in other places. I am aware of that. The repetition is deliberate. It is often only in hearing something over and again that the message sticks. And until the message of reciprocity is certain, there can be no further development.

I had a student called C. He was so offended by the concept of karma that he stormed away from a class I was holding when the subject of divine reciprocity was introduced. When I caught up with him (he was flustered and angry, and fled to the car park) I asked him to explain his impetuous exit. He made his complaint, and it went something like this: C had once helped a friend who was starting a fledgling business. He did so, he promised me, out of the goodness of his heart. He served his friend from a place of love, he expected nothing in return. Later his friend's business found worldwide acclaim along with the fiscal return you might expect when a business finds a global platform. This same friend, C said, *did not lift a finger to help me when I needed him.*

C was not seeing his situation from a true place.

He'd convinced himself that his was an act of genuine kindness, when in fact it was a common barter, with all the implicit expectations that bartering infers.

If it was a true act of kindness, there would be no expectation of return. He'd have felt neither anger nor disappointment when his friend did not offer reciprocation; C would have just been happy to play a small part in his success.

For the divine economy to operate at potential, service has to be completely selfless and not performed from a place of expectation.

There can be no agenda.

The exchange must be pure.

When it is pure, the return is guaranteed, but it is not expected.

It is an absolute given that profit will be forthcoming, although the return may not, *and often does not*, come directly from the source of your service. It may be a *referred return* that comes via someone else. It might be a *triangulated profit* that finds its way home through several often disparate people before it reaches you. It could come back to you from a seemingly unrelated place or person and at a completely unexpected time. Even though it will come back to you in like measure, it may not return to you in kind. You might gift someone money and it comes back to you in the form of a kindness, or good health, or an opportunity, whatever the economy deems of optimum benefit to you and to nature at the time of repay.

If the act is selfless, it will always return, and it will always return with profit.

At the prime level, the service itself is the highest reward.

When the service comes from love, genuinely from love, it does not come *from* us; rather it comes through us, from our Source, from the abundance that always remains in abundance, from God.

We do not contain the commodity of love, but this body is a vessel, a perfect conduit for love.

When we serve from love, we draw love through every delighted cell in our body as we deliver the love to others. Selfless service coats and sates and saturates the server with bliss by proxy of the fact that we are delivering and processing love for other people, from Consciousness.

If this process is interrupted at any point before, during or after delivery, what began as a genuine desire to serve can quickly turn into a greedy need for ownership or profit.

Our service can be hijacked by the false ego at any point, and the process spoiled.

If this is the case, we fall out of divine exchange and into the common barter that can leave both parties feeling bitter and short-changed. They are bitter *because* they have been short-changed. They were promised love and received instead something less; a facsimile, a cheap copy of love.

Some people are hijacked before the act of service. Perhaps they do genuinely feel the desire to serve from a selfless place but then, before the service proper, the ego kicks in with its greed and conniving – *there could be something good in this for me*

– and immediately breaks the divine link and stops the delivery of essence entering them.

They may interrupt the transaction somewhere in the middle of the process for similar reasons. This is worse because by this time they have received the divine essence, it is already in process. Unwittingly they allow the whispering ego to talk them out of their divine service and covetousness enters; instead of delivering the gift (of love) that was vouchsafed for someone else, they hold on to it. When this happens the undelivered essence spoils and internal pestilence ensues..

It'd be like a postman taking credit for all the letters and parcels he delivers, pretending that he is the gift-giver, rather than the agent engaged to post the goods. Or refusing to even deliver the gifts in the first place, because he forgets that they're not his, and that he is simply the deliveryman.

What is even more common, which was the case with C, is that the desire to serve does genuinely come from a pure place at the time of service, it *is* aligned, but afterwards an ego-bitterness creeps in when the recipient of their kindness does not appear to reciprocate.

This comes from ignorance of the law.

The first ignorance is when we fail to understand that we have already been paid.

The bliss we receive when we process divine essence is the ultimate reward.

We receive our profit when the divine energy infiltrates and energises and heals and coats our being during the processing period.

The second ignorance is not recognising that the law is infallible, it will always return with profit, every selfless service, unless it is interrupted by human covetousness.

But, as I said, often it does not return directly or immediately or even necessarily in kind. It will be always be an optimal and proportionate return; but what you give in one form may return in another.

I once sent a free book to a random stranger, a university student (called Nic) in South Africa. He was struggling financially and wrote to me asking if I would consider gifting him a copy of *Watch My Back* because all his money had been spent on student fees. I felt great joy in sending him the book. There was no expectation of return. There was no agenda. I felt the intuition to serve him. I followed my intuition and I never thought about it again. We didn't even stay in touch. Ten years later an unsolicited invite to appear on a very popular online podcast landed on my virtual doormat (email). It was a very cool podcast called London Real, and they wanted to interview me for their show. I was pleasantly surprised. London Real has millions of followers and they only usually invite very high profile guests to their studio. I had a cult following, but high profile I was not.

When I arrived at their London studio one of the hosts introduced himself. His name was Nic. He was the South African student I'd sent a free book to a decade before. He wanted to repay my kindness, he said. I went on to do two great interviews on this fabulous show (with Nic and Brian) and the subsequent return I received as a result amounted to thousands of pounds.

Not bad for an investment (in the divine economy) that I had made so long ago I'd almost completely forgotten about it.

I may have forgotten, but, the *economy* had not.

On another occasion I spent a morning of my time mentoring a young lad (Ben) who worked in a bookshop. I'd never met him before but he'd read my books and – after a talk I'd given for the shop – he asked me for some advice; a little direction on how he himself might become a writer. I felt an intuitive connection to the lad, so I arranged to meet with him a few days later. Some weeks after our meeting, he introduced me to his sister (Natasha), who by sheer coincidence happened to be a film producer. This divinely orchestrated return led to me making two acclaimed films with her, and us winning a BAFTA.

The most common disruption in the pipeline of divine decree is undoubtedly post-service, when a person works from a righteous spiritual stance but afterwards feels short-changed because the recipient of their charity had not reciprocated.

Or, even more common, after the service, the ego feels the need to announce his charity. He can't stem the urge to brag about his good deed. You've probably heard it a million times when people say *I do a lot for charity, but I don't like to talk about it...* but of course, they just did.

My friend Raphaela is of Brazilian decent. She told me that in her culture they have a delicious saying relating to this phenomenon: **the fish dies in the mouth**. It is basically referring to the ego when it tries to take credit for the work of the soul.

When we brag about our service, the fish dies in the mouth. When we expect and court reward or praise for our service, the fish dies in the mouth. If we feel disappointed, or become bitter, because we feel we have not been rewarded for our service, the fish dies in the mouth.

The divine economy is perfect in every aspect.

It has its own ledgers and records.

It has its own accountant who delivers the returns – good or bad – that are due.

It is a body-absolute, a complete reality with schools and teachers and books. It has its own plan of which we are all a part. The divine schematic is not visible to the majority so they neither know about it, understand it, nor utilise it.

But, it is there and it works despite our ignorance of it.

For those who have awoken, this economy is real. In fact it is the only thing in this temporal reality that is real and it becomes their infinite source of energy and learning. Once you become aware of the divine economy, you start to work with it, you start to invest in it, it becomes the only thing you rely on.

Eventually you create a covenant with the divine economy, officially and consciously utilising its unbounded resource as a divine satnav. It is like an ethereal satellite that links into your individual dharma and guides you faultlessly through the bardo of this existential world.

When you do eventually link to it (more about how, and when and why later), it automatically reads who you are, where you are, what your bespoke purpose is, what needs to be reduced or increased or removed or included in order for you to expose and fulfil your purpose, how fast you are able to grow, who you need as a teacher, what books you should read and what texts you ought to avoid. It knows every intimate detail about you. It is in possession of your personal blueprint. It knows your part in the plan, and its raison d'être is to prepare and position you so that you can fulfil the potential that is your divine inheritance.

The *potential* is simple in principle, but difficult in its execution.

It is heavily invested in this process, because when we are nourished, It is nourished.

The plan, the ultimate potential, is to help lift you to a density of Love.

It does this by helping you to identify, process and jettison the sandbags of negative and accumulated karma, and then navigate your path through this territory on your way Home.

We are meant to be here, but we are not meant to stay here.

We are not instructed to change this place.

We are only called to refine our soul, sharpen consciousness on the whetstone of duality, and in doing so win our exit from this forest of delusion and return to our Source.

The divine economy will provide clarity for you regarding divine reciprocity.

The proof will be clear and undeniable and this will enable you to work unhindered and unfettered by personal doubts or general confusions, so that every exchange you make in the world – business, personal, familial – will come from the same frequency of love.

Once you get it, once you are in ownership of this certainty, the temporary reality we know as the world becomes a different place, a wonderful nirvana. With your expanded eye, you will see that every encounter offers the opportunity to download love from its source place. It offers you the gift of processing that love ecstatically through the body-infrastructure. It allows you to then deliver it to the recipient of your service. And you will know, without any doubt, that the reciprocal universe will reward your service at a time and a place that will most benefit you and It.

Knowledge of the divine economy also gives you unequivocal certainty that all negative actions will be equally and oppositely returned.

As a man who has committed more than his fair share of sin, I can tell you that this is sobering information. Understanding it makes you very discerning indeed about how you live in the world. Knowing that everything eventually returns to sender, you will be highly alert to every thought, every word and every single volitional deed.

Once this is established as a certainty, we start to self-discipline and self-regulate, and more than anything else, we stop relying on our small fallible intellects and start to call on divine Intellect (capital I) when we feel unsure of our actions or our direction moving forward.

Charity, *true* charity, only comes from one place – Love. Knowing this, we no longer look for solutions in the world, we learn instead to access the Akashic folders in the larger economy.

You might think that making this work in the world of men is very difficult, when so much of our service is tied up in fiscal commerce and politics and the physical exchange of products and services. These very evident concerns are not taken lightly. Wise discernment is called for when the reality of *no expectation* intercourses with the capitalist world of great expectation.

The divine economy is privy to all the workings of the

world. It is patently aware that in the current climate (the 21st century), coin is still the primary means of exchange. Money still moves from hand-to-hand, fiscal deals are still being struck and human economies vacillate with the needy waves of economical intercourse.

The secret is to recognise that in truth there is only one real economy – the divine – and if we are diligent and get that one right, the second economy will fall into perfect order and the world at large will look after itself.

You may look at the chaos in the world, the human vicissitudes, and feel helpless or overtaken. It is tempting, I know, to believe that no order exists or *can* exist anywhere in this fathomless realm, let alone in an ethereal economy that exists beyond the usual human senses. But the world we live in is the world we create and recreate every hour of every day. It is the manifestation of collective and personal reciprocity. Whilst you may not be able to make sense of the world around you or immediately change your current circumstance, you do have a definite choice in how you react to your immediate situation. You have the capacity, the ability to choose what you think and say and do in this moment. Your choice will affect your current mood, and your current mood will determine your future outcome.

Also, if your current situation is very challenging it will create the perfect opportunity for you to investigate the divine economy for yourself. You may feel very stressed or frightened right now. All external doors might be closing to you. Perhaps every option for relief has been withdrawn. From my experience, this often happens in order to encourage (even compel) you to look inwards for the solution instead of out.

I suffered from depression as both man and boy. At times it was painful and debilitating and very lonely. Often just leaving the house would fill me with every kind of anxiety. At first I reached outwards for help – doctors, friends, family, books – but

I knew, even as I reached out to them, that none of these people could help me. I understood deep down that my solution did not exist anywhere in the manifest world. Every external door closed to me too, leaving only one door left to try; the inner door. I had a moment of clarity, an intuition, a radical idea; instead of running away from the things I was afraid of (something I had always done, something that had clearly not worked) I would instead run towards them. I decided to write down all the things I was afraid of and confront them, one by one. I can still remember that moment, the decision, and the anger that rose in me. I was so weary, I was so very tired of feeling bullied by my own mind, by my own feeling, battered daily by the bodily-reactions to fear, that I exploded: **I'm not having this anymore. I am not having it.**

That's what I said. I actually said it out loud.

The moment I stood up to my fears, the divine economy opened up to me, it created a field of energy that furnished me with every tool I needed to gain sovereignty over fear. It proffered me inspiration and aspiration. It fed me ideas, it led me to books that taught me practical exercises that I could use to understand and thus gain desensitisation to adrenalin. It was as though the divine economy was just waiting for me to ask, urging me to turn inwards instead of always turning away; it was waiting for me to help myself, rather than crumbling under the pressure and begging the help from some external source.

Suddenly a world of darkness, void of all potential, became a wonderland of exciting opportunity. My small act of defiant courage automatically connected me to a whole other world. This eventually took me from where I was then – depressed, imprisoned by an obscure view of the world, living in a terraced house, in an unhappy marriage, working as a factory labourer – to where I am now: living my life with a clear view, as a covenant-making, creative, happy, healthy, thriving, self-employed writer of truth.

The circumstance I found myself in did not immediately change. Only my attitude to it was altered, only my perception. Like Francis of Assisi, I was implicitly assured by the Greater Good that the things I hated at that moment I would later learn to love. The amber light of limbo and hesitation and the red stop-light of fear changed and became the shining lamp that instructed me to go, go, go.

Once my attitude changed, of course, my altitude changed with it, and once my vantage point elevated, the world around me shape-shifted in accordance and degree to my own adjustments.

The world at large is unfathomable, no doubt, but yours need not be.

A clear view is available to you here and now. It is our birthright, our Ground of being, and it is available to all. Your ability to choose your mindset, challenge old perceptions, connect to the Original Perception in the divine economy, even (perhaps especially) amid personal crisis and world-chaos, is always there; it is a steady constant.

Certainly, from my experience, it is often when we fall or when we experience a crisis in our lives that we are able to see this.

## Chapter 3

# The Divine Fall

Jalalad-Din Rumi, the 13th century Persian poet, wrote: *"Birds make great sky-circles with their freedom. How do they learn it? They fall and in falling they are given wings."*

It is often not until our life meets with a crisis that we either discover or begin the search for something better; a new way, a view of life or a method of living that is better than the one we are currently experiencing.

One of the reasons I write books like this one is in the faith that one day a soul in crisis might find words of balm here, some kindness, an instruction that comes from the pen of certainty, and shows them *the treasure in their ruin*. If that's you, if you are that soul, I want you to know that this book has been formed especially and specifically and entirely for you. Somewhere, out of time, out of space I am resurrected from these sleeping pages and I appear here at your service. I manifest so that I might talk with you and pay-forward some magic-sound, words that ring with the *singing bowl* of love and compassion.

And when I say, just for you, I do mean exactly that.

This is just for you.

In your current situation these words appear for your eyes and your ears and for your benediction.

One of my own beautiful teachers, Etty Hillesum, is sat before me as I write these words. She is visiting me. She is with me for a brief and yet eternal moment. When I too am going through trying times, challenged and tested by the changes in my own life, her words are sobering, her words are awakening, they are balm. She gives me perspective and the inspiration to wield this slender fountain pen (to paraphrase Etty) *as if it were a hammer and my words will have to be so many hammer strokes with which to beat out the story of our fate and of a piece of history as it is and never was before.*

Etty was a Dutch Jewess who was sent to the Nazi death camp Auschwitz in 1943. Her chronicles survived. I am holding her legacy in my hand right here, right now. Unfortunately she did not physically survive her ordeal. She was killed by the Nazis in November 1943, a few shorts months after entering the camp. Her story deserves its own read, but basically, she was a woman who used severe crisis to find, one might say *demand*, equanimity in and from one of the most depraved locations in the history of our species. Just before and during her incarceration, she was delivered into the realms of Consciousness, and communicated there directly and intimately and purely with God, not despite her inhuman situation, rather because of it.

If there can be hope in that dark place, Etty is showing me, in the cauldron of death, there can be hope anywhere, there is hope everywhere.

Similarly, Viktor Frankl, a Jewish doctor, shared the same death camp as Etty Hillesum; although not the same fate. He survived. He was able to leave the death camps of WW2 with both his life and a written testimony of the events that is still rippling through the world now, some 80 years later. Viktor, like Etty, made it his sole purpose to write and lecture and spread his learning about the Holocaust for the rest of his life. In his seminal book, *Man's Search For Meaning*, he talks about entering completely alternate densities whilst in the camp. He accessed realities and dimensions, usually only spoken of in esoteric texts, or science-fiction movies. He was able to access his wife – who had already died, unbeknown to him at the time, in a different camp – and hold deep and meaningful conversations with her, sometimes for hours on end. It was, he said, as though she was actually sat there with him in Auschwitz. The situation in the camp was so severe that all external calls for assistance were suspended, and it was because of this severe restriction that Viktor was able to access a power beyond human reckoning. He connected to a field of energy that protected him from illness, deemed him almost invisible to the camp guards, and kept him alive. He missed the death marches and the ovens and the random assassinations often by seconds or yards. For his duration in the camp Viktor reported that he was able to live and work with impunity, courtesy of the divine economy. He carried with him a copy of the Torah (the Old Testament) which is said to contain the blueprint of the whole universe, and he read pages from it every day as holy balm. When the prison camp guards confiscated the book, Viktor was told by a quiet, inner voice: *We don't want you to read the Torah any more, we want you to be the Torah.* Rather than accessing the holy book, he was called to go directly to the Holy of Holies, his God.

Most of his fellow Jews were so consumed by the horrors that they were unable to do this.

What was it that made Viktor and Etty different from their fellow prisoners?

In a word, Purpose – or what Viktor referred to as Logos – which was one of the Old Testament words for God.

Purpose connected them both to a kind of immunity where human laws, world laws and known scientific precedents were superseded.

In human terms they fell, and in their falling they attracted invisible support. It gave them metaphoric wings, and with these wings they were lifted high above the world. *If we can be lifted on high*, the scriptures inform us, *we will draw things towards us.*

*Lifted on high* means lifting yourself above the grasping desires and greedy ambitions of the temporal world. When we let go of worldly wants heaven descends to earth.

It means to work through love, as these two magnificent people did.

When the memory, the intellect and the will all work in alignment to love, it gathers everything together.

In Viktor and Etty's case, they drew towards themselves (amongst many other things) an immunity-shield, a divine protection from the unspeakable depravities that assailed the camp prisoners. They absorbed 99% of the resident evil, and in doing so, were able to puncture through its illusion.

They opened the door to Consciousness, by working from love.

All of my own personal epiphanies have come through either existential challenge, or personal crisis.

On some occasions a life-crisis transformed from despair into a moment of clarity, and at other times a moment of absolute clarity triggered a life-crisis.

When I suffered deep anxiety, as a young man lost in depression, the clarity only came when I leaned into the sharp edges of my fear; when I did this a door of light opened to me that I would never have otherwise seen.

Another time, in a moment of divine clarity, I was shown the possibility of all things and a crisis of painful dissonance immediately followed.

Ultimately, both situations eventually led to an expansion of awareness because they each, in their own way, demanded of me change.

In the former, I had to muster the courage to lean in to my pain and go through the door of light. It demanded that I make hard choices and effect difficult changes, to accommodate my new truth.

In the latter, I had to study rigorously, cogitate intensely and wrestle hard with some very challenging contradictions, in order the clear the dissonance.

Breakdown, breakthrough; same difference.

I can identify too, in my own life, that purpose was always the driving force.

Purpose opened the door to that *other economy*, what Dante called *the Real world*. To access the divine economy you need the courage to embrace your *fall* – the depression, the illness, death of a loved one, the business collapse, the marriage failure, a crisis of faith or loss of confidence – embrace it, step through the fire-and-thorns of resistance, submerge and drown in your ocean of pain. Only the drowning man sees Jesus; the man who kisses his leper will dissolve into consciousness.

The fall is a highly vulnerable time. It is wise to understand this. It is a forewarning. There will be two opposing energies vying for your attention at this time of potential. One of these forces wants to lead you into light and the other wants to drag you into darkness.

These two energies are represented by disparate voices: the quiet voice of love and the garrulous voice of fear.

It is important to stipulate here, that both energies are ordained; both energies are necessary ingredients in the growth of consciousness.

It is easy to imagine that the dark energy is a force of evil and that it has a separate autonomy from God.

Nothing is separate from God; neither can anything be inherently evil. Love is the only constant, evil is the false belief that love is lost.

If we allow ourselves to be consumed by the negative, of course, it can and it does lead to dark and painful outcomes in our phenomenal world.

In reality, the negative energies that rise are the whetstones we need to sharpen our virtues and bring us back to the equanimity of our human nature, to love. They are our own mind-projections: they rise to consume, or be consumed; to claim, or be claimed; they rise for incarnation or for liberation.

This is entirely our choice.

They have no reality unless we allow it.

In esoteric practice this is known as **feeding the bear**.

If the negative force (the bear) rises and we are tricked or frightened or seduced into emotional engagement, or identification, the bear feeds off us, it consumes us.

If we are able to observe the bear as it rises, and refrain from identification or engagement, the bear feeds us; its nature (fear/lust/vice) is liberated, and its effulgence is transferred over to us – we literally consume the essence of the bear.

Regarding the negative energy, her first voice is the song of the siren. She is the temptress of mythological lore, who would seek to seduce. She lures her prey into the boudoir of carnal relief, temporarily numbing their pain with any and every vice – drink, drugs, and sex; all the usual suspects.

This imposter promises relief but delivers only damnation.

I have witnessed many close friends and blood-family bled dry by the sirens of drink and drugs and sexual extremes.

The second is less of a voice and more of a roar. This is the roaming lion, St. Francis' demon of scripture, who feeds off vice and fear and shrinks its victims into apathy, filling them with feelings of hopelessness, sinking them into depressive impotence.

I have experienced falls like this. I have to admit that many times, in my darkest hours, I felt like giving up; I just wanted to run away.

It happens. It happens to us all.

But we can learn from this, of course we can, and that's the point. Falling is the best way to win wings; that's often why it happens, that's how we earn certainty, it is how we become experientially schooled and metaphysically nourished and spiritually strengthened – especially when the fall is painful.

When I feel like running from my own pain, my teacher Rumi always reminds me to stay, he asks me to observe (and in observing strengthen my observer), and instructs me to melt into the pain, because *the pain itself will crack the rock and let the soul emerge.*

What I have learned and what I know is this: it is important that you are not tempted or frightened by the specious voices and the fear-masks that present at such times.

Recognise that they are projections from your own mind.

They will feel very real, they will make themselves appear mighty and potent, but, they have no reality other than the reality you afford them.

They become real if you allow yourself to be tricked into identification; you offer them breath the moment you emotionally engage them.

Do not emotionally engage them.

Do not identify with them.

Just observe them, with no judgment, no opinion; observe them with no connection.

Do not try and change them, or lose them, or hide from them; don't attempt to (try and) get rid of them, neither barter with them nor beg, and never attack them.

Remember, they are not real.

But, if you engage them – now then – if you engage them, they can become a mighty evil and you will make the unreal, real through you.

Just objectively observe.

Notice them, observe their rise, watch as they ply their wares, see how they hustle to win your attention, notice how they fall when attention is denied them.

Pay them no heed.

When you are able to recognise that these fears are your own mind-projections, *recognition and liberation* is simultaneous.

If you fall, if your life meets with crisis, consciously and objectively observe your condition, watch the fearful voices as they rise, resist the fear they elicit, and do not recoil or be herded into the wrong mindset or taken to the wrong actions because of them.

Beyond the posturing, behind the fear there will be a faint light, a small inspiration, hope – this is consciousness, the backboard of all manifest and un-manifest things.

Follow that light, trace that feeling, feed it with your undivided attention and it will grow brighter and brighter until eventually a *way* will open up to you, a new doorway that you can enter.

A friend called me recently. His old workmate P had lost his job in a company shake-up. He was suddenly and unexpectedly assailed by the wild and uninvited voices and visions of doom and despair. He had no defence against them. Subsequently he fell into a dark hole of depression, a fall he struggled to rise from. He asked if I might send P something to read, a book that might inspire, something to lift his gloom.

I'd recently published a book called *Warrior: A Path to Self-Sovereignty*, which I knew would help. P believed that losing his job was the end of the world, and his untrammelled internal-dialogue reminded him incessantly of this every waking hour. In fact he was waking every hour in the night worrying about it. He was a middle-aged man, not in the best physical shape and he believed that the loss of employment *at my age* left him few, if any, life options.

Reading *Warrior* sparked a light in P, an inspiration. He fed that light, capitalising on and expanding it by reading other similar books.

By taking instruction from the books – winning his fitness back, giving himself goals to aim for *a purpose* – he began an amazing new life in a direction that he had never before envisaged.

When the voices of doom assailed him, he engulfed them with the light of inspiration, by reading a book (in this case mine) written by a man who'd experienced similar falls to his and found a way out.

Another email landed in my in-box only yesterday. It was from a pastor (Adrian Laws – Warfield Church), who runs a meeting for people suffering crisis. A gentleman came into the church, he told me, who was near suicidal. Adrian offered him one of my books (Adrian has his own supply), which the man went away and read five times. When he returned, the gentleman said he was *totally transformed by its content* and wanted *to meet to plan going forward.*

Garish and posturing fear appears foremost at the time of fall and it is no surprise that people are tricked into engaging and identifying with it as though it was real, as though it was going to last forever.

As convincing as it often is, it is not real.

Anything that changes is not real, it is temporal.

Nothing Real can change, because the Real *is eternal, it is indestructible, it is immutable* (to paraphrase the Gita).

Our perceptions are the ever-changing ideas we engage, the interim truths we identify with, they are the impermanent, unsatisfactory programs sitting on the changeless backboard of our human nature – they are not Self.

The changeless backboard, the Original Perception, our human nature is Love.

Love is the only constant.

You will hear this a lot throughout the book.

You may have to hear it several times before it sticks.

Love is the invisible energy field that permeates all; it never changes and that's how you know it is Real.

When a book, or a talk, or a film, or a song, or a poem, or a gesture, or a righteous charity, or a nod of encouragement, or a smile of appreciation, or an anchoring touch, or the Prophet in scripture, or Jesus in oils, or David in marble inspires you, *when it inspires*, when anything connects you to spirit, it opens the door to Love, and it allows you to be both witness and proof to the eternal.

Light can save you.

Light will save you, be in no doubt.

And it is there, light – awareness, consciousness, Truth – it is there and it is a constant and it is yours, it is your Ground of being.

Fear is not real.

Fear is the belief that Love is lost, it is like veils of false-belief covering love with deceptive rhetoric – lies – telling you that light is not available, that inspiration is folly, that Love is a soft-option for the socks-and-sandals brigade, or love is the whimsical weakling looking for an easy solution to the hard problem.

Love is not only Real, it is all that is Real.

And you can enter it.

This is what you need to remember when you fall.

There **is** a doorway, your job is to reveal it, your task is to open it and walk through.

Your *inner opponent* will try and convince you in times of trial and times of testing and of mental confusion that there is no salvation, and that Love – if it even exists at all – is elitist. It will tell you that love is aloof and unavailable to *someone like you*.

Not true.

The centre of Love is everywhere: its circumference does not exist.

You can enter it here and now. You can enter the womb entrance of Love in this eternal moment, especially if you are suffering.

In my own life, suffering was the clarion call to Love.

I might never have looked for it, had I not been awoken by the strongly expressed demand and request for action.

Inspiration is there for you.

Ask for it.

Seek it.

Knock on the mind-door, and it will be opened to you.

I know that this might sound fanciful, a little poetic perhaps, but it is Real, it is undeniable, and it is right in front of you.

All I am saying is pick up a phone and make the call for help, read a book, or send out an internal call, a prayer for assistance, a request for intercession.

What you are looking for is there, it is everywhere, as we said earlier, eschatology tells us that it has always been there and it is ours.

What a waste if we don't take what has been eternally vouchsafed for us.

Even one small candle is able to kill a legion of dark.

Light a candle.

No shadow would dare present itself before the glare of the afternoon sun.

The voice of the whisperers, those conniving, internal, assaulting voices, who thrive in the darkness of crisis, will convince you that there is no light, there is no inspiration and that hope is snake-oil, it is snake-oil sold by snake-oil salesmen; cheap charlatans flogging illusion to desperate fools.

They lie.

I can tell you this without fear of contradiction because I am in possession of certainty.

**I am certain.**

You don't have to believe what I say is true. In fact I don't want you to. It would not help. You need your own certainty, and that's something that can be encouraged by a book, it can be briefly evidenced in the presence of an enlightened teacher, or by the door-opening inspiration of a line or a paragraph or a page, but it cannot be permanently gifted, it has to be experienced personally.

All you need to do is be curious enough about what I say to look at.

Experience it for yourself.

Be your own proof.

If you are feeling inspired now, reading this chapter, you have already experienced it. You already have proof.

Capitalise on it.

I will reiterate: the voice of fear is often very convincing, but its promises and threats are gossamer thin. With the light of original perception, their deception will be torn-apart like a web, they will be burned-to-sunder like a balsa-bonfire.

I'm not making light, I've lost count of the amount of times that the devils in the bardo have tricked me and stolen a day from me to untruth, or a week to anxiety, or a long year to fear and misery and depression.

It happens.

Even the sages of lore, the biblical prophets and Kings of scripture, at times, temporarily lost their alignment because they listened to fear, even at the level of sainthood.

The difference with the adept is that he quickly recognises his astray, and urgently and immediately realigns himself.

If it can happen to the saints, it can and it will happen to us all.

When we fall into fear, the sea of nescience, that forest of delusion, we haemorrhage seminal energy. Our vital fuel spills like a divine river and we will be *noticed*.

Leaking essence always and immediately attracts the attention of beast and fowl; we draw towards us misaligned energies (people and otherwise) that will feast on our spill.

The fall offers us access to an aperture, a wound, an opening into another room (in the house of 100 rooms). It encourages the expansion of our consciousness, our experiential knowing. It offers us the chance (as Huxley said) to cleanse the doors of perception.

It is also worth mentioning briefly at this point (more later) that once we enter into the Absolute, all talk of human consciousness, and expansion, and certainty will become redundant, it will be mute, it will mean nothing because in that place everything is everything; it is beyond phenomena, it is above human understanding and articulation.

In the meantime, to open the door, to enter, we have to pass through *the fires and thorns that surround His garden*, the gargoyles, those guards, the scary house-ghosts, whose job it is to protect the entranceway, the gateless-gate. They frighten the unworthy away and allow in only those who have proven themselves ready. And they do this, these shadows, by rearing up in us like the Lions of scripture with their sharp claws and gnashing teeth and growling scare-masks, whispering premonitions of doom and prophesising false promises of hell and damnation.

But, each time they rise, these *pain-bodies*, with their need-to-feed, looking to engage and lunch on the energy of our drama, when they approach with their threats of *terrible tomorrows*, torturing us with reminders and exaggerations of our past-failings, the false-ego and its legion of helpers – unchallenged concepts and beliefs – it shows its hand.

It gives away its game.

And… we are better informed because of it.

Now we see it. Now we are privy to its bag-of-tricks and subsequently we are better prepared for the next time it approaches, and the next time, and the next, looking for engagement.

The devil, the divided thought, does not exist in consciousness.

Mevlana Rumi reminded me of this beautiful idiom, just now: *Fear knocked on the door. Love answered. There was no one there.*

It can only enter existence if we have matching-elements within us, on our conscience, or stored away in our blood and bone and organs and sinew. Errors that we have not yet processed, that we have so far failed to atone. These hidden elements, incubating somewhere in our psyche, are like iron-filings to the magnetic, negative voice in our head. Once we cleanse ourselves of unfinished business (more on the *inner purge* later) we will no longer attract feeders, there will be no outstanding issue that can be leveraged against us. We can't be blackmailed by the dark elements of our past, if we ourselves have consciously brought the shadow into the light of the present.

What we expose to light, must itself become light.

When we engage inspiration – a book, a film, a conversation –

the connection acts as a religion, a raft of connecting light, a link to the divine, a bridge that we can walk across. Once this bridge is formed and solid, once it is in situ, we can cross it at will; we can rise above the manifest world, we can leave the reality of time and space and causation and we can enter the silence and the stillness of the Real.

In this place we will find equanimity, one moment and one thousand years are not different.

Big and small do not exist.

In the Absolute, we can access all knowledge, we can find the solution to all things – more specifically, we can see with a clear view. Then, once we are practised in forming this bridge, we can cross it for clarity whenever we like.

And other people, too, can cross the bridge to the divine economy through us.

As Al-Ghazali said, *those who look into the face of the man who has looked into the face of God, also look into the face of God.*

If you have created a bridge, you become a bridge.

How do you build this bridge?

In Christian theology, Christ was known as *the living bridge.*

Christ is the divine connection between here and there, earth and heaven. When the bridge was drawn, heaven and earth became one.

Christ represents God-nature and human-nature as coexisting in the same body; Christ is consciousness.

Consciousness, awareness, becomes our bridge.

Once we become aware that there is a bridge, we are able to access and cross it. The reason most people fail to do this already is, as I mentioned earlier, because they either don't understand the concept, or their conditioning has taught them to eschew and ridicule the notion of a heaven on earth.

Many of the people I meet these days are apostates – they are anti-religion.

They think of faith in all its denominations as either

fundamentally evil (the cause of all wars) or some kind of silly socks-and-sandals escapism.

*You can't cope with the world,* they accuse, *so you create a fantasy world to escape to instead.*

This is a common accusation, but it is an accusation without substance.

People use these complaints like house-ghosts to scare themselves and others away from personal connection with the divine.

There is no rigour here, no qualification.

Religion exists, it is real.

We all practise religion every day in one form or another. We are all religious fanatics. Conditioning makes us so. We all *align* to an idea or a belief and then fight with our very being to defend it; in the case of fanatics, they will fight to the death.

One of the translations of the word religion is *religare.*

It means to reconnect, man to man, man to his Source.

It can also mean connecting or aligning to a belief, a truth or even an untruth.

People like Hitler or Stalin were dogmatically religious in their murderous beliefs because they were aligned to the wrong ideology. Their fervour was so strong that whole nations fell under their influence. For a time, legions, powerfully attracted to their rhetoric, joined their religion, and killed millions of innocents in its cause.

Most of us walk around every day dogmatically aligned to the lives we live, the social mores, the rules and regulations of society, the norms, the repressive pressure of public opinion and cultural dictation. We care more about what other people think of us, about being in a tribe, than we do about our own lives. Many people kill themselves, rather than challenge the soft-inheritance of their schooled beliefs. We are so busy contributing to cultural and national and tribal and social-religion every day that we rarely take time out to consider what we actually think ourselves; what our deepest thoughts and desires are, what we would really love to do with our lives if it wasn't for the work or the family or the city or state or country.

I spoke with a schoolteacher on the phone some years ago. Having read some of my work, he'd reached out to me for a little advice. It became very quickly clear that he really only called to tell me what he wanted to hear, in the hope that I would hear it and then feed it back to him as truth. He was in the middle of a fall, a life-crisis that brought into question his place and his purpose in the world. He wanted to be a writer. He'd always dreamed of becoming a writer. The dream was to spend his days composing words on a page. But he was torn. Even though he had no love for teaching, he felt it was his absolute duty to elucidate schoolchildren and assist them with their education. He was adamant that it would be a complete betrayal of his moral obligations if he gave up teaching in order to follow his own dream of becoming a writer; he was hoping that I would concur.

But what was he teaching his children, this lovely man?

He was teaching them a lie.

It was implicit, of course, I am sure he didn't consciously intend it, but, it *was* a lie.

In settling for a job that he had no love for, he was teaching the children *by proxy* to do the same. He was subliminally teaching them that they too should settle (like him) for less than their due. He was not teaching them to follow their personal dharma; he was schooling them in the art of social conditioning.

If the teacher can't live the dream, what chance the student?

Rumi cautioned me yesterday to *never take directions, from a man that has never left home.*

When I suggested this to the teacher, he fought ferociously for his limitations; he defended his point vigorously and refuted everything I'd suggested.

But he was fighting for a specious title and a tin hat.

He was battling for something that was of no real value to him, he was arguing for something that he did not even want.

If we are not following Love, what else are we courting other than a lie?

We make the gravest mistake when we try to sit anything other than love on the seat of the throne.

Paul tells us, in his letter to the Corinthians (1 Corinthians 13), that even prophetic powers, and understanding all mysteries and having all knowledge are little more than *noisy gongs and clanging cymbals* if we do not have Love.

Usually, we live a lie because living with deception is easier than seeking the truth.

And regarding truth, we are often guilty of looking very hard for it but in all the wrong places.

We go around and around (as it says in the Hikam) like a donkey at the mill, the place we are travelling to is the same place as we are travelling from.

I remember a lovely story I heard from the Islamic pantheon that illustrates this beautifully. One evening, after dark, a man is seen searching for something under a street light outside his house. His neighbours notice him in his frantic hunt, and one of them asks, *"What are you searching for, neighbour?"*

The man tells them that he has lost his keys and they kindly join in the scout. After a fruitless hour, one of the exasperated helpers asks, *"Neighbour, are you sure it was here, that you lost your keys?"*

*"Oh, no, I didn't lose them here,"* he tells them, *"I lost them in the house."*

The neighbours are confused.

*"So why, if you lost your keys in the house, are you looking for them out here?"*

*"Because –"* he tells them *"– there is a light out here."*

The message of the story is clear: if we look for solution – the lost keys to our lost Self – in the external world we will never find them.

At the metaphysical level, *all needs* (to paraphrase the Hikam), physical, material, emotional or spiritual, *are coded messages from the One Source requiring attention, awareness and hence (us) calling upon Him for relief.*

When we lose our small-self in crisis, we can find our True Self in recognition. By breaking the code and heeding the call, we turn inwards for guidance instead of out.

If we look *in the house* of ourselves, instead of under the street lamp of the external world, we will locate our lost keys.

That is the essence of this chapter.

In fact it is the essence of the whole book.

If you are in crisis, if you are suffering a fall, ask yourself this: what is the coded message, what am I being called to recognise?

Breakdown can miraculously become breakthrough if you turn in for the help and stop wasting your time searching for the Unfamiliar in familiar places.

Religion (alignment to the Unfamiliar) is about sitting down, doing the deep internal rigour and actually drawing out and aligning to your true purpose.

People ask me if I am religious.

Their asking often betrays a sense of suspicion or inferred ridicule, as though in embracing religion I've fallen foul of something terrible, something silly or cultish; or that I am a simple mind tricked into the fantasy of God.

From my experience, the Truth is always ridiculed; it wouldn't be the Truth if people didn't ridicule it.

Religion might be a source of ridicule for some, but only until it is felt.

Once it is felt, it is no longer a source of ridicule.

Ridicule is a common house-ghost.

It scares away those who just don't want it enough.

Don't fall for it:

We connect or reconnect to the divine by first cleaning away the prejudices we hold; any prejudices, *all* prejudices. Go in with an open mind and the sharp sword of discernment. Be inquisitive. Don't take anyone else's word for anything, and certainly don't take mine. You need your own proof, your own certainty. If it is borrowed from someone else, it might satisfy for a while, but it won't stick for long.

Other people can be good for inspiring you and creating a temporary link to inspiration (inspired means *to be connected to spirit*). For that link to become permanent you have to create it with your own certainties and forge it with your own links.

Complete stillness, silence, is our ultimate aim.

It is only when the chitter-chatter of the ego-mind has completely stilled that we are able to access consciousness.

## Prayer and the Inner Life

How do we achieve this?

When people met the personality Jesus Christ or the holy Prophet Mohammed or the Tibetan saint Milarepa or more modern day saints like Saint Teresa of Calcutta, they would often automatically fall into an inspiration. This is because these saints were on the **carpet of proximity** – they were close to God. If you stand by someone who is on the carpet of proximity, you too are on the carpet of proximity.

So be around or place yourself in the proximity of people who are established in their proximity to God. If you can't be immediately around them, access them through their secondary bodies: their books and DVDs and their online talks.

Talk to God, meditate, contemplate, pray.

If you are unfamiliar with prayer, or if the word *prayer* fills you with conditioned trepidation, look at what prayer is in its broader context.

Any intercession can be considered a prayer. If you feel inspired by music, music is prayer because it connects you to spirit. If reading this book, or others like it, fills you with the feeling of hope, then you are already praying. My dharma is to write books, and make plays and films and deliver talks that act as an intercessor, a prayer for people that are not accustomed, for whatever reason, to traditional prayer.

The most concentrated form of prayer of course is always going to be direct, and the purpose of all works of intercession is ultimately to deliver a spiritual discourse that aligns you directly to your own Source.

Start the inner conversation; dialect with your highest self.

Literally turn inwards and use your internal dialogue; ask questions.

If you are unfamiliar with biblical prayer, make it up; even if you don't know what you are doing or feel a little silly, still try. You could start by saying (inwardly), *look I feel a little silly, I don't really know what I'm doing but...*

The internal dialectic is the beginning of what is known as the inner life.

Often the very best times to access your Source, directly and immediately and intimately, is during a fall; crisis opens a wound, and through the wound you can find a direct link to consciousness.

As Leonard Cohen so succinctly said in one of his beautiful lyrics: *"Sing the song you still can sing, forget your perfect offering, there's a crack in everything, that's how the light gets in."*

A character (a priest) in my latest musical stage play, *We'll Live and Die in These Towns*, tells a debilitated and frightened singer (suffering stage fright) who has come to him mid-crisis for help, *"I hear God in you."*

The singer scoffs, *"I don't think so. I am full of weakness."*

*"Well yes of course,"* the priest replies kindly, *"God's power is perfected through weakness."*

We are weakened by crisis.

The ego collapses. It doesn't just lose control of the world, it recognises that it never had any control in the first place.

An opening occurs.

This is an invite to the inner life.

Other than the tweet-tweet of constant and unconscious internal dialogues most people do not have an inner life, they have never even heard of it.

Once you establish the inner link, it becomes the most enriching source of direct, teacher-less knowledge.

## The Bibles

Inspired books will also link you to the Unseen. Read the bibles, expose yourself to the scriptures, they are full of arcana. I have been proved and enriched and expanded and exalted by my exposure to the Old Testament, the New Testament, the Torah, in its own right (the Torah constitutes the first five books of the Old Testament), the Zohar, the Gita, the Mahabharata, the Srimad Bhagavatam, the Dhammapada, the Guru Granth Sahib; I could go on. The list is beautifully endless, and the tomes are full of the inner knowledge that will feed the inner life. And it comes direct from the quill of our very own sages, our very own prophets and saints. It is all there (and often free to access). The only thing standing between you and them is the house-ghosts of modern conditioning.

## Art as a Bridge

Writing or painting or music, any kind of art can also link you to the divine economy. You see people all the time who are *lost in the music.* They intercourse with their art. Many writers and painters and sculptors enter the creative space and struggle to leave it again because the divine link is so strong. For the most aligned artists, those that make art their bridge, it becomes all they do; nothing else matters, nothing else even exists. They orchestrate their entire lives so that they can connect to divinity (or what the artist Yves Klein called **the abstract**) as often as possible. At this degree of commitment, the level of the adept, even the money-shape becomes an annoying distraction as does any form of acclaim or accolade associated with worldly success. Once you have felt the Real thing, you will recognise that the world has nothing valuable to offer (other than as a winnowing tool), compared to the inner life.

## Rhythm and the Abstract

The aforementioned artist Yves Klein connected to the Source via both his art and his martial art (he was a 5th dan Judoka). He talked about practising uchikomi (perfect repetition of a single technique in an unbroken rhythm) until the movement connected him to the abstract. He said, *when you return from the abstract, you are not the same person.* He used Judo to take him into the abstract and, whilst there, he connected to his purpose, and on his return he would bring back with him genius. He would then produce pieces of art that had an altogether ethereal nature.

I find the same connection in martial arts training, specifically, like Klein, through the uchikomi of Judo and the atemi (hand strikes) of karate or boxing. I can create a rhythm through both that connects me immediately to the divine.

I can also produce the same effect for my students.

One of my elite students, a lovely and powerful fighter called Wayne, is a specific example of the power of rhythm. He is a gentle soul but very physically capable. He worked nightclub doors for a time, as a bouncer, and later hired his weight out as a collector of unpaid debts. Both of these employs favoured his physical demeanour but they sat uneasy with his quiet nature.

In one particular class, I was teaching a punching routine on focus pads to demonstrate the efficacy of rhythm as a bridge to the abstract.

One of my critics had scoffed; *tell Geoff Thompson he won't find God by hitting a focus pad.*

I have never laughed so hard; the only reason I hit a focus pad is so that I can connect to God.

To demonstrate this connection I called Wayne out to the front of the class. I instructed him to strike the pad I was holding, in steady repetition, building up rhythm and power as he progressed.

I focused on Wayne intently. I closely mirrored the rhythm of his punching hand and I matched it with my receptive pad-hand, synchronising his energy with my energy until there was no distinction between the pad-holder and the pad-hitter; we were as one. We were so intently focused on the perfection of the rhythm that we erased every other student in the room. They no longer existed in the space we shared. After a minute or so of steady, powerful, connected rhythm the room vanished and then I disappeared too. The rhythm created a bridge to the absolute.

When we finally ended the routine, the room reappeared and everyone attending the class broke into spontaneous applause. I looked around the sports hall (we were sharing the space with badminton players); everyone had stopped their game to watch us. They all felt the stillness of consciousness because we invited divinity into the room with our display.

Wayne was so moved by the shared experience that the next day he gave up his job as a debt collector.

He had experienced something Pure and it did not sit well with his current employ. Wayne is now working in youth development, helping troubled kids.

Personally, I find my richest, most direct link to the abstract through the pen and the page.

Writing to me is a form of intercession or prayer.

It's my way of having a conversation with God.

Mother Teresa of Calcutta captured it beautifully when she said, *"We are all merely pens in the hand of God."*

People also find the connection through nature, or more specifically, through their gardens.

The martial arts mystic Morihei Ueshiba discovered a powerful link between the divine and agriculture. After a prolific life of travelling and promoting Aikido (a non-aggressive martial art he created) he and his wife eventually retired to a small cottage with a garden, just so that he could develop his connection with God directly through the nature.

## Conversation

Conversation (I have found), when it is aligned to the good, is a prime way of connecting to the abstract. If the conversation is in the spirit of progress, and there is a sense of collective evolvement associated with it, If it can be kept to the positive, and those partaking avoid any kind of rhetoric or dogma or gossip, it will create its own positive field of energy that will facilitate our learning. To avoid the conversation taking a downward turn, it has to be monitored; at least one of the parties involved needs to be 'awake' and he or she must diligently keep a measure on the nature of the badinage so that legitimate talk of the mysteries does not revert to a titillating feast on conspiracies in all of their delicious forms. It is also very easy for processing – vital cogitation used to clear dissonance and remove obscuration – to decline into gossip and drama, which feeds the very confusion that you would like to remove. The conversation can be planned – we get together with people of a like mind and nourish each other on the protein of an elevated exchange of ideas – or it can be a spontaneous conversation that breaks out between two or more people, who happen to *accidentally* converge in an amenable space. I meet with certain people every week (I have for many years), specifically to hold these planned conversations, but I also often cross paths serendipitously with strangers and pleasing energy is exchanged in the form of a casual chat. In the case of the latter you will have something to pass onto them, and they will have something to pass on to you. Again, even with conversations of the spontaneous nature, you have to be careful to not allow the junk-food of everyday drama to break through. This occurred only yesterday, when I bumped into a delightful cyclist whilst out running. I'd stopped by a local brook to stretch, he was passing on his bike and an exchange took place. The conversation between us was lovely; he was an older man (69) who had found great freedom riding his bike around the continent. When he talked about the joy of being in nature, just him and his cycle, I found him very inspiring. Within a few short moments, however, his conversation fell from the spiritually nourishing to the unappetising and mundane; he started to talk disparagingly about *that fella off the telly* who was earning obscene amounts of money, whilst his elderly neighbour had to *exist* on a very small state pension. Generally, people cannot converse for very long before gossip and opinion and complaint find their way to the table looking for a feed. Before his spark of rhetoric caught fire and razed our beautiful encounter to the ground, I killed his complaint by gently reminding him that, unless we are omnipotent, we are in no position to do a value judgment on the *greedy newsreader* who earns £400k a year. I reminded him of how free he was, and that perhaps he shouldn't spoil that freedom, by getting angry about something he'd read in a popular newspaper. He's been baited by a deliberate tabloid-tasty, and it was giving him spiritual indigestion. Slightly chagrined, he agreed with my philosophy and we reintroduced inspiration back into the conversation.

If there is a genuine desire for enriching enquiry, elevated conversation is a direct way to connect to the Akashic library for answers.

## Talking to Rocks

At the highest level when you have an understanding of eschatology and the connecting worlds, you recognise that the doorway to divinity is everywhere. It exists specifically in the present moment, the here and now. You could just as easily connect to God through the act of washing dirty pots as you could from praying over the tomb of St. Peter in Rome.

When you have entered the divine economy once, entering it a second time becomes easier and a third time easier still. Eventually, you will not need to *enter and leave* because you will be in a constant state of prayer. Connected at all times. Conversing – as Solomon did – with a rock or an animal as easily as you would converse with your neighbour over the garden fence. At this level of Siddha, you can ask questions of the landscape, you can talk to stones and rocks or share dialectic with animals; even the sun itself will respond to your inquiry in the most profound ways.

I am aware that I am already exceeding the context of this chapter. I will expand on my experiences of Siddhas in the relevant place. It is enough to say that in the higher echelons, limitation is redundant. You will have all sorts of strange and beautiful experiences that will feel (at the time) completely normal to you, even though they might exist outside of (the usual) human reckoning or beyond current scientific nous.

## Meditation

For a direct link to the divine economy – and this has been the most efficient method I have found – start practising meditation.

Again (before I expand on meditation), I don't want to lose connection with the fact that this chapter is about the fall, and that it is personal crisis which has led us to this place of looking in instead of looking out. At the time of crisis, all external means of help might be withheld or withdrawn or otherwise unavailable. When this occurs, there can be little doubt that you are being called. You are being invited inwards. In this sense, the fall is good. Crisis is beneficial. Everything that happens to you is good, if you are able to decipher the hidden code and unlock the door to relief. And whilst I would never underestimate the suffering of people – I know first-hand how painful physical and mental breakdown is – it does offer the opening to purpose, a better way of living, that would not, perhaps could not have occurred otherwise.

If you are being called inwards, meditation is an excellent and structured practice that will take you there.

There has been much said over the years about the pros and cons of meditation, some good, some not so good.

I have decades of experiential proof that it is powerful and effective.

Not just as a method of bridge-building, but also as a method of healing.

As one of many examples of the latter, I am currently working with an uchidechi of long standing. He started practising TM (transcendental meditation) at my recommendation in January 2018. By July of the same year he had cured himself of high cholesterol and type 2 diabetes. His level of consciousness expanded from the very first session and continues to expand every time I see him. The physical healing was not the aim of his meditation practice, merely a very powerful by-product.

Of all the methods of bridge-building, meditation is definitely potentate; it is a compound exercise. It connects you immediately to the divine economy (or what Jung called the *collective unconscious*) and it registers you there. When you connect to the Source with your own unique pass-code, it knows exactly who you are: *this is Joe Blogs,* it says, *this is where he is, this is where he needs to be, this is why he needs to be here, this is the pace he is able to work at, and this is the work he is called to do.*

Whether people are conscious of it or not, all forms of external help – mentoring, physical training routines, meditation classes – are ultimately intended to achieve one specific goal: to connect you to your inner guru, the inner tutor.

Intuition is a true method of locating and following your own unique path.

I am no man's guru.

I don't want to be.

My only job is to deliver a spiritual discourse – through

writing, through talking, ultimately through simply being aligned myself – in my own personal vernacular in order to align people, not to me, rather to their own inner guide.

I don't know your plan.

Why would I know your plan, we have never met?

I don't know my wife's plan; I don't even know my own kids' plans.

But I do know where the blueprint is.

And the quickest, most direct connection to it is through consistent meditation.

Just a quick scan of the World Wide Web will show you that there are a million different methods of meditation out there, and they are all claiming to be the best.

They can't all be right.

How do you choose?

There are so many different methods that people tend to either butterfly from one form to another, never really establishing a constant bridge or any meaningful results, or they become so logjammed by endless choice that they fail to choose at all.

This is why I advise choosing one method and sticking with it.

Transcendental Meditation (TM) is my personal recommendation but only because I have experiential proof of its efficacy.

This is the one big decision you have to make.

But if you listen, your intuition will already be directing you to a method that will suit your sensibilities.

Once your practice is constant (consistency is everything with meditation, compound returns are only achieved through regular practice), this compound exercise will deliver exponential results, I guarantee it.

All of your subsequent decisions and directions will come directly via your own link. The moment the bridge is built and communication between you and the divine economy is initiated, instruction will start to download from the unconscious to the conscious.

Then the work begins.

The instruction will become clearer and clearer as your bridge becomes more and more established until eventually you will develop *acoustic clarity*.

The messages you receive will tend to come primarily in moments of inspiration (these are messages from your inner tutor), flashes of divine insight, moments of clarity, or head-on, full-fat epiphanies. Sometimes the message will be delivered by a sage internal-voice, often you will experience serendipity and synchronicity; God will speak to you through any and every medium. Being an omnipotent, omniscient and omnipresent force, there is nothing It cannot use as an instructional tool.

Once we establish a divine covenant with our Source (more on *the covenant* later) every molecule in the living universe will fall at your feet, ready and eager and willing and desperate to serve you in order that you may 'do the work of many' from a divinely aligned place.

I am certain of this because I have experienced it.

**The fall is the call.**

Put it on a T-shirt, print it on a bumper-sticker, make inspirational posters from it.

The modalities that you are being drawn to (in this chapter, in this book, in works of a similar ilk) have been proffered not despite your fall, but because of it. This is why the fall is important. If you are currently suffering a crisis, congratulations, you have been noticed, you are being called.

My previous statement about *doing the work* begs a telling question: who is it **in us** that does the work?

When I recommend that you turn inwards, who am I talking to?

Who is it that starts a dialogue, and creates a bridge and makes a covenant?

Who is it that actually takes the instruction from these pages and *actions* the trillions of individual cells in the body to follow its lead?

The **divine ego**, of course.

## Chapter 4

# The Divine Ego

I've personally lost count of the number of books I've read on the esoteric and the exoteric, the physical, the physiological, the psychological, the sociological, the religious, the spiritual and the metaphysical. They have all offered good advice and proffered sound instruction on all things self-help and self-healing and psycho-spiritual, but **who are they talking to?**

Who is it that receives the information, and follows or fails to follow the advice?

Who is it that actions the instruction?

There seems to be a presumption that the person they are talking to via the pages of their book, or in the audience at their seminar or through the computer screen on their YouTube channel is singular identity.

It is not.

Usually they are addressing a collection of disparate personalities and sub-personalities all gathered together in one body.

There is more than one of us in here.

The mystic Gurdjieff believed that inside every being there were countless different personalities, some dominant, some idle, some dangerous, some relatively harmless, and some of them dormant, only rising to consciousness periodically when summoned by a particular stimulus or triggered by a specific arousal.

These personalities are myriad and varying, and they are largely unaware of each other.

They all think that they are you, all of them.

At their most destructive they battle away inside you, fighting for dominance.

Many of these separate selves (or I's) have their own agenda, their own aims and ambitions and their own very individual desires and standards, which may sit in stark contrast to the wants and needs of the other personalities.

The greater issue here is not that we have a community of disparate selves living in us; the real danger is that we don't know it. So, when an angry personality, or an envious voice, or the echo of rage rises in us, we tend to think and believe *this is me*. We make the mistake of assuming that these dissonant and disorientated and often disreputable personalities are acceptable, if uncomfortable, elements of ourselves. We fob them off as romantic quirks, or harmless aberrations, or normal personality traits. And when one of these shadow-characters brings us to disrepute in the phenomenal world we use rationalisations like, I was out of character; that wasn't like me; that's not who I am; I lost myself in a moment of rage; something just came over me. I have even heard people say: I was not myself when I did that (whatever unacceptable thing 'that' was).

The emphasis here is on the prefix 'I' and the identification of this I, in all of its many presentations and associations, as us. What I have learned from my own internal rigour and what I know is this: they are not us, they are not I, certainly not the true I, the authentic self of which there is only one.

I have literally observed people as they shape-changed into their rapid and violent, sometimes subtle and covert identity shifts. As I was developing, I also observed myself manoeuvring from one I to the next like a master quick-change artist.

Only, it is not the costume that is changed, it is the whole personality.

It is absolutely fascinating to observe.

I have witnessed it in myself when a certain fear or a specific arousal has called forth a complete stranger *in me*, who ends up writing metaphoric cheques that I, the true I, cannot possibly honour.

The transformation is astonishing.

During these shifts, people's gait, their posture, their language and syntax, their actual facial features, their moods completely change and you find yourself thinking, *who is this stranger?*

The first real experiential recognition I had of this phenomenon was after a major epiphany I experienced many years ago. I'd been invited to teach a martial arts seminar for the movie legend Chuck Norris, in Las Vegas, Nevada. The invite was the culmination of a lifetime's dedicated practice of my art, and at the time I felt it was the greatest honour to be invited. All I had to do was turn up, deliver my truth and it was an instant place on the world martial arts stage, guaranteed.

I won't go into the minutia of the visit itself, because it's described comprehensively in my book *Notes from a Factory Toilet*, but the essence of the story is this: I was frightened to go. In fact I very nearly cancelled because the fear became so acute; it took every ounce of my courage to cross the fear threshold (and the Atlantic) to take my place on the world stage. I stretched and strained every muscle and sinew inside and out to get myself *over the pond* to deliver a seminar to a personal hero and 500 of the top black belts in the United States. Embracing and overcoming this tremendous dread triggered the epiphany that I would like to relate.

It happened in the middle of the night, two weeks after the seminar, when I was back home in Britain. The experience left me floating in the divine economy for nearly two years. It was as though my whole world had changed or, more precisely, *the* whole world had changed. I awoke with my chest expanded and aglow, and I experienced my infinite connection to and the possibility of all things. It was so clear to me, so obvious, and if I wanted more proof, all I had to do was look out the window at the magnificent and bewildering and boundless universe spread out before me like an exotic creature – the evidence was there for anyone to see. I understood all at once and with complete certainty that the secret to perpetual motion was selfless service. During that honeymoon period, nothing could threaten my peace because I knew that I owned nothing and so nothing could be taken from me, and in owning nothing I had complete access to everything, in fact I was everything.

The Hikam sums up my experience perfectly: *when divine inspirations descend upon you they demolish your (selfish) habits,* *"Surely the kings, when they enter town, ruin it."*

As an addendum I would say this: *when inspirations descend* *they also demolish all your (selfish) personalities.*

After the kings entered town in this midnight parade, all my sub-personalities jumped-ship. They all temporarily evacuated. I remember looking out of my eyes, at the world, for the very first time as one self. It was as though I suddenly realised how unique this was. I kept trying to explain to family and friends (who I think were convinced that I'd had a breakdown) that *I'm* *the only one looking out of these eyes, only me.*

They didn't understand what I was trying to explain.

Perhaps that was because, at the time, I didn't fully understand it myself.

It is only now, some 15 years later, that I can fully comprehend what had occurred.

For that two-year spiritual honeymoon, I was the only person looking out of my eyes. Not the small I, we are not talking about the personality known as Geoff Thompson, he was not even in the frame; I was looking through these eyes as the observer, in fact I was the observer.

For that short, blissful period I experienced what it was like to be one I. Not sharing this body with the multiple personalities that, up until then, had inhabited my body-home, and presented themselves to the world as me.

At times, they even convinced *me* that they were me.

## The Sentinel Ego

This I, the authentic self, I later labelled the **sentinel ego** (or the **divine ego**).

In Christian, Judaic and Islamic mysticism this sentinel ego is often referred to as the *lower soul*.

Most adepts accept that there is a lower and a higher soul. They exist like twins, separated, one resides in the body, and the other is outside the body, in consciousness. The lower soul is situated in the physical body. In its porous nature, it could be likened to the multilayered, flexible plastic surface of film, coated with light-sensitive ingredients (silver atoms), that cause a photo chemical reaction when exposed to light.

Both the film and the soul are highly sensitive to impression. Film records only the images it is exposed to.

With the lower soul, the form and character – its personality – are too entirely determined by its strongest impressions.

These 'strong exposures' are the building blocks to our inner structure. They are delivered through the lens of the human senses and derived from the hard and soft-inheritance of our parents (genetic influence, and familial teaching and conditioning); our formal schooling; peer influences; the media in all of its many manifestations; and of course culture and religion which are a strong determinant of a person's inner and thus outer reality.

Once these impressions are accepted, and in situ, they form what Freud called the super-ego, or internal parent. These powerful impressions constitute the inner life of the ego, and the way we view the world is via direct reference of these conditioned impressions.

This inner life determines the shape, and texture and quality of our outer reality.

Once the beliefs are impressed on to the lower soul, our outer world is determined, just as surely as the movie playing on our local cinema screen is fixed by the images beamed through the projector.

Once we understand this, once we recognise that the ego is not the enemy, we realise that the battle is not *against* the ego as society would have us believe, rather the fight is *for* the ego. Instead of allowing the lower soul to be assailed by any random impression floating in the atmosphere, we start to protect it from the carnal-impressions spewed out to the masses as news, as objective fact, as entertainment or as education. Instead we deliberately and consciously and methodically cleanse the old impressions and concepts from the lower soul – like removing old programs, and redundant files and viruses from your computer backboard – replacing them with kind impressions; the images that you would like to project on to the screen of your world.

As I mentioned in the last chapter, this usually happens when – through crisis or clarity – we suffer a falling; the lower soul wakes up to who it really is, recognises its sovereign identity, and goes into battle to win back its kingdom.

Once this war (known in Islam as the Greater Jihad) begins the lower soul, cleansed of wrong impressions, infused with Love, connects by steady graduation to consciousness.

The lower soul ascends. And in rising it is noticed. It is noticed by higher forces. It is noticed by the higher soul, who descends, and joins the lower soul in union. When this occurs, we experience heaven on earth, because heaven and earth – the properties of human nature and God nature – communicate.

I will go into this in greater detail as the book unfolds.

I was talking about my Chuck Norris awakening. I mentioned that after my first, major, post-Vegas epiphany, I enjoyed a period of time where there was no internal war with opposing personalities. No battles with the will. No dichotomy of choice. I was connected to the divine network, that was all. The intuitive commands came down the divine pipeline. They were received by the sentinel ego, who commanded my body, my mind, my emotions and my senses, to carry out those orders in the world.

In Vedanta, they employ the metaphor of a horse-drawn

chariot to represent this internal human command structure. The horses represent the senses: the reins are the mind: the driver of the chariot is the ego and the chariot itself is analogous to the human body, the physical infrastructure. The passenger in the chariot is represented by the higher soul, who ultimately dictates the purpose and destination of the vehicle.

It is the case with most people that the horses (senses) are wild and untrained. They are more likely to pull the chariot off the road, in all sorts of opposing directions, or crash it, than they are to follow a true path.

The reins (the mind) are unruly and tangled, and thus, incapable of receiving tactile instruction and direction from even the soberest driver, which means that they have no instruction to pass on to the horses (senses).

The driver himself in this analogy (ego) is either drunk or asleep (or both). This makes him dangerous and unreliable. Certainly he is not fit to receive cohesive direction, let alone pass it along through the reins and from the reins to the horses.

You don't have to look hard to see that, with many people, the chariot itself (the body) is either not kept in good working order – it is damaged and in ill-repair from lack of maintenance – or it is in splendid order, it is pristine but remains unutilised, like a timorous Ferrari, hidden under dust sheets in a locked garage for fear it might become damaged or tired or stolen if it is taken on to the open road.

And the passenger of this metaphoric chariot is literally any alluring or convincing impression. Like a taxicab for hire, each journey is determined by the punter who climbs in from the street and pays the fare.

In order for the chariot to serve its true purpose, the horses-of-sense need to be broken and trained.

The reins of the mind need to be untangled, straightened and ruled.

The driver must be awake and sober.

And the chariot itself needs to be kept in perfect repair.

Once the four bodies of the chariot are ordered and in aligned communication with each other, it becomes fit to attract and carry a royal passenger: the higher soul.

Once in residence, it is the higher soul who directs the chariot to its ultimate potential.

It will not enter the passenger seat until the chariot is in perfect order.

In the New Testament the prophet Jesus tells his disciples: *for where two or three gather in my name, there I am with them* (Matthew 18:20).

When the lower soul wakes up, and remembers its divine mission, he recognises that in order to fully realise his dharma or duty, he must first win back command of the 'chariot', then reunite or *gather together* and unify the disparate parts of his divided vehicle.

Prior to the awakening, the bodily-house was divided, and subsequently it was always at war with itself.

After the awakening, the sentinel ego, recognising that it no longer holds sovereignty in its own kingdom, sets to work on winning back its throne. He does this first by captaining a second body to his cause, the tangled and disordered mind.

He controls the mind initially through control of palate, he masters the appetites: what we eat; what we drink; what we ingest. Everything we imbibe through the five senses is brought under control, and placed on a strict, healthy regime.

Vice in all of its many forms, anything unwholesome is routinely rejected.

Virtue, anything healthy becomes its staple.

The moment the mind is controlled through the palate, a third body (the sensual) is automatically gathered into alignment. Because we control the mind through the quietening of the senses, the two gathered together (the lower soul and the mind) automatically become three.

When we control the palate (Gandhi advises) the senses fall into line.

When we control the senses we control ourselves.

Once we control ourselves, we literally control the world.

The moment two or three of our bodies gather together, as the gospels tells us, we automatically invite in the higher soul, or what the Muslims call the Ruh, and through the soul we immediately connect to the divine economy, and consciousness itself.

Once the lower soul awakens and controls the mind and senses, God will be present.

The fall that I spoke about in the last chapter acts as the spiritual shock that rudely awakens and sobers the sleeping ego and kick-starts it into action. From its place of crisis, the lower ego suffers; and through suffering, it acknowledges viscerally and painfully: *I don't want to live like this anymore. I can't live like this.*

The I that suffers after the shock, the Self that *refuses* to live like this anymore, starts to make changes. As I said, he wins back control of the mind, kicks out the bad habits and starts working only from virtue.

This is the **real I**.

This is a pivotal moment.

This is where the lower soul, painfully recognising its impotence, turns inwards, calls out for help and guidance, *even mercy*, and connects to the higher soul.

This is the true voice, your divine soul personality, **the sentinel ego**, that is elected to take over the running of this fleshy spaceship, to grab the wheel, demand control and action and relay the commands delivered intuitively by the higher soul.

In esoteric parlance the higher soul is called **the witness**, or **the observer**.

In many spiritual and psychological texts we are encouraged to go to war with the ego, as though it was an enemy that needed to be subdued. As I mentioned earlier, when I spoke of Islamic mysticism, from my own seeing, I have observed that the fight is never with the ego, the fight is always for the ego.

We fight to win the ego back.

We war against ignorance, to win our kingdom back; we aim our arrows of truth at the nescience which obscures the ego from its true identity.

The ego is not our enemy, although if left unprotected, it can easily and quickly become the most deadly nemesis.

If there is an enemy, it is the negative impressions that seduce and usurp the ego. The lower ego is gossamer, it is delicate and it is innocent. It cannot discern good from bad any more than this page I am writing on can discern between holy words and murderous rhetoric. It simply records the ink that is impressed upon it. The only thing that dictates its final nature – a book of horror or a ream of verse – is the hand that writes the words.

The ego has two forces acting on it at all times.

Each force is vying for its favour, usually both at the same time. All of our mythology, all the scriptures and even the modern epistles – *Harry Potter*, *The Lord of the Rings*, *The Matrix*, *Star Wars* – depict in metaphor the battle that is going on inside each of us. The ego is the gatekeeper of the body, the unwitting guardian. He controls the inlet from divinity and the outlet in to the manifest world. In this beautiful human tabernacle, the mobile carrier of divine essence, the ego is the caretaker, the controller, the king of all he surveys.

As I mentioned before, the only problem is he doesn't know it.

He has no idea of his true identity.

Like Cinderella, who doesn't know that she is the true queen in waiting.

And Rapunzel locked in a high tower, hidden from her true identity as a princess by her wicked stepmother.

Luke Skywalker works as a labourer on his uncle's farm; he

has no inkling that he is the last of the revered Jedi Knights.

The ego is the greatest prize.

It is the forgetful keyholder to the kingdom.

It is anaesthetised. Thousands of years of conditioning keep it asleep to its true sovereignty.

All of the scriptures, old and new, are directing us towards our true identity.

The sleeping masses – also unaware of their divine nature – are manipulated and manoeuvred and herded by powers they are completely unaware of. This human tabernacle, the housing of the divine soul, has access to unbounded treasures but this truth has been kept from us.

Entire worlds can, and have been, and still are being created, maintained and destroyed by the human engine. Our energy is seminal, its potency is hugely creative. This makes us valuable prey to people and energies that would capture and exploit and usurp the power of the divine ego.

Once this occurs, like the Israelites forced into slavery by the Egyptians, the ego becomes a serf in his own kingdom.

The two powers who fight to influence the divine ego are archetypal in nature: they are the dark and the light, the destructive and the creative.

The lower primal energy seduces the ego into darkness and binds it to the earth. The carnal seductions eventually bring its energy under the sovereignty of Al-Shaytan (the false-self).

The creative presence that fights to win the ego is a benevolent force. It urges the ego to take back control of its own territory. It encourages it to clean out the defilements that have inadvertently corrupted it. When this occurs, we have a marriage: the communication of properties, a divine covenant between the lower and the higher soul.

The ego automatically becomes **the sentinel ego** when it awakens to its true position and takes on the task of winning back, and preparing, the human tabernacle, so that it is worthy of the divine marriage.

But how does it do that? What are the modalities?

I mentioned earlier that the waking soul vies to win back control of the mind and senses, so that the three bodies *gathered together* will attract the divine guest, and become host to the holy spirit of God.

The *gathering* is achieved through a process of reduction.

I worked in a chemical factory for seven years when I was a young man.

Our job in the plant was to reduce large vats of weak acid (18% strength) to its neat state. To do this we used a method of testing that saw the weak acid being put through a series of extreme heating and cooling tanks in order to separate the pure from the impure. Basically, anything that was not neat acid was removed by these processes. Once completed, and the impurities extracted, we would be left with tanks full of 98% neat acetic acid.

Of course, in the process we lost 82% of our original volume, but what we were left with was pure.

## Apophatic Theology

Apophatic theology – the theology of negation – is a similar process, but it is used for divine testing as opposed to chemical purification. We employ it in the process of winning back, and reuniting, our heaven and earth. With it we separate the pure from the impure within us.

In the biblical lexicon, it is a means of identifying God via negation.

We identify who God is by identifying first who It is not.

In Vedantic theology this is called **neti neti** (pronounced ney-tee ney-tee). It means to understand the nature of Brahma (the ultimate reality) by first understanding what Brahma is not.

If we accept that God is our own Ground of Being (the seed of God as existent in every being) then Apophatic Theology is the search for God, by negation.

We identify who we are, by identifying first who we are not.

The practice is simple enough in concept; if you locate and remove everything in you, in your life that does not meet with your highest moral duty, eventually you will be left with the pure essential Self.

As my teacher Etty Hillesum told me just this morning, *unless every smallest detail in your daily life is in harmony with the highest ideals you profess then those ideals have no meaning.*

Etty was a gifted seer, and if you practised incongruence in her company, she did not hesitate to tell you: *why do you dream about creating a new world,* she asked a friend, *when you are poisoning your own world with God-knows how many cigarettes a day?*

We humans often like to talk a good game, we dream of the fantastical, but, like Aesop's fabled turtle, we contemplate flying above the earth, when we are not yet able to walk properly on the ground.

We can often be guilty of trying to clean the world *out there* whilst we live quietly, desperately, perhaps unknowingly in our own cesspit.

As long as we are not *one* with ourselves we are wasting our time trying to make the world and its people become one with each other.

Etty believed, as I believe, that each of us, ultimately, has just one moral duty: *to reclaim large areas of peace in ourselves, and to reflect it towards others. And the more peace there is in us, the more peace there will be in our troubled world.*

It has to start with us.

I remember reading a story about the beautiful beat-poet, Allen Ginsberg, a staunch anti-war campaigner during the American invasion of Vietnam. In a bid to separate himself from the violence and the chaos of his troubled country, Ginsberg bought a small farm outside New York for him and his fellow poets to inhabit, in peace.

Within days of them moving into the farm, there were fist fights.

Some of the poets violently opposed the views and the habits of their fellow farm-steaders. A microcosmic war erupted in a community of pacifists. Ginsberg was perturbed. If he couldn't prevent the conflict in his own home, what chance was there of him stopping the war in Vietnam?

In this world (which is beyond fathom) our only job is to create peace in ourselves. And that is a big job, right there, a large job full of heavy lifting.

You will have contributed the optimum peace possible in the world, if you complete this one moral duty.

Whilst you are still at war with yourself, with your family, with your neighbour, any effort to change the world out there is folly.

The theology of negation is the go-to method of self-work for any serious student of the esoteric. Its main artillery is **observation**: we observe and we scrutinise every aspect our own life, our own behaviour, our own habits and beliefs and we eliminate those behaviours that do not meet our highest divine standards. We eliminate them, one by one, until all that is left is the pure Self.

## The observer

As I said, in theology the authentic I is called **the observer** or **the witness**.

The observer is consciousness.

Whilst you might initially experience the observer as an individual witness, looking only through your eyes, my experience has shown me that the observer is Absolute, it sees through all eyes, and all things, at all times simultaneously. This is why it is possible to experience yourself momentarily as a bird, or a horse, or a tree or as another person or people. Consciousness is present in every cell and in every mote of dust.

The moment the ego wakes up, we automatically start to experience intermediate flashes of the observer (or consciousness observing through us). We quietly recognise that it is present all the time, it always has been, and it always will be; it is the constant. We just didn't notice it before. This is the higher soul, slowly introducing itself.

Through the theology of negation, we strip back, we reduce, we contract and shrink until we are able to see the world completely free from concepts. It's not that concepts are not there anymore, but we can choose whether or not we engage them. If we are disciplined and expanded enough, we can even choose to change or reverse concepts; the burn of a hard training session or difficult learning curve can be re-seen (or re-envisioned) as exhilarating rather than painful, or stressful. Our discomfort then becomes comfort, even pleasure, because we flip the concept, by adding dimension and purpose to our actions. If I am able to see and associate a run with health and fitness, or the painful-burn of a weight-training session with muscle growth, or the intellectual stretch of a job change or university course with expansion of my life-potential, I will relish the endeavour because I have changed its aspect.

I can remember once, many years ago, literally talking myself into being a bad flyer because I had one choppy transatlantic flight. I had always been a good flyer. I loved it, until this one negative encounter with turbulence. Afterwards I told people so often I was a bad flyer, that eventually I taught myself to hate flying, to the extent that I no longer wanted to take a plane anywhere. I became scared of flying. When I realised (the power and the folly of) what I'd done, and how silly it was, I reversed the process. I began telling everyone (and myself), over and again, how I loved flying, how long flights were a great opportunity to read more, and relax etc. and I repeated it until I once again became a good flyer.

My friend is a long-distance runner. In the past she struggled in her training sessions with hill-work (sprinting up ascents). When I saw her, she would talk about her running with a sense of verve, but she always complained about the hills. She'd tell me and just about anyone else who'd listen how she hated any kind of incline. If I asked her how the run had gone, she would invariably use loaded adjectives like: *not pleasant*; *hard*; *tough*; *torture*; *murder* or *terrible*. The quickest way to place a negative concept on an otherwise neutral action is to label it with painful or uncomfortable adjectives. Who in their right mind is going to enjoy a running session that was torture? The hills (or her perspective of them) were stripping the enjoyment out of the runs. Her unchecked rhetoric started to spread; eventually it was not just the hills that were torture, the run itself was filling her with dread.

As a friend she asked me how she could bring the joy back into her running.

I encouraged her to *change the language*; tell herself and everyone else that the hills were exhilarating, they were her favourite, and she loved the hill-work. If people asked, *"How was your run?"* she should immediately say, *"Great session, great burn, exhilarating, the hills were amazing,"* etc.

It is very powerful.

It works.

If you ask me what I love most about holidaying on a cruise ship around the Caribbean, or the Mediterranean, it is not the pool I'll be referencing, or the summer sun or the 24-hour access to ridiculously good food; I will light up, I will fill with a tangible joy, and I'll tell you that the thing I love most about being on a cruise is the running. I run around the deck for three miles before breakfast every morning. I love it. If I go to the travel agent to book a cruise, and the ship does not have a running deck, I won't go. That's how much I love it.

It is not hard. I don't find it taxing. It is completely exhilarating. The daily run makes my holiday.

I have taught myself to love it by placing a healthy concept on my daily holiday run.

Reverse the adjective, and over time you will change the concept.

Say it even if you don't mean it. Say it even if at first you might not believe it. Eventually by changing your language, you will change your concept, and something that you once hated, you will learn to love.

The enlightenment being of course goes entirely beyond concept.

He levels the hills, and he fills the valleys (to quote the Christian canon).

As you expand awareness, you find equanimity in the whole manifest world.

At this level, good and bad, right and wrong, pain and pleasure present themselves simply as waves on the surface of a fathomless ocean.

*There is a field beyond right and wrong,* Rumi tell us, *I will meet you there.*

This field is consciousness.

The more we expand, the more aware we become of our observer.

Instead of your life being driven by disparate personalities, each with its own agenda, your life, instead, is directed by the divine economy, and steered solely by the one authentic you.

Your power is no longer watered down, spread over myriad personalities. As Blake said, all the subsidiary roots are pruned so that the sap can rise powerfully in one direction.

Our seminal energy is concentrated in the One I and this makes it potent and productive.

When I worked in the chemical factory, once a year all of the machinery was closed down for an annual clean of the containment tanks. The residue was so caked on, it had set against the copper interiors like concrete and only the most powerful cleaning tool would remove it.

What do you think the most powerful tool was?

Water.

We used water.

But this was not just water swished around a soapy bucket, and thrown on to the residue with an indiscriminate slosh followed by a wipe with an old sponge. This was water driven by a powerful motor through a tiny aperture at the end of two-inch solid rubber hosing.

The force was so powerful that the water coming through the nozzle could cut wood.

This is analogous with the principle of divine light or observance, projected through the one I, the single aperture of the human consciousness: it is immeasurably powerful.

When we develop the ability to concentrate and sharpen our consciousness on to a definite target, and with an aligned and certain intention, it can be used to clean even the most baked-on internal residue and it can also be employed to create the most splendid realities.

If the same water nozzle had twenty, or a hundred or a thousand outlets, its cutting power would be proportionately weakened. And if it lacked the powerful motor of singular intent, all the water in the world would not increase its capacity, because it is indiscriminate, it lacks concentration, it has no purpose or drive.

I have just finished working on a spiritually muscular play (a musical) for the theatre.

It is so divinely astute and aligned and conscious that it has had hundreds of patrons either crying, or cheering, or laughing, or singing along, or on their feet in rapturous ovation (often, all of the above at the same time) every night for three weeks. It is a rare spectacle to see a whole auditorium in singular alignment; the stage, the set, the design, the nine actors playing 13 different characters, the lighting designers, the sound technicians, the ushers, the bar-staff, the ticket office, a whole professional theatre all working in unison. And all of this manifest magnificence was squeezed through the nib of a pen when I made myself available to intuitive instruction; when I sat down, and made myself a vessel for the words.

I sat there, in the theatre, most nights watching this beautiful creation unfold before me and I was dissonant, because I knew, but could still not completely comprehend, how all of this was delivered through a human tabernacle, employing the vessel of a biro pen and its tiny nib-opening to lay the inky manna of our creation on the page.

It came through in such concentrated form, because there was only one Self sitting at the page, scribing the words.

There was not ten of me at the pen, each with a different idea, or separate agenda; there was no expectation, no demand for money or acclaim, no wish for accolades, there was no lethargy, and certainly there were no claims of ownership.

There was one command.

There was one writer.

There was one pen and one page.

There was one story.

The story was singular and it was the story I was instructed to write.

What I wrote was as surprising to me as it was to everyone who read or watched it.

As I was writing the words I was receiving the words.

The first time I heard the story was when the story came through the nib of my pen and alighted on the page.

When the divine force comes through the one I, it is so concentrated that, like the water-sword at the factory, it can cut through any blockage and it will create at the highest level.

While the energy is coming through several I's, it's always going to be compromised, it will always be weakened by division. Once the opposing I's have been subjugated, you become a powerful single force that can act on the world with tremendous efficacy.

The concentration is a force to behold.

The theology of negation is not about testing other people, it is not about reducing the world, or separating the pure from the impure somewhere out there.

It is about working local; it entails testing yourself, it is all about separating the pure and the impure in you – sorting the wheat from the chaff, as the gospels tell us.

But where do you start, with this internal purification, where should we begin?

In my own life, I looked at the elements (or elementals) of my collective being that I absolutely knew were not me.

That's where I started.

It might be confusing to take a concept as unfathomable and as divisive as (the word) God and then try and identify exactly what God is. It is perhaps just as difficult to locate who *you* are.

But, just as it is not difficult to know who God is not, it was not hard to know who I was not.

All of the great books suggest that at the level of union, man and God merge into a singularity where *my father and I are one*. So if we are able identify who we are by negation, we will surely be closer to identifying who God is through the same process.

In the old days I definitely did not know who I was but I absolutely did know who I was not.

This is how I started; this is the self-statement I made.

**I know without question that:**
I am not jealous.
I am not anger or rage.
I am not self-pity.
I am not envy.
I am not greed.
I am not criminal.

I am not a hypocrite.

I am not a liar or a cheat.

I am no thief.

I am not covetous.

I am not slovenly or gluttonous.

I am not violent.

I could go on.

My own list of personal vices was embarrassingly extensive.

I am not, I was not, and I refuse to be any of these impermanent, unsatisfactory identities.

They are not who I am, they are not Self.

And yet... and yet for a time I did still allow all these vices to live in me.

I permitted them to live through me and from me and even as me.

For a long incarnation I did allow that.

I didn't consciously permit defilement. Like most people, I was in denial. At the time I unconsciously blocked myself from seeing these misaligned elements because seeing them caused me discomfort. In retrospect I can see that I used a whole array of different defence-mechanisms to cover my faults: denial, rationalisation, blame, projection, reaction-formation, self-pity, anger bubbling over occasionally into uncontrolled rage. I used sex and sexual pornography, I drank lots of alcohol, and I consumed excessive food to anesthetise my pain-bodies.

For a long decade I even used violence as a defence mechanism.

I often made the mistake of viewing my sub-personalities with a romantic or sympathetic eye in order to deflect from what they actually were. It was easier to deal with dark personal energies if I called them quirks, character traits, or harmless anomalies. They could be tolerated, or understood or even forgiven if I was able to kid myself that they were *just part of my personality*. Naïvely, I even employed perverse pride with some of my shadows in order to shield me from the glare of honest appraisal. I lauded and celebrated my volcanic, Hulk-like temper. I would grin and gurn like the village-fool when people told tales of *Geoff Thompson's uncontrollable rage*, as though it was some kind of twisted virtue and not an ugly carbuncle.

I kidded myself that these aberrations were acceptable.

I told myself that they *weren't doing any harm, not really*.

I would convince myself that I wasn't greedy, I was just *a big lad, with a big appetite*. I rationalised and projected my self-pity on to others; it wasn't my fault, it was theirs: *they're just not recognising my talent. I'm not being rewarded for all my hard work*.

Or when things in my life fell apart, and I refused to take responsibility, I'd whine and complain, *why has this happened to me? I haven't even done anything wrong*.

I'd marinate in juvenile-dissonance, shake an angry fist at the sky, and register an unqualified complaint about not being looked after by an *unkind and random God*.

I was not a criminal, I was not a liar, and if you'd accused me of being a thief I would have been outraged. I would tell you in no uncertain terms that *everyone fiddles their taxes; everyone doctors their expenses; everyone tells 'white' lies, and buys bent goods, it's not really dishonest, it is not really stealing...*

The first thing I had to do when I started work on the theology of negation was dismiss all of these *weak*, unqualified, base-level rationalisations.

They dishonoured me. They were cowardly. They were below my game.

It is not someone else's fault if I am angry.

It is not government business laws that force me to cheat on my taxes.

There is only so long I could keep using the trauma of my past as an excuse for my present behaviour.

I was brutal in my cleansing.

I sniffed through all my hidden places, like a bloodhound.

I looked deeply at my life and my faults, at what *internal rigour* really meant and what a ruthless personal inventory actually entailed.

I went below the surface.

**Jealousy** is not acceptable.

It is a leak of energy that consumes.

Jealousy of sexual partners, jealousy of other people's successes (leaking out in cynicism and judgment) is an assault on Love.

**Anger** and **rage** are acts of subtle violence.

It is an abominable abuse of my essential energies when I spill them. And if I spill them on my kids in anger or impatience, I have to be brutally honest about what that actually makes me: it means I am a violent parent.

My wife is 48 years old and she still fills with a paroxysm of corrosive and dangerous fear-chemicals every time her elderly father raises his voice.

He schooled her in this dangerous Pavlovian response when she was a small, malleable, helpless child.

Anger is violence.

**Self-pity** is a childish and amateur spill of energy that disempowers.

It is the epitome of powerlessness and projected blame.

When we engage self-pity, we surrender our power to a squirming parasite that dines on the delicious energy of *poor old me*.

**Greed:** if I am overweight, and there is no medical reason why, then I am greedy.

It means I consume more than I need.

It tells me that I have no self-control.

Greed in one area opens the door to the greed in all areas: greed in relationships, greed in business, greed in life.

When I am greedy, I am not honouring my vows.

We take energy in with the implicit agreement that we will expend it again in volition. We invite pestilence when we do not behaviourally expend what we have physically consumed.

**Stealing:** you don't have to break into a shop or rob a bank to be a criminal.

Some of the biggest businessmen I know wrangle their way into millions of pounds and stay as close to the edge of judicial law as is humanly possible without breaking it, but they decimate myriad human and divine laws and morals and ethical standards en route.

You can be a mighty success in the world of men and still be a spiritual criminal. Wearing a charity coat twice a year will not negate the ethical laws we break every time we conduct business that is not righteous.

I don't need to go into detail here; if you are in business then you already know the moral laws that are trashed daily in the bid to increase net profit.

**Judgment:** you may not literally steal from your neighbour but you commit the greatest crime when you fall into judgment of them, or gossip, or envy or covet what they have.

There is no honour in this kind of behaviour; there is no intelligence in it either.

In the New Testament Joshua tells us that *the way you treat the least of you, is the way you treat me.*

How do you treat the least?

It is good to look at this, because the way you treat others is also the way you treat yourself.

All that caustic judgment, the cynicism, the unkindness, it is processed in every cell of your body before you dish it out.

And reciprocity means of course that we process everything at least twice: once when we deal it out, and once when we receive back the effect of our cause; the Karmic return.

## Hypocrisy

We are all hypocrites.

Unless we meet our highest ideals and set heady standards

with exemplary acts, every day, we are hypocrites.

Believe me, this is as painful for me to say as it is for you to hear; we are all hypocrites of the first order.

## Lying

Are you a liar?

If you rationalise your bad behaviours, you lie to yourself, which is the worst error of all because to lie to yourself is to not know yourself.

## Cheating

Are you a cheat?

If your thinking and your saying and your doing are not in righteous alignment, you are not congruent, and if you are not congruent, you subtly lie to everyone and cheat them in every encounter.

## Stealing

Do you steal?

When we gossip we steal energy from others.

When we lie, we imbibe (energy) illicitly, and we steal.

When we eat meat, we steal the muscle and flesh and fur – the body and limbs – from a fellow being.

We steal their right to life.

When we eat dairy we play our part in the violent and invasive and torturous treatment of animals and the children of animals.

If you doubt this, please don't demand proof from these pages, it is beyond my remit. A short internal dialectic with your conscience or a visit to the World Wide Web will give you all the evidence you need. It is there for anyone to see.

(Free range farmers) allowing chickens and cattle to run free in the field every now and then in no way negates the fact that, at some point, these beings will be herded, they will be shot in the head, or 'stunned' to death, then decapitated, then hung from meathooks, bled, dismembered and slapped on a dinner plate so that a more *elevated species* can dip their chips in the animals' blood.

There is no room here for self-congratulation.

There is no scope at all to feel proud of ourselves because the meat on our plate ran around a field before we killed it.

Yes, I know; I didn't like looking at it much either.

And none of this is written with any undercurrent of judgment.

How could I ever judge anyone?

I have committed the most heinous crimes during my sojourn on this spinning rock; against man, against animals, and against God.

The question we have to ask ourselves, the question I had to ask myself was, do you want to see the truth or not?

We can't work on the theology of negation, unless we look at the cold hard truth. We can't find out who we really are, until we look at those very coarse parts of who we are not.

I did look, and very closely (I am still looking).

In my bid for absolution, my goal of revealing the one authentic Self, I started by addressing my obvious and overt defilements first.

As we eliminate the aspects of ourselves that grasp and avert, we start to see our clear nature, and in seeing our own clear nature we are able to see the clear nature of things, without distraction and without judgment.

There can be no judgment when we see clearly, because there is nothing to judge. Things just are as they are, without concept.

In my own practice of negation, I exposed the things I grasped for, and the things I was averse to, one by one, over a period of time.

It does take time. It's a process that should not be rushed.

Once they were exposed, I stopped engaging them.

When the urge rose in me to partake in a defiling action –

grasping or aversion – I simply did not engage it. Recognising that they were no longer traits that I wanted to associate with, I distanced myself from them and instead encouraged their opposite.

In this way virtue replaced the vice.

In the beginning this was tough.

I'd fed and housed these habits and concepts for so long that they were very strong, they had a reserve-store of energy that allowed them a period of autonomous momentum, even if they were unable to feed from my emotional engagement. But without the feed of my identification, this store soon depleted and the defilements – those devils of habit – got weaker and weaker until eventually they either left of their own accord, they died or they were evicted or they transcended.

## Dialectic at the door

With most of my own shadows I have been able to remove them (usually by piecemeal) simply through the process of individuation: bringing the unconscious into the light of conscious awareness, and either integrating them into the whole, or dissolving them. Occasionally though, when a false personality is very strong and threatens to literally take my attention by storm, I have to forcefully stop it at the doorway and talk it down. To do this, I use the strong, trained internal voice of my sentinel ego to engage the invading element in a preventative dialectic.

This involves standing at the doorway to engagement with a conscious awareness, perhaps (when it feels appropriate) allowing the rage to vent, even giving the vice a voice, and allowing it to speak its vitriol (without my emotional engagement).

I will relay a particularly dangerous situation I had with a rage element that I was struggling to evict. This occurred many years ago, but I will retell it now, by way of example. Allow me first to offer some context to the situation in question.

An old friend – I will call him Bam – had threatened someone very close to me, someone I loved very dearly (I'll call her G).

G had committed a crime that she immediately and deeply regretted. She put her hands up to the crime, accepted full responsibility for her remiss, was taken to court and justly punished by the law. There were no complaints. G committed a crime, she expected to be punished and when she was she took it gracefully. It was a very difficult period for everyone that loved her, because she suffered intensely for her error. Bam watched this very personal crisis unfold from the periphery, and to cut a long story to its synopsis, he decided in his wisdom that the law had not punished G adequately enough. He also felt, insanely, that G, in committing this particular crime, had somehow betrayed him personally, and he was going to redress the issue by doing something about it. He did this by recruiting two other old friends of ours, and outing G in a social media hate campaign. By proxy of course, this threatened me: any attack on G felt like a personal attack on me. Bam was an old and trusted friend, so for me there was also a large degree of dissonance regarding his actions, which muddied the cerebral waters somewhat. Part of me just kept thinking, *why would my friends do this?*

Often in situations like this, there is no specific *why*. People are overtaken by their own rationalised weaknesses and rigourless rhetoric, or the pervading negative energies possess them, and for a time they are not themselves; even they probably don't know why they behave so abhorrently. You have to (learn to) be comfortable with this ambiguity.

After the fact, when Bam rang me to try and rationalise his actions, I felt such an overwhelming and uncontrollable surge of rage that I thought I might kill him. It took every ounce of my willpower to stop myself from become physically violent. I have never felt such homicidal anger. I realised of course that this was not me, and I knew that to allow myself to be the vessel of any violence would be wholly inappropriate. I also recognised that I was being presented with an opportunity. If three men as weak as these could trigger rage in me so keenly and so quickly, something in me was clearly amiss, and it needed to be addressed.

They acted as a poultice, these three men, which drew out a fear-element in me that I might not have seen otherwise.

At the time, my rage was so violent that I knew objective observation alone was not going to stop it. I needed a different technique, one that would cool the smouldering edges off this bubbling energy-ball, in preparation for dissolution via observation. So I took myself and my rage, and I sat in a very quiet room (in the basement of my apartment in London). I accessed the rage, and I let it say its piece. I sat before it like an internal counsellor and I allowed it to fully vent. I am aware now in retrospect that I placed the rage-element before my observer, the holy gaze, but used the voice of my sentinel ego, as a sort of fireguard, a buffer, or filter. Every time the rage voiced what he wanted to do to Bam – smash him, punch him, snap his bones, stamp on his throat, inflict every kind of heinous violence – I asked the rage: *and then what? What will the consequence of that action be to him and to you?*

The rage answered angrily (using copious expletives): *He'll be battered. He will bleed. He'll be broken. He'll be unconscious.*

I asked the questions, and allowed the rage to answer without edit and without interruption. Ultimately we got to the point where the rage acknowledged and admitted (and didn't care) that, if it was allowed to fully vent, Bam would be dead in the ground, he would be a corpse. I would end up in prison. I would lose my wife and my children, along with my liberty. Bam's gorgeous children and his sensitive wife would lose him.

My world as I knew it *and his* would be no more.

I relentlessly and objectively questioned the rage for a full hour before its energy dissipated and it was fully spent. Then, when the moment felt ripe, I asked another question: *Are you going to allow weak men like Bam to control you like a puppet? Are you going to allow them to take everything away from you?*

I felt the rage personality fall into a place of rationality, regret followed, and then compassion – not just for my life, but for the life of my old friend, and his family, and my family.

My true self emerged.

*Would it be worth it?* I asked, capitalising on the moment. I could feel the old part of me, the frightened, angry, afraid personality, shake his head in the negative; it would not be worth it. When compassion rose in me, I also felt the invading negative energies, that were trying to capitalise on this weakness, decamp.

When the rage had gone, all that was left was a vulnerable energy signature that felt like a gaping wound. I stopped talking and allowed the full force of my observer, consciousness itself, to alight on the wound and witness it, and the wound was washed.

There and then the rage was liberated. It has never returned. The wound was healed. Whatever the rage was, and wherever it came from didn't seem to really matter. It was gone, that was all. And the vacuum it left was filled with consciousness.

I exited the basement room calm, a new man. I walked upstairs. My wife hugged me. She said quietly, *well done.* She knew exactly what had gone on and the healing that had occurred.

I realised that, sometimes, if we allow an aberration to fully vent, in a safe place, if we just give it form, without doing anything in particular, it will show you its true nature. Once its nature has been exposed to light, it must itself become light.

In other words, if we allow the rage etc. to fully emerge – head, body and tail – and create a vacuum of non-doing for it to enter into, it will dissipate, and at the tail end of its hurricane, it will show you its wound.

In exposing its genesis, it is healed by consciousness itself, without any work from us at all.

Whether the rising was a surge of rage – I had a strong element of fear and anger in me for the longest time – or an attack of lust, disproportionate sexual arousal (it comes from the same carnal store as rage), mattered little. If the untamed energies of the lower soul rose in force, and threatened to take my engagement by storm, and my usual tactic of detached observation failed me, I learned to talk myself down.

As a younger man, unaware of any of these concepts, I often became uncontrollably angry, or overwhelmed by so much sexual lust that it physically hurt to me to contain it. These two primal energies did not come up all the time, but when they did I simply didn't have the wherewithal to stop them.

There are two schools of thought when it comes to eliminating aberrations like these. One is **source-healing**: we trace the feelings back to their source, and heal whatever wound is causing them to rise.

The other is **juncture-healing**: in this method we need not concern ourselves too much with genesis. We just meet the energy at the juncture point (the neck dent), where it vies for our engagement and seeks a behaviour release in the manifest world, and rebuff it.

The danger with the former is that defilements, as they present themselves, are not as they appear. They are usually symptoms of a deeper ailment; the effect you meet at the doorway is not the original cause. The energies that rise are often referred or triangulated. They may also have multiple causes, or the original cause might be something that you inherited, so locating the genesis within your present life cycle is unlikely..

As I have already suggested, with juncture healing it doesn't really matter where the aberration comes from, whether it is referred or triangulated, multi-sourced, genetically inherited or even if it is a negative external energy-form looking for a meal; it still relies entirely on our emotional engagement for its sustenance. It can't live for long, or experience any behavioural existence through us if we stop it at the juncture point and refuse it engagement. It may be strong, it may have a store of energy that allows it enough autonomy to attack our stronghold several times, without the replenishing feed of our identification, but its store is surprisingly finite, and without our engagement it will weaken and eventually perish.

When I think back to my days of manning nightclub doors, we (the door staff) didn't need to know where the troublemakers came from, or what sourced their aggression, when they demanded entrance to our club. If they were undesirable, we stopped them at the door, we fought them at the door if need be, it was as simple that. They did not get past us. They didn't enter our establishment. Some of them might chance their arm and come back more than once, if they were persistent, but this was quite rare. Once the criminal element knew that we ran a fierce-tight door, they learned to avoid us. We made our club a hard target. Why get into an affray with a hard target, when there were so many soft target clubs, all around the city centre?

You can employ either of these methods, or a combination of both if it suits; it's up to you. For the record this is my advice; any aberration or defilement (or energy signature) that rises contains its own genesis, its original nature and its own means of healing. No need to search too hard for it; if you observe them for long enough they will offer it up to you. You just have to be prepared to witness it in stark silence, without identification or judgment, and it will be healed.

I say this as though it is as simple as the words imply. I hope it goes without saying that it takes tremendous courage to guard the mind-door against attack, because you often have to sit in a cocktail of anxiety throughout the process.

The main thing from my perspective is that you clean your vessel, and sharpen your awareness so that your body and mind are inhospitable environments for the wrong elements – and make sure that the doorway to your heart is always heavily guarded.

Each time I was able to evict a sub-personality, my authentic self moved in to and occupied the vacated space and I got stronger and stronger.

As my authentic self expanded, took up more room, and grew in strength, I was able to take on more challenges, both in my body and in the world. My newly situated Self could act with ever-growing freedom and autonomy, without being hijacked and depleted by those old evicted personalities.

## Reality at the level of engagement

As you will have discovered from the last few pages, the practice of negation taught me that the reality of our sub-personalities only exists at the level of engagement.

If I engage negativity, I give negativity life for the duration that I keep engaging it.

If I engage Love (which is the ultimate aim), if I identify with selflessness, with kindness and charity, I give consciousness life; again, this only lasts for the duration of engagement.

I get to determine the colours and the shades and the tones of my reality by actively choosing what I want to identify with and eschewing what I deem unworthy of my association.

To reiterate; it is not just a matter of simply engaging a thought or emotion or an energy form and then experiencing it for the period it is engaged. It is much bigger than this. It is recognising that, when I engage anything, I give it life *through me*; I am the doorway to the world. If I allow these energies in I literally become incarnated into the form that I have engaged.

Engagement, identification, is a womb entrance and we should be very careful about the womb entrance we choose to enter, because it leads to an incarnation that is wholly determined by the nature of our engagement.

This incarnation might last for five seconds or it might endure for five or 55 years, depending on how quickly we recognise our remiss and how able we are to extract ourselves from it.

During that brief or long incarnation we accumulate karma

– good or bad according to the womb entrance we enter – and that karma, the debt, will have to be met at some point, now or in the future.

How many people have ruined their life by engaging a negative desire that has led to an action which has drastically altered their whole incarnation?

I had a friend who, in a moment of folly, decided to engage in a little drug dealing. He was desperate for money, and this (he felt) offered a quick solution, but it led to the greed and violence we all associate with crime and now he is serving two life sentences in a category A prison. His new *home* is so secure he can't receive or send letters without a mile of paperwork and weeks of processing.

His greatest sadness, he told me, was that he will never get to see his mother again, not in this lifetime. And he will not get to see his children grow up. By the time he leaves prison, if he leaves, his young children will be young adults, no doubt with their own families.

Another friend, a super-fit Marine, in a moment of drunken reverie dove head-first into a swimming pool after a night out with his friends. He didn't know that the pool had been drained for repairs that day. He landed on the concrete-bottom of the empty pool, on his head. His spine was shattered. He lived the rest of his very short life (he died a few years later, in his thirties) as a paraplegic in a wheelchair.

I would argue that the dangerous energy here, the one that ultimately stole his life, was not the one that compelled him to dive into an empty swimming pool. By then he was already compromised, his mind was no longer his own. It was the energy that drove him to the bar at the end of every workday that was to blame. Mind-altering stimulants (alcohol, drugs etc.) confiscate our ability to make rational choices. The driver of your chariot is drunk, he has fallen asleep, which means that any malcontent can climb into your passenger seat and determine the state of play. As I may have already stated, if you let in one vice, you let in all vice; a leak anywhere is a leak everywhere.

Once you really understand the power of your own personal engagement and the many incarnations we put ourselves through, even in a single day, you begin to urgently monitor the energies that bid for your attention and you only let the right ones in.

The large defilements, once removed, reveal the more subtle shadows, those that hide themselves behind the doors of our defence-mechanisms.

Eventually, with practised discernment and laser-keen observation you are able to evict all of the old sub-personality-squatters, knock back any invading temptations that court your engagement, and retain complete autonomy over your own kingdom.

Once this is achieved, the ego becomes the sentinel ego that mans the doorway of your heart.

The Chinese general, Sun Tzu, said that we should keep an army for a hundred years, even if we only use it for a single day.

The work is not complete just because the kingdom is cleaned of undesirables.

Like the devil of scripture, if you kick out one, he will return with ten more.

Now that your inner-city is clean, the gates need to be constantly guarded.

You have taken your sovereignty back, but your throne needs to be maintained.

As a security expert, in my early thirties, I was once recruited to a nightclub that was overrun with local villains. I ran a very tough team at the time, and we were brought in and paid to clean the place up. This entailed evicting and barring the existing troublemakers from the premises and guarding the door against other potential troublemakers who might try to get in. It took us about two months and some bloody and frightening encounters, but eventually we made the club clean; the gangsters kept away and the club became a haven for the locals who wanted to enjoy an evening out without the threat of violence.

However, the moment the place was clean of rats, the owners of the club – like the cheating citizens of Hamelin – did not want to pay the piper. They decided they no longer needed our services. In short, they let me and my team go. The very first night that the bar was left without security, the gangsters returned in force. They not only invaded the space again, they also forcefully took control of the door, and by proxy the club; they became the new security.

The locals who had briefly enjoyed the peace of their clean local, left en masse.

The pub eventually fell into disrepair and closed down.

It was derelict for many years before the land was bought up by developers.

The club is now a block of flats

The security you have created needs to be maintained, even strengthened.

While you are in a body, this will always be the case.

In theology this process of inner cleaning is called kenosis.

It is a method of self-emptying.

We self-empty in order to create clean space for the higher Self to enter.

If the sentinel ego is the manager looking after the infrastructure of the human tabernacle (the body) then the higher self is the CEO.

The divine CEO.

Before we meet the CEO, let's first explore the Divine Covenant.

## Chapter 5

# The Divine Covenant

Whether we are consciously aware of it or not, we are in covenant with what the Chinese sage Lao Tzu called the 10,000 things (the world). These are the overt contracts we make, with mortgages and loans, with work or insurances, with banks or mobile phone networks. It is also the implicit agreements we make with family, with friends, with the social mores and religious and cultural dogma. Or even the implicit, often repressed or suppressed protocols we honour with our own sub-personalities – what the mystic Eckhart Tolle calls *pain-bodies*.

Pain-bodies, or shadows, are the alter-egos that exist in everyone (they also exist as incorporeal, free-floating energy forms that pervade the atmosphere around us) and they feed on the drama and chaos and pain of the causal world.

As I mentioned in previous chapters, they rise up inside us, these false impressions, they rise or they approach from the outside in order to be fed; if we engage them, they incarnate through us and feed from the spoils of our essential energy – specifically energy expended in painful or salacious human experience.

It doesn't take a genius to see that the world runs mostly on negative energy.

These *adverse forces* of negativity feed on melodrama, they dine on the pain of human existence, Sri Aurobindo assures us, and this is where they create their greatest havoc; they use it to bring about in us a state of depression, playing with a very old teammate within us, who Sri calls *the man of sorrows* (the self-pitying, sleeping lower ego) *who cannot help but loving melodrama even as he cries out for relief.*

Negative energy is easily accessible to these *adverse forces*.

Almost anyone can be tricked out of their energy and forced into an emotional intercourse, an intimate exchange of energy, against their own will. As little as a well-contrived TV advert or provocative news bulletin or an unkind Facebook post can trick you into expending essence in the form of anger or judgment or emotion.

As Tolle says, this equates to *pain bodies feeding off other pain bodies*.

We are under attack by these covert forces, at all times, whether we are able to acknowledge it or not, especially those of us who are heading for an enlightened destination. If you look closely enough, you will see evidence of this illicit and covert exchange everywhere; it is going on right now, inside you, outside you, and all around. Your anger is triggered or your fear spiked or dissonance aroused by an unkind word on your Twitter feed, or a curt email from a friend or associate; suddenly you engage in, or you are tricked into engaging in, an angry intercourse (internal or external: same thing) that can completely deplete your energy reserves within a few heated exchanges. A whole day's worth of human, seminal energy can be spent without profit in an unconscious instant.

Sometimes the attack comes from external forces, other times it comes from a weak human source, or inhuman forces, working through a weak human force. The raison d'être of these adverse forces is to keep humanity asleep, in a herd mentality, where we are easy pickings for the roaming lion. It would be easy to imagine that these forces – devils, demons, divides, shades etc. are entirely malign, but as I understand it, they are ordained, everything is ordained, our Source is omnipotent and omniscient and omnipresent, there is nothing that sits outside of Its domain. In Islam these negatives are known as *God's master swordsmen*, and they are sent to teach us how to perfect our weapons. If we understand their nature, we are able to recognise that they serve us, by keeping us in holy-alignment with the use of divine shocks if we stray beyond the virtue-borders.

If we stay in holy alignment, these forces are of no consequence, they are impotent against anyone who is aligned to Love, and unless we err, we are invisible to these forces. Virtue is our invisibility cloak.

However, we become vulnerable to assault if we fall out of alignment; as Al-Ghazali warns, *if we court vice, we will be noticed.*

Online they call this kind of arousing provocation *baiting.*

You are drawn into an exchange of energy by the tasty-bait of a heinous comment or a titillating image or salacious gossip; you impulsively reply to the comment or you press the link to reveal or see more and suddenly you are engaged.

Engagement leads incrementally and subtly and covertly into deeper and deeper identification until eventually you realise that even if you switch your computer off, the parasite that baited you, the image that captured your eye has already been implanted on to your impressionable ego. Like a direct debit, it draws down on your energy every time the (stored) comment or image fires off in your brain; it feeds off you every time you engage it.

This kind of human-siphoning (or bleeding) is so potentially damaging that it can deplete your essence until there is more parasite in you than human. Eventually it lives inside you, as a fear, as guilt, as an arousing trigger or a festering wound. It eats you from the inside out until all that is left is a robot doing the bidding of those possessing-impressions. Either that, or it cleans you out and leaves you as an empty husk.

Many people – as we all know, as we have all witnessed – end up so depleted by these parasites, that they terminate their own lives.

Shockingly, this is common.

Everyone knows someone who has committed suicide.

It is happening under our very noses every day.

This human bleeding is inflicted on you and me every time

we consciously or unconsciously engage a negative emotion. It can hook you, this parasite, with clever advertising, with garish imagery; specific and contrived sounds can be used to steal your attention: fear, sexual arousal, idle curiosity, voyeurism, dissonance and a thousand other tricks are used to draw you. Often, online trolls will post heinous comments about you or about other people that are almost beyond human comprehension. Often it is so difficult to process (which is how it's designed) that it creates a cognitive dissonance. The moment we engage and try to unravel the fear that mental confusion causes, we are, once again, engaged; pain-bodies are feeding off pain-bodies and a frenzied exchange of energy ensues.

While we are distracted and raped of our vital energies, it leaves us little time or power to wake up and recognise what is happening.

Every time we are tricked into engagement or identification – the energy-exchange – we unwittingly create a covenant with the object of our engagement. That covenant might be a one-off exchange of energy, or it could be a Trojan horse, a seemingly harmless *gift* that sneaks a hidden army of defilements through the gates of our psyche.

This is pretty much how all addictions start. Light titillation, flirtation, leads to a fully-immersed, life-threatening addiction: to food, to drink, to people-pleasing, to drugs or sex, or gambling etc.

Most people harbour several parasites.

They sit inside them, hidden (or vaguely visible) but ever-active; in the case of addiction *highly active*, or dominant. Sometimes they might lie dormant for long periods of time, rising periodically for a feed.

There is a singular defence against these dark energies: love. Love everyone without exception. Love your life, every single day.

We spoke in the last chapter about the idea of kenosis, the

art of self-emptying; this is a method we consciously employ to unearth the repressed, suppressed, or hidden covenants that take regular energy-payments from us. Kenosis is a method of exposing and severing every negative covenant. Once we have exposed, and purged and broken these myriad contracts, we are then in a position to create a single covenant with the One, the Absolute.

This singular covenant creates a complete paradigm shift.

It is simple enough in principle, but all-consuming in practice; it asks everything of you, everything, everything, everything.

But of course, our little worldly *everything* is as but a drop of dew when compared with vast oceans of divine return; the rewards are unbounded.

It is worth mentioning here that my own covenant with God has been gradual; it has increased exponentially over a long period of time. I have been practising kenosis for decades now, and each time I was able to break a negative covenant, it automatically made room for expanded consciousness and placed me in a deeper covenant with the Divine Economy. But there is (I have noticed) a tipping point. In our practice we reach a critical mass, where your covenant with the positive finds dominance and starts to outweigh your covenant with the negative. At this pivotal juncture you are proffered the opportunity to make a covenant-proper with God. You go from serving two masters – the world and the divine – to serving only One.

In the divine covenant, your dharma is to serve the higher force. All personal ambitions are sidelined. You no longer work from personal volition, or for individual gain. You graduate from self-service to selfless-service.

At this level (as I have mentioned) your job is simply to receive instruction and follow it, unquestioningly. Your intuition will be so clear and your faith so strong that you won't need to know the reason for or the consequence of your instruction, only that it has been ordained. You will receive a command, and you will follow it, trusting that the highest potential will come from your actions, either now or in the future.

Like the postman of my earlier metaphor, you will deliver every letter and every package in your bag, taking no credit for the delivery, and seeking no detail of its content or purpose.

In the covenant proper, all your means – capital, a roof, transport and supper – will be provided, at the exact time of their need. They may (and usually do) arrive at the eleventh hour, from unexpected sources and in unfathomable or unfamiliar ways, but they will arrive.

My own covenant-proper was initiated after I had a major epiphany some years ago whilst workshopping a play I'd written, at the National Theatre Studio in London, England.

The National is seen as a Mecca for all things theatrical, so I knew from the very beginning that my invite into this auspicious space was Godsent, it was leading me to a station, densities beyond the National itself.

One afternoon, whilst working on the play (which later became *Food Order*), one of our wonderful actors (Patrick) delivered a monologue that was a part of the story. As soon as he started to recite the words I felt the room, and then the world, fall away; my heart expanded exponentially and I experienced the definite presence of God.

I was in rapture. I remember thinking in astonishment: *am I the only one witnessing this?*

I looked around me, and I saw that the director was crying.

A voice in my head spoke quietly: *get rid of everything now, and just do this.*

The words were as few as they were simple, but their intent was profound, and detailed and undeniable. I knew in this one simple line of instruction that I was being called to make a commitment – a divine covenant – to change everything in my life, in order that I could dedicate my entire self to a deeply personal esoteric quest that would be realised (at least initially) through the art of writing.

In retrospect, I can see that I had been expecting this moment of clarity. I'd anticipated an absolute covenant for some time. Whilst I had been outwardly successful in the world for a couple of decades, lately I'd felt stuck in a frustrating limbo. I knew in these few succinct words that an entirely new direction was called for, a completely different way of living in the world.

On the way back to my apartment that night, walking over London Bridge, I excitedly rang my wife Sharon. Looking out across the Thames, I told her what had happened.

*"We have to sell everything,"* I said urgently, *"I have been instructed to dedicate my life to writing."*

She simply said, *"OK, let's do it."*

Yes, ladies and gentlemen, that is the kind of amazing girl I was blessed enough to marry.

The instruction continued to unfold over the next three years; we sold and repaid the mortgage off our London apartment, and used the profit to pay off my mum's house (one of our three mortgages) which left us with a very small mortgage on our own house (which we planned to pay off as soon as more funds made themselves available). By doing this, my need to make money was vastly reduced, leaving me with time and energy to concentrate on making myself a clean, singular vessel for the writing – bearing in mind that the writing *was* an essential tool for my personal kenosis. I was downloading words and sounds and symbols from a divine place, and the essence cleaned me as it came through me.

As well as selling my apartment, I closed the mail-order company I was running. I stopped teaching martial arts classes. I let go of nearly all the people I was mentoring (other than two long-term uchidechi). I severed all connections with social media; I changed my email address and my phone number.

The Mexican shaman Don Juan Matus would call this *getting rid of your personal history.*

In order to become the authentic Self, you have to subjugate all the old selves; you can't create a new reality without first destroying the old, in fact it is with the old that we rebuild the new.

I let go of anything and anyone that I intuitively considered extraneous to my instruction, this included personal ambition.

It is not that I actively eschewed material gains; these are a natural and exponential effect of working with a divine covenant, and I celebrate and appreciate and enjoy them as and when they are delivered; it is just that I was no longer aiming for them anymore, not specifically.

So, I suppose you could say I embarked on a divine fast, reducing everything in my life, internal and external, to make more room for God.

The process was tough.

I was not making decisions based on the world anymore. I was taking instruction and direction that the world would not necessarily understand or agree with. My friends and business partners and associates could not possibly fathom some of the decisions I was making. I let go of 90% of my immediate earning potential, because where I was earning money was no longer congruent with where I was being called to work.

This was, of course, very worrying for my wife, and remained a point of great anxiety for nearly three years.

My accountant was also dismayed at how much my top-line had fallen: *terrible year, Geoff,* he said, *terrible.*

*No not terrible,* I tried to explain, understanding even as I said it that he wouldn't understand, *it's not terrible, it was planned, this was expected.*

As I briefly mentioned, part of my new, singular covenant was that I would do the work requested of me, and the money and the means to live would be supplied; people (I was assured) would feel the urge to give me capital when I needed it, they would pay me, for books, for plays, for films, or they would simply feel the overwhelming desire to patronise me.

Money would appear.

Not everyone liked what I was doing.

Very few people understood what I was trying to achieve.

Some openly criticised me, others felt that I must be dying; why else would I abandon Twitter, why else would I voluntarily exile myself?

I didn't care what anyone else thought.

My agreement was no longer with them, my covenant was with God.

As I removed the elements of my old life, I created an internal vacuum that was automatically filled with consciousness. This gave me the extra energy I needed to carry out the dedicated work I was being called to do.

Cancelling my worldly covenants also removed blocks in my spiritual perspective. This afforded me a *clearer view*. In other words, when I removed the veils of worldly obfuscation – business dealings, money worries, imagined success-trajectories – I was able to see true. I was able to understand (a little about) who we are (as a species), why we are here, what we are here to do, and how and when we are called to do it.

The effects of kenosis, my spiritual fast, were enlightening.

My writing went to another level; the words coming out were definitely from *that other field*. Many other gifts came to me in revelations and realisations and introductions and an expansion of awareness that showed me categorically what I am here to do, and the importance of (me) being a vehicle for essence.

In short: the reduction (or fasting) resulted in the gift of a personal covenant between me and God; I follow Its instruction (usually via Intuition or inspiration or signs) and It delivers the wherewithal for those instructions to find voice and form in the world.

I have (and I am still working on this) surrendered my personal sovereignty, and given it over to God.

Instead of trying to make my way in an unfathomable, sign-less reality, street-by-street, road-by-road, city-by-city, I plugged into the Divine Satnav.

This was *my* personal covenant.

Yours, if you are called to make one, will be different to mine, no doubt, but it will be just as personal, no less demanding, and equally rewarding.

As I said, it is very simple in principle; you are no longer negotiating your own way through the labyrinthine corridors of this world territory.

You offer up your personal freedom, and surrender it to your highest potential.

In Christian mysticism this is known as *freedom under authority*.

It might not sound very appetising when you read it off the dry page, and there may be a danger of this sounding religiously dogmatic, and servile.

I look at it differently.

I see it in simpler terms.

I view this covenant as a joining, a gathering together.

It is nothing less than plugging your radio into the main's electric, or using a satnav in your car to make your journey on the roads easier, or employing the Google search engine to connect you to the World Wide Web, or plonking a satellite dish on the side of the house so you can access innumerable TV channels on Sky.

I was simply plugging in.

I was reconnecting with my highest potential, an elevated version of myself who knows the why, the where and the how, and can guide me faultlessly to my Idyll.

All I have to do is hear the command and follow it.

As for instance: If I was pure light, and I wanted to travel from object to subject through water, from a frog on the bottom of the pond to the eye of the beholder on the side of the lake, I could spend lifetimes manually calculating the trillions of possible routes looking for the most direct, or I could connect to Nature, and allow Her to do the sum instantaneously and proffer me the optimal route.

Making a divine covenant is nothing more and nothing less than connecting to Nature and allowing It to map our perfect trajectory.

As I am sure you can see, the divine covenant is all-encompassing.

It is also a very serious business.

We need to clearly understand the ramifications of such an agreement before we fully commit to it. The divine covenant comes with a caveat that cannot be negotiated, and it includes penalties that will not be escaped if at any time we break our vow.

The caveat is this: we will serve only one God.

The warning that we have fallen out of alignment with our covenant is the **divine shock** (more on this in the relevant chapter), and the penalty for breaking the covenant completely is (possible) spiritual exile – we (in effect) evict ourselves from *our Eden*.

In the Vedanta classic, the Bhagavad-Gita, Lord Krishna, the Godhead, warns his ward Arjuna Pandava, who has been tricked out of alignment by fear, *that those who find the soul and then lose the soul are lost to the future and to the past.*

In the first book of the Pentateuch (Genesis – the Five Books of Moses), Adam and Eve fall into temptation. They break their covenant with God, by tasting the forbidden fruit from the tree of knowledge. As a consequence they are evicted from Paradise.

By agreeing a covenant with the world (eating the apple) they automatically broke their covenant with their Source.

In effect, they pulled the plug out of the wall, and disconnected themselves from the mains-electric.

They self-exiled.

They disconnected from Power when they chose to eat the

apple of knowledge.

The covenant says that we cannot serve two masters.

Trying to serve two masters creates an immediate cognitive dissonance (which haemorrhages essential energy and attracts *beast and fowl*). It creates an internal conflict, where two diametrically opposing truths compete in the same creative space.

This is a simple, neurological precedent; it is not the work of a jealous God.

It is also an esoteric precedent: two masters equate to internal duality. Duality is the manifest world that we live in.

The divine covenant is an invitation to exit duality, and matriculate into a singularity.

In the Zohar, the exegesis of the Torah, it tells us that there are three realms of man: the masses exist in **the vegetable realm**. The businessmen, the entrepreneurs and politicians exist in **the animal realm**. The spiritual adepts, those who have transcended the lower densities and seek only to serve, exist in what is known as **the human realm**.

Unless they wake up, the vegetable realm cannot access any other realm than their own. Those in the animal realm can move in and out of the animal and vegetable at will, but (unless *they* wake up) cannot access the human realm.

The human realm (because its occupants are fully awake) can move in and out of every realm at will, but they only do so in order to serve the greater good.

The divine covenant is an invitation into the human realm.

In the lower realms, duality is the constant.

Duality, in esoteric parlance, means to be divided. In the macrocosm, this equates to a world – its people, its cultures and its countries and continents – that is divided against itself.

In the microcosm, it spells internal division; man is divided against himself.

*We are divided.*

The common biblical idiom tells us rightly that a house, divided against itself, will fall.

*Divide* is the root word for devil or demon.

When we fall into division, we are possessed by demons.

When Jesus cast out demons, he literally removed the dissonance or internal division from those possessed by opposing concepts. Christ was spiritually aligned, so in his presence, those who were divided automatically became aligned to him, because his was the most dominant atmosphere.

Jesus (or Mohammed, or Krishna, or Buddha) was the tuning fork that attuned those who were out of key.

In repairing their divided beliefs, he removed them from duality, and aligned them back to unity.

He plugged them back in to the mains electric.

We become a walking, talking, quarrelling contradiction when we are divided, and our troubled and confused ego projects its corruption on to the manifest world.

The divine caveat might look at first glance like the thundering command of an old testament God, the jealous Logos of scripture.

It is and it is not.

God *is* jealous, not in the human sense of covetousness, but in the absolute sense of exactitude. The caveat has to be absolute, it has to be obeyed; but not to satisfy a greedy or insecure god-figure; rather it is there for our own protection and the protection of the soul.

God is *not* jealous, but only in the sense that it is not a man-projected sovereign-figure demanding total loyalty without reason or qualification. Instead, It is a familial energy trying to protect us from the pain of disconnection, a father or a mother figure, who metaphorically holds our hand across a busy road, or keeps our fingers protected from sharp objects.

The holy-covenant is not an emotional adjunct to a list of juvenile, hysterical human rules; it is a life-saving, soul-protecting, benevolent essential, an instructional dictate that sees the danger ahead and sets out to forewarn us of it.

I am not an overbearing father simply because I keep my children away from dangerous energies, skulking and lurking on Internet message boards.

I am not an unkind authoritarian if I shout a warning at my young offspring when they venture carelessly towards a busy road. I am not dogmatic when I demand that they heed my command first time. I am urgent and insistent because I love them and I don't want to see them hurt.

Am I a jealous alchemist, when I absolutely demand that my students employ the greatest protection and care without compromise, when they are dealing with acids, and caustics and other elements and poisons that can kill as keenly as a blade or a bullet?

I mentioned earlier that I worked for a time in a chemical plant. It was a highly flammable environment, with huge signs everywhere warning employees and visitors not to use any form of naked flame. On one occasion, a worker – it was his very first shift on the plant – was being shown around on a night-shift by the plant foreman. As he was showing him the acid vats, he complained about the lack of light around this particular part of the factory at night, and promised to show the new worker around in the morning, when the sun came up and natural daylight prevailed. Thinking that he was being helpful, the new worker took a cigarette lighter from his pocket, and immediately lit the flame, to try and better illuminate the area.

He was instantly sacked.

He was dismissed on the spot and sent home.

Some might argue that this ruling was unkind, the absolute law of a jealous factory boss demanding complete and unquestioned adherence to the plant rules. I would suggest that the rules are there for a reason; our unwitting and thoughtless worker could quite easily have blown the whole place up and everyone in it with this one careless act.

What am I saying?

I am saying that the divine caveat is there for our own protection, for the protection of the resident soul. When we test or prove our vessel, the tabernacle, we invite the higher soul to descend, to communicate with the lower soul and take up residence in the body.

The higher soul is powerful; no doubt, all of the Siddhas, the creative miracles and the agency of God itself occur because of its presence in the body.

But the soul is also highly vulnerable to the careless, the unwitting and the abusive: it is as fine as gossamer; it is as sensitive to negative exposure as film is to light.

The divine covenant, with its caveat of *one master*, is in place to protect, not to aggressively dominate, or unnecessarily govern.

In the human realm, we take our instruction from a singular source, from the one master. To take instruction from the world as well is to fall out of alignment, and attempt to serve two sources at the same time.

You will, I am sure, already have had your own experiences of the soul dipping in and out of your world; those moments of high inspiration and clarity and stillness; the feeling of deep unconditional love is a sure sign of the present soul. But it is an elusive and private energy, the higher soul. It does not enter easily, and it will not stay in a human arc for long if it is not cleaned of human duality and elemental stench, if it is not guaranteed the protection of a fiercely loyal and highly-trained sentinel ego. Even if, and even when, everything in the body and mind is cleaned and prepared there is still no guarantee that the divine CEO (the soul) will take up permanent residence immediately.

In my own case, I made a definite covenant with the divine and the CEO entered me to the exact degree that I made space for it, to the level of my work on continued kenosis, and the around-the-clock protection I vouchsafed it. I was shown early in my development that I could have as much of God as I wanted (and the CEO is certainly the bridge to God) but I had to make room for Him – this is my ongoing process.

As I said, once the higher soul is in residence it is vulnerable.

If you break your covenant and fall into vice in any of its forms, it is living torture to the soul and, of course, because the soul is now in you and communicating with the lower soul, its pain is your pain. Its shock is your shock. Its agony is your agony.

I have experienced first-hand the torment of the soul when exposed to vice.

It is completely disproportionate to anything I have ever felt before and it is in no way commensurate in degree to the offending vice.

As little as a single exposure to excess (porn, violence, greed, judgment etc.) is torture to the soul. This might sound overly dramatic or an exaggeration of the facts but why exaggerate when the truth is enough. The experience is not unlike touching a live electrical cable. The shock of a light touch can throw you across the room as keenly as a full grasp.

The caveat is there to protect the soul and to protect you.

If you agree a divine covenant, but also worship false Gods – engage in vice – not only will it be painful for all involved, but the higher soul, unable to abide defilement, will quickly vacate the body; this is both unfortunate and dangerous.

If we break the covenant we may never get a chance in this particular body to create another, and a kingdom without a king will be quickly overrun.

There is also the very real danger of the higher soul vacating halfway through the process of integration with the divine ego, leaving the latter in an addled state, neither here nor there, neither this nor that; a half-cooked hybrid of something and nothing.

I have seen many people fall into this misshaped, ill-formed state, half hatched and spiritually dissonant, unable to function in the manifest world but at the same time disabled from operating in the divine.

Many end up in mental hospitals, or like Tootles in *Peter Pan*, wandering in a nether-world looking for their lost marbles.

You may accuse me of giving more weight to the process than it needs or deserves.

I say only as I see.

I speak only of what I have personally experienced.

I have lost friends under the wheels of peak-hour Tube trains, I've seen other very worthy people end up at the mental asylum because they rushed their development or tried to serve two masters.

The knowledge is esoteric for a reason.

The gate is deliberately narrow; many are called but only a few will enter.

Why?

Because this covenant asks everything of those who enter.

The divine covenant itself is a natural and organic extension of waking the sentinel ego and cleansing the body.

The sentinel – like the new broom that sweeps clean – breaks the old covenants with the world and chooses instead to break bread with virtue.

## You Will Be Noticed

When you elect a sentinel ego and he takes charge, you will be noticed.

Like will attract like.

When we live in the world and we fall into any kind of vice, we are noticed too, by people and elemental energies that exist in the same frequency.

This should be no surprise to anyone.

If you walked into a rough bar, or wandered in to a disreputable area or visited an illicit website on the World Wide Web, you would not be surprised if you were noticed by the locals, by the inhabitants of the site, and by the webmasters themselves.

It goes without saying, I hope, that if you walk down a dark alley at night or kerb-crawl in a red-light district, your chances of being attacked or propositioned increase exponentially.

Similarly, when we entertain vice, we will be noticed by visible and incorporeal energies; beings that peddle in the dense energies we court, adverse forces whose purpose it is to derail human evolvement.

Why would anyone do that?

As I mentioned earlier, these energy forms are fed and nourished by unconscious, negative energy; if we evolve and stop supplying their sustenance, their store of easy-meat will be withdrawn. They are invested in keeping everyone asleep because their existence relies on it, we are like farmed cattle to them, so they will make every effort to disable any individual or group who tries to help people wake up and evolve.

Similarly, when you start to court virtue, you will also be noticed by visible and invisible guides that will help and encourage and protect you.

Whichever path you choose, you will be noticed.

To protect yourself against the lower energies, simply make yourself invisible.

You make yourself invisible by not only eschewing all association with them, but also by actively courting their opposite.

If the adverse forces congregate on the frequency of **lower-hell-radio** and you are tuned into **higher-heaven-FM**, the higher becomes invisible to the lower. In fact you are invisible to all the other frequencies other than the one you are tuned in to; it will be as though you do not even exist to the lower bandwidths. It is only when we start playing with the dial and flirting with different stations that we fall out of frequency and once again become noticed. And, if we do enter the lower frequencies, we will be seduced, attacked or assailed.

Similarly (and of course a wiser choice) the moment you are noticed in the higher realms, you are courted by the higher potentials.

When you are *doing the work*, as Gurdjieff would call it, it will be noted that you have a sentinel ego in place and that you have a cleansed vessel.

When you are noticed, manna in the form of instruction – books, teachers etc. – will be subtly presented to you. No tricks, no coercion, just the offer of a guide on your path. If you accept and engage and identify with these gifts, you have opened an account with the divine economy and an informal covenant with higher power is made.

It is worth stipulating that these gifts, these offers of reciprocal exchange, occur because of the work already done; your esoteric rigour has elevated you to a finer density, a locale that is shared by other energies vibrating at the same ratio.

They approach because you have been noticed, you are seen.

You are *in the room* because you put yourself in the room.

The more you court virtue and Love, the more virtue and Love will court you.

And the faster you move and the harder you work, the faster the divine economy will move and the harder it will work to serve your development.

There is a beautiful line in the New Testament: *if you take one step towards Me, I will take ten steps towards you.*

The covenant starts off casually and increases in intensity according to the investment you bring. As I invested ever-increasing amounts of time and energy in my spiritual development, ever-increasing amounts of instruction have been placed before me. Exoteric books led me to esoteric tomes, books and tomes led to dedicated practice; practice led to teachers – all sorts of wonderful, mysterious guides – knowledge followed and awareness expanded. This, in turn, placed me into ever-refined frequencies, which contained the next level of work, and books, and talks, and gurus and Sufis.

When I was studying Hinduism, I started out with a small handout offered to me on an Edinburgh street by a devotee of the Hare Krishna movement. I devoured the pamphlet, and the inspirational words from Vedanta led me to read the Bhagavad-Gita; the Gita led to the Mahabharata, which in turn guided me to the 16-volume Srimad Bhagavatam. The moment I ordered the Bhagavatam (my children bought it for me as a gift) I was contacted by an esteemed Hindu Pujari (priest) who wanted to meet me.

I had been noticed.

He gave me information and instruction about my path that no book could have offered.

What he told me was both personal and prophetic.

It was as though he had read my mind. He knew exactly who I was and where I needed to go next and why. He sent me to a temple in London and the Pujari there added layers of instruction and guidance beyond what the books had offered.

Each time I accepted the gift of their guidance and did the work, another level of covenant was formed.

Whilst in the lower regions, my covenants were all with the world and were at best selfish and fear-based, at worst corruptive and carnal and dark and *ultimately* enslaving.

The higher covenant was the mirror opposite.

It was benevolent, it was patient and kind, it was gentle and nurturing and completely transparent.

I was not tricked, like the worldly covenants secreted into my mind by the adverse forces, and led into ever-decreasing circles of fear; I was simply invited into higher and higher levels of bliss, until I reached a point where I wanted to make a full commitment; I needed to create a full-fat covenant with God from which there could be no turning back.

As I already said, at this level you are no longer working

from the stance of individual ambition or for personal gain or profit or acclaim – though all of these are often gifted to you as an exponential effect of your covenant – rather, you are working under the guidance and from the direct instruction of consciousness.

At this level, we stop relying on the unfathomable world and instead give all of our autonomy over to the inner tutor. In return we get to live the optimum experience: heaven as it is on earth.

With a divine covenant you are led to your true life purpose.

Your part in the divine plan is revealed and your optimum path proffered to you. Your job, then, is to heighten your singular vision, clarify your inner hearing until it is acoustic; you have to sharpen your imagination (imagination in its true sense, which is the ability to decipher the encoded *images* you are shown in visions), you have to read the signs and identify the symbols and words, and break the codes that will be presented to you by way of instruction and understanding.

Even, and perhaps especially, when the covenant is in place, there can no longer be room for complacency; we still have to constantly clean, we must still continually guard the heart and conscientiously remain alert both to the divine messages *and* the roaming lion of negativity, who is always on the lookout for a wayward soul to tempt from the path.

Cleaning at this new, elevated level no longer involves manually wrestling with your defilements, like Jacob at the top of his divine ladder. It is very easy to muddy the waters if we keep regurgitating the same sins, trying to clean them again and again. Rather, the cleaning or healing now comes directly from grace itself. When defilements (or their residue) rise, as they will continue to do, we no longer engage them at all; we simply access complete silence and stillness, and they are individuated by the God force, consciousness itself claims them.

It is difficult to articulate in a book but, in the covenant, every aspect of your life will be quietly and intuitively dictated to you:

what you eat, what you drink, what you do, where you go, who you associate with, who to avoid, whether you turn right or left or go straight ahead, when to push, when to yield, when to readily agree and when to firmly rebuff.

## Cleansing Stations

Periodically, the divine satnav will also direct you to *cleansing stations*.

These are specific places or environments where the prevailing atmosphere acts like a poultice, to draw out residual weaknesses. You may be guided to a place you fear to go, you might be given a platform of human power and privilege that further tests your virtue, or perhaps you will be placed before a temptation that draws out a hidden weakness.

Defilements will be drawn out of you and revealed so you can forgive them or *give them over* (allow them to be dissolved by God) so that you can continue to make more room for consciousness.

These stations also act as whetstones, on which you again sharpen and prove your consciousness.

I always do my best to accept these invites, even though I often don't want to. I take the invitation with gratitude, because I want to be cleaned, I want to make room.

You will know if it is an invite to a cleansing station, by your own reaction. The very fact that you won't want to go, your unrighteous resistance to accept will be an indicator that you should rally towards your instruction. Adverse forces, coupled with the lower parts of you (that *man of misery*) that have not yet been converted, will undoubtedly throw up lots of resistance. They will assail you in a thousand different ways, and whisper copious legitimate reasons in your ear as to why you should not, or could not or simply will not go. These rationalisations are usually underpinned by indignation or fear, or disproportionate anger or cognitive dissonance; certainly you will be urged to act rashly, to take urgent action, to refuse the invite as quickly as possible. You will feel railroaded into making your decision *right now*, this moment, immediately, in a bid to assuage the obvious discomfort that is being piled upon you.

When you meet this kind of savage resistance, you automatically know that you are being drawn away or scared away from something very important.

Make no rash decisions.

Take some time away from the situation. Sit in the quiet. Ask yourself, *why are these adverse forces so afraid of me accepting this invite?*

Then, when it is clear that you need to take the invite, accept, say yes. Then be very vigilant. Keep your guard tight. These forces are nothing if not persistent; they will keep trying to scupper you, and will not stop until you have found certainty absolute (in which case the adverse forces will immediately evacuate – recognition and liberation are simultaneous), or until you have actually arrived at the station.

Remember too, when the whisperers are in your ear, you are not without help. At this sensitive time you have direct access to divine assistance, even if you feel convinced (or you have allowed yourself to be convinced) that you do not; ask them for help, call on your angels for clarity and guidance and they will speak to you.

If you say yes, if you go, I can promise you this: the things that you hate now, prior to accepting the invitation, you will come to love later.

The station might manifest as something simple, like bumping into an old friend, who draws out a hidden lust, a passion or a temptation that you were unaware of; something that you didn't know you were still harbouring. It might place you in front of a group, or a culture or an association that reveals a hidden judgment that needs to be removed. You might spot an old enemy across a supermarket aisle, someone you still hold a grudge for; this is the divine economy highlighting an area for your immediate attention.

This happened to me only recently. I was invited to a family occasion. I knew that a particular relative, a person that had caused me great pain in the past (someone I thought I'd forgiven), would be there. The invite triggered an exaggerated anger in me. It alighted at first in the form of dissonance. My confusion quickly spilled into righteous indignation and outright anger, fuelled of course by those instigators of darkness, the adverse forces.

My disproportionate reaction alerted me immediately to the fact that I still had work to do on forgiving this person.

Saying you have forgiven someone and actually properly forgiving them is not the same thing, they are two entirely different beasts.

There is a progression to forgiveness, I have found. We rarely forgive people clean, in one fell swoop. First we do the big forgiveness. We look at the situation and we look at the person who has hurt us from as many angles as we can – the light *and* the shade. We acknowledge that they are human, and that it is human to err: no one is beyond making mistakes. Even if we don't entirely believe it at first, we acknowledge that forgiving them is a good thing to do, it is healing for us, because forgiveness is the letting go of anger and pain and dissonance, and that has to be a healthy thing to do. We say the words *I forgive you* in our sub-vocalisation (even if *initially* only to ourselves), we test them out, we see how the words taste on the tongue, and we notice what emotions they invoke in us. It doesn't matter if, at first, we don't fully believe it, we say it anyway and we practise saying it until we do believe it.

We also look at ourselves from as many angles as we are able. We acknowledge that we too have made mistakes, we have hurt people and been unkind, and we acknowledge the universal truth: we can only be forgiven for our own sins, to the level that we are able forgive others.

We all want to be forgiven, right?

If you can do the big forgiveness, do the lesser forgiveness – let go of the details, the minutia – and if you can manage that, do a lesser still forgiveness, and if you can do that do a still lesser forgiveness. This way we work from the most basic to the most profound forgiveness, which requires us to detach our ego and surrender to the correcting balance, the self-levelling universe, where the real healing is done.

In *The Physicians of the Heart*, it tells us this: at first you will see only grudge, shadow. You see the worst ugliness, when you look at the 'unforgivable place'. Then you notice light and shade, good and bad, because the wider understanding of fault comes in. Eventually, when you turn away from the fault and turn to God, all footprints are blown from the sand; you no longer have any negative connotations, all imprints and impressions are erased.

We also have to acknowledge that the emotional distress and pain, the assured condition of refusing to forgive, is narcotic in its nature, it is a delicious drug that feeds the *man of misery* within us all. It can be highly desirable to hold on to pain, it gives pleasure to our lower element, the false ego. Misery could be likened to a form of grotesque love, an ugly mode of energy that might be coarse, and polluted, but it is still energy, and, as with all energy, it has a divine signature at its core. This might not be palatable to the ear, but I have found it to be very true. I once spoke with a young woman who was highly distressed, to the point of mental illness and depression, by how badly she had been treated in the distant past by her ex-husband. She assured me that his actions were indefensible, and she could never forgive him. When I suggested that forgiveness was a potent form of healing, she became extremely angry, and said *you have no idea what he did to me*. I didn't need to know what he did to her; I only knew that whilst she held on to the abuse, she would continue to live a life of spiritual penury. But that was the whole point: she wanted to hold on to the pain, because the pain-body inside her was nourished and pleasured by her complaint. And for this reason, she chose to eschew any form of help. At a level just below her conscious knowing, she did not want to get rid of the pain. When you don't want to get rid of it, you will attack all forms of help.

When you definitely do want to get rid of the misery caused by abuse, you will be open to any and every form of healthy redress. That's how you know you are ready to heal.

How do you know personally when you have forgiven?

You will know that the seeds of grudge have been removed when negative emotion no longer rises at the mention of their name, or at the sight of their face in a crowd, or when you hear through the whisperers that they have been talking unkindly about you again.

You will know you have forgiven when the flower of compassion grows in you, in the place where weeds of anger once prevailed.

**You will feel compassion for the people that wronged you.**

The moment compassion rises (love) you become invisible to assault, you are immune to attack, the sling and arrows of threat will not find their mark in you because there will be no target to aim at.

Even the master archer loses potency when he has no target to aim at.

At this level, your eyes will be so illumined that the darkness of error – yours or theirs – will be dissipated by your holy gaze.

As I said, forgiveness is a process. Process by its very nature implies time. It may take several cuts with the axe, before the timber of grudge falls.

We have to assail our disease with ruthless and targeted precision. Like a surgeon removing a tumour, we can leave no trace of our emotional cancer behind.

My reaction to the invite alone, whether I accepted it or not, showed me that I still had some cleaning to do with this man. I knew that if I left even the root of the root of the root in my soil, the weed would grow again in its season, because I neglected the rigour, I had not removed it wholesale from my being.

I was also assured, by a strong, internal voice, that if there was a barrier between me and even one person, there was a barrier between me and God. This was incentive enough to place me before any challenge.

I accepted the invite. I met the man in question with gratitude and with love. In the space of one evening I completely forgave him, evicting all traces of residual anger from my mind once and for all.

It would be more accurate to say that I simply turned up with a good heart, and the *disturbance* was removed from me wholesale by the holy Surgeon.

I'd like to assure you, too, that whilst you will be asked to go to the places that scare you, you will not be asked to go alone.

Wherever you go, your perfect companion *Intuition* will walk with you.

And behind intuition of course is consciousness.

God will walk with you.

Like an honour guard, It will be by your side, ever at your right hand and always ready to protect you, settle confusions and guide you.

When Francis was instructed to kiss the leper in Assisi, he agreed to the task, but he also demanded that Grace walk beside him.

We cannot do any of this alone.

We need our companion, the divine assistant; higher power is an essential.

In my own life, I have been guided to make such drastic changes that I am sure some people think I am *out there with Pluto*. But the direction is so certain that when I hear it, I heed it – I follow the instruction and trust that *"all will be well and all will be well and all manner of things will be well."*

Once this covenant has been established, you become Religio, the bringer of joy.

You no longer follow religion, you *are* religion.

You are no longer multiple, disparate selves abiding in one body; you have become one with the One, a unified being following a singular path.

Now that the bridge between heaven and earth has been established, and a communication of the properties begun, you will be delivered the first of many spiritual gifts: **The Divine Sword**.

Chapter 6

# The Divine Sword

Once the connection is established, and a covenant made, a growing and deepening communication between the lower and higher properties begins, and the divine economy starts to deliver you divine potentials, the first of which is **the gift of human and spiritual discernment**.

It is just one of many gifts you will receive, but it is possibly the most important, because discernment is an enabler, it allows you to discriminate between the voice of the divine and the voice of the enemy. No matter how elevated you might become, there will always be a danger of hearing and listening to the wrong voice. The roaming lion is not disqualified just because you happen to have a covenant with God. On the contrary, he is more vigilant with the adept than he is with the novice. Of course he is: a highwayman gains more when he robs a rich merchant on the road than he does when he steals from a pauper.

Also, as I mentioned earlier, now that you are awake, you are able to awaken others, you are a holy whistle-blower, and this is a real threat to the *adverse forces* that rely entirely on unconscious beings for their supper; they do not want people to be awoken, so you become a real threat to these forces.

The more elevated you are, the tighter your game must become.

This is true in all walks of life, not least in the spiritual realm.

I practised Judo for a time, at a high level. I trained in a full-time class, with Olympic standard players, under the auspices of World Judo Champion Neil Adams. At this density of play, you could not afford a moment of error in your game, let alone a bad day on the mat. Even the slightest gap in your technique would be manipulated by these elite athletes, and engineered into a gaping hole. As little as a millisecond of lapsed concentration and you would find yourself on your back from a throw, tapping out with an arm-bar or knocked unconscious by a strangle or a choke.

Spiritual discernment is a powerful Siddha: it is the eye that sees all.

In esoteric parlance, this is known as *the sword of discernment* or **the divine sword**.

The sword enables you to cut through negativity and dissonance and fear like a reaping-sickle. It allows you to recognise any kind of (inner or outer) unrighteous voice or threat when it appears or as it approaches. Like superhuman X-ray vision, it also enables you to see right through the cloak of even the best-dressed wolves when they approach your borders dressed as sheep.

Wolves always tend to approach in disguise.

If, for even a second, you were able to see the hell-forms that try to secrete themselves into your heaven, you would be immediately alerted and take all necessary measures to forbid them entry. So concealment is the order of the day for invading parasites, but subterfuge no longer works against you when you are in possession of the divine sword.

You are aligned.

You are the inlet and the outlet for divine essence, coming through an undefiled vessel.

You are a human tabernacle, the portable vehicle for heavenly manna.

You are immeasurably valuable, you are also a great threat.

You are full of divine treasure; of course you will be singled out, and it goes without saying (I hope) that you would be the greatest prize for any would-be pirate.

Where, before *the gathering together*, you might be fooled by these clumsy disguises, now, with your heightened discrimination, all you need to do is quietly observe, and studiously listen and diligently sense everything that approaches, looking for a little engagement and you will be able to identify defilement under even the most elaborate disguise.

It still takes courage of course, you must be brave. If you are aware of and awake to these threats – we are all under spiritual attack, be in no doubt – but are too afraid to oppose it, what chance the ignorant, those lovely people that are still spiritually uneducated.

It takes valour to stand in front of a shade, and say, *I see you, no entry.*

I practised this for many years, in the external sense (external, internal, same difference), when I worked as a bouncer, manning nightclub doors. Spotting the potentially violent and the criminally inclined in a queue outside a club entrance was simple enough; but to stand in front of them, toe-to-toe, nose-to-nose, with their posturing demeanour and say *not tonight* took tremendous courage.

Most of the other clubs in our fair city were overrun by the villainous element because the door security was either weak or they themselves were part of the criminal clique. The weaker doormen knew the criminals but were just too frightened to stand up to them. Instead, they kowtowed, and tried to befriend the gangsters by letting them in. They curried favour, not realising that (to quote Churchill) "you cannot negotiate with a lion while your head is in its mouth."

The internal dynamic is no different.

If fear or passion or temptation rises up in you, looking for a little engagement, vying to enter your heart-space, it takes tremendous spunk to place your foot on its neck and say *not today, not any day.*

These monsters can be frightening to look at. It can be a terrifying prospect, and it takes a true David to stand his ground against the Goliath of fear.

It is at the point of confrontation that you have to remind

yourself: you are aligned. You have Truth at your back. Consciousness is your corner man. Anyone challenging you would be taking on the whole universe. It would be like spitting into a tornado.

You are in possession of a David-Sling, and a bag full of truth-pebbles that will fell any giant.

This is absolutely true. It *is* true... but is it true for you?

You need to know that it is true, and remember that it is true and live your life like it is the only thing in this world that is true. When we allow ourselves to be convinced by the whisperers that we are vulnerable, and that we are without protection, and that we can be assailed, we fall into (what the Kabbalists call) *the forgetting*.

Remember it. Remind yourself constantly.

The sword that sees true also cuts true.

The same power that exists in your discernment is also present in your authority

This is another truth that needs to be constantly reiterated, to save from the forgetting.

If you deliver your rebuttal with certainty, you will not be challenged.

You have to know this, you have to trust this, and of course, ultimately you have to put your sword to the test in order to be certain of its potency.

At this point in time (now), you might be still developing your skills; perhaps you are not yet the full article (who is), if so, then daily reminder and diligent practice are imperative.

## Merging Souls (the communication of the properties)

As your covenant deepens the higher soul continues to merge with the lower soul, the divine ego.

The Concentrate and the dilute communicate.

The union is at once ecstatic and challenging.

It can be exciting, but also very frightening.

When your worldview radically changes, as mine did, and you start to see things that other people are blind to, it can be extremely disconcerting. I've had moments when I've looked up at the sun, and realised that *the sun is not the sun* (my wife always warns me, *don't tell the sun story, not one will understand if you tell the sun story*). The sun is no longer a disparate orb blazing indiscriminately in the sky; it is a sentient, familial and personal energy source watching over me from the edge of my consciousness.

As varying aspects of the higher self manifest in the lower self and communicate and integrate, it triggers an evolution of our whole physiology. Old energies shift, often unwillingly and uncomfortably, and new energies enter as the redundant vacate. Like ousting an outdated government and replacing it with new leadership, not all of the old school will leave without a fight.

During this transition, understanding and great courage are called for. You needed heaps of bravery to get this far; no one takes control of their own kingdom and kicks out the old order without the most exemplary acts of bravery.

Being in possession of the divine sword is all fine and good, but you still have to lift the sword, you still have to wield it.

You are a prize.

I have said this many times, I will say it again until it sticks: you **are** a prize.

You are the honeycomb of divine essence, and as such, a bounty for any burglar, a rich-haul for every thief.

You'll attract elements that will go to any ends to win that prize.

One of the subtleties of spiritual discernment is complete self-awareness: you will be conscious of your true nature, your priceless value, and the need to protect your divine cargo at all times.

You are also the direst threat. This too cannot be stated enough times. You are a menace to disparate beings, the inner and outer adverse forces, who harvest your essential, creative energies, with little or no resistance. Anyone who is awake, more so anyone that threatens to awaken others, challenges the status quo, and so becomes the target of attack from these negative forces. And the more noise you make, the more you will be noticed.

This is fine as long as you are aware of it. This is all good, as long as you are prepared to live your life in the bravest manner, never allowing yourself to fall outside the narrow bandwidth of virtue.

When I worked as a bouncer, I knew that the very act of policing a busy nightclub in a major city would make me a living target for any malcontent, any criminal, any social parasite that stood to benefit from an un-policed club.

I knew before I started, that working as a bouncer would mean, in effect, I was taking on all comers. No doubt. This was standard knowledge to anyone that had given it any level of reflection. To not understand this from the start would lead to grave danger, if not sooner, certainly later. I had a student of mine who wanted to become a bouncer for the money, for the challenge, for the local celebrity, perhaps for the female attention that even ugly bouncers received. He had been offered a job, and came to me for advice; should he take it? I asked him one question: *how would you feel about a 4am phone call from someone you have thrown out of the club, who threatens to shoot you dead, who threatens to shoot your wife dead, who threatens to kill your children?* This might never happen, but equally it could happen on the very first shift. This, and similar threats, had been levelled at me more times than I care to remember. My friend went pale at the very thought. *I wouldn't want that*, he said. *Well then*, I said, *you shouldn't become a bouncer.*

Policing your body and mind and soul is no less serious, especially once we are awake. Control of the thoughts we engage, and the thoughts we reject, is what keeps us protected from attack.

As I said somewhere else, if you stay in perfect alignment you will remain invisible to threat. You will not be noticed by negative forces. They can only see you (or smell or sense you) if you wander out of your divine frequency and into theirs.

But we are still in a human body, and by this very fact we will err, and it is when we create errors that we will be seen so we must remain ever vigilant.

In my own life I have learned to be invisible whilst actually standing right in the centre of potential threat.

My work has placed me in the very environment where defilements congregate with humans. Often, I have been called, in my divine instruction, to talk in juvenile institutions (to troubled kids, and criminal youths), prisons and the hallowed halls of big business, where (sometimes) the businessmen I worked with turned out to be bigger crooks than the convicts I met in criminal institutions.

I have been called to pass on my learning to people who are so possessed by vice that you can physically smell it and see it and sometimes taste it oozing from their bodies. In these dangerous places, the eyes of the misaligned sweep over you like a scanner, probing for leaks, searching for breaks, hunting for weaknesses that they can manipulate. Damaged females might try and gain entry with the use of sexual allure. Rich businessmen will use the clout of money and their business connections to seduce you. Criminals and the violently inclined will swab you for traces of fear or greed or any other human weakness and use your *fracture* as their entry through your mind-door.

For a few years, I had the honour of serving as patron to a local addiction centre. I frequently visited, and offered counselling to the sufferers there. When I was first invited to take the position, I remember how nervous I felt. I innately knew that if I entered an abode of this calibre and was not completely aligned, if I did not have my divine sword to hand, I would quickly be noticed, and routinely devoured.

It was an amazing but uncompromising training ground. God placed me there so that I might serve these troubled souls, whilst at the same time, tempering my sword. Every time I sat with them – their addictions ranged from gambling to sex, right through to drink and drugs – I could feel their eyes and ears all over me, probing for any vibrational match. These were damaged people. Most of them were at the very end of their last chance. They had lost everything to their addictions and were left only with the impaired bodies they walked around in. Some of them were empty husks, devoured from the inside out by their parasite of choice. More than one of this group would lose their final battle with addiction, despite all the help they were being given, and either die due to disease or end their own lives out of despair.

Not everyone makes it out alive, not even with the best help in the world.

The defilements were not only in these folk, consuming the very last of their humanity, they were also all around them, pervading the air.

*The devil lives in the atmosphere,* Francis told me when I studied with him for a time; *he is in the atmosphere.*

Eckhart Tolle believes the same. He said that as well as the individual pain-bodies that most people harbour, there is a world pain-body, a collective residue of free-floating negative energy that lives in the atmosphere, and is always looking for a similar energy to align with.

You could certainly feel it in the atmosphere of this room.

When I say that these people had lost everything, it would be more accurate and more truthful to say that they had given everything away – including all their social edits. There were no niceties in this place. If you were incongruent, if they disagreed with what you said, if they didn't like the cut of your jib, or the tilt of your hat, they would let you know soon enough. Given even half-a-chance they would trample your pearls under their feet *and turn and tear you in pieces.*

And why not?

What did they have to lose?

They had nothing to lose.

This made them perfect whetstones for anyone wanting to sharpen the blade of their virtue, or the edge of their divine sword.

The only time I fell short at one of these meetings was the day I took blind-arrogance with me to the centre instead of my humility-shield and the divine sword of discernment.

On this particular occasion, I was in a busy rush (always a mistake when you are on divine duty) and I'd shoe-horned my appointment at the centre into a tight schedule of *other jobs* that needed to be done. My poor planning and complete lack of respect left me little time to prepare my own atmosphere before I entered theirs.

When two atmospheres converge, the strongest or most stable will dominate.

The stable atmosphere will have the consistent quality of love and compassion. It has an inner quality (to paraphrase *The Physicians of the Heart*) that is awakened in a similar manner to the way steel is tempered in the process of forging a sword. It is not a passive calm. It faces hostility, slander, and corruption with serenity, while at the same time it has a soothing effect that reaches the core of the apparent enemy.

My preparation (to dock with this stability) consists of a meditation – as I mentioned in the previous chapter – that aligns my lower and higher soul. Once aligned, the sword of discernment is armed.

This day I failed to prepare and I paid.

Halfway through my talk, one of the older addicts in the group noticed incongruence in me; he spotted a corruption in my talk and in my manner and he angrily pulled me on it. I'd allowed myself to drift away from the higher soul and ended up instead waffling like a clever-fool through the rhetoric of my false-ego. Instead of talking about healing potential, I spoke about earning potential. One of the younger addicts in the group was obsessed with making money and I'd inadvertently allowed myself to fall into his atmosphere. In a boastful and naïve bid to satisfy his curiosity, I bragged about how much money someone could make in the world if they were aligned.

It was a stupid, rookie error.

The older guy, a recovering alcoholic, interrupted my talk. In front of everyone present he shot me down. He had absolutely no interest in money (he told me). Of what use was *filthy lucre* to him, he had lost everything; he was *fucking dying*? Why was I talking about something as trite as coin when he had lost the whole world and everyone in it that he loved? He had no interest at all in fiscal matters, he just wanted to live again, he just wanted to breathe free air without having to filter his oxygen through a thick fog of anxiety and pain and regret.

I lost his confidence. I lost the confidence of the whole group, because I did not take my sword with me.

Most people would probably look into a room like that and see the dregs of society: druggies, prostitutes, gamblers, thieves and alcoholics.

I doubt they would see fathers, mothers, sons, daughters, sisters and brothers.

They would not have seen a loved one, a wife or husband, a granddad or grandma at the sharp end of each dirty addiction.

My brother was a beautiful, beautiful alcoholic.

The disease killed him at the age of 42. His death was both violent and tragic. He left four young children and a family that loved him very much. I was with him when addiction snatched his last breath. It was not a good end, my brother's. Certainly it left his children with the mistaken belief that he chose the bottle over them.

He did not.

Though these gorgeous kids will have to discover this for themselves, as they live out their own lives and have their own children and watch them too make unconsidered decisions that will affect everyone they love, just as keenly as it will affect them.

My brother was a powerful teacher for me, even if my learning was only by proxy of his mistakes.

At the addiction centre, I shared a room with troubled, damaged, hijacked souls. Every one of them reminded me of my brother.

Perhaps that's why I loved them.

I have to tell you that they too were my best teachers; they were my very best gurus.

If there was even the scent of incongruence in me, even one in a billion parts, these reaped-souls would sniff it out, they would draw it forth, and, if I failed to dissolve it, they would manipulate and engineer it until it was a gaping hole that a legion could march through.

They were my finest tutors.

I survived my skirmish on this occasion, because I quickly saw the error in my preparation, and adjusted accordingly. I apologised to the older gentleman after the session; I agreed that he was right and I was wrong and my honesty brought me back into congruence.

I won back both their trust and their ear.

I saw two healers fall foul of this group because they approached without a sword.

One was shot down after his very first session; a pretty addict seduced him and then complained to the organisers that he had *tried it on with me*. Another man, a fine motivational speaker, didn't even get through the front door. He'd offered his services, gratis, but was so incongruent that the organiser kicked him away.

The first healer ended up crying down the phone to me and

blamed the girl, even though he admitted that he was very attracted to her and *I did feel a chemistry*. I reminded him as kindly as I could that he wasn't there to feel chemistry; he was there to administer healing.

The second blamed the organisers; he argued that they didn't even give him a chance, but he too missed the point.

The seductive girl and the discerning organiser were the spiritual teachers of both these healers. They showed each individually where they still needed to work on themselves, before they could enter the room and help others.

What both men failed to take into the room with them was love.

One was always unconsciously trying to meet a woman. He was a gifted healer but he could not hold his sword because he had a greedy parasite in him that was desperate for female company.

The other brought neither love nor goodwill. He was another good man who was not yet fully aligned. He wanted to conduct a talk at the centre because it would boost his ego and look good on his CV if he could show that he was working with addicts.

The difference between me and these two gentlemen was that I had enough sense to be afraid.

I *was* afraid.

I knew what I was being called to do, I was in no doubt.

I understood the atmosphere I was entering. It would demand divine alignment, nothing less would suffice.

Go in with your sword in your hand, or come out with your head on a spike.

I wanted to work with these souls because I felt great compassion; I wanted to serve them because I'd been called to do so. But I also *needed* to work with them for selfish reasons. I knew that I was walking into a room full of elite teachers. They would help me to locate any weaknesses that were still hiding in me; and they did.

On another occasion I made exactly the same mistake, this time though with a different group.

In my defence I was still learning and I hadn't yet fully grasped the concept of the divine sword and its importance when working with people who have active covenants with vice.

I ran a small writers' group in Coventry.

Actually, it was less of a writers' group and more of a healing circle where we used the pen to bleed pain on to the page. Unlike the prisons I'd visited and the addiction centres, this group was not full of overtly addicted or criminal elements, they were just lovely people who, on the surface, wanted to become writers or certainly explore their potential.

The naïve, dangerous mistake I made was allowing myself to believe that working with this group would be a walk in the park. I kidded myself that of all the groups I was currently assigned to, this was the easiest.

Before I continue, please allow me to offer a little background on the nature of the other groups I was working with to add some context to the current story.

At the time I was working with lots of different and disparate people. I had several martial arts groups (I was joint-chief instructor to an international self-defence association) and my students visited Coventry (where I held courses) once a month from all over Britain – some from as far as Australia and Dubai – to train under me. Whilst they believed they were there to practise the lesser Jihad of physical martial arts, they were actually partaking in the greater Jihad, the inner work. I'd set the class up to run once every four weeks for between 6-12 months. The lessons were orchestrated in such a way that each of the students would bump into one or more of their defilements at some point during the course.

It was a metaphysical class, martial arts at the level of Budo.

The class itself was a manufactured environment, devised to draw out inner weaknesses and reveal hidden strengths in the students. This was the deliberate design and definite intent of the class, so of course I expected confrontation and I was prepared to deal with.

The other groups, similarly, were places where I fully anticipated meeting people with problems, and positioned myself accordingly.

As an aside, you might be surprised to know that in my martial arts classes the greatest opposition came from the most unlikely people: my own instructors. Those who were meant to assist, mostly ended up opposing me and the material I was teaching. I should have known this might happen, but I didn't; at the time I wasn't experienced enough to know that in an aligned room everyone is affected. I have to tell you it was a shock to me, although I learned masses from it.

The divine nature of the class, cleverly disguised as a martial arts workshop, drew out the defilements of anyone who entered the room; not least those who were previously my most loyal guards. The nature of my teaching had always drawn heavy criticism from a martial arts fraternity that had its own standards, both explicit and implicit. It was a community with its own unique mores, and had positioned itself in such a way that teacher and practitioner alike, if they so desired, could hide from their own shadows. It is not unusual to see obese, violent and vice-laden men and women even and especially in the higher echelons. I should know, before my own encounter with the honest-mirror I too hid my gross underbelly behind a big right cross and some very convincing rhetoric. But when you start to see the faults in others, when you are able to see their lies, you cannot help but see your own faults too; you cannot escape your own dishonesty.

You can't speak the truth without hearing the truth.

The criticism I got – which was expected, the material was so potent that it exposed negativity in people who only read about my teaching – spilled on to many of my own instructors by proxy and they lost sight of who they were and why they were there.

Many of them went on to actively and openly attack me on social media platforms. This surprised me at the time but of course it should not have, again that was my own naivety. I tried not to take it personally but it is hard to be objective when *"the slings-and-arrows of outrageous fortune"* come from people you love. At the time I tried to warn them that they were *not themselves,* and that they were placing their own defilements on an open platform for people to view. But they were stuck in the forest of delusion and I was unable to pull them out.

In these places it's not difficult to anticipate push-back.

That's why you are there.

In the writers' group I didn't anticipate any of this and so I failed to prepare.

I went into the room unarmed. The sword of discernment was not at hand and the room I'd set up as a writers' group drew out one of my own shadows – arrogance.

I was the teacher here. People looked up to me and I made no bones about letting them know on the first session of a six-month course that I was going to make it a very difficult experience for them. I intended to set them writing assignments and exercises that would intimidate and frighten them so much that *most of you won't come back for the second session.*

That's what I said to them.

To my deep shame and scalding regret, those are the exact words that left my lips.

The fish had definitely died in the mouth.

Writing this now, sat in my comfy home-office, I am embarrassed by my own arrogance and disturbed at how quickly and how easily I became tricked by the adverse forces and ended up a fiend in a class of people who had surrendered themselves to my care. I was not running the class. My arrogant ego-shadow was running it, and consuming the fear and the anxiety my words had triggered in the room.

I could see the worried look on all the faces before me, and it felt good.

I am ashamed.

Did I say that already?

Just in case I didn't iterate it enough, I need to reiterate it just so that you are in no doubt that I was an arrogant fool.

Suddenly a very large man (his head was the size of a bottle-bank), his face blood-red and bloated with fear and anger stood up and said: "*That's not why I'm here. I haven't come here for this. I've come here because I want to write.*"

He looked around the room. He spoke to the other attendees, attempting at this very early stage – minutes into the first session of six – to not only disrupt the class but draw the attendees into an open mutiny against me, with him as their new captain.

Adrenal dump!

I suddenly experienced a shock of fear that coursed through my body like fire.

It was absolutely disproportionate to the situation I was facing. It took all of my experience in fear-management to stop it from completely overtaking me.

Later I would recognise this as a *spiritual shock*, a prod of terror with a divine signature, sent to alert me to my remiss.

At that moment it was raw and unadulterated fight-or-flight; I was the antelope and this lump was the lion biting at my hooves.

Within the first minute of the first session my arrogance had inadvertently yanked a violent shadow out of one of my students and I was not prepared for it. I managed to stay controlled and talk to him down and calm him and gather the class-energy back to a centre space, but the man in question was so emotional that he got up, walked out of the class and stood outside by the road. It took him an hour to calm down. I sat in the room, swimming in adrenalin, carried on teaching as though I was completely fine, but I knew in that moment I'd made a grave error and that the error would live with me for the next six months. I knew that every session for the next half-year, I would experience adrenal build-up in anticipation for the tension I had created in one moment of blind arrogance.

After the class, I could not clear the fear from my body.

I'd had people threaten to kill me when I was a nightclub bouncer, people *had* actually tried to kill me and it never felt as bad as this. I was confused by the disproportionate nature of the fear, I didn't understand it. I spoke that evening to my friend Steve, a priest. I told him that my body was under some kind of attack, a satanic siege, and I didn't know how to defend against it. Steve gave me a prayer-card and that night I went deep-sea diving and had a face-to-face dialectic with God.

*What are you showing me, Lord?*

These were my exact words.

I was granted a vision. The vision was of my folly. It was laid it out in front of me like a life-review. It was so clear that it felt other-dimensional. It was like a rerun of my mistake in super-HD, where the image you are viewing on the screen is actually clearer and more pronounced than the life all around it.

These people, He showed me, were not in the room with me just because they wanted to write. They had travelled from all over the country to bravely put themselves in the room with me, so that their tormenting fears might emerge. I was meant to be there as a careful, loving healer. I was there to serve.

My job was to **serve!**

I was there to help facilitate their healing process.

Instead they turned up, these very lovely people, to find a bullish, thoughtless, clumsy surgeon.

I was shown how afraid these people were, coming to my class not knowing what they might find. He showed me how incredibly courageous that made each of them.

I had completely underestimated this.

I was informed that the disproportionate amount of fear I was feeling was exactly the level of fear they felt every time they set out to come to my class. Every time. In the very middle of my fear, God was saying to me, *how you are feeling right now is how these people are feeling every time they turn up.*

I had shown them no respect.

I had given them no credit.

I had left my divine sword at home because I didn't think I'd need it in this *easy* class...

My compassion was missing on that day, missing presumed dead.

I had taken their unbearable fear and I had added to it tenfold with my careless, thoughtless, torturing hubris.

When I was shown this, I was full of remorse. It is hard to describe the level of regret and sadness I felt at my casual mistreatment. The anxiety did not let up until the next session when I was able to stand before my class and apologise.

The man in question, the angry one who'd pointed out my error, did not attend the second class.

In fact he only attended one more session out of the next five. When he did turn up, I pulled him to one side and apologised unreservedly for my mistake.

On that first session back I sat in front of the class and I apologised profusely: *on the last session I was arrogant and clumsy,* I said, *I should have been gentler. I should at the very least have been kind. I was not and I fully apologise. That will not happen again.*

My confession lifted their anxiety. I felt the room breathe.

When their anxiety lifted, my anxiety lifted too.

The biggest shadow that came out of that first session was not from any of the students in the class, it came from me; it was a bloated, pretentious shadow that I did not even know was there.

It existed because I entered the room without preparation. I did not align. I did not bring my sword, and this left me open to the *adverse forces* who entered me through the door of arrogance.

This was one of the biggest lessons I was ever gifted. I have never forgotten it.

*You are dealing with souls,* God reiterated to me, *and you are dealing with Al-Shaytan, the nemesis of all souls and his adverse forces. Never ever be indiscriminate with the former, and underestimate the latter at your peril.*

As I mentioned before, the devil, divided energies, live in the atmosphere and will pervade anybody that is not protected. If you go into any room, knowing this is so, you must prepare first, your sword must be tempered, your sword must be drawn.

On the doors of Coventry nightclubs, this awareness was an absolute standard. No question. If you lost your awareness, you could lose your life.

After teaching coal-face self-defence for several decades on the world stage, I learned that the greatest tool we could offer people for their own protection was awareness.

Awareness translates as consciousness.

We taught our students to be ever-conscious of potential assault, conscious of the modus operandi of the criminal element – their preferred hunting ground, their purpose, their big bag-of-tricks, their methodology – how their own bodies would inevitably react in stressful situations and the best method of practical defence should a situation spill into a physical assault.

Simply by being aware, you automatically reduce the potential of attack by as much as 95%.

Awareness in self-defence *is* Religio.

It is what you align to the moment you leave your home, especially if you are working in a volatile environment.

The world of men is a divided place, no question. This means that it is always a potentially volatile environment.

In some of the locations I worked, you could feel defilement as a palpable force; it was treacle in the air, it had a sickly humidity all of its own.

In the clubs I worked in my home city it was like walking into a sickening fog.

Anyone that doubts the fact that these defilements live in the atmosphere would only ever have to walk into a club like this *once* to be entirely convinced; it is so tangible it is physically stifling.

## Hard-targeting

In external self-defence, your awareness of potential threat, your awareness of the enemy attack-ritual is your divine sword; it is your greatest protection. When a would-be assailant becomes aware that you are aware of his pre-assault ritual – they rely mostly on artifice and surprise – your awareness closes them down before they can even get started and they wander away looking for a softer target, someone who is less aware.

(I mentioned this earlier) we called this process **hard-targeting**.

You make yourself a hard target for potential attackers, with the tool of discerning awareness. The nature of potential miscreants is to seek out easy targets, someone who looks weak, or injured, who is old and infirm, or young and incapable, or distracted or unaware, or vulnerable; someone who is separated from the herd.

The inner game and the outer game are really no different.

As you become more and more adept in the world of the metaphysical, you see less and less distinction between internal and external reality, you also learn to see no difference between corporeal and incorporeal assault; the latter are really just a more covert version of the former.

If you are diligent and disciplined, you can sharpen your sword to such a degree that eventually you become invisible to attack.

The three magi, who attended the birth of the Joshua in the New Testament, were said to have travelled from distant lands to witness the birth of consciousness; the nativity of the Redeemer. On their journey through dangerous territories, across foreign lands, they protected themselves using only their thoughts.

In my previous incarnation as a self-defence teacher, I learned and I taught every variation of empty-hand and weapon-based physical self-defence known to man, but the most effective tool I developed and taught was the sharpened sword of awareness.

Your sword needs to be drawn at all times.

Never leave the house, enter a meeting, meet a client, negotiate a deal, or walk into any establishment without it.

If you do, you are vulnerable.

If you break your covenant, you disconnect with spirit and that will leave you without your protection.

If you break a vow, your sword is lost.

If you court a vice, you have been disarmed and your sword is confiscated by the nature of your vice; you offer your weapon to the enemy and it will be used against you.

On the doors we had a rule, as taught to me by my grandmaster John Anderson: *presume that everyone is a potential threat. Presume that they are all armed.*

In that overtly dangerous arena, we presumed that everyone was a potential assailant, and we assumed that everyone was carrying a weapon.

This was our rule.

It kept us safe.

It kept us alive.

Those friends and colleagues that were murdered, and there were many: they died because they forgot this rule.

At this level, you only had to lose concentration for an instant and death would pounce.

Several close friends lost their lives; they were murdered not because they lost a fight, rather they paid the ultimate price because they lost their awareness.

Our awareness in those days was so sharp, so alive, that we could scan a group of fifty people in a nightclub queue, waiting to enter our establishment, and know absolutely by behaviours (even very subtle behaviours) who would be starting trouble in the next three minutes and who would be causing mayhem within the next five hours.

Using this awareness, we would stop them from entering the club before they'd even reached the front door. One of the more experienced members of the team would walk along the queue, do their assessment of the customers and remove the person(s) they knew to be future troublemakers.

With the eye of the sword, we were able to look into the future; we could predict outcomes with our razor-sharp discernment.

With the decisive cut of the sword, we could pre-empt trouble minutes or hours before it even happened.

Of course the person in question would rail against our ruling, claiming they had done nothing wrong. It is hard to convince people that we were kicking them out of a club, before they even got in, because we could see that sometime in the next few hours they would commit a crime on our premises.

The prospective offender had to go, even if they believed they'd done nothing wrong.

We could see the future.

We could predict outcomes.

We had a choice; we could intervene and prevent the future from happening, or, out of fear, we could leave it and be forced to meet the threat again later, when it had matured, when it had gathered support inside the premises – then you really did have a fight on your hands, one that you were not guaranteed to win.

What I learned as a nightclub bouncer and as a teacher of self-defence have carried over. The door I protect now though is not the neon-lit opening to a heady dance club; rather it is my inner door.

The inner nemesis is of an altogether more subtle nature, although it will often and may still work through other people. The *adverse forces* will inhabit and work through any available body in their bid to invade the heart-space of other people. External or internal, approaching from without, or rising from within, once you recognise the enemy in its many disguises, they all look the same, and they all get cut down by the same divine sword.

My own ritual of protection, the method I use to connect heaven and earth and bring forth the divine sword, is simple enough in its method, and thousands of years old in the practice.

In worldly self-defence, the technique was to switch on my awareness the moment I left my house.

Actually, even within my own home, awareness was (and still is) a constant. It is enforced with locked doors and bolted windows and an alarm box on the outside wall.

When I venture outside, I am constantly aware when I walk down the street, when I enter and leave a building, where I stand in a bar or sit in a café. Even when I use a public toilet, awareness is paramount. I never use the urinal; I will only ever *vacate* in a locked cubicle. Wherever I go, I am aware of the people around me, their actions, and their atmospheres and their moods. If I am in an establishment, a café, a shop etc. I consciously assess the location and its inhabitants for potential threat. In my days of door protection, when violence was a constant potential, I would even practise *commentary walking*: as I walked down the street I would sub-vocally describe where I was, what I was doing, and who was around me etc. In the end these internal-coms would be so usual that it would occur unconsciously, it would feel as natural as placing a seatbelt on in the car.

We are not talking paranoia here, just situational awareness.

Spiritual protection is pretty much the same, other than the fact that I am not just looking out for the potential of physical attack, but also the possibility of a non-physical assault. I scan for shadows, or sub-personalities, working unconsciously through people. I also observe my own behaviour to check for shadows or ghosts rising up in me.

To prepare and protect myself, my awareness consists of placing a circle of light all around me: in front, behind, above, below, from the right and from the left. I visualise it in my mind's eye, and as viscerally as possible, so that I can actually see a protective light-shield surrounding me. The more I practise this technique, the more palpable it is and the stronger the protection becomes.

You can think about this as a visualisation technique, if my description feels too esoteric. Imagine that you are fitting actual protective armour all around your body. Or you can read it as a simple exercise in personal awareness, arming yourself with the heightened cognizance of a soldier going out on patrol – either way, it will work, it does work, it works very powerfully for me.

Once you become practised at this technique, other people will feel the energy around you, even if they can't physically see or articulate what it is they feel.

Some years ago I experienced a challenging situation with a potentially violent man that illustrates this very well. I will call him G. He was a big man, and he had taken an instant dislike to me. He was aggressive and rude and it was evident that, if I didn't quickly interrupt and redirect his intention, it would spill into a physical attack (him attacking me).

I have seen enough violence – thousands of assaults in clubs and pubs – to recognise a pre-fight ritual and to know when an assault is imminent; I can read violent-intent with my inner touch like air-braille.

It is important to stipulate here my own glaring error; the reason this situation occurred in the first place was because (again) I had gone to a location (a boxing gym in London's East End for a film shoot) that I should have known would attract attention. Not anticipating this, I failed to prepare adequately. If I'd given this situation half the respect it deserved, I would have been invisible to this behemoth, and the situation would never have happened.

As it was I didn't prepare, and it did happen. For no specific reason G (six feet tall, 18 stone, hard-of-thinking) noticed me, and out of all the other crew members on the shoot that day, he chose to use me as his punching bag. He was blunt, he was blatantly rude and openly aggressive. When I politely asked if I could use some of his focus pads for the boxing scene we were about to shoot, he literally squared up to me, poked me in the chest and said, "This is my gym, and I'll tell you what pads you can and can't use." In the world of violence, this was as good as a challenge to fight; this was a base man posturing, to show everyone else in the room who was the boss. He was slaughtering a chicken to train a monkey, as the Chinese say. What is interesting, and also disturbing about this encounter, was how quickly other people picked up on the energy. The room became thick with tension, people looked nervous, and everyone (at some level) knew that, now this man had insulted me without redress, the situation would inevitably escalate, and eventually spill into physical violence. Malcontents at all levels of play tend to test the waters with mild insult or ambiguous rhetoric before they make their play proper. If their opening gambit is accepted without response, they will use their initial probe as an entry point to greater abuse. This is true both in the microcosm of the individual life, and in the macrocosm of the world at large.

G was a boxing trainer, he taught young kids in the very room we were filming; many of them were there to watch the shoot. The disturbing element of this story is the fact that one of these kids, he was about 12 or 13 years old, having just watched G insult me and get away with it, thought he could do the same. He approached me with a smug grin on his young face and said sarcastically *so you're going to teach us how to hit the pads then are you?*

"Pardon?" I said. I was shocked. After watching G attempt to dominate me, even this young child assumed I was fair game. It showed me categorically and without question how very quickly the *adverse forces* advance when a weakness is exposed, and how readily they recruit, how insidiously they will enter and enlist anyone, even children, to their cause. It demonstrated too how vulnerable we make ourselves if we fail to protect our space at all times; it is imperative that we recognise the subtle (or not so subtle) precursors to abuse, and *dash the little one against the rocks* before they have time to mature into full-fat attacks.

Pre-emption is the order of the day in any kind of defence situation, be it external or internal, physical or physiological or metaphysical. The legendary Japanese swordsman Musashi called this *the pre-emptions*. He recommended that when we intuit an imminent attack we interrupt it, and strike first. There are three methods of pre-emption: attack first, the moment you sense that your opponent is thinking about his attack; attack as he is physically preparing his attack; launch your attack simultaneously with his attack. As I said earlier, we can only utilise pre-emption if we are aware of the prevailing atmospheres, and can spot the potential of attack before it occurs. In the case of G, I missed this opportunity because I did not engage my divine sword; I was not aware, and so had to resort to other techniques to eventually quell the situation.

The ultimate pre-emption, of course, is invisibility. If you stay in spiritual alignment, you will not be noticed.

At the time of this situation, the language of violence was not foreign to me. I understood the territory very well; my history was steeped in it. I was a seasoned *speaker*, I was once fluent in the vernacular, but no longer used it as a form of problem solving. I consider physical violence to be coarse and unacceptable; certainly it was below my current game. Of course none of these people knew this. None of them knew of my violent history, or my long standing as a veteran martial arts guru. All they saw was a middle-aged, balding man (they assumed I was an actor I think) who they thought they could bully.

I could have chosen to be physical with G, that was an option (I had the tools), but I absolutely refused to go there. I ruled violence out instantly, and where G aimed low, I aimed high. I took myself to one side. I went through an accelerated version of my meditative protection. I placed a powerful and immediate arc-light of awareness around me. I surrounded myself with a ball of light, I could feel it (almost see it) rippling out from my body, and filling the room. I accessed a guardian spirit, the Archangel Michael, as a protective archetype (coming from a Christian background, this suited me culturally). I actually spoke out loud to Michael (low enough so that no one else could hear): *this man needs to feel you in this room,* I said, *he needs to feel you now.*

My part in the film production was a small acting role, where I played a crooked boxing trainer trying to convince a young boxer to throw a fight. I had to take him on the focus pads, whilst at the same time convincing him to take a dive in his next bout. I climbed into the ring, focus pads on my hands ready to shoot the scene with the young actor playing the boxer. I heard G outside the ring, mumbling insults, so that everyone in the room could hear him. I ignored him until the director of the film called **action** and then I let rip. I banged the leather focus pads together twice, creating a cacophonous *crack* that echoed an authority across the room that was other-dimensional. In slapping the pads together, I aligned myself completely to my inner core (the Quakers call this technique *centring down*). It is so potent that it creates a field of energy around you, a bubble of protective light so profound that, if you are walking down the street, people walking towards you from the opposite direction will give you a wide berth to avoid your invisible shield; they won't necessarily see it, but they will sense and feel it. Instantly, the moment I started to work the actor on the pads (I had done thousands of hours of pad work in boxing both as fighter and as trainer) I saw G step back away from the boxing ring, and exit the room. He left so quickly it was as though he was dragged out by a rope. I had no further problems with him for the rest of the day. In fact he made it his job to try and befriend me.

After shooting the scene the atmosphere in the room was transformed. A crowd quickly gathered around me, excited with questions about the scene we had just shot, and the method of pad work I used and the philosophy I lived.

It was not me they were seeing any more, but Christ in me.

G had gone, and the young boy who had temporarily joined his tribe had gone too. I never saw him again.

Energies, atmospheres, good and bad, are real, be in no doubt, and either you manage them by stabilising your own or you will be dominated by the other energies in the room.

If you don't believe me, if this sounds fantastical, try to recall a situation where you have been in the company of someone with a malign, or dark, energy, and how oppressive and frightening it was. Remember if you can how quickly you felt like leaving his or her space.

I once sat in a talk radio studio with the late gangster Mad Frankie Fraser, a former henchman for the Kray twins. I have never felt such a powerful, invasive energy, it was palpable. A very small man in stature, he literally filled the room with his menace. I had the very real sense that one wrong word, or a micro movement of judgment on your face, could trigger a wrath of violence from this man. Even with all my past experience in handling unstable energies, I still felt discomforted by him.

Similarly, in days of old (another lifetime ago), when I was writing heavily about violence and about conflicted men, I found myself in a series of unlikely telephone conversations with Reggie Kray himself. Again, even over the phone (he was calling me from prison), I could literally feel his dark energy scanning me like a living thing, looking for a matching frequency that he could connect with and control.

Our energy fields – dark or light – are very real, they are a force, and they can be developed and expanded and strengthened.

Building spiritually protective armour follows the same

principle as the gangsters I met, but using light-energy, the frequency of Love, as opposed to darkness.

The dark energy is low-frequency and destructive, it draws from the lower echelons, the carnal, the base; it is not a kind energy, it is used to intimidate, pillage and manipulate.

The light energy, the high-dimensional force (a higher love), draws not from the world, but from our very Source. If there is a duel between the two energies, light will always prevail, it will always overpower darkness, there is no question about that, there is no competition: Light is the ultimate protection.

I also use this same method of armour-building with rooms that I might be visiting. If I have a meeting arranged somewhere, an office, a bar, when I was teaching martial arts it might be a sports hall or a gymnasium, I take some time out before I arrive to meditate. I locate the room in my mind's eye and I place the same shell of light around the perimeter of the room as a security. In my mind's eye I visualise light at every doorway, light at every window, light pouring in from every corner and crevice of the room, light from the ceiling, light from the floor, light from every wall. I basically flood the room full of luminescence so that before I even arrive, the room is cleansed and I am protected.

Even if I have never been to the place before it doesn't matter.

I locate the room, via meditation, in time and space.

I take myself there remotely and I go through a protective ritual. I have often located rooms in my internal vision that I have never visited before and in my mind's eye saw specific features that, when I did finally arrive at the location in real time, were exactly the same.

In Islamic mysticism the practitioners follow a similar ritual.

They first take their heart to the location of their choice, in a kind of mind-reconnaissance.

They look around the locale, and make sure it is safe.

Once they know it is safe, they return, rejoin with the body and then take the body to the said location.

Similarly, human pioneers went out and found the new lands, they colonised them, and once it was established and safe, they sent back for their kin to come and join them.

As an evolving species, we do this all the time and in so many ways, from improving our diet and fitness, to expanding our intellects, upgrading our abodes, heightening our morals and ethics, right up to proving and sharpening our consciousness. When we live in an exemplary manner, we become pioneers of the soul. We reclaim large areas of ourselves, and bring peace to them. In doing so, we give others not just the permission to follow our example, but we also leave them a trail to follow.

Preparing yourself, or (as I like to call it) *preparing the room*, is an essential in spiritual practice. Even when I've been working with troubled kids, I still follow the protective pre-visit ritual. In fact I have learned through hard experience that often vulnerable kids and young adults need more preparation time than their older counterparts. Some of these kids can be more challenging than hardened criminals.

As an example (and an aside): I had a strange experience some time ago working with a group of teenagers; in fact it was a startling encounter that I have never fully shared before, outside of this book. I use the word *startling* in a considered and sober manner, and without fear of exaggeration. The reason I haven't shared this experience before is because I didn't want it to be true, even though it was so patent I was almost blinded by it. I was still learning at the time, I was still making mistakes – I still am, that's the path I am on – so, again, when I was invited to talk to a bunch of delinquent kids, I made the (very familiar) mistake of thinking, *kids! How hard can it be?*

I've worked in violent nightclubs. I have talked with murderers and bank robbers and drug dealers in prisons. I've conversed with gangsters – I have *worked* with gangsters. I've mentored CEOs of powerful eight and nine-figure companies, worked on elite bodyguard courses, taught in military camps, personally tutored the chief self-defence instructor for the LAPD; working with a bunch of kids for an afternoon was going to be tea in the park by comparison!

It was one of the most difficult sessions of my life!

But the difficulty was of my own making.

Once again I failed to prepare (no sword: *it's kids, I won't need a sword*), and my lack of diligence prepared me to fail.

These kids were aged between 16 and 19. All of them came from troubled homes and abusive families. Each had been kicked out of regular school. They were in this particular college on this specific course with these expertly trained teachers because no one in regular education knew how to deal with them.

They were only young but already they had learned to eschew authority. And in doing so, they had dismantled every framework that had been set up to help them.

I didn't understand this entirely until I turned up. Naïvely, I was expecting to find a captive audience. Kids love me, how difficult can it be? When I entered the room, several of the teachers flanked me; they were there (I later realised) to keep order if indeed order was lost. I was met by a room full of kids that did not know who I was, did not care who I was and did not want to spend the next sixty seconds looking at my face let alone the next hour listening to my voice.

There were probably 15 kids sat at disparate desks in a regular classroom. One or two of them actually sat underneath their desks as I entered, rather than engage me; it was an open, if unconscious act of rebellion. One kid refused to sit down at all. He was wandering around the room like a confused Pac-Man lost in a maze of tables and chairs. All of the others were chatting nonchalantly amongst themselves, or lying on their arms on the desk either feigning sleep or actually trying to sleep.

I was unable to immediately bring the room to order, it was like trying to herd wasps into a jar. When one of the teachers asked the kids to pay attention and be quiet, he was immediately shouted down by a youth who was the biggest and the oldest in the group.

The teacher encouraged them to pay attention, I was there (he told them) out of the goodness of my heart. I'd come in especially to talk to them. They should at least do me the courtesy of listening.

The big, garrulous youth – I'll call him D – was clearly the ringleader. Everyone else in the room including the teachers were afraid of him. He was loud, he was confrontational and he was openly aggressive. But I had met aggression before, I had dealt with *hard*, and this was not it. He was just plain scared. In fact, I could see that he and every other kid in the room were afraid, though each of them was displaying their distress in different ways. Pretending to sleep, sleeping, randomly walking around the room, sitting under a table, posturing and, in the case of the teachers, constantly placating the kids: these were all subtle displays of fear.

With the kids of course, I understood why they were scared. They didn't trust adults. Every one of them had experienced varying degrees of abuse at the hands of trusted adult carers. Why would I be any different from all the other grown-ups they'd encountered?

D was the most aggressive by far, but in his defence he had been exposed to the most abuse. His father was an extremely violent man. He'd beaten and assaulted D's mother ever since D was born; he'd even tried to kill her before he was eventually arrested and sent to jail.

D had a qualified and violent mistrust of every male authority figure, not just in this room, but in the whole world. Now though, he was no longer a defenceless boy having to helplessly watch as his father beat his mother, rather he was a disproportionately large young man who used his size and his sound to either push people around or to push them away. Because of this no one could help him. He wouldn't let them. He didn't trust a soul.

This in turn meant he was destined to stay in this undeveloped state for the rest of his life.

Recognising that D was the key to the rest of the room, I focused in on him.

He accused the teachers of not caring. He said that none of them were really bothered about him or the other students; they were there for the money and nothing else.

I called him out on this. I asked him to qualify his statement.

The other teachers were not keen on my direct approach, but I was not bound by the same fears or the same college etiquette as them, so I pressed my point.

*"All of these teachers could earn twice as much in standard education as they are earning here,"* I told him. *"All of them are taking a pay-cut to work in this room with you."*

D looked puzzled and angry that I'd challenged him.

*"None of them care,"* he shouted, clearly unable to qualify his accusation.

*"They all care,"* I said firmly, *"I care, and I'm here for free, I am here for nothing."* I drove home my point. *"I'm not being paid, I'm here because I care and I don't even know you."*

He didn't have an answer to this so he shouted and postured a little more, like a large dog without a bite.

*"Why are you so scared?"* I asked.

Now he was genuinely confused.

Scared!?

He was the biggest, scariest kid in the class, even the teachers were afraid of him.

*"I'm not scared of no one,"* he said.

*"You are scared of everyone in this room,"* I challenged, *"if you weren't, you wouldn't be making so much noise."*

Silence.

An uncomfortable impasse.

One of the teachers called a tea-break to give everyone a chance to calm down.

I requested that they filter D out for me. I wanted to sit with him and talk one to one. I felt he was primed. I knew I could get through to him.

I connected to my divine sword (better late than never), before we sat together, me and this damaged boy. We had a heart-to-heart. I inspired him by explaining the huge potential he had available to him. His power was sitting just beyond his fear.

He wanted to hold on to the fact that no one could be trusted, no one at all. I gently pointed out that he had no right looking for trust from others whilst it was obvious that he could not even trust himself.

This shocked him.

*"You are bullying these teachers,"* I said, *"in the same way your dad bullied you and your mum."*

I let this settle for a few seconds.

*"Do you want to be a bully, like your dad?"*

He was absolutely adamant that he didn't.

*"Then stop acting like your dad. You are a big man. You are frightening everyone in the room when you kick off."*

I suggested a new strategy: gentleness. Kindness.

I assured him that there was true power in gentleness, in kindness especially when it was administered by someone as big and physically capable as him.

The concept of being kind, simply because he could, moved something in him and he softened.

*"Let these people teach you,"* I suggested, *"let them help you to realise the full force of your potential."*

During the second half of the session every kid in the room was hanging off my every word.

I cleared the room of fear with the divine sword.

But, this was not the startling element of the story that I alluded to earlier.

This was not the anomaly I witnessed with my spiritual eye, it was not the peculiarity that I did not want to witness, and found most difficult to accept.

Because these kids were young and overtly out of control and there was no punishment for their bad behaviour, I was able to see in exaggeration what was present, but less obvious in other areas of society. I was able to see the head, body and tail of their shadows. Even in the jails I'd visited, the pain-bodies of the inmates were obscured behind enforced protocols. Prisoners were always on their best game around visitors. Bad conduct was punished by withdrawal of prison benefits and the suspension of early release for good behaviour, so everyone wore their best mask.

This is what I witnessed: these kids were physically and psychically damaged, and because of this they were all leaking essence, badly leaking.

I was able to see this very clearly.

I would go as far as to say that I was called to this place specifically to see it.

I saw (in my mind's eye) incorporeal energies gathering around every one of these kids, entering them, feeding from them, acting-out through them in order to trigger arousal in others – drama, fear or otherwise – so that a feeding frenzy of essential energy between unconscious people could ensue.

I could see that these kids were consumption for the *adverse forces* looking for a free meal.

Francis of Assisi warned us that the *adverse forces* are airborne, and will enter wayward souls through the smallest fractures in their psyche. These negative energy forms will be drawn to fissures as surely as rain gravitates to a crack or a split or a loose roof tile in an old building.

I could see, just from looking at these boys and girls, that they were vulnerable to every kind of defilement, human or otherwise.

Eckhart Tolle, in his books and seminars, talks comprehensively about *pain bodies*. I mentioned this earlier. Carl Jung called these elements *shadows*. The bibles label them as devils (derived from the concept of the divided self). The Buddhists refer to them as defilements. Gurdjieff called our inner demons *sub-personalities*, and it is these *teammates* (as Sri Aurobindo calls them) that the *adverse forces* bait, and feed on; the whole world, Gurdjieff said, ran on this exchange of negative energy.

On this day, in this room, I was able to witness this as a truth, I saw them unhidden, and in their full regalia. I could feel energies around each one of these broken kids, waiting for a moment to enter. It was so obvious and so palpable that it was impossible to deny. By bringing a balanced energy to the room, one that neither sought nor took advantage of the essence oozing from these kids, I was able to use the divine sword to empty the room of any inbound or airborne defilement. These energies, whether in the air or in the body, are absolutely repulsed and affronted and beaten back, often completely obliterated by the frequency of love.

I was shown clearly that, in future, I should never enter any room without my sword; without spiritual alignment. If I had any dormant defilement in me, these energies in and around the kids would have scanned me, located them and entered at the exact frequency they were emitting; fear at the level of fear, anger at the level of anger, dissonance would feed off dissonance, lust or greed or self-pity would automatically have docked with its matching energy and the feed would have begun.

It was demonstrably obvious to me that you cannot heal anyone, until you are first healed.

You cannot free people, if you are not free.

You can't help them, until you have first helped yourself.

How can you balance anyone if you are out of balance yourself?

You need to be the balanced tuning fork that those around you resonate with.

I was able to understand, too, why so many people in these

areas of expertise – teachers, carers, prison guards etc. – had become cynical, deeply bitter, corrupted and some of them very ill; it's because they too have been assailed by invisible energies that they didn't have the wherewithal to deal with.

I have lost count of the number of unbalanced policemen I have met, and prison guards, and teachers, and doctors and nurses, and parents. It is concerning, because they are in charge of the most vulnerable members of our society.

I saw all this very clearly.

The seeing itself, I realised later, was a spiritual Siddha (which I will expand on later), one of the gifts of consciousness.

I saw it, but at the time I did not want to admit what I saw.

I didn't want to see because the clarity of seeing was raw. It was unadulterated. It felt foreign to me, and it was painful. The revelation was far removed from our general workaday view of the world, the standard conversations, the gossip and the daily news bulletins we are served as our daily-bread.

These kids showed me, in no uncertain terms, that the world at large is fractured; it is divided and people are *not themselves*, they are leaking.

People who leak are prey for beast and fowl. They are without defence.

They are without even the understanding of the need for personal defence.

Through these leaks energies enter. Human perception and human volition and human autonomy are hijacked.

The divine sword allows you to discern this. It shows you how to see true, and how and when to cut true. I have said this already, but you have to be very brave too, brave enough to look truth in the eye and not balk at it, or step away or turn away from it because it is confusing, because it is outside of our usual frame of reference. We are often guilty of using weak rationalisation to deny the obvious because it is easier to look at a lie.

If you open your spiritual eye, you will find evidence of this anomaly everywhere. It can be seen every day in our own lives and in the world news.

At the lower end of the spectrum, you will see that the masses are depleted or sated by this unrighteous and unholy energy-intercourse, depending on whether they are the dominant or the dominated. Their energy is reaped by stronger atmospheres, or, if they are the negative and dominant presence in the room, they dishonestly reap the energy of others.

Anyone that disempowers or disrespects or undermines you is pillaging your energy.

More specifically, you are allowing them to.

If you disempower or disrespect or undermine someone else, you pillage theirs.

If you are spiritually asleep, you will be doing this yourself, very subtly, in a thousand different ways, usually without even knowing it.

The angry father pillages when he dominates the home with his intolerance.

The insecure mother pillages when she uses withdrawal of love or affection in order to get her own way.

The friend who gossips about the friend pillages.

The viewer who judges the viewed pillages.

The husband who slams doors when he is denied conjugal sex, pillages.

The wife pillages when she exchanges loveless sex for material security.

Whilst we are incongruent – our thoughts, words and deeds are not in sync – we pillage.

Etty Hillesum said that the boss she worked for, at the onset of World War Two, held a searing hatred for Adolf Hitler, but, she noted, he was a mini-fascist in his own office; he bullied his own staff.

I have friends who would be loath to admit it, but they are fascists in their own homes.

I was loath to admit it too when, many years ago, I recognised that I was an insecure fascist in my own life; I was a subtle bully.

When we deny people their autonomy, because of fear, or insecurity or arrogance, we steal their energy.

At the denser end of the spectrum, in the world news, deranged men and women enter school buildings with automatic weapons and take innocent lives.

At the college I visited, with these damaged kids leaking all over the classroom, I saw all of this in microcosm, and it was discomforting, because at the time I was still afraid of *seeing*. I didn't want to look at it because that would mean I'd have to *really* look, I'd have to *see* with the true eye of rigour, I'd have to dive deep below the waves of human conformity, where I knew deeper truths would be revealed to me, truths that were still harder to see.

Perhaps (I feared) I would see the same *adverse forces* consuming people close to me, the people I love, which would mean I'd have to do something about it. In taking the field against them (as in: fighting on the side of love), I would surely become their target and that really scared me, just as standing on a nightclub door all those years before had; taking on all comers placed me neck-deep in the brown stuff.

I realised, too, that what unnerved me even more than this – I had duelled with murderous forces when I worked as a bouncer, and sat easy at that station once I understood the terrain – was the fact that in accepting that invisible, conscious, malign forces existed in the world, would be to accept that there were other dimensions or densities existing in the same space as our four. This would mean an absolute and complete paradigm shift; if I accepted this as a truth, everything in my life would change, everything. What I witnessed sat in complete opposition and direct contradiction to current scientific law. Who was I to contravene known law?

Actually, who was I not to?

In reality, what these kids showed me was what I already knew but, until then, had not clearly articulated, or certainly I had not fully accepted. Like most other people in the four-dimensional world, I pretended these other densities and the beings that inhabited them – good and bad – weren't real, they only existed in allegory, or metaphor, or in bible stories or horror films or fantasy magazines on the extremes of society. The only difference was, now I was fully acknowledging it.

I had witnessed this *other dimensional* phenomenon before, many times, but even then didn't want to admit it, not fully; I did not want to accept it.

I stood on nightclub doors for nearly a decade and watched every kind of depravity acting from and working through the damaged or the impaired or the intoxicated human psyche.

I already knew that people were often *not themselves*, me included.

This situation just enabled me to consciously recognise and clearly define it.

And what does it matter anyway, if energy-forms are airborne or earth-bound, corporeal or incorporeal, it all amounts to the same thing at the end of the day.

If it is not noticed and dissolved, it is dangerous.

And if a specific aspect of this energy makes us afraid, then it needs to be investigated and understood and the fear liberated, otherwise we will remain stuck, like latter-day cavemen, afraid of the fire.

I later realised, and Sri Aurobindo confirmed, that *God's negations are as useful as his affirmations* and that all forces, human or otherwise, have their original signature in God, they all come from the same place, and they all play their part in the human evolution. In laymen's terms, the forces that would seem to defy us are actually beneficial. Like the gargoyles standing sentry at the gateless gate, they keep the unworthy out, and allow only the worthy in. This is for our own good. If we were to access the energy-streams at these higher dimensions before we have proved our physiology, we would likely fry. I have witnessed it. I have seen people attempt to *hack the system* using fast-track measures, or drugs etc. as a battering ram to break open dimensional doors. Some were severely impaired by their experience, others paid the ultimate price, when energies way beyond their *pay grade* addled their minds, or took their lives.

The adverse forces, as dark as we might like to paint them, protect us from premature exposure. And – if we choose the narrow gate as our way – they will act as the forge through which we might temper our blade.

From this perspective, then, everything that happens to us is good.

The Kularnava Tantra tells us that, *"By what men fall, by that they rise."*

*And if these perturbing forces yank the little coats* (that we put on to avoid seeing) *a little too violently, it is not random or with wanton malice, but to open our eyes and compel us to a perfection we might otherwise resist... these rather ungracious forces are instruments of progress.*
(Sri Aurobindo)

They always catch us, these forces, when our defences are down. And that is the point right there; our defences should not be down. And if we were firm, if we were very certain and *one-pointed in our development, they would not shake us,* not even for a second, if fact we would not even register with them.

Certainty is the invisibility cloak of mythical legend.

And if we are not certain, and we *are* caught unawares, we should look to ourselves for the source of error, instead of blaming the world and the devils in the world for our woes. If we were wise enough do this, we would find that everyone of these attacks exposes an unproved element within us, a leak that needs urgently addressing. They may feel like hell, these adverse forces, when they alight at the doorway of our heart, but they are our very best teachers, and we should thank our Source every day for sending his master fencers, to help us perfect our divine weapon.

And what is that weapon?

We deal with the adverse forces, the same way we deal with all the other vibrations: with silence, the inner stillness that blows all footprints from the sand.

The adversary will disappear only when he is no longer needed in the world.

The adverse forces are elite training instructors, the personal coach that we hire to train us to our absolute spiritual potential. Whilst we allow old hysterical thinking to dominate our view, we will never be able to recognise these forces for the ordained teachers they really are.

Sri Aurobindo discovered that, when we are able to perceive these vibrations, and distinguish between them, it enables us to *"manipulate them, quiet them, avert them or even alter them. Once we are able to control them in ourselves, we are automatically able to control the same vibration anywhere we meet them in the world."*

Whilst we are afraid of anything we will not grow, and the **divine plan** will always be kept from us, and this will be for our own protection.

*Yes*, there is a divine plan.

This was the final perhaps most important truth that the sword of discernment revealed to me.

There is a plan, and I have a specific role to play in it. So do you. We all do.

But this secret will remain hidden from us, behind *the thorns and fire* of obscuration, and we will remain in limbo, stuck in the existential bardo until we make ourselves ready.

## Chapter 7

# The Divine Plan

There is a divine plan.

I don't know what the divine plan is.

Not the whole plan.

Not exactly, not entirely.

I am certain that there is one, but my intuition informs me that it is less of a plan and more of a map, a detailed chart that can guide us through the bardo we call existence.

I don't have the whole map in my head but I don't need it, any more than I need a detailed roadmap of Europe in my memory if I am following the satnav in my car.

The divine plan operates on a need-to-know basis. As we journey through the arc of our life, it delivers the street-by-street, road-by-road direction as we travel.

At first I suspected that the divine plan offered a personal itinerary, an ideal route through the vicissitudes of the human condition; just as a satellite navigation system might chart a traffic-free, safe-passage through an uncertain terrain.

Later I was gifted a broader realisation, which I will come to shortly.

All truths are interim in this temporary abode and the rules that apply are apt to change the very moment we think we've grasped them.

*If you see the Buddha on the path, kill the Buddha*, the popular idiom advises.

The moment we think we have grasped the absolute, we know that we have not, because the abstract is beyond objective articulation.

The true truth can be experienced, but it cannot be relayed.

Gurdjieff was warned by his sage grandmother to *never follow anyone else's map. Only follow your own map, and even then, never use the same map twice.*

Before I expand on the divine plan as I see it, I should first explain a little about the reciprocal universe, for context. The former won't make much sense without an overview of the latter.

I am aware that I have spoken about this twice already, but repetition is the mother of learning in this realm, and of course, each new telling of the same material – as in the New Testament – brings a fresh angle on the same subject.

Understanding reciprocity is foundational; nothing else can proceed until we first find certainty in its laws.

## The Holy Wheel of Karma

The Buddhists believe that the reality we inhabit is karmic by law.

We don't have to look very far to see proof that this is both true and obvious.

They propose and I concur – that in each new incarnation we inherit the karmic credit and debt, carried over from the last. At the end of each day, each week, each month, each year, certainly at the end of every lifecycle, our credit and debt are accounted, and the balance carried forward to the next day or the next life.

In Sufism, the mystic arm of Islam, they call this law *Ya Muntaquim* (pronounced yaa mum-TA-kim, also recognised as one of the 99 names of Allah). It is the balancing force that is completely reliable and totally uncompromising. Ya Muntaquim (to paraphrase *The Physicians of the Heart) is the embodiment of the principle of reciprocity, the holy wheel of karma, as described in the Dharma traditions.* It suggests that whatever you put out into the universe comes back to you. The force of Ya Muntaquim equalises and seeks to create harmony in the universe in ways that might appear tragic and violent from the human perspective.

In other words, all debt has to be repaid, and the universe will determine the optimum way to right that balance. Even if, to our human sensibilities, it appears disproportionate or unqualified, from the omniscient perspective, it will always be reliably fair and perfectly balanced.

None of this should come as a shock.

It certainly should not be hard to believe in credit and debt, or even reincarnation for that matter. Everyone has witnessed the birth of a child and the death of a friend or relative, we know that people exit from and arrive at our planet every day in their millions.

And the karmic balance; it's really no different to the usual fiscal exchanges we make in our everyday dealings with the world. If you earn more than you spend, you will stay in credit. If you spend more than you earn, you will accumulate debt.

It is not hard math.

And debt has to be paid. If it is not paid, you will be taken to debtor's court, or sent to prison.

Similarly, if you lie, or steal or cheat, if you break the law, legal reciprocity – the judiciary – will haul you into a courtroom and bring you to book.

The difference with divine karma is that nothing ever gets missed. No one gets away with anything. No debt goes unpaid, all credit is honoured: everything is accounted for.

The law of karma states that if we die to the body, with any debt left unpaid, we will be reborn back into the world, into new life in a new body, and that debt will be carried over.

The quality of our new life will be wholly determined by the quality of our old life.

If we live a good life, if we are kind and act righteously in the world, this will be recompensed and in our next outing we will be elevated because of it.

If we live a negative life, if we are unkind and unrighteous, this too will be recorded and the next incarnation will be coloured by the last.

The level of your next station is determined solely by you.

Like school, or college, or university, each next academy of learning will begin at the level reached in the last.

A-star students and no-star students will each enter universities that reflect the quality of their past learning.

The Buddhists believe that people live and die and live and die again, ad infinitum, until they are able to neutralise their karmic debts, whereupon they are released from Samsara, the eternal and unsatisfactory wheel of existence; they can then head towards Omega Point (Home – union with the Source).

The atheist will argue that nothing exists beyond the body.

I can already assure you that this is not true.

I was taken out of my physical body, whilst I was wide awake. I was gifted experiential proof, so I am already certain that life exists beyond the mortal coil. I have witnessed dimensions beyond the physical realm.

As I said earlier, most religions talk about heaven and hell and the in-between place, the waiting room or bardo, as places that exist beyond physical death; but each has their own theory on how this manifests and what it means. No one – in or out of religion – seems able to concur on a specific belief.

It can be very confusing trying to discern truth from the pick-and-mix of believers and non-believers who are each adamant that *they* have the truth and everyone else is living a lie.

When I read the plethora of conflicting theories – theological and secular – proffered by the esteemed and the learned, and I find myself once again dissonant, I do what I always do, I turn away from the theories and beliefs of others and I revert instead to what I know, what I have individually experienced.

This next example might seem peripheral to the subject at hand, but I will tell it anyway, because it acts as a tremendous reference point for me (and hopefully will for you too). When measuring personal yaqeen against the borrowed or inherited or hand-me-down truths, bandied about by the experts, there can be no competition; the only one real certainty is experienced certainty.

When I was an ardent martial arts (MA) player, training at local club level but with the aspiration of going much higher, there was much debate in the MA circles about self-defence. The disagreements centred specifically on efficacy, and more generally on what particular martial art or MA technique might work best when faced with a determined attacker, a real assailant in the street. Everyone had their own particular theory, each favouring their own specific art (there are many different martial art systems). Many of these theories were proposed by the most credible and the most able martial arts players on paper. Some of these theories were proffered by my own teachers and by their teachers before them; some of them were practically gods in the martial arts pantheon. These were people whose opinion really meant something, and as an aspirant you didn't dare challenge them. If you did you might burst immediately into flames for your blasphemy. You could not question the system. To question was to doubt, and to doubt what you'd been taught in the dogmatic world of martial arts was an assault on etiquette and this was deemed deeply disrespectful.

Etiquette (I have found) is often little more than dogma dressed up as protocol. It is an implicit stop sign, a red light that forbids honest scrutiny.

Unanswered questions kept the martial art myth alive. This mystique allowed pseudo-masters with bloated egos (and bigger bellies) to parade like sovereign-kings in large halls full of conditioned followers, converts who can't see that the emperor is not wearing any clothes.

Very few people want to see true, for fear of looking stupid.

Forgive me if this sounds disingenuous or cynical, that is not my intention.

I have a lot of close friends who practise martial arts. Many of them are fine athletes and dedicated teachers, but the truth remains: there are as many opinions about MA efficacy as there are practitioners, and that's because people take *yes* for an answer, when they really should not be so trusting or so gullible; they are allowing other people's beliefs to stop them from finding their own.

The opinions on workable self-defence are delivered by seniors with such deep conviction that it is very hard to believe that they're not telling the truth.

They can't all be right.

What I have learned and what I know is this: most of them are not overtly lying, they are just not telling the truth.

What does this mean?

It means that they are not lying, because they really do believe what they are saying. But they are not telling the truth either, because what they are saying is unqualified and untested outside of the practice hall.

They are simply passing on what they've been told. Or they are testing and qualifying their art in a controlled and conditioned arena (the dojo, the sports hall, the gymnasium) and presuming that what works on dry land, will be automatically be watertight when it is submerged into the ocean of reality. Or they are using any random exception to prove their rule.

As a young karateka, I didn't know who to listen to or what to believe.

All I was sure of was this: I witnessed a savage, dogfight in a local pub when I was 15 years old, and I knew even then as a lower grade purple belt that the *very tidy, very organised* MA we were being taught in the dojo would not sit well in the messy debacle of a beer-sticky pub brawl. Almost as soon as I'd noticed this glaring anomaly, my martial arts conditioning kicked in and rationalised my true seeing as the naïve and blinkered ignorance of a low-grade-nobody who didn't know what he was talking about.

The instant I noticed the truth, I dismissed the truth.

I immediately reminded (or reprimanded) myself never to

question the masters again. My frightened ego told me to get my head down, train harder, get my black belt (in Shotokan karate, one of the toughest martial arts systems in the world), open my own class, and pass on the lie that I'd been taught by the instructors before me. I was assured by my own conditioned rhetoric that it would all make sense in the end.

It did not.

The honest-true I'd seen as a 15-year-old neophyte was now buried under a thousand new "killer-techniques" and a teacher's certificate.

And so the lie perpetuates.

It was only after suffering a debilitating depression in my twenties that I was able to be brutally honest and admit that I was scared of everything. My new black belt didn't help matters. In fact it made me even more scared because there were so many more expectations of me now that I was a supposed expert.

In truth I had absolutely no idea what would work consistently in a real fight because I'd never had one, not since school. Even light skirmishes with violence, low-grade confrontations left me so overwhelmed by adrenalin and fear that all I wanted to do was run away and quietly disappear.

The point I am making is this: all of the experts, all of my teachers, my MA heroes were wrong.

They were wrong.

I loved them. I admired them. I respected them immensely, even hero-worshiped some of them, but they were wrong.

They were not telling the truth.

And the only way I was really going to know the truth was to scratch below the surface and find the truth for myself.

Which I did...

I took a job as a nightclub bouncer.

It was a complete and absolute paradigm shift. My whole world changed.

I learned more truth on my first night than I'd learned in the previous 15 years.

That my MA masters could be so categorically and utterly wrong was both shocking and freeing.

The very next day I went back to my karate class, to my students, and I said, *we are doing this all wrong.*

It was true – we were doing it all wrong.

And in seeing or confirming a truth that I'd always known but denied for fear of looking stupid, or offending my art, I changed the landscape of martial arts.

I certainly changed the landscape of my own life.

How could so many people be living in such absolute denial? It beggared belief.

And… it was so very inspiring to me.

If these splendid athletes were all in denial about something as relatively unimportant as the efficacy of a specific recreational martial art, what else were they in denial about?

What else was I in denial about?

What other things was I taking everyone else's word for?

Of course, as is often the way, I revealed my findings to the MA world, and I became just *another* martial arts voice, one of the many, one more strong opinion to add to the confusion. But the difference with me was that mine was no longer *just an opinion*, it was a truth backed by a raft of empirical evidence that could not be denied. And my message to them was not *follow me, I know the truth*, my word was *don't follow anyone. Go and find out for yourself.*

It won't mean anything if you don't find out for yourself.

This brings me back to the exciting revelation that the truth is out there.

But the spiritual truth is bespoke, it is individual, it is so unique to each person that no one else can tell you what it is, only encourage you to experience it for yourself.

People often say to me, in reference to my revelations: *I need proof.*

Well, yea, of course you do, but *your* proof is not my job, it's yours.

So... go out there and get it.

I've got my proof, go out and get your own.

Taking the word of someone else as a belief will also stop you from finding your real truth.

It will never be certain until you feel it for yourself.

It will only ever be a nice idea.

All written and spoken truths are interim, but you can experience a certainty that is impossible to articulate or put into words.

When Nelson Mandela was imprisoned on Robben Island for nearly 30 years, he experienced absolute certainty.

I spent some privileged time with Chris Lubbe, a man who shared prison time with Mandela. Chris later went on to bodyguard for him in his years as president of South Africa (SA).

Chris, Nelson Mandela and their fellow dissidents suffered many abuses at the hands of ruthless prison guards on Robben Island, including torture. Through this painful and regrettable experience Mandela was able to pierce many truths, not least of which was that there is a divine plan.

He confessed this to Chris and Chris passed it on to me.

Nelson Mandela did not reveal the exact details of the plan, only that it was real and it was undeniable and that Chris' part in it was to go out into the world and (to quote Mandela) *tell our story*.

And what was his story, Nelson Mandela?

What was Chris' story?

What is my story?

Ultimately, what is your story?

What is the story you need to discover, live and then tell to others?

What story was Nelson Mandela telling Chris Lubbe to pass on to Geoff Thompson so that he too might go out and tell other people?

What was the story?

I don't just mean the story of political oppression or the story of apartheid or his story about *the prison years* or even those years beyond where he eschewed the violent terrorism of his past, and took his seat in history as the first black president in South Africa. These stories are all splendid enough, but it has to be bigger than the story of one man, or the liberation of one nation, so what is the gist?

If you wrote your learning down on the back of a pebble what would it be?

What is its essential reduction?

What has *this* man learned, the one sitting here with a pen, bleeding the ink of his experienceon to the page?

Mandela told Chris a very interesting story that gives us a clue.

Nelson Mandela had suffered at the hands of his oppressors for years in prison; they hated him.

These white SA prison guards despised their black, terrorist prisoner.

Mandela hated them right back.

It was hate that first convinced Mandela to reach for arms, for weapons and bombs in the fight to win freedom for his people, instead of grasping for convincing rhetoric.

Hate fed hate and pain fed pain and so the violence perpetuated, to the point that hate and pain were destroying a whole country and making news (being noticed) all around the world.

This conflict concluded with Mandela spending nearly three long decades in a prison cell, on a small island, doing the internal rigour on his situation.

On one occasion, Mandela was being tortured by some of the new guards. These were young, angry white South Africans, who had picked up the baton from the old guard and wielded it with gusto. It was in the middle of a particularly excruciating torture (Chris told me) that Mandela had a realisation; these guards, the men torturing him, were young, they were way too young to have been anywhere near the troubles in South Africa when they first erupted and when Nelson was first sent to prison. There was no way they could have known anything about Nelson Mandela personally, other than what they'd been told or had heard or read; they only knew him through the negative conditioning that been handed down by their forebears. These men could not really hate Mandela; they could only hate the effigy of him that had been sculpted by other hands, they could only hate him as a concept.

The moment Mandela realised this, he had an epiphany.

These young men were victims of apartheid, just as much as he and his fellow black South Africans.

They had been infected by hate.

They had been weaned on hate.

And hate needs hate in order to exist.

Hate feeds on hate.

In *The Tibetan Book of the Dead* they have a powerful and profound saying: *recognition and liberation are simultaneous.*

The moment you realise the unreality of fear, the illusory nature of hate, you are instantly liberated from it.

In his moment of realisation, Mandela replaced his own hate with compassion, with understanding. Ultimately he replaced ignorance with love and he was liberated.

The moment he accessed Love, the torture stopped and it never returned.

He realised that unless he fed into the hate and fear of his oppressors, they could not harm him. These young men never tortured him again, and later like the rest of the world, many of them came to love this man of peace.

Of course hate and fear are seductive.

They have roots in human conditioning that go back tens of

thousands of years; they do not give up their sovereignty easy.

As Nelson Mandela was driven through the prison gates of Robben Island, back to freedom after 30 years of jail, he (said he) still felt the stirring pull of hatred in his heart. He knew that if he didn't leave those feelings at the prison gates, there would be no hope for him, and ultimately there would be no hope for South Africa.

Then and there, as the car left the compound, he let go of all his hate and the world was changed.

So what was his story?

What was the story he wanted Chris to tell me?

What was the story he wanted me to tell you?

Legends of the world are created in the sharing of stories, but that is not their true purpose.

In the classic novel, *The Odyssey*, there is a moment when Odysseus, the hero of the story, visits Achilles (the famed warrior) in the underworld. It was said that Achilles traded a long life full of peace and contentment for a short life full of honour and glory. But he tells Odysseus that it was all a mistake.

*I just died,* he says, *that's all. There was no honour. No immortality.*

He promises Odysseus that, given the chance again, he would choose differently the next time around, he would choose to go back and be a lowly slave to a tenant farmer on Earth rather than be what he is – a king in the land of the dead. He said that whatever the struggles of life were, they were still preferable to being *in this dead place.*

Living without Love is like being in limbo in a dead place.

The telling and retelling of our stories is vital, so that we can mine their truths and reveal the divine plan, an ethereal schematic. Not one that will get us *through* this bardo, or lift us out of this existential nether-world, but rather, a map that will reveal a magical formula that transforms our hell, our bardo, our purgatorial limbo into the heaven on earth that has been foretold by every prophet and saint since time in memorial.

There is nothing to escape.

There is no territory to negotiate.

There is nothing to seek.

There *is* a divine plan.

The divine plan is Love.

Love does not need to be nurtured; the soul, *which is pure love*, does not need to be trained, it is already fully functioning and ripe with the sap of divine love.

It just needs to be fully revealed.

The plan, the map, the direction, the instruction is Love.

If this seems a little too simplistic, it is because it is.

It is only because we are conditioned to believe that truth is complicated that we have been looking for Reality in the complex.

The truth is always simple.

It is so simple that it is almost offensive.

But that does not mean it is easy.

*Love is not a subtle argument,* Rumi reminds us, *the door there is devastation.*

As I mentioned in a previous chapter, in order to access love, we first have to remove, or refuse (or devastate) those elements from our life that are not love.

We have to devastate the *many* truths in order to reveal the One. When I put to question martial efficacy on the door of a Coventry nightclub, the answer was so simple, so basic that many people are still offended by it, and still denying it, and still violently eschewing it even today, some 30 years later.

They are offended because the answer was too simple.

Mandela defeated his torturers by changing his own atmosphere. He cleared the fog of his hate, and in doing so, he revealed Love, and he met their hate and he met their fear with Love.

Love is the still centre that all things will be drawn towards. It is the primal atmosphere that all other atmospheres surrender to. When we dwell in the one place (love) all multiplicity will swim around that one still point.

If love sounds like a soft answer to a hard question, it is because you haven't yet grasped the true concept of love as the panacea. I understand why you can't see it. It took me an age. I had to remove many determined obscurations before love revealed itself to me. Even though it is in plain sight of everyone, it is revealed only to the few.

The concept is so basic that it slaps you in the face, and yet it still took Mandela 30 years of incarceration and degradation and torture before he was able to see it. And even then, the root of the roots still had to be dug out and it would be many years even after his release before he was able to fully control his legendary temper and stop himself from falling back into conditioned hate and learned fear.

Love will not reveal itself to us until we have denied its opposite. We have to absorb 99% of the hate and anger; we have to expose it *head, body and tail* before it reveals its true nature, gives up its sovereignty and falls back into consciousness.

Like Mandela with his prison guards, the hate has to be enfolded in a loving embrace, before it gives up its strength.

If there is even an ounce of hate left in us, a legion of hate will feed off it for a calendar month. It can march a battalion through a pinhole of hate and fear. It will colonise us before we even realise that we are the victim of a personal coup.

Francis had to kiss the leper of his manifest sin before the hideous defilement transformed into the beautiful Christ.

Like Prince Arjuna, in the Bhagavad-Gita, Mandela did not eclipse fear and hate from a classroom, he transcended it whilst in the tortured battlefield of Robben Island.

I too had to stand nose to nose with violence before it would reveal its evanescent nature.

If love is the plan, then love must become the goal.

Hate blocks love, as surely as cloud covers the sun.

Whether the hate rises in us or approaches from an external source is of little significance here. Fundamentally they are the same. It is whether or not we engage or identify with hate that determines its fate, and with it ours.

If we do not engage it, it dies in the air, literally.

If we are able to observe without engagement, we become the vulture of Mayan mythology, the death-eater, a being that converts death into life, hate into love.

This is why the Mayans consider the vulture to be a symbol of cleansing, of renewal and transformation.

When we refuse to engage defilement, any defilement, it dies; the nature of the defilement is liberated and the effulgence, the energy it contained is transferred over to us.

The answer is love.

The divine plan is love.

It always has been and always is, and it always will be.

We negotiate our way into higher dimensions, we enter the heavens, with the ever-reliable compass of love.

The rest is just detail.

The truth has been hidden in plain sight.

It is so obvious that, as Churchill said, people have been tripping over it for millennia, getting up and walking away as though nothing happened.

I have already written a brief synopsis of the next experience I'd like to share, in a previous chapter, but a comprehensive telling at this juncture will hopefully illustrate the transformative power of love.

I had an enemy.

Let me rephrase that; I *thought* I had an enemy.

I'll call him L.

I hardly ever saw him anymore. His world and mine were separated by a betrayal that cut right through to my marrow. I prided myself on the fact that I'd forgiven L. I said all the right things about him and our shared but difficult experience; what

I'd learned from the historical incident, what part I myself had played in it, my own faults, the fact that I was in no position to judge him, I'd committed as many mistakes as he had etc.

I said *all* the right things.

And yet... whenever his name came up in conversation or in company, or even in passing, I still felt the ever-so-familiar tingle of adrenalin in my stomach.

I told myself and I told others (and I had even told him) that *all was forgiven*, but my body signals, the alert of judgment and fear, said otherwise.

Then, out of the blue I had an invite. He wanted me to attend a function he was holding, a party. My anger and dissonance bloated to the forefront of my consciousness like a boil ready to burst.

*I've forgiven him,* I said to my wife very angrily, *but that doesn't mean I have to go out to dinner with him.*

I was dissonant.

This man had made it public that he hated me, so why the hell did he want to sit with me at a public function?

God spoke to me in my intuition. He reminded me of kenosis, self-emptying.

He also reminded me of my covenant, to follow His instruction, to heed His guidance unquestioningly.

Then he added these spiritually cutting words, the coup de grace to any resistance I had left in me: *if there is any obstacle between you and even one person, there is an obstacle between you and the One.*

I did not want any obstacles between me and God.

I did not want that, I could not accept that.

So I willingly and gratefully and immediately accepted the invitation, and agreed to break bread with my enemy.

When you have a divine covenant, obedience, taking instruction, even when it doesn't immediately make any sense, is an imperative. Miracles occur when you take the instruction;

*even water will grow solid under the feet of the obedient man.*

I went willingly, I went thankfully, but I still went nervously.

When we met, I immediately saw sadness in his eyes.

I felt compassion in my heart, love.

Any anger, any dissonance or hate evaporated.

Together we entered an eatery that looked as though it had been drawn from a nirvana-painting and made real just for this occasion.

I said to him kindly, *you look tired.*

He melted.

Let me take two steps back.

Let me retreat a little, otherwise the rest of the story will not make the complete sense it needs for me to articulate my point.

The entry point was love.

I followed my instruction because I love God.

I entered the meeting carrying the atmosphere of love and because of that, not despite it, all I saw in the eyes of a nemesis was love.

The atmosphere of love took me out of conceptual time and into (what is known as) *essential time,* where everything slowed down and I was able to experience a dimensionality different to relative time. Time as I knew it stopped and I was able to experience post-eternity. The room we sat in, the folk who peopled the establishment, the waitress who took our order, the barman who served us drinks, the food that arrived on the table and the company we kept for the rest of the evening was all converted into the most stable and dominant atmosphere in the room: Love.

Love was the atmosphere that I brought with me, or should I say, the atmosphere I brought *in* me.

The food was so delicious I found myself mentioning it again and again.

I'd never tasted a banquet like it – there are simply not enough superlatives to capture the culinary delight.

The food was the product of the energy, the atmosphere I exuded – love.

I have sat in other places at other times, while I was carrying a dark atmosphere, in times of conflict, during difficult cleansings and the atmosphere I met and the food and drink I was served was as dark and as putrid as the atmosphere I brought with me. I remember a period in my life when violence still owned me and I rationalised my base behaviour, where I sat in a dank restaurant eating a poor plate of *something* and a cockroach fell out of the ceiling tiles, landed in my food and wiggled around until I buried it in mashed potatoes.

This is not a metaphor. a cockroach literally fell from the ceiling on to my plate.

I paid for the meal and left without complaint.

I think even then I must have known that the parasite in my food was created by the parasite in my mind.

This day, eating with an old enemy, my new atmosphere delivered divine delights.

It showed me once again that when the veil of vice is removed, love reveals itself, it reveals its plan; my plan and *the* plan is the spiritual panacea that is love.

The truth will always reveal itself but we have to be prepared to absorb 99% of the lie before it gives up its tenancy.

I have repeated this I know. It bears repeating.

Absorption of the lie in order to reveal the truth takes courage.

## The art of doing nothing

There is a belief at the top-end of esoteric practice that in order to realise God you don't have to do anything at all, nothing.

This is absolutely true.

God is omniscient, He is omnipotent and omnipresent; He exists in every conscious atom and molecule in the whole universe.

To search for Him is to lose Him because there is nothing to search for. The part of you searching is also illusory, an amnesiac-periscope poking its eye out of the sea of consciousness looking for its source. Everything we are looking for is already here and if we abandoned our search and dropped our plethora of very fine techniques and sat still and quiet for long enough, we would see this in an instant.

Do nothing.

As you will have already noticed, there is a hell of a lot of work in doing nothing.

You must develop the courage to be still. That's first.

Next is the patience you must develop to wait for complete silence of the mind. To do this you need to know and give an allowing to the *you* that waits, the witness, the one who observes.

Third on the list of *not doing* is to engage nothing that tries to rise, and rise to nothing that tries to engage... that is a big job right there, a large job, weighty.

Doing nothing takes tremendous wisdom.

It also demands strength, and a wide understanding of process.

Siddhartha, before he became the Buddha, exhausted every search and observed every posterity, and practised every esoteric technique and perfected every asceticism before he finally gave up on it all, sat under the Banyan tree and did nothing, refusing to move until enlightenment presented itself.

Shall I tell you what I learned from spending nearly a decade working in a life-threatening employ?

May I tell you what I learned about physical self-defence and its efficacy in the microcosm of war?

I became a bouncer to end my depression, by facing down the fear of violent confrontation. It was my bid to prove the techniques of martial arts, and remove the fear of ignorance. I told you this much. During that ten-year semester, I was able to reduce the workable techniques down from the thousands available to one principle: the pre-emptive strike.

This concept would allow an average combatant to survive countless confrontational situations with one simple punch.

If this was all I'd learned from the university of confrontation, I'd be pretty disappointed with myself.

What I did learn that was of significance and what I am certain of is this: if I'd done nothing at all, there would have been nothing to fight for and no one to fight with in the first place. Everything in that violent bardo, including the bardo itself, would have disappeared. All of those monsters and the infrastructure where the monsters congregated were merely aspects of my own mind, my own damaged psyche.

*The Tibetan Book of the Dead* informs us that monsters are projections of our own mind. It also warns that when they present themselves they will seem very real, you will be able to hear them, see them, touch them and smell them.

They appear real, but real they are not.

Had I the insight and the practice and the wisdom of an adept, I'd have been able to just sit in my Coventry home and annihilate every one of those defilements as they petitioned for my engagement, without ever having to leave my own front room.

I am sure of this.

I am reminded of Etty Hillesum again: *"I do believe it is possible to create, even without writing a word or painting a picture, by simply moulding one's inner life. And that too is a deed."*

These wise words are true. They have always been true, they always will be. But I know that Etty only discovered this secret when she was incarcerated in a Nazi concentration camp, during World War Two. Whether this would have ever been revealed to her without the pain-stimulus of her *troubles* is unlikely.

In my own case too, I would not have had the great understanding or the seasoned wisdom or cast-iron will to practise nothing, to know *how* to practise nothing or even to know what practising nothing meant, without the vast experience that came from first trying to practise *something*.

Ironically, all of the virtues that I did eventually develop were honed on the dualistic battlefields created by my mind-projections.

I suspect too that the Buddha may not have developed his own powerful insight into nothingness without first sharpening his *eye* on the 10,000 things.

Once this truth is realised and we no longer feel the need to search for our grail in worldly locations, tilting lances at imaginary monsters, and drawing swords against metaphorical dragons of lore, what is left?

What *is* left?

Now we can see that the mind, as Milton said, *is its own place* and that it can make *a heaven out of hell and a hell out of heaven*, what do we do with that?

Make a heaven out of hell of course.

This, it seems to me, is the most obvious and immediate course of action.

And, if called upon by divine covenant to do so, assist those making a hell out of their heaven to see their remiss, and reverse their process.

But before this, why not practise the art of nothing, why not start now, this moment, go directly to it; if the adepts are assuring you that this is the direct route, take it and be the proof that they are right.

Many sages and gurus have gone down blind alleyways to earn this information, so that you do not have to.

Silence the mind and still the body and simply wait until those ungracious *somethings* withdraw. They *will* withdraw. They have to; otherwise they will be incinerated in the *white snow* of your atmosphere, when they make their approach; it'll be as though they've walked into the whole universe. And if you are to make this philosophy one of worth, hone it in the world of men, where the strong and determined opposition to your silence will become the very force that proves and perfects it. Your ability to create silence even in the midst of typhoons is already vouchsafed, you just have to go out there and take it.

Either way – and this is the point I am labouring to make – while you are in the world, you will not be able to avoid the world, so one way or another practising nothing will always involve doing something. Once we understand this, every encounter becomes an exciting opportunity to practise silence.

Just the usual vicissitudes of this world will provide the whetstone you need to perfect the art of nothing. When you can do nothing whilst in the middle of doing something, you will have cracked the technique.

*Nothing* is the centre that all things are drawn to.

The nothing I speak of is God, or Grace, or Singularity.

If I was to reduce this force to one name I would call it Love.

The divine plan is Love.

The divine plan is to reveal Love.

You will find it in silence, in stillness.

Wherever we are, whoever we are, and whatever we are doing, this is our only practice.

Love is the constant.

I was reminded in meditation that I *am* love, so I too am the constant.

The divine plan is realising this and, if called upon, assisting others to do the same.

Being aligned to Love is the greatest service we can ever afford our fellow humans, because being aligned to Love is not just the Law, it is the whole of the Law.

When we are in religion with Love, just being in the world is a service to the world; when we connect to God, everyone benefits, everyone is better protected and better inspired because of it. Even if we never leave the house, the world consciousness is lifted because we are lifted.

If we *are* called to assist others, how are we to do this?

What tools do we have at our disposal to serve this calling?

How can we make our work effective for people who are still struggling to meet their basic needs?

We follow the divine covenant of course.

That's the start of it.

Instruction will guide us, it will tell us where to go, who to talk to and what to say to them. We will also be given otherworldly tools to carry out this service, *the work of the many*.

These working tools are the Siddhas, the supernatural gifts, the mysterious by-products of expanded consciousness.

# Chapter 8

# The Divine Gifts – The Siddhas

It's very easy for a book like this (and its author) to be accused of exaggeration or fantasy.

With that in mind, in this book – like all the books I write – I'll be sure to stick to what I know, what I have personally experienced rather than what has been reported or read in a book or heard in a sermon.

It is also common to read the saints and follow the prophets and hear-tell of the miracles that occurred in their presence and pass it off as a mere metaphor or pay it forward as incontrovertible truth.

My own perspective is that either everything is a miracle or nothing is.

My problem in this book is that I have experienced and continue to experience so many miracles every day that I don't really know where to start. Some of them are the ordinary miracles that we hardly even notice happening, and others are extraordinary, what you might regard as *miracle* miracles, the biblical kind where no rational explanation can be found for what you have witnessed. But even these I have noticed are quickly relegated to the realms of coincidence by those too afraid to say and admit and process what has occurred.

My beautiful wife – who is not really comfortable with the word God or the idea of miracles – once, in a moment of spontaneous courage, accessed the God she was not sure existed and asked Him for a proof. *Something tangible,* she said, *something that I can't pass off as coincidence.* She added as a promise that if her wish was granted, *I will never ask again.*

She asked God to let her find a £20 note, sometime in the next twelve hours. She wasn't really bothered about the money per se. £20 is neither here nor there. She just wanted to witness something tangible, something that she understood and that was very specific to her request.

She was out on a training run when she made the proposal and confessed to me later that she felt a little silly even as she asked. Almost immediately after making her prayer she found a £5 note on the floor. She smiled, was someone teasing her?

This occurred in the morning, in London, whilst I was in town at a business meeting. Later that same day, bearing in mind I had no idea that Sharon had asked for this sign, we met in Islington (where we had an apartment). We walked down the road together, on our way to a local restaurant. We'd not walked more than a few feet when I saw £20 lying on the pavement in front of me. £20! I said. I picked up the note and handed it to Sharon. She became very quiet for a few minutes before finally revealing to me what she had asked for that very morning.

I smiled.

She had her miracle.

*I'll never ask again,* she said to me, *I don't know how this has happened or how it works and I don't need to know. I have my proof.*

Within two weeks Sharon was already putting her miracle down to *a strange coincidence* and *probably not anything miraculous.*

She had already forgotten how powerful it felt to witness a miracle.

Like most people, I think she was afraid of looking silly, or of being duped, or appearing evangelistic, like some recent convert, a pilgrim who has seen the light.

More likely, she was afraid of the paradigm shift that would necessarily occur if her model of known laws were suddenly challenged by this unknown phenomenon. When a miracle challenges scientific law, it can cause dissonance, because it begs more questions than it answers.

I understood. Her reaction was very common.

When miracles happen, I find, there is always a little wriggle-room left for those of us who might become dissonant if the laws of physics as we know them are suddenly defied by the unfathomable miracles we evidence.

## The Siddha of temporal reality

The first and the most obvious Siddha is the temporal reality we create every day of our lives.

The body that we stand up in, with all of its trillions of working, conscious cells, is an absolute miracle of mind.

If you don't think so, take a look at how many people maintain or destroy their bodies every day, simply with the miracle of engaged thought. How many people have you witnessed destroying themselves, with the behaviours they choose – cigarettes, alcohol, food, drugs, pornography, violence etc? It is popular to laugh at the idea of making money just with our thoughts. Or healing illness and disease, by the power of the mind. Or finding the perfect partner, with positive affirmation.

Just in my own life I can offer testimony to the miraculous potency of engaged thinking; I have made myself desperately ill, just with the consistent power of negative thought. I have healed myself of the same ailment, with the same process reversed. I have created wealth with powerful thinking. I have lost businesses because I allowed my thoughts to drift into greedy capitalist thinking, or adopted a scarcity mentality. I have won the most amazing relationships with my charm and my loving attention. I have decimated the same relationships when I engaged the caustic thinking of jealousy.

We are creating and destroying whole realities every day with our rudderless minds. Be in no doubt that the ability to create, maintain and dissolve the reality you live in is the greatest Siddha. And when we master this human reality-maker, we can make all of our clay-creations with the hands of loving kindness.

This miracle is missed by most people, as I said, because they do it so often and so unconsciously, that they no longer see the miracles they create.

## The Siddha of technology

Most of the adepts I know could not tell you the science behind their miracles, only that they happen, and they happen frequently. But then I couldn't really explain to you in any qualified technical sense how I can access people and information and maps from satellites in space, and how I can pull the rabbit of money and food and just about any other physical amenity I desire from the technology-hat I carry in my trouser pocket. Even 20 years ago my smartphone would have been the greatest mystery. As little as a century before that, you might have seemed alien and physically attacked for owning such a device.

We think we have invented the new technologies and we cope with this daily-magic by showing the lineage and history of clever inventions. This enables us to cope with the modern miracle without our heads exploding into a jumbled psychosis.

In eschatology, the premise is that our existential reality already contains all things. Everything exists, right here, right now; it is already available. We do not invent any of it, we simply become aware of it, and then call it invention.

All future technology already exists.

It is just waiting to be revealed.

I know this sounds strange and it might seem a little off the wall, but everything already exists. It is already here. It comes into view, when we open our eyes wide enough to see it.

Imagine if you will a small tribe of natives, living in an undiscovered part of the world. They are still working with rudimental tools, just coming to terms with fire, hunting with spear and bow; how miraculous would our very mysterious world be to them? *You* currently processing *me* through the ink on a piece of paper; me travelling from Coventry to London on a Virgin train in under 60 minutes; 500 people flying across continents in a jet-powered smarty-tube at 614 miles per hour;

astronauts travelling interstellar, faster than the speed of a bullet.

Ours would be an absolute and verifiable world of miracles to the less-developed tribesmen.

If one of those lovely natives was to wander from his remote village and happen upon society with all of its *modern-miracles*, he could not be said to have invented the mobile phone, or the piston engine, or aviation, or space travel, or satellites in space. He simply opened the door to a series of new rooms. He expanded his conscious-net wide enough to discover and explore what was already in situ. It would be naïve to say that I and my fast train and my powerful hand computer do not exist, just because the natives in this small village are unaware of them, just as a housefly on the screen of a TV would be naïve to deny the reality of the picture on the TV (and the TV itself) just because he is too close to see it.

If there are tribesmen in the world who would view us an advanced and miraculous race, then it stands to reason that there are beings, in different dimensional rooms to ours, whose advancement would make us look like cave-dwelling Neanderthals by comparison.

We are surrounded by so many unnoticed miracles that we are in danger of being blinded by the very miracles we deny. To be able to create food and drink and other material, temporal things with the use of sound and symbol is in itself a miracle. You enter a shop, you communicate with sound, you show a plastic card or some paper notes with symbols and numbers on them, and people hand you food and goods and services. This might not sound like a miracle and it perhaps doesn't look like a miracle, but it really is.

The whole transaction, whether you buy a coffee or a new home, is conducted with nothing but a written or spoken vow which is delivered by the medium of sound. It might seem like we are just *spending money* that we have earned, but in actual fact we are not. If you trace money back through the sound and the symbols and digits on your card and the numbers in your bank, if you follow the crumbs, you end up with nothing but sound, a vow that we speak, a promise we make to pay or repay the bearer of our note a proportionate amount of energy, in the form of a product or service. We exchange service for service, and the money-system simply keeps an account of where we are in credit and where we are in debt. The whole world of exchange with all of its promissory notes and its ledgers and accounts is based purely on vow, on perception of value and on the trust that the exchange we propose will be reciprocated.

This is *exchange* at the level of commerce where trust is only guaranteed by a lawful contract and nearly everyone is out for profit.

In the divine economy, as I mentioned somewhere else, notes and accounts are redundant because every single transaction of energy-exchange is recorded; no account is missed and all debts are paid – if not now, later.

Everything in the economy, divine or otherwise, when you strip it back and reduce it to its raw essential, is simply an exchange of energy, an intercourse of essence, which, unless it has been polluted by agenda and expectation, is ecstatic.

Nothing else exists other than this.

Everything else is temporal.

It forms, it is maintained for a variable duration, and it expires.

Over and above our most basic needs, the temporal things are neither good nor bad, but they are not real, not in the sense of eternity. They do not bring us certainty or any permanent sense of love or achievement. They definitely don't make a heaven out of hell, although they can do the opposite. They are the temporary by-product of the exchange of energy, which is the only thing that is real. The ability to produce temporary things in the world is a party-trick that everyone does every day to some extent. Some do it better, or bigger, or shinier than others, but we all create, maintain and eventually dissolve manifest things in the world.

To create anything takes a lot of energy.

To maintain it over a period of time takes a large expenditure of energy.

Dissolving what you have created will also cost you, especially if the dissolving object deceases when we least expect it, when we don't want it to, or when it returns to dust seemingly against our will.

Even if we choose to dissolve something consciously – a business, a friendship, a habit – it takes an enormous amount of seminal essence.

Sometimes, if the withdrawal of our engagement or identification contravenes the status quo, it can create an all-out war in the world and with the world, or in and with ourselves. As I am sure we all know, there is nothing like a war for depleting and exhausting vital resources.

I recently dissolved a business that I'd built up over 20 years because I was changing direction. It took me three years from start to finish, at the cost of copious amounts of emotional energy, spent in confab with established customers some of whom did not understand why I was withdrawing my services. Also, there were internal wars with parts of myself that had formed habits with the perceived benefits and promised security and sense of self that the business brought me. Even selling our apartment in London took close on 18 months of consistent effort.

I've seen many people sent into emotional freefall and suffer the mass exhaustion of seminal energy when they have engaged in illicit activity – personal, business or both – because the engagement and maintenance of the said activity demanded disproportionate levels of personal investment. Others have lost vital energies and even their lives when, realising their folly, they tried to withdraw from the engagement, only to realise that cancellation was no longer an easy option. This is especially so with addictions, be they to substance abuse or to people in damaged, symbiotic relationships, or with cults or institutions.

This is no less so with the creation, maintenance and dissolution of perceptions and cognitions. Our perceptions live, they are semi-autonomous thought-forms, and they enjoy life in the body and mind of you and me. Most of these beliefs are inherited (known as the gift of inheritance or the curse of ancestry) or they are learned. We come into the world with tens of thousands of years' worth of conditioned beliefs; these are usually re-established and reiterated in our early education. Each of these perceptions contains a vast amount of energy-power, certainly enough to maintain the living reality all around us. They are powerful because they create and maintain our model of the world every time we wake up in the morning and climb out of bed. We share this creation with every single person and influence in our own personal world. This means that we have an implicit covenant with them too, we are bonded to them by these beliefs and we literally feed off each other every day of our lives. Not just with the bread we break and share from the corner shop or the supermarket; this is the least of our foods. I'm talking about the emotional exchange of energy that keeps tribes, not only together, but also alive.

We are conjoined by our shared beliefs, so changing them or challenging them places us in opposition to our internal world and our external associations. If you stop believing what they believe, you are no longer able to exchange energy with your kin or share food with friends at a level you or they are able to digest, and this might get you kicked out of the tribe. Your tribe is your protection. It is your food, your drink, your means of emotional and physical intercourse, your ability to procreate – it is your means of survival.

The threat (or belief) is clear enough: if you get kicked out of your tribe, you die.

This is why it is so hard for people to challenge or change any aspect of their race, their religion, their culture, their schooling, their education, their governance and their indoctrinated version of God.

Challenging the tribal precedents can trigger the fear of death, even the threat of death.

I have personally witnessed close friends who have committed suicide because of the overwhelming dissonance experienced when they tried to challenge their cultural mores. It takes tremendous strength to confront accepted standards, because we are not just challenging what we have learned in this lifetime, we are going to war with beliefs that have been established for thousands of years.

People are taking their own lives every day, because they expressed or read an opinion on an Internet message board that is in opposition to the accepted gestalt. This has resulted in trolling and personal hate campaigns that have tipped them into mania and depression and ultimately suicide.

Every minute of every hour of every day there is news of people being pilloried or assailed or murdered for trying to challenge, or change, or improve or debate social, religious, personal, gender or cultural issues.

When I first left my employment as a factory worker to live out my ideal as a martial arts teacher, it was so difficult, it took me three attempts. Leaving what was known and safe and comfortable created tremendous fear and judgment and confusion in me and in my associates, especially close friends and family members. I wondered at the time why it was so difficult. I realised later that it was difficult because I was not simply changing jobs, I was shifting paradigms; I was challenging everything and everyone I knew, a whole lineage of belief. I was literally changing identity. It might not sound like much, but when you realise that your personal identity is connected to everything in your personal world – your wife, your parents, your family, your friends, your employment, your class, your religion – you start to understand why seemingly small changes can trigger disproportionate amounts of fear and trepidation.

Later, when you start connecting to the divine economy and you are asked to let go of *all* identity, believe me, it is harder still.

The ability to create, maintain and dissolve is nature's gift to us.

It is a wonderful and natural magic.

The reason people don't make more use of this ability is: 1) because they are not fully aware of their Siddha, and 2) they don't understand the extent of change; that they will not just be changing their perception they will be changing their world.

Someone asked me only today, *if what you say is true, why aren't more people free?*

They are not free because they are afraid of being free.

(To paraphrase Maslow) people are afraid of the godlike responsibilities that come with their godlike potential.

They are nervous of all the work that comes with personal freedom.

It may be our absolute right, but it is also our greatest fear.

Rather than taking freedom with all of its exciting potential and its very hard work, they instead place their autonomy in the hands of a family tradition, social mores, government politicians, employers, banks, advertisers, royalty, actors, or the new-royalty – pop stars; they give it away to any kind of convincing authority figure.

They sell their autonomy for a promised security that does not exist.

The only security available is the knowledge that if it exists at all, it exists in you and through you and from you. Any promised external security is pseudo security, and those on the promise-end are selling you a pup.

People believe that money provides security, that a home is safe, or that *the 10,000 things* will bring them comfort or stature or the acclaim or renown that they think will afford them security.

None of it does.

None of it can.

False perception sells you this idea.

But perception is malleable, it is temporal, it is an ever-changing interim-truth that is hijacked every day by society with its capitalist or communist, or socialist (or any one of the *ists*) ideas. There is only one real certainty, and of all the Siddhas, perhaps knowing this is the    greatest miracle of them all: **you are the magician.**

You are the one pulling the rabbit of 10,000 things out of the hat.

You are the one through whom the world unfolds.

Your own mind creates the slum you live in.

It is your own mind that creates the heaven you may enter tomorrow.

Once you understand this, and remove the squatting doubts, those old scripts, the beliefs that insist freedom is an idealistic lie, then you begin to *see* the world through different eyes.

I don't mean to literally see the world differently with the eyes, I mean in the metaphysical sense of *seeing* something into existence.

*Seeing* is the creative heart of your reality.

This is the greatest miracle of all.

If you own the apple tree, or if you are an apple tree, you don't need to worry about the supply of apples.

You don't need to beg, steal or borrow apples from other people.

You no longer need to worry that you are going to starve for want of apples.

You won't have to sell your soul to get an apple from someone else.

No longer will you fall for, or be hijacked, or disabled, or disempowered, or frightened by those who operate your belief-system through the dark-magic of their rhetoric.

You are the apple tree.

The apples come from you.

That this is true is in no doubt for me... but is it true for you? Getting from the world of perception to the world of Reality is not easy.

Knowing and doing are not the same.

Simply knowing about the existence of electricity will not qualify you as an electrical engineer. The adepts dedicate lifetimes to perfecting this ability, and even then, the illusion of the manifest world is still often so intoxicating, so seductive that they too can fall back under its spell, or *fall asleep*, as they say.

Reading a book about Morihei Ueshiba does not suddenly make you an expert in the martial art of aikido.

Reading the information can be a good starting-point though, an inspiration towards your practice, or perhaps a confirmation of what you already suspected, but were afraid to consciously acknowledge.

Once you understand the temporal nature of material things, you will recognise that over and above the magic-sprinkle of concept-dust they have been coated with, they are worthless.

They are worthless trinkets, the shiny-keys that you have just exchanged your vital energy for. The exchange only works because the same people have bought into the same beliefs. If we all agree that gold bars are valuable and that paper money has a certain worth and that a chunky watch makes you look important, we will all be rushing out and expending a whole lifetime of energy, 40+ hours a week, for 60 years, just so that we can park a posh car on our drive and purchase a larger space, surrounded by muck and bricks that we can say we own.

It is all perception.

I watched a beautiful documentary once about Michael Palin travelling to remote places on the earth. In one episode he was talking to a native woman in a small African village. She was beaming.

*"Why are you so happy?"* Michael asked her, intrigued. She indicated behind her as though the cause of her glee should be evident to all. She was pointing to a small, shed-sized abode with a tin roof, *"Look at my beautiful home,"* she said.

Perception is all.

What we have access to, what we inlet and outlet, the divine essence that we are a vessel for, is a precious commodity. With it we are able to meet other beings and exchange energy at many levels, the least of which is material consummation, the highest is where energy is exchanged at the level of love.

The exchange of love may be as little as a kind acknowledgement and it could be the most valuable exchange we ever make. Equally, we could make a gesture that feels enormous, raise millions for charity and it not even register in the divine economy, because it lacks alignment, it is service with agenda and not from a place of genuine love.

I spoke with a friend just recently who was going through a difficult business expansion. The smooth transition was interrupted at a crucial point by one of his business partners, who unconsciously sabotaged the process. He was sexually suggestive with a member of staff and it threw his integrity into doubt. The partner in question was already suffering ill health and the rapid growth of their business only added to his struggle. The inappropriate behaviour was (I suspected) his way of compromising his position in the business, forcing the other partners to either sack him, or buy him out. He was desperate to relieve his unbearable pressure, but had neither the self-knowing to understand this, nor the gumption to acknowledge it, and either ask for help, or step away gracefully.

Better to be removed by force than leave by choice, at least then he can blame others.

My friend complained about the *very bad timing*. It was inappropriate and thoughtless, he said, and the partner's chances of retaining his position were rapidly diminishing. He concluded by saying that he wouldn't be surprised if this desperate man *topped himself.*

It would be easy to dislike or hate the partner. His bad behaviour was sexually orientated, and the quickest way to send the public at large into a feeding-frenzy of hatred is to mention any form of sexual misdemeanour.

It would also be easy to judge the timing of his action as thoughtless and selfish, but this would be to miss the obvious; the action and the timing was *his* and it enabled him to step away from the overwhelm without the perceived shame of saying, *help, I can't cope.*

I'm not in any way condoning this man's actions or rationalising what he did or when he did it. What I am saying is this: at the very centre of this drama is a human being and he is in pain. How he got there, why he got there, whether or not he deserved judgment is none of my business. *He is in pain.*

Everyone was turning away from him in droves; he would be alone very soon. Perhaps he *will* kill himself.

*What are you going to do with that?*

This is how I counselled my friend. This is what I asked him.

I could see in a clear-instant that the business, the expansion, the exotic holidays, the posh cars and the high-figure income were tat when you compared them to one man, even a criminal, who is suffering.

What are you going to do with that?

This is the measuring right here.

Not the public charity work we do (and if we tell even one person about our work, it *is* public), it is not the work we do with the homeless, it matters little how many old ladies we help to cross the road, or how big the benefit-ball we hold is, or the amount of old clothes we stuff in a donation bag for the local charity shop.

Can you turn to a man or woman, who everyone else has turned away from – even if only in your prayers – and treat them with compassion?

When you serve a prisoner you serve God.

When you serve the man that society has eschewed, you are *really* serving.

These are the things that count.

When we enter into the heavens, these are the only pebbles of favour.

How we exchange energy in these vital moments is all that will matter, because exchanges of selflessness, of Love is the only worthwhile profit we carry forward from one day to the next, from one life to another.

The ability to see this is in itself a miracle, and those conscious enough to act on it are the real miracle makers.

I told my friend that he was being presented with an opportunity to do something of significance. If he could help his friend through this difficult time it would be the greatest service, especially when everyone else was very busy abandoning him; even if he just talked to him kindly over the phone, or met him for a coffee, or made sure that, if he did leave the business, he was fairly remunerated.

*"What should I do?"* my friend asked.

*"Do the right thing,"* I said.

I knew that he knew what the right thing was.

When it comes to the divine accounting, one simple kindness for this man, for any person in need, will be worth more than all the worthy accolades, and titled medals, and public approvals that come from working in the world.

When you can see this, when you can act on it, you are exercising the greatest Siddha.

And you won't have to wait long to receive divine reciprocity. We carry the instant reward for kindness in every cell of our body. Kindness invites love into our fleshy abode; it perfumes us with the indescribable fragrance of God.

One of the more subtle Siddhas is the ability to identify

a person's pain beyond the obfuscation of aggression and antisocial behaviour and crime. You will see it nestling there, just below the loud bravado, a layer beneath the cut-and-thrust of business and profit.

You will develop the eye to see it, and the will to do something about it.

Another Siddha is the ability to know *what* action you should take, and muster the courage to take it; even and especially when the masses approve of and rally towards the wrong action.

If we are collecting karma-pebbles for the *master of the scales*, these actions are the only ones that will carry weight; they are the white pebbles of spiritual pursuit. It is only the essence or concentrate of rare opportunities taken that will carry forward, everything else will be lost in the fire.

Business and life accumulations are mere playthings in this existence.

You can play the business game, the life-game if the spiritual ends are justified by the material means, but nothing will ever be more important than how we treat beings, especially when they are in need or in pain or in dire straits.

One famous writer I know quipped that he had written three very strong films, and if there is a heaven, these would guarantee him a triple-A-pass through the gates of pearl.

I knew they would not.

How you treat other beings is the only thing that lets you in or keeps you out.

All the other gifts I am going to talk about or make mention of or allude to are only important if they are utilised in the service of God, in the service of others.

If they are not used in this way the spiritual boons will be quickly removed, or more precisely, the divine CEO will withdraw from your home and along with him the gifts.

These following examples are some of the supernatural gifts that I have personally experienced as a result of expanded consciousness, the connection to and the integration of my lower and higher self.

## Heightened intuition

This might not seem like a siddha in the traditional sense of spiritual miracles. It is a subtle kind of magic that has gifted me internal direction and intuitive cues and codes that I have found immeasurably helpful. Fully matured ideas – sometimes complete film scripts that I would later go on to produce to great acclaim – have dropped into my consciousness like a coin falling through water. Other times exasperating enigmas that I've been struggling with have corrected themselves in meditation and the answer to my problem has just fallen into place. One film script I'd been struggling with for many years had me and everyone else involved stumped. We had a world-renowned script editor working with us, and even he couldn't work out a through-line to our story arc. One day, on the set of another film I was shooting, I mentioned to an old friend that we were struggling with this other script and boom! Without another word being spoken, the problem solved itself, there and then; the film literally fell into perfect alignment. All the elements of the script that did not serve the narrative simply fell away. That's how it looked in my mind's eye, like a sheet over a statue falling away to reveal a perfect sculpture. Some bits fell away, other elements reversed themselves or placed themselves in different positions in the script. The moment I arrived home the next day, I made the changes and the script was absolutely perfect. I could feel it. I immediately sent it to an acclaimed director, and he optioned it on the spot. I had to do nothing other than follow the instruction that I'd seen in my vision.

As is always the way, there was no problem to solve, I just needed a clear view, and that was proffered to me.

My intuition also prompts me with people I meet and interact with; it might tell me what they need to hear, or direct me to what they need to read, or generally what they ought to notice about themselves in order to clear their own view.

The intuition I receive is very specific.

I have learned not to question its methodology, its intentions or its potential outcomes. If I am directed to speak with someone in need, for five minutes or five hours, I follow the instruction. If I'm advised not to meet a certain person at all, or keep them at arm's length, I don't question it.

Before this gift came to me – or when I was first learning to hear the intuitive command clearly and heed its call – I would meet anybody and everybody who asked, and stay with them for as long as they wanted, whether it felt right or not.

I was a people-pleaser.

I was afraid to say no for fear of seeming unkind, or worse, for being judged unspiritual. My wife (who is my spiritual counsel) would ask me, *why are you meeting that person? I could tell by your voice on the phone that you don't need to meet them.* Other times she would insist, *you really must speak to this person, why are you avoiding it?*

I later developed acoustic clarity with my intuition so that I neither miss nor misinterpret the message.

Intuition – schooling from my inner tutor – has directed me towards better diet, healthier training, the right influences, the correct books, life-changing lectures, informing newspaper articles; it has led me to a plethora of exact places in order that I might receive the specific information or direction I need.

Often if I was hurrying – I learned eventually never to hurry – I would miss the *small quiet voice* urging me to take notice of a person, take note of a place or examine an anomaly. I might be a hundred yards down the road, or 20 pages ahead in a book, or ten minutes on in a conversation before I caught the inner prompt. Then I'd have to stop and retrace my steps and look at what I was guided to see.

Similarly, when I am writing a book or a film or a play, or

even an email to a friend, things that I need to mention or extend, or clarify, or rewrite, or take out completely will quietly present themselves to me; details not to be missed, whole stories to be included or an entire segue to follow – they will bid for inclusion and I will have to make a separate note of them, there and then, or they might be lost forever.

On the last book I wrote – *Notes from a Factory Toilet* – lots of ideas for other books or films were intuited to me as I placed ink on the page. I had to keep a separate pad within open reach so that I could note them down as they presented. On one particular day, I took a break from *Notes* and walked down to the local health food shop (the Chinese takeaway) for my Tuesday night mushroom curry. On the walk, an entire short film was dictated to me in small segments. I had to keep stopping, writing the notes down in an email, and sending them to myself so that I didn't forget. The intuition was so urgent that by the time I got home I had a very specific film written over twelve separate emails, for a very particular person (I also had a very hungry wife; my usual 40-minute walk took me over an hour).

Acoustic intuition is my prime mode of communication between my lower and higher souls.

I have trained myself to listen out for it; I have learned to rely upon it.

I have learned also to trust it and be excited when an idea is downloaded because it always leads to something special.

Intuition tends to present clearest and most prolifically when I am either in complete silence, or when I am on the carpet of proximity, when I am inspired (fundamentally they are both the same, as both situations engender silence). Knowing this to be the case, I make every effort to place myself in the silence of inspirational atmospheres as often as possible.

On one particular occasion, feeling flat and tired and uninspired – the aftermath of an exhausting project – I visited a London art installation to deliberately place myself on the carpet. Art always inspires me. I went to see a Man Ray exhibition but, on entering the gallery, I was immediately captured by a sculpture of two life-sized men, having a conversation on a bench (*Double Bind and Around* by Juan Munoz): it was mounted at head height on the wall as I walked in. I looked at the sculpture and noticed that the light hitting the images projected large wing-like shadows on the wall behind them.

Angels!

It was so visceral, so other-worldly, I almost gasped.

I said to my wife, *"Look! Angels,"* and pointed dementedly at the shadows on the wall.

*"Where?"* she said. She could see no angels.

I could see them, she could not.

I was elated. I approached the gallery coordinator. I pointed to the sculpture and the angel wings behind it.

*"I love the way you've lit the sculpture,"* I said, *"so that the shadows project out like wings."*

She furled her eyebrows, looked at the sculpture confused, *"Wings?"*

She could see no angels either.

She apologised, *"I'm so sorry,"* she said, *"it's not supposed to have any shadows; it has not been lit up correctly."*

She picked up a brochure featuring the same sculpture on the front cover, less the shadows. *"It's supposed to look like that,"* she said.

I immediately bought two tickets, abandoned Man Ray and went in to view the sculptures by the divine artist, Juan Munoz.

All of the figures in his exhibition had angel wings behind them.

I was high for the rest of the day.

I didn't know why my intuition had led me to this place or to this particular exhibition, but I was inspired and I trusted that it would all make sense in the end.

In my next stage play *Fragile*, I was inspired to use four

portraits of the Munoz sculptures to illustrate the changing dimensions of the lead character.

In my next book *Hunting the Shadow*, the Munoz Trust gave me permission to use several of his images to illustrate my work; one of them I used as a beautiful cover mount and another I actually named a specific chapter after: The Munoz Ball.

I had no idea what or why my intuition placed me in a London art gallery on a hot summer afternoon. I didn't need to know and I could never have guessed that my next two pieces of work would come directly from it.

When I am mentoring people – I have worked with world-class businesspeople, martial arts instructors, kids struggling at school, right through to convicted murderers and bank robbers and drug dealers, writing from their prison cells – intuition is the tool I reach for first. It enables me to see defilement hiding in someone's dialogue, as clearly as you would spy a fox in a henhouse.

As the wonderful Mooji said, *there are no dialogues, just a single monologue, coming from a single force, working through the many outlets.*

If I am quiet, if I make myself very still before I meet the people I am working with, if I *connect* to the divine sword, all I have to do is observe and they will tell me exactly what they need to hear. Sometimes, if a big defilement is going to present itself, I will feel the disturbance in my body minutes, hours or even days before the appointment.

When I am with my students, over the period of a session (anything from one to three hours), they will unconsciously repeat a telling phrase several times. They may come to me with a specific issue, only to reveal with a spiritually-accentuated word or phrase that the issue is something entirely different from what they thought it was.

One student – a very liberal and learned healer – wanted to talk about a block she was experiencing in her development as a counsellor but found herself, instead, inadvertently telling me all about the unacceptable antics of her young, Asian workmate whose inappropriate behaviour was troubling her. Whilst she insisted that she was not in any way racist or judgmental, the pronunciation and syntax of certain key words she used rang out to me as loud as gunshots. I pointed this out to her, and at first she wriggled like a worm on a hook, and tried to escape and deny any form of judgment, but then, realising that she had been betrayed by her own rhetoric, she admitted that her workmate had drawn *something uncomfortable* out of her.

It's important to state at this point that this lovely woman was at a spiritual crossroad, she was ready to transcend to a higher path of service, but certain unconscious defilements were obscuring her passage.

Once she'd acknowledged this unconscious bias (I sensed that it wasn't actually her bias, it was a cultural unkindness that had been passed on to her, and she'd failed to block it), and agreed that it was unacceptable, we were able to determine that: 1) her workmate was a powerful teacher for her; 2) the fact that this situation had literally landed on her doorstep meant that she needed to decode its message as a matter of urgency; and 3) her workmate's behaviour was nothing to do with her workmate's behaviour (things are never what they appear to be), rather it was a distorted and exaggerated projection of something that was hiding in her. The standard rule in professional counselling is this: if you harbour any kind of judgment towards your client, even if it is deeply hidden, at some level they will know, and their knowing will disqualify you from working with them.

You can't serve anyone if you hold a negative judgment towards them. Judgment automatically breaks your religion, it disconnects you from the Source of healing.

Because this lady was being called to a new density, it was important that she harboured no judgment at all, not just to her clients, but to anyone. As it was, this healer was meticulous, the model of professionalism when she was working with clients, but out of counsel she was the same as everyone else; she was being lulled into judgment left, right and centre.

In the higher densities, you are called to be always in prayer. Every minute of every day has to be lived as though you are communing with God.

Judgment causes spiritual obesity. You will not squeeze through the narrow gate while you are fat with vice.

All judgment had to be refused, if she was to be promoted, all of it.

I promised her that this troublesome workmate would disappear – or her issues with him would cease – the moment she heeded the message and refused any form of judgment.

She went away and meditated on what we'd discovered, and within weeks she received an inner calling for a new, elevated path.

She has also had no further problems with her workmate; in fact they have become fast friends.

## The spiritual poultice

One of the effects of being on the carpet of proximity is that, often, the people who stand close to you will unconsciously and unknowingly be on the carpet too. *Those who look into the eyes of the person who looks into the eyes of God, also look into the eyes of God.* One of the side effects of being on the carpet is that it often causes people to reveal their darker, hidden thoughts seemingly against their own will and their shadow will reveal itself.

Divine proximity sucks it out of them like a poison from a sting. It is often very uncomfortable to witness, but it does show you what you need to see, and – if they are under your care – share with them what you have witnessed.

I saw a very dark sub-personality emerge from a man I sat with one day in St. James's Park, London.

I have to say before I share my recollection, that when he was himself, he was one of the loveliest men I have ever worked with. He was polite. He was generous. He was extremely charming. But, on this day, he was *not himself*.

Interestingly, an hour before our planned meeting he emailed me to cancel. Perhaps he sensed that something in him would immerge, and in a bid to avoid being exposed, he tried to postpone. I'd travelled to London specifically to meet him, so I told him that if he did cancel, he would lose his payment, and he'd have to wait until my next visit if he wanted to meet me again. Not wanting to be out of pocket, he decided to honour the schedule. Recognising that he was spilling, and intuitively forewarned that this would lead to a difficult session, I went to St. James's Church in Piccadilly before I met with him, just to pray for an hour and get myself connected to Religio.

We were sat on a bench in the middle of the park, halfway through the session. He'd spent the first hour subtly posturing, quietly trying to distract and intimidate me with his theological intellect. Like a nervous pre-fight pugilist, shadow boxing in the centre of the ring to spook his opponent, he orally machine-gunned his vast knowledge of esoteric knowing – everything from secret Masonic initiation rituals, right through to his intimate understanding of the 6,000 shabads of the Guru Granth Sahib (considered to be the final, sovereign guru of Sikhism). It happens. When people are insecure about what they know, they often resort to verbose recitals of what they have read. If they have something to hide they will throw up intellectual smokescreens to try and obscure your view. I'm used to it. As I said, this occurs a lot. When people share space with someone whom is in proximity to stillness, it exposes their defilement like a bug under a microscope.

I created a vacuum of silence. I held the silence until he was spent.

Sat on the bench, his eyes darting and dissonant and his garrulous chatter reduced to short distracted staccatos, he was quieter now.

Then it happened.

A pretty girl jogged past us. His eyes were altered in high arousal. A different character poked through his soft facial features. I no longer knew him. I was sitting with a stranger. He completely lost me for a few seconds. It was as though I was no longer there. He broke off our conversation mid-flow and followed the girl's bottom with his eyes as she ran along the path. His tongue flicked fast and snake-like and lasciviously on his lips, simulating cunnilingus and he hissed dementedly about how he would like to *lick her out* (please forgive the language; it is a direct quote). When the girl disappeared from sight, he came back to himself, and resumed our conversation as though the interruption had never happened.

I immediately knew what I was dealing with. I understood that he would have to remove this squatting-defilement, before his core self could be revealed.

As a mentor, this unconscious spill is very helpful; it allows the dog to see the rabbit, as the Irish are apt to say.

I was unable to able to help him with it this time around, unfortunately. That was the last session he booked with me. He has not contacted me since.

This has happened to me a lot. People completely changing personality halfway through a conversation. And the more stable I have become in my own being, the more it has happened. At first I was unable to completely comprehend what was occurring, only that it was occurring more and more often.

Later I was able to fully recognise not only what was happening, but also why.

Sometimes you become aware that people in your proximity sense (in themselves) this urge to spill, and resist it for the duration of your mentoring session. But, interestingly, if you deliberately run over the allotted time, they reveal their secrets in the dying seconds or minutes. It is as though at some level the pain-body senses its vulnerability, factors in the time it is going to be in front of you, and then hides until the time has elapsed. Often as little as a few minutes over, and the shadow emerges, and starts to act out, or speak out through your student, without them consciously knowing that it's happening. A completely different person appears, and when it does, you have to notice it, and draw their attention to the anomaly.

I worked with one very dynamic young man, who could walk or sit with me for a three-hour mentoring session, and be word perfect in everything he was saying. He was honesty itself, he was very polite, and generous; he was the model student. If I let the session run over by as little as 15 minutes, a different character would immerge through him who'd refute and argue over everything I'd said (and he'd concurred with) in the previous three hours.

All the work I did with this man was conducted in those last 15 minutes.

One very reluctant businesswoman I worked with was corpse-grey when we met. She complained about everything: the hotel we met in was too dark, the catering staff who served us were inattentive and the drizzly weather greatly offended her. As we walked around the country park, on a planned three-hour session organised by her boss, she extended her locational protest to a more inclusive grievance about the world in general, and the world of business in specific. She railed about how difficult it was, as a female, to *get on* in such a male-dominated environment. As I listened, it became very clear to me that excelling in business – male-dominated or otherwise – was not really her issue. Three times in one hour she mentioned her young school-aged son. Specifically that her son was her main priority, in fact he was her only priority. She was more than taken aback when I suggested that, from where I was standing, I could see that her son was her least priority.

*Even when you're off work, in your downtime, at the park or at a restaurant, you're not present with your son; you are either making business calls, or you're receiving business calls, and if you are not on the phone, your mind is drifting away from him into the workspace. Even on holiday you're not present. You are either reading reports or working on your laptop.*

I pointed out that, being with someone, spending time with them, especially children, involves a lot more than simply turning up with your body, with your child-friendly schedule and sharing the same location for a few hours. To *really* be with someone you have to be present. This necessitates that you switch off your technology and your very busy mind for an hour or so and be entirely situated with them.

She was stunned into silence, and in the prevailing silence her intuition told her that my observation was correct.

She left our meeting an hour early so that she could be with her son.

The next time I saw the grey-lady, she was beautiful and effulgent and colourful and so full of joy I hardly recognised her.

I recently bumped into a brilliant young woman (an old friend – I'll call her Q) who desperately wanted to be an artist, but was just not breaking through. Q confessed to me in a hundred-mile-an-hour spill of excitable chatter that she was frustrated to the point of near insanity. She knew exactly what she had to do in order to realise her dream, but she kept letting herself down. She wasn't (in her own words) *doing the work*, even though she promised herself faithfully that she would. Without breaking rhythm, she immediately and unconsciously diverted her manic stream-of-consciousness on to a different subject, one that seemed at first completely unrelated to her own dilemma. She told me about a recent heroic spat she'd had with a local government official. The councillor in question had made certain political promises that he later reneged on, and Q organised a large protest march to bring public attention to it. She was very proud of the fact that she'd publicly called this man out. She even challenged him to a debate on local radio (which he declined). When Q paused for breath, I suggested that her actions were very good, but they were all aimed in the wrong direction. If she really wanted to make a difference, she needed to organise a protest march against herself, not this councillor. She should call herself out, challenge herself to a dialectic about her own incongruence; after all she had reneged on all of her own campaign promises, she was breaking her own personal vows.

Q presented her dilemma, and in the space of five minutes, unconsciously delivered her very own solution.

A beautiful man booked a mentoring session with me after watching a talk I gave on a popular online podcast. He'd heard me talk about love as the panacea and, as a successful businessman himself (a multimillionaire, he pointed this out several times), he wanted to meet me. As it turned out, he really did want to meet me, but only to tell me that, whilst he liked me personally, and enjoyed much of what I'd said on the podcast, I clearly didn't know much about the world of business, which is *cut-throat and full of c\*\*ts.*

Again, please forgive the coarse language, it was his vernacular, I am relaying it here for authenticity.

*"Love won't work in my world, Geoff,"* he said, *"because it is full of c\*\*ts who will walk all over you."*

As he spoke – or ranted, I created a spiritual vacuum.

Basically I fell into silence; I didn't emotionally engage or identify with any of his rhetoric.

Because his vitriol found no emotional docking-point in me, his *misaligned sound* was left hanging in the air and was consumed by the vacuum of space that I'd created.

His belief was this: if you are soft in business, if you are kind to *anyone,* if you care for people too much – especially your employees – they will take advantage, they will devour you.

This was his *unquestioned* belief.

His investment in this concept made it true (or true for him), and it kept him perpetually unhappy.

When he stopped speaking, I left a pregnant pause before I spoke.

Eventually I said flatly, *"That's a very powerful story you have there... but that's all it is. A story."*

He looked at me long, and quizzically, and then became very quiet.

My truth entered through the open door that silence had created and consciousness shone through.

The spiritual vacuum acted as a poultice. It drew out a powerful, parasitical belief that kept this fiscally rich man very poor in spirit.

He was desperately perplexed and unhappy despite all his material success.

He listened intently for the next three hours.

By the end of the session he was crying.

I have never met a man with so much love to give.

This one unchallenged belief kept him suspended like a hungry ghost in his own self-erected bardo.

I didn't know this man.

I had never met him before this day, and I have never met him again since. This one session was enough for him to see what he needed to work on. It showed him that the love we exchanged during our three hours together could become a constant in everything he did, including his business. But this would entail him looking at every aspect of his life, not just his business; his loveless marriage, his dysfunctional symbiotic relationship with his mother and his brother, his addiction to sexual porn, and his false belief that money was a panacea. When you lift up a rock, you often find lots of uncomfortable creatures crawling around underneath that you didn't know even existed.

There would be lots of undesirables to look at, no doubt, but they can all be remedied with the same power: silence, stillness (love).

Many of the people I have mentored over the years – sometimes for as little as a single one-off appointment – are strangers to me when we meet. There is no way I can know anything detailed about their lives, their relationships, or their businesses.

I don't need to know.

My proximity to God is the force that reveals the element they need to work on. My intuition will show me the exact line or phrase or belief or opinion or observation or action that will betray their imbalance.

It will spot the anomaly and prompt me to *pull him about that, explore this, ask her to qualify that belief.*

One man came to see me with a business dilemma, but throughout our conversation randomly and unconsciously broke away from the subject at hand to tell me about his young son, prefacing each anecdote with the confession that *I'm not a very good father myself but...* His comments were very telling, not least because they were peripheral to the nature of our meeting. It was as though something unconscious needed to be spoken, and the frequency or energy-field we had created offered the perfect space for that need.

At the third time of mentioning, I said, *"You keep saying that you're not a very good father. Why are you not a very good father?"*

If you want to be the very best father all you have to do is be entirely present with your child when you are with them.

Another man, a senior manager of a large conglomerate who wanted to explore his fear of promotion within the company, suddenly announced out of the blue, *I can't say as I have ever really been myself in front of my boss.*

I asked him, *why haven't you been yourself?*

*What would happen if you were yourself?*

*If you are not yourself, then who are you?*

Finally, the killer question: *when are you your true self?*

It turned out that this delightful man wore more masks than

Zorro, but he was startlingly aware of it. He managed, through our conversation, to identify that he was only ever truly himself when he was with his son, *and* when he did a bit of stand-up comedy, for fun, at his local pub.

These were the times he felt truly authentic.

These identifiable moments became his reference points. I suggested that he use them to introduce authenticity into all of his roles in life. If he could be himself with his child or on stage at the pub, he could extend these moments into every aspect of his life, so that eventually, he would be authentic all the time.

A CEO, who seemed to fit uncomfortably in his particular line of business, once said to me, *it'd be nice to do what I really love as a job, but the world just doesn't work like that.*

I asked him: *is that really true?*

*Can you qualify that statement?*

*Who says it doesn't work like that?*

*It works like that for me. I do what I love for a living.*

*What is it that you would really like to do?*

*What's stopping you?*

*Why aren't you removing the things that are in your way?*

Intuition is the most powerful Siddha.

It does all the work for me.

It spots the obfuscation and suggests a method for removing it; all I have to do is voice what I have been shown.

I turn up, intuition leads me to the right questions, and the right answers are delivered like milk-and-honey to my tongue.

## Sound

Aligned sound is a wonderful Siddha.

It is one of the very strong gifts.

Sound becomes more effective the more you expand your conscious net.

Everyone uses sound, of course, in one way or another.

We create realities with our ability to convey sound.

I mentioned sound already, in the last chapter; in brief, but not in detail.

The ancient Egyptians had their own name for the use of divine sound.

They called it **Heka, which** translates as *magic sound*.

The adepts use it to both create and furnish their world; they employ it to inspire their followers, and heal the sick, and ultimately to transcend the one-room world.

The Japanese adepts also practise a system of perfecting sound: **Kotodama-Gaku**. This translates (again) as *the use or practise of magic sound*.

Masters in the acoustic arts, those who are schooled, can command very large fees to deliver their Heka to an audience in speeches or organised lessons or public lectures and masterclasses, or even – as in the case of sound baths – for healing. If the sound is righteous – as in *aligned to spirit* – it can transform lives. People have been inspired to greatness after hearing a powerful speaker; others have been healed by receiving sound delivered through a clean-vessel with an ordained alignment. Equally and oppositely, orators of evil have started wars and caused great human tragedies by using sound that aligned people to ignorance and hatred.

As I mentioned earlier, the lower soul is influenced by any powerful impression, and for want of a holy-aligned word, it will quickly be seduced by the next strongest sound in the room.

The inventor and futurist, Richard Buckminster Fuller, one of the greatest visionaries of his generation, reported that it was not until he experienced a nervous breakdown in his early forties, after a family tragedy, that he fully understood the power contained in words. He said, on realising this truth, that he didn't speak for six months, in fact, he refused to speak again until he knew exactly what he was talking about.

Fuller recognised the power of words.

Especially if those words were spoken by a being of influence.

Even more especially, if words of kindness and balm were delivered to a fearful or vulnerable person.

Sound can destroy just as easily as it can create, according to how it is used.

We take our destiny very lightly when we fail to recognise the power of sound.

We commit the gravest error when we listen to and engage the wrong sound, or use our own sound indiscriminately, or even worse, when we use it to deliberately hurt or slight others.

What you are reading here, now, what you are *collecting* with your eyes, from the ink on this page, is sound.

It is sound, saved as letters, and symbols and words.

It is sound written in an aligned rhythm, recorded on paper and held in inky-suspension until someone opens the book and reads them. Then, once again, the words become sound.

When you read this text, you will convert the letters, words, sentences, symbols and meanings back into sound again with your internal voice. You will sub-vocalise them into your own sound, in your own head.

Sound heals, of that I am sure: I have reams of experiential proof.

Only yesterday a man introduced himself to me in a café. He told me emotionally how, in his last job, he was very unhappy to the point of nervous exhaustion and depression. He read one of my books (*Stress Buster*) and the sound it created in his mind, the meaning it conveyed, was the very beginning of his healing. He left his old job, and found an employ that was more in alignment with his spirit.

Be in no doubt that sound can also act as a catalyst to violence.

Every day we read about gullible, vulnerable men and women who are seduced and brainwashed into killing others, by terrorist rhetoric.

Sound can also be the cause of disease.

I can offer personal testament to this: I have talked myself into illness when, with an undisciplined mind and with the misuse of sound, I herded myself into psychosomatic illness that became so acute it eventually showed up in blood tests and on X-ray. Realising the error of my ways, I was able to reverse the same illness with the use of positive sound.

Uncontrolled and negative self-talk caused my illness.

Controlled, positive affirmation healed the same sickness.

We are constantly being influenced by sound.

We are consistently being herded and bombarded by noise.

Our senses are ignited on a daily basis by auditory arousal; seductive sound that contrives to move you *here* or shift you *there*. Subjective but highly focused acoustic stimulates you to *buy or sell*, to *stay where you are* or *move urgently*, to *be excited*, or *be afraid*, to *be aroused*, to *keep your authentic self quiet* or *let your angry sound roar*; it coerces and convinces you to exchange your energy with this person or that person, or with this product or that service.

Sound is all around us. It unconsciously influences us every time we engage or identify with it. One prisoner I spoke to recently was serving a life sentence for murder: he killed a fellow singer who had *dissed* his brother in a lyric.

One man's ill-conceived sound lost him his life.

One man's perception of another man's sound caused him to murder.

As a consequence, one man ended up dead, in the muddy hole; the other dead to his liberty in a prison cell.

The extended family and friends of both men were damaged by proxy.

Once we understand sound, we can start to choose the sound we listen to, and we can choose the sounds we make.

If we can control sound, we can start to control our own reality.

The most important sound to control of course is your own sound.

Your internal dialogue (which usually spills into your spoken sound) is influencing every cell in your body every time you engage it. Just by identifying with a rage-sound, you can stimulate the release of enough stress hormones to trigger heart attack or stroke. An angry outburst can also send shockwaves through every being in close proximity, yourself included; don't forget, every sound you emit has to be processed through you before you speak it to others.

It does not take advanced logic to deduce that ill-conceived, uncontrolled or hostile sound (internal or external) can be the direct or indirect cause of psychiatric diseases like depression and nervous breakdown, and to killer physical diseases, including cancer.

At the most basic level (for instance), sound that is delivered as threat can trigger an avalanche of psychiatric response. The psychiatric is directly linked to the psychological, to the physiological and in turn to the sociological. People can become very ill when sound is used in a malign manner. Even sound relayed through a Twitter feed, or a Facebook post, or a message board comment can be enough to send people's central nervous systems into spasm. Many people become depressed, suffer nervous exhaustion, and even kill themselves because of someone else's clumsy or deliberately malign use of sound.

When sound triggers the perception of threat, stress is the expected result.

During stressful episodes, your body automatically goes into a state of fight-or-flight. The sympathetic nervous system is activated and (amongst myriad other physiological changes) the immune system closes down for the duration of the (perceived) threat. While the immune system is deactivated, the body has no defence; there is absolutely no resistance to invading viruses, including cancer and all the other unspeakable diseases.

Of course, blood pressure rockets during fight-or-flight too, which greatly heightens the chances of suffering stroke and heart attack.

The chemical cocktail released during the *sympathetic response* can also be deadly. Stress hormones are secreted into the body, we are all probably aware of this. But, because most stressful situations demand neither fight nor flight (the modern threat is psychological rather than physical), the dangerous chemicals – specifically cortisol – are not behaviourally released. This means they stay in the body. Cortisol, if is not behaviourally utilised, acts as a caustic on the smooth internal muscles, like the heart, the lungs, the intestines, the bladder etc. It also finds its way to the brain and attacks/kills neurotransmitters (cortisol has been linked with dementia and Alzheimer's disease), it scratches the inside of the arteries, and the fatty acids released during stress get caught up in the grooves; this leads to heart disease and angina. The list goes on.

And all of this can be triggered as a result of misused sound.

This would not be such a big problem if the sympathetic response only lasted for a 30-second physical emergency, as it was designed to do, because the stress hormones would be burned up as fuel and behaviourally exhausted during fight-or-flight. It becomes a very real danger if we remain in a state of alert for hours, or in the case of people living in challenging environments or working in stressful jobs, days or weeks or even years. This is especially so if these situations offer no behavioural outlet, and the damaging hormones are not evacuated from the system.

This is a big subject, and out of the context of this particular book. It needs its own read; it can't be covered in a few paragraphs. I would recommend you read my comprehensive book *Stress Buster* if you'd like to explore this subject more.

It is enough to say that when sound creates stress it is dangerous to our health, but it can be countered.

Equally, and more powerfully, an aligned sound, emitting from the intention of love, can have the most profound and healing effect, not just on everyone who hears it but also on everyone who hears *of* it.

Of course, as I have said, it also has a profound effect upon everyone who speaks it.

How many healings have been triggered by the retelling of the Prophets' testament, or Joshua's story, or the Buddha's enlightenment under the Bodhi Tree?

I was once lifted from deep depression, when I read the inspirational novel *Watership Down*. The story of a small rabbit (Hazel) overcoming great adversity and becoming the leader of his warren against all the odds facilitated my healing. It called me to courage in the face of anxiety. The sub-vocal sound of the author's aligned words penetrated the obscuration of my depressed thinking and allowed the light of inspiration (spirit) to shine through.

The sound you use will determine your whole life, for better or for worse. It can get you the girl or lose you the date; it will win you the job or get you the sack; it creates health and wealth and prosperity, but it can also destroy all three like a tsunami. I have personally made lots of money when I used my sound in an aligned manner. A wonderful benefactor once handed me a £50k film bursary after he heard a spirited speech I made about making movies to serve people in pain.

Before I knew of this power, I lost more jobs and more money than I can shake a stick at when I let arrogance and ignorance speak my sound instead of humility.

I have won love with aligned sound.

I have killed, smothered and suffocated love when I let myself be taken over by the toxic sound-vibration of jealousy.

Sound is corrupted when sound carries duality, or agenda or expectation.

If it is contrived, it is corrupted.

As the Hikam reminds us, *a heart cannot accept worldly desires and Divine Love at the same time.*

When you deliver your sound from a spiritual stance, the acoustic is so powerful that, frankly, there is nothing that could not be achieved through it.

The whole of the Quran is said to be one long holy sound, as directed from Allah Himself to the Prophet Mohammed on the mountain.

To use sound from a righteous place, of course, must mean that the sound is coming from the right person, the right I, the authentic self, as detailed in the chapter on the divine fall. Once the authentic self is located and in situ, you won't need to train yourself to use sound correctly because the correct sound will be intuited to you by you from the correct I.

In between times, as most of you will have probably noticed, our sub-vocalisation chatters away constantly in the background. We engage copious and random thoughts from the ether, and those thoughts bounce around in our heads like lottery balls, vying for our identification. Some of them *whisper* at the doorway of the heart, some of them win our engagement and enter the heart, and for the duration of engagement – five minutes, five hours, a lifetime – they become us.

Very few people have control of their sub-vocalisation, or indeed have the ability to stop themselves from engaging rogue-thoughts that infect them with the insanity of repetitive worry.

Sub-vocalisation is automatic, and unless consciously interrupted, it just plays on repeat like crap background Muzak in an office lift.

You can change this.

## Manual sub-vocalisation

You can manually take over your sub-vocalisation and change its settings so that, if there is any background noise at all (silence is obviously the optimum state), it is put there by you and it has your flavour or your beat, rather than a 20-year-old rerun of an argument you had with your partner or a historical *slight* delivered by a friend or the *bad news* that entered your thinking over breakfast this morning when you were watching the TV.

Manual sub-vocalisation, again, might not seem like an obvious Siddha, but even just understanding that you can control your internal voice is in itself a sign of expanded awareness and has a magic all of its own.

If you are not convinced, ask yourself this question: how many people do you know who even understand what sub-vocalisation is, let alone have any control over it?

Probably not many.

Count them and you'll still have fingers left on a single hand.

Just knowing this is a gift, and exercising it is practical magic.

Reading these words will not be enough on their own.

Much practice will be needed in the beginning. The sub-vocal voice has been in residence all of your life, it will not give up its seat easily. Also, the more you observe your own inner life, and the more you connect to your higher faculty, the clearer this will become and the easier it will be to practise.

Ultimately, we are aiming to interrupt and dissolve any current, negative inner thoughts (or vibrations) and replace them with a new voice, a new sound, a better vibration, or ideally, when control is deepening, the ultimate background noise: **silence**.

Silence is the Original sound.

Silence is the sage of all sound.

Silence is consciousness. It is vision. It is healing. It is instruction.

When you connect to silence, you will recognise your own signature there.

If you trace *every* sound back to its origin, you will see that all of it, without exception, comes out of the infinite ocean of silence.

Silence is home.

It's not only home, it is you.

Silence is the constant.

The constant **is** you.

Silence is what each of us is looking for.

It is the balm that we all long for.

And... it is available.

All you have to do to receive silence is stop engaging sound.

Eventually the waves of noise will settle into the depths of consciousness.

What I learned to do was *watch* sound, and imagery, and impressions. I learned to observe them as they rose up from inside me, or approached my mind-door.

I watched them intently to see where they entered me and I located the doorway where they congregate looking for engagement. I also observed the myriad impressions, especially the very strong impressions, the ones that I found hard to resist; I followed them too, I observed to see where these thought-forms went if I refused to engage them.

You might be interested to know that all internal impressions – sound, vibrations, energy etc. – rise from out of nothingness and, if we refuse to engage them, if we simple observe them, they eventually return back to nothingness.

When the adepts talk about *doing nothing* as the ultimate defence, this is what they mean.

If we do nothing, if we refuse to engage, or we resist identification, all stimulus will eventually be consumed back into nothingness.

Ultimately, it is the same with external stimulus, sound and impressions approaching from outside of us (eventually we will see that *out and in* are the same; there is no dichotomy between the two). If we have the wherewithal to refuse engagement, all impressions must return to their source.

If we are insulted and we refuse to engage insult, it will not affect us in the least.

We can choose what we engage and what we do not engage.

We determine what we offer breath and what we refuse life.

## The Heart

Allah (speaking through the holy Prophet in the Quran) informs us that, "the heavens and the earth do not contain Me, but the heart of my lover contains me."

The heart does not contain God; rather it is *the heart of my lover* that contains Him.

This is an important distinction and it emphasises two important words: the verb – **contain**, and the noun – **lover**.

## Contain

The Cambridge English Dictionary defines *contain* as "to have inside" to "include" and/or to "control". It means to be "a vessel for something". What we become a vessel for, what we have inside us or *include*, that we become. By definition, the human heart holds a godlike capacity, but only if it intercourses with the divine.

## Lover

The Holy Book does not tell us that we contain God when we love God. It says distinctly that we must first become *God's lover* before we are able contain Him. We have to intercourse with God.

The Cambridge English Dictionary defines *intercourse* as "the communication between individuals, or between individuals and groups".

Intercourse is, in its definition, communication.

This aligns with the previously mentioned Communication of the Properties, when the lower soul intercourses with the spirit, resulting in Christ-consciousness.

To intercourse means to surrender; we surrender to our lover.

When we surrender to the Concentrate, we contain Its essence, and by extension, we contain in our heart, not only God, but also the heavens and the earth.

In the Vedic classic, the Srimad Bhagavatam, Lord Krishna (the Godhead) promises his servant, that *if you surrender to Me, I will have no choice but to serve you endlessly.*

The heart-space itself does not automatically contain God. In and of itself, the heart is just a hub of soft internal muscle, a fleshy pump that drives blood through our veins, and supplies life-giving oxygen to the body. We can gather and store any of the myriad available vibrations in the heart (this is our free will) and, subsequently, feed our trillions of conscious cells with the content of our choosing: good, bad, healing, diseased, indifferent, human or otherwise.

The heart is not the important factor here; it is what we ally the heart to that counts.

What we allow into our hearts, we automatically allow into every other aspect of our being. And what we allow into our being, we cannot help but project on to our world. The individual human heart, then, is also the global heart; it pumps blood and oxygen into all the organs of the world.

Hence, when you hear the words, *change yourself, change the world,* it is not a pithy aphorism, it is a literal truth.

If we contain God in our hearts, how can we but transmit love and joy into the world?

I would assert that it is worth our ceaseless effort to be a lover of God.

What we engage or identify with, therefore, is what we allow into our heart, into our being and subsequently into our world.

If we engage or identify with sound – a whispering insult from an enemy, the loving intercession from a friend – it will enter our heart-space.

The heart-space is a vast cavern, a human TARDIS, situated in the breast area. It appears small from the outside, but inside it is an infinite tabernacle, a kingdom in its own right.

What exists in the heart of a person can be judged by what is existent in their external landscape.

*They can be judged by their fruits,* the New Testament tells us.

His or her external life is entirely the product of the heart.

What we engage, what we identify with, we give permission to enter the heart.

Impressions enter via a specific entrance: known by the Desert Fathers as *the doorway of the heart* (sometimes called *the mind-door*).

When esoteric texts caution us to *guard the doorway of the heart,* they are not talking metaphorically, they are referring to the heart *and* the doorway to the heart as specific locations.

Once a negative impression enters the heart, it incubates and – if not quickly removed – it eventually colonises us. We become its host. If we do not remove it immediately, it incarnates, it literally becomes us, and we are *reborn* into the nature of our association.

Thoughts and impressions can alight anywhere; they approach from outside of us, and can land in multiple locations on and in the body. Anywhere that we have senses, they can register, to garner our attention.

But, they can only enter the heart via one very specific doorway.

There is only one doorway to the heart.

Everything that enters, enters here.

Everything that leaves – our own words and impressions – leaves from here also.

We have to guard what rises from inside us too; those thoughts that engage us, that seek expression in the world, through us. This is just as important.

What exists in us – every perception, every concept, and every belief – needs sustenance. It will seek this via engagement with what exists outside of us; this is how it feeds and perpetuates, this is how it propagates.

This is good news; if there is only one door in and one door out, this means there is only one location, one entrance that we need to protect.

This is the *narrow gate* of scripture, the doorway where impressions engage us and try to enter (or leave) the heart.

This locational doorway is called the **suprasternal notch**.

It is also known as the **jugular notch**, the **Plender gap** or the **neck dent**.

The doorway to the heart is situated in the large, visible dip between the neck and the two collar bones.

Any thoughts that rise in you or any impressions that approach from an external source through any of the senses – eyes, ears, nose etc. – have no corporeal life unless you engage them at this **exact** point.

As I mentioned, the thought may originate or initially alight in your head or in your stomach or anywhere else that the human senses fan out to, but they are not able to incarnate the heart until you consciously (usually unconsciously) engage them at the neck-dent doorway.

Just learning of this doorway and its location is a Siddha of the first order, a gift of consciousness.

It is vital that we know where the doorway is.

If you don't know where the doorway to the heart is, how can you stand at the doorway, how can you possibly protect the heart?

## Sound mantra

Back momentarily to the sub-vocalisation (I will return to the heart imminently); in order to manually take over the sub-vocalisation you have to choose a soundscape – a mantra, a prayer, an affirmation – and consciously lay it over the automatic sub-vocalisation that is currently in situ.

Thich Nhat Hanh, the Vietnamese Buddhist monk, simply uses the words **thank you**, which he repeats with every step he takes as he walks.

If the sub-vocal noise is going to be there all the time anyway, and we know how much sound can destroy or create, it is best that we use a simple *gratitude* sound as our audio-wallpaper. Once you have spent a few days constantly repeating the mantra, laying the foundations of this manual sub-vocalisation, it will quickly become automatic. If you ever find your mind drifting and invasive thoughts start to congregate, you simply switch on your manual inner voice again and block it out.

Never forgetting that at the highest level, silence is the ultimate backboard, it is the premium background noise.

Although the conscious mantra is not silence, it is a positive sound of your choosing, and, if we place our entire focus on the mantra, it will lead to the quieting of all other background chatter, and the emotions they trigger. Eventually, you will be able to cease even the conscious mantra, and enter complete silence.

The mantra is a boat that leads your mind into the deep waters of consciousness.

The Desert Fathers and the great aesthetics from Christianity use the Jesus prayer as their automatic sub-vocalisation (**Lord Jesus Christ, son of God, have mercy on me**). They manually repeat the prayer as a powerful inner soundscape that protects their heart from idle and damaging chatter, and also connects them to the abstract.

You can switch the mantra off, if you want to contemplate, or pray, or work something out with an internal dialectic; all which of course are forms of manual sub-vocalisation.

With practice, you can also actively enter complete silence, which dissolves all sound and all impression – this is consciousness itself, the place beyond concept.

The main thing to remember is this: on recognising the power of sound on the psyche, we learn to choose and control our own inner soundscape and only engage and sanction external noise that we personally feel is righteous.

The Buddhists have a beautiful soundscape-mantra that

I have found particularly powerful, not just to protect the doorway of the heart and the heart itself, but also as an effective weapon against undesirable and invasive thought-forms that try to tempt or trick or scare you into identification.

The moment a negative thought or image or emotion arises, you literally direct the mantra at it; you saturate the negative thought-form in the conscious sound mantra.

It acts like a fire extinguisher, it strips the oxygen out of a spreading thought-blaze the moment it fires up.

The mantra is a simple affirmation of the unreality of all manifest things.

It is a statement of knowing.

It is directed at the ghost of negative thought-forms, and it says, *you are not real, I know you are not real.*

We know this is true. We can acknowledge that this is true, because all temporal things are unreal.

The only thing that can be real is that which does not change, that which is constant: consciousness.

The mantra is only four words long, but as a directed sound, it is very powerful.

**Impermanent.**
**Unsatisfactory.**
**Not self.**

It is quick to remember, simple to annunciate and very easy to direct at a negative vibration. It acts like a water-cannon that extinguishes the fires of nescience.

Your mantra, your sound-guard, can be any of your choosing. Practice-time with specific sounds will direct you towards the ones that work best for you.

Once you have the mantra, the key now is not to use it just as a manual sub-vocalisation but also to direct the sound so that it sits at the doorway of your heart, the neck dent, where it acts as a security detail. I see it as an aligned energy source, a force-field or vibration that sentries the doorway of your heart. It's a bit like placing a team of burly bouncers at the door of a nightclub, or perhaps a detail of armed guards at the border of a country, or the gates of a palace.

If you visit Buckingham Palace, the central London home of our British queen, you will see that the palace gates are heavily guarded. There is a veritable platoon of armed and trained guards at the doorway to our monarch's home.

What we have to protect – the heart, the inlet and the outlet to a creative reality – is very precious, much more so than the queen or the prime minister or the president.

But what is shown to us in exaggerated form (in the world) is what we need to see in miniature, in us.

The English monarch needs a trained guard.

Our inner monarch needs a trained guard.

This is one of the most wonderful Siddhas, the knowledge that everything in the manifest world is a mirror, and it reflects everything that is in us, good, bad and indifferent. In this sense, the world and everything in it becomes our teacher. All we have to do is look for the signs and decipher the code, and there is nothing that we cannot learn from something that already exists; whether it is a book of words or a garden weed. For instance, when I first woke up, everything spoke to me in its own unique language. I read Sun Tzu's *The Art of War*, and it was no longer a book about negotiating external warfare, and the relationship between general and captain and between captain and soldier. It read instead as an instruction manual on the greater jihad, the inner battle, and the relationships we forge between the soul and the sentinel ego, and the sentinel ego and the senses.

I was parking the car on my drive one day, when I saw a weed looking up at me. It was growing out of the tiniest speck of soil in the tarmac. I was amazed. How in this arid and soilless black landscape, a veritable desert for any kind of green life, had this weed managed to find enough soil to grow in.

I tried to pull the tiny weed out, but to my shock and surprise it resisted my every effort. Incredibly, I was unable to remove it, even though I was tens of thousands of times bigger and stronger than the weed.

The weed had bedded itself into a speck of dirt and used it as working capital. It grew roots that spread deep beneath the tarmac, where there was a whole bed of hidden soil. I was trying to pull this tiny weed from the ground, not realising that it had anchored itself into a ton of tarmac.

In bedding itself into the tarmac, it had become the tarmac.

The weed spoke to me implicitly. First of all it reprimanded me: it was not a weed (it insisted), it was a life-form, and it had every right to its place on this earth. The idea that it was a weed was little more than a human concept.

It taught me several other things too: in a garden full of black tarmac, it could grow and sustain itself on the smallest amount of soil. It used the initial soil as capital, to grow its roots, it used its roots to fan out and source more soil, which in turn strengthened its roots. In its slow and steady process of growth and search, it was able to penetrate even the densest material in its bid for life.

It offered me both a warning and an inspiration.

A warning, because a pain-body is not unlike a garden weed.

It too is a life-form (all energy is life), even if it is an unwelcome one in our body. It wants to live, and it too will do everything in its power to do so. It will feed its roots on the smallest amount of human conflict, burrow deep into the human psyche and bed itself there. Once established, like the weed, it too will resist every effort to remove it.

An inspiration, because what is true for the weed, must also be true for the flower. Goodness wants to grow in us. All it needs is a little assistance, the tiniest amount of help, and it too will grow roots, burrow deep into our being, and in wedding with consciousness, it will take on the power of consciousness.

I was talking about a manual sub-vocalisation sound; you direct your chosen sound so that it sits right at the opening of the heart, so that it nestles in the neck dent.

You can and you must also direct your attention to the doorway too. Just by observing the doorway, by locating your concentrated attention at the opening, you afford yourself protection; but the sound-guard also guarantees you an added layer of security.

The mantra is (what you might call) a resident sub-vocalisation. It needs to be of a very positive and empowering and connective nature. The mantra acts as a static guard, but it can also act as a crusading army that we direct to parts of our body where energy may be stuck or diseased.

Often pain-bodies lodge and stick in prominent places in the body. They might present themselves as injury or illness, to draw our attention. They may throb and ache and cause pain that is as real as the pain you feel if you hit your thumb with a hammer, or dash your knee on a table edge. Sound can be used in mantra form to locate the anomalies, break them down and dissolve them.

I am not a medical doctor, so I can only refer here to my own experience of this anomaly, but my own pain-bodies have presented at one time or another with the symptoms of myriad major and minor disease, including cancer.

At one time, in the middle of a very raw cleansing process, I was so vulnerable that my guard was completely non-excitant, the doorway to my heart was wide open; if anyone simply suggested the symptoms of a disease, I would experience those symptoms in their full physical force in the specific part of my body suggested. I remember a time – again this happened when I was vulnerable and had no conscious guard in place – when my mum inadvertently placed three specific killer-disease symptoms into my mind (and subsequently my heart-space) just by suggestion; the instant she told me the symptoms (with the implicit suggestion that I had a hereditary vulnerability towards them), they instantly presented in my body. I have to tell you it took a real fight and a great deal of internal work to get them back out again. At the time this happened, I felt as though the whole world – particularly my mum, who was obsessed with hereditary cancer – was attacking me with symptoms of disease. My vulnerability, my unprotected heart-space was like an out-of-control centripetal force that drew symptoms to me like metal filings to a magnet.

It was very disconcerting, but it was also profoundly instructional.

It was (I realised) a rare opportunity to develop my guard, and perfect my attack.

What better place to develop and prove defence and assault techniques than in the field of combat.

What better time to work out what was of practical worth and what was practically worthless, than actually in the theatre of internal conflict.

I would argue this is the only time we can test and refine efficacy.

I didn't learn the true art of self-defence until I placed myself on to a nightclub door and put my arse on the line and my skills to the test.

As a bouncer, I hardly had to do anything at all; the environment itself was so demanding that it shaped and sorted and proved my skills for me.

Our internal foe works in invisibility; it is a sniper, sharp-shooting at us from hidden places, it is adept in the art of disguise, and its weapon of choice is artifice.

We can't defeat what we cannot see.

In the midst of the battlefield, however, fear becomes blatant; it is no longer hidden, it is out in the open, fully exposed. It is so arrogant and so sure of victory that it no longer bothers to hide;

this is when the pain-body is at its most vulnerable.

This is when we can claim it.

When you are being attacked from all quarters, even through the people you love, you soon find out what works and what does not work. When an internal attack presents itself, you can locate the ache or the block or the fear-signature in your mind's eye and direct your sound-mantra right on to it, right into it. You can intellectually strip the labels off the anomaly – pain, illness, disease, fear, anger, rage – because labels only give your ache power. If I allow myself to think *threat, illness, penury* etc. these labels add a tremendous load to my worry; they spider out with all the perceptions that I (have been conditioned to) associate with these words and they anchor themselves into as many fleshy-places as they can and start to expand. If we strip the label away and look at exactly what it is we feel – ache, pain, fear – then strip even those labels away, all we are left with is a block of energy that is intelligent and autonomous enough, like a virus or a parasite, to locate somewhere, anywhere in our body where we feel particularly vulnerable, and then feed off us.

In the case of my mum, injecting cancer symptoms into me that grew into real pain: she was only able to effect this level of suggestion because there is a history of cancer in my family, and she was a parental force that I had been trained to listen to unquestioningly. In my mum's eyes hereditary is synonymous with certainty; to her it meant that my brothers and I would definitely, at some point, contract the disease. Without even knowing it, I'd bought into this belief. Subsequently, I invited in an internal parasite, a hungry thought-form that housed itself somewhere around my bladder. The thought-form spread by leading me via quiet, whispering suggestion towards worry.

Worry progressed into symptom-hunting (in my body, on the World Wide Web).

This led me to anxiety and the urge to verbally express my fears to family and friends. Before I knew it, all I could think about all day, every day was cancer.

Consciousness is determined by what you completely focus on.

My worry and the disease symptoms grew worse and worse, until eventually two-thirds of me believed I was dying.

I can categorically tell you that negative sound put me into this dark place.

There is no doubt about that.

I can also tell you just as emphatically that, once I finally managed to arrest the situation, it was the magic of positive sound which got me out of it again.

When I was absolutely on my knees, when even getting out of bed took the greatest effort, I said to myself, *right, this is where you find out what works and what does not work.*

The magic of correct sound is what reversed all my symptoms until I was once again perfectly healthy.

Since then, I have capitalised on the lessons this situation taught me and started to practise sound as the foundation of my life.

When you strip away the subterfuge of labels, all you are left with is energy, and all energy has the same origin. It is neti neti, neither this nor that, it rises out of the sea of consciousness, it looks for engagement; if it finds none, it falls back into the depths. It has to, it has no choice.

If you are able to locate the energy at the point it is blocked, and deeply penetrate it, go into the very heart of it with your silent, observing mind, you will be able to dissolve it completely by offering it no emotional engagement.

Or, you can absorb it, control it, then reconstitute it, clean it through the filters of creativity and make it into something beautifully conscious.

## Absorption and positive displacement

Spiritual absorption (and subsequent displacement) is a fine

Siddha in and of itself. You can turn the sow's ear of any negative energy into a silk purse, by soaking up the energy of negative elements – criticism, fear, worry, doubt – without emotional engagement, process the energy through your body, and make something beautiful from it.

This is advanced play. It is not easy to do, and not many people perfect it.

Somebody harshly criticised me once (this by way of example) down the telephone. It filled me with a mixture of their negative projection, and stress release. I was able to contain both energies in my body together, without labelling them, and with no emotional engagement. I kept the negative energy in a separate holding space inside me, away from the heart, until I was ready to positively displace it. When I was ready, I reworked the energy; I cleaned it by writing an article about the situation, which I sold to a magazine for £500. I took the raw material of a negative encounter, put it through the recycling plant of my own body, and repurposed it into hard cash.

This process works with all raw energy – positive or negative – but it does take a practised adept to pull it off; not many people can consciously carry negative energy for very long without it corrupting them. It is not easy, but it is possible and it is accessible. I know because I did it many times. I am doing it now. The words on this page are the product of (a mixture of) energies that once colonised my body. As a young frightened man, I negatively absorbed, emotionally engaged and negatively displaced the same energies and used them to enact violence.

All energy has its source in Love.

All energy, if directed by the divine ego, can be led back to Love.

Love is the only constant.

Energy only becomes *other than love* because it is allowed to go through the divided and polluted filters of a dualistic mind.

My very prolific output as a writer is living proof of this

process, and it is a gift.

For the adept, even the darkest energy can be transformed back to Love.

You can take the scrap metal of any emotion and make it into money, sculpture, art, literature, work-ethic, manual labour, love, anything.

This is a mighty Siddha.

More on this later.

It is enough for now to recognise that you are talking to yourself all day, every day. What you say to yourself becomes what you make of yourself.

So be careful about what you say to yourself.

What you say to others, likewise, can create or destroy.

Choose to create.

What you do to others with your directed sound you automatically do to yourself.

I am certain of this.

It is obvious.

What you do or say to others has to be processed through every cell of your own being first.

The hate you give is the hate you get.

It makes sense then, surely, to give others only what you would give to yourself.

Love, love, love.

## Sound as beings

*Sound is not sound.*

My wife always warns me, when I get on to the subject of all things metaphysical, *don't tell the beings story. People won't understand if you do the beings story.*

She is worried that people will think I've lost the plot if I share some of the more esoteric things that have been revealed to me.

I'll take the chance.

This revelation, gifted to me in a moment of clarity, is that sound is not sound as we might ordinarily know it. It is powerful – as we already discussed – and I know this, because I have personally damaged people with clumsy and unthinking sound and I have healed others with aligned speak. But sound is not just a noise that we conjure in the mind and process through our lungs, project through the vocal cords, shape with the tongue and emit from our mouths. This physiological, rudimentary reduction of what sound is would be both inaccurate and disingenuous.

Sound is not sound, or should I say that it is not *just* sound.

Sound, as I was shown, is a collection of billions of sentient beings, a literal army that we send to work in the world of causation every time we utter even a single syllable. Every minute particle of sound is a collective of individual living beings, each endowed with consciousness.

The first time I was given this vision, it filled me with inspiration – all of these beings, expending themselves in my service.

At the same time I was filled with fear, or perhaps *awe* better describes it. Awe because I realised that a waste of words was literally a waste of life.

I will relay my vision here in the hope that the recollection might add some clarity to the very grand statement I have just made.

I'd just finished a yoga session.

Yoga is an amazing tradition for yoking or joining the higher and the lower souls, heaven and earth.

Straight after the yoga, I meditated on a Zen mantra for about 40 minutes.

I find that meditation when practised directly after a yoga session is always deeper.

After the meditation, I went for a warm shower where I continued my mantra, this time it was the Jesus prayer: *Lord*

*Jesus Christ, Son of God, have mercy on me.* I repeated the mantra (as I washed) over and over again, slowly, carefully, trying to emotionally connect with the words, focusing on the texture of the sound as it vibrated through my inner body.

I was saying the mantra but I was not fully feeling the mantra. It was as though I was just repeating the word-sounds by rote.

Then, suddenly, the strangest thing occurred. I was no longer in my body. It would be more accurate to say that I was no longer contained by my body: I was no longer myself, the personality known as Geoff Thompson. He had disappeared, he was gone. The individual I knew as Geoff Thompson was actually a convenient illusion, a brilliant collection of beings, trillions of them, connected together like conscious-Lego, into a tabernacle or processing plant, an evolvement chamber for the beings to transcend through.

The real I was simply witnessing everything.

In this eternal moment my observer was the omniscient witness. It was everywhere (and nowhere) all at the same time, quietly watching the minutia of the manifest world and beyond. I was able to experience the observer as a sort of Omega Point, that all other life is moving towards.

At once I (the observer) became aware of a towering man, he was above the world, above everything – he was the size of a mountain. My person (stood in the shower) was no longer there. He was gone. The Man was imperious and looking yonder as though in contemplation of some unseen horizon. I could see this large being as though I was an internal observer looking outwards at the magnificence of my own span.

The mantra, which up until this point was merely a sound projected by my sentinel ego, transformed into a numberless-community of individual beings – the size of sand grains by comparison to the Man – chanting the Jesus prayer in unison, like a church congregation.

As I noticed the imperious figure, the sound-beings noticed

him too.

In reverential awe they all turned as one and directed their mantra to him.

This was no longer a mere sound-jumble habitually repeated, it was a rhythmic prayer marinated in Love.

These beings literally fell at his feet in divine ecstasy.

I could see and feel that each individual being and the whole ensemble of beings were desperate to serve this God. In fact liberation, their holy-transcendence, was wholly incumbent on their sacrificial service to him.

I could discern also that opportunities for discarnate beings to transcend were rare and could only be transacted at this particular level through an incarnate and conscious being. They could be, and they were, consumed over and again, by living beings, in the everyday acts of combustion, but consummation *and* liberation were wholly reliant on the conscious act of selfless service, on the part of the embodied being they were working through.

It was only selfless service that leads to Brahman.

This was the truth I was prompted to remember. It was very important, because it contained a secret: energy-forms will fall at the feet of anyone who serves selflessly. You will not have to seek them out. The means to meet your spiritual ends will be supplied. It will be drawn to you, and will actively and gratefully sacrifice itself, and consume itself in service.

As is the way with divine vision, I was shown and understood so much all at once that it is hard to articulate it.

I'll tell it as best as I can.

In an eternal moment I was shown that sound and everything else, animate or inanimate, was sentient.

Everything contains consciousness, everything *is* conscious.

Even more than that, every cell of every *thing* was an individual being that desperately desired to be consumed in the holy fire of divine service.

Sound is not sound; it is an army of sentient beings, looking for, praying for a moment of human alignment so that it could be liberated through the sacrifice of love. When it sacrifices itself in service, it transcends in the process.

The water coming from my shower was not water; it was billions of beings, sacrificing themselves to clean and maintain this body so that this body could better serve God. Even my body itself, the skin, the muscle and flesh and sinew, the bones, the nervous system is trillions of individual beings forming one collective body, throwing themselves into the fire of volition to power this body, so that this body could serve God.

The showerhead, the water pipes, and the glass cubicle I stood in, the bathroom, the house that contained them all, *the same*: billions of beings all were serving me so that I can serve God.

I was given a vision of my smartphone, of my car, the train that takes me to London, aeroplanes that transport me at speed from one country to another, every manifest thing had formed itself purely so that I could live, so that I could communicate and travel across distant lands in order that this body, the soul ensconced in this body, could be of service to God.

Every single, living, sentient, conscious cell's raison d'être was to be consumed in the service of God and in doing so became One with God in the process.

I could feel that it was the greatest privilege, the entire purpose of every sentient being, to sacrifice themselves in service, in order to become one again with their Source.

Then I witnessed another beautiful moment: when the Man of giant proportion noticed that the *sound-beings* were falling at its feet in service to Him, He tilted his head slightly towards them and proffered the most beatific smile.

This gift of clarity allowed me to see that everything, every living cell, is yearning to evolve, to transcend, to go Home, and if we align to Love, if our service is righteous, if it is connected to or ordained by heaven and earth, everything technological, everything fiscal, everything material and infrastructural, would not only be made readily available for our use, it would literally fall at our feet in its race to serve those of us who consciously and unconditionally serve Nature.

It benefits everything to serve us, because in serving us it serves its Source, and transcends in the process.

It was so obvious.

I felt such certainty, that after finishing my shower all I wanted to do was get to work on proving my alignment and orchestrating my life in such a way that I could better facilitate this beautiful process.

Sound is not sound.

Sound is a community of sentient, conscious beings.

Seeing this, knowing this, is a wonderful gift, a true Siddha.

Everything you see around you now is living, this page, these words, the ink on the paper, the table you sit at, the muscles and bones and ligaments in your fingers that hold this book, the eyes that read the page and the book itself.

All of it is sentient; all of it wants to serve anyone who aligns to the divine economy, those who surrender themselves to the God economy.

The superheroes (and their powers) you see on the cinema screen are all drawn from esoteric literature.

The ability to defy scientific laws are displayed by the enlargements you see on screen, because if there are any supernatural powers they will be shown to us in their exaggerated form, so that you might better recognise their subtle potentials in us. They (and their abilities) feature in every scripture: Old Testament and New; the Bhagavad-Gita and all of its supporting literature (some 500,000 Vedic verses); the pantheon of Buddhist adepts – from the Buddha, to Patanjali and Milarepa right through to modern day mystics like Thich Nhat Hanh; Rumi, The Prophet, Al-Ghazali, Rabia (in Islam); Julian of Norwich, Teresa of Ávila, Catherine of Siena in Christian mysticism; Gurdjieff and Ouspensky (the Fourth Way); their teachings are all spilling with stories of Siddhas.

Here are just a few of the superhuman powers that have been written up throughout the history of esoteric literature: superhuman speed – the ability to move faster than might seem humanly possible is known as the *100 mile boots*; shrinking and expanding – the ability to make yourself very large or very small, by the act of will; reading other people's thoughts; healing people by your presence or your touch; visions of the future or past; the ability to communicate with animals or even (as in the case of King Solomon) rocks and other inanimate objects; tolerance to heat or cold and pain; the ability to control your appetites; the ability to control energies; invisibility; knowing the mind of others; drawing people to speak their hidden thoughts; control of natural forces; the ability to affect machinery... I could go on, but I think you get the picture.

For those who don't believe in a Panpsychic universe, where everything holds consciousness, the very idea of communication outside of normal human interaction probably seems ludicrous.

And talking to stones!

Who ever imagined such an idea?

I have friends out there right now (you know who you are) who will be absolutely outraged at the very idea that such Siddhas exist, and they will demand my proof.

Of course they will, that much is predictable.

I have proof, my friend.

If *you* want proof, lovely people, use your outrage as an entry point to internal investigation.

Outrage is always a sign of fear.

Fear is a doorway.

Get your own proof.

Despite human scepticism, the history of esoteric practice and of aesthetic adepts is full of examples of people who defied every scientific law, wrote about their miracles, even demonstrated and performed them in front of many witnesses, but still, the scepticism remains.

That is how it is with miracles.

That is how it has always been.

And please remember, they are only miracles until you are able to experience and understand them. Then they become the extraordinary-ordinary. You too will become extraordinary, which is actually your natural (ordinary) state.

Proof is individual.

Proof is a fingerprint.

It certainly is not affected by opinion.

It doesn't need or look for or depend upon or recognise or curry favour with any human limitations or governing bodies or respected journals.

It doesn't need them.

It does not need or rely upon the safety of peer review.

You get your proof from the fruits of rigour, or sometimes simply through the gift of grace. And when you get it, it's so certain that other people's applause or approval or confirmation or testimony is not only unnecessary, it is redundant.

The very need to have your miracle sanctified by a recognised body automatically tells you that the fish has died in the mouth; the ego wants to own or see proof of something that the soul has produced.

It is so obvious when you experience it that looking for validation would be a little like asking someone to validate that the T-shirt I am wearing is grey or the ink I am scribing with is black.

The truth is so obvious that validation is unnecessary.

It is so ordinary too. When it happens, it doesn't feel supernatural, it is just normal.

With siddhas, none of the usual rules apply.

You have to be your own proof.

You have to be your own validation.

You have to be your own peer review.

When you *know* it, you will not seek the safety of validation.

If you seek the safety of validation, you can safely say you do not yet know it.

Once you recognise, as I have been gifted to recognise by direct experience, that every single mote of dust is conscious, you are no longer in communication with a rock, or a tree, or a wasp or a bird or anything else seemingly inanimate or insentient, you are communicating with consciousness itself.

Instead of limiting your communication to human interaction, you interface with everything.

You are communicating directly with the motherboard of consciousness and she will reply to you through any one of her trillions of sentient outlets. You can just as easily communicate with a tree as you can your wife or your brother or your neighbour over the garden fence.

In fact the intercourse will be more profound because it is not limited by the language or the intellect of the person you exchange with. It is certainly not hijacked or filtered through the muslin of expectation, or agenda. When nature gives, it gives without expectation, because it innately understands reciprocity.

I will briefly illustrate some of the countless examples of siddhas that I have experienced and some of the creatures and inanimate objects I have communicated with.

## The wasp

I was struggling with a personal *behaviour*.

This was many years ago, when I was newly awoken, and working on my inner clean. At the time, I couldn't discern whether or not this behaviour was an addiction, a harmful habit – in which case I would work to dissolve it – or if it was simply a harmless flirtation. I sat in my garden contemplating my dilemma, whilst drinking a fresh orange juice. I swallowed the last of my drink, and put the glass down on the table.

In my sub-vocalisation I asked the question, regarding my dilemma, *is this behaviour harmful to me?*

Almost immediately a wasp landed on the edge of my empty glass. I watched as it sipped the residue of juice, around the rim. The wasp flew away, and then returned just a few seconds later. This time he was a little braver. He went deeper into the glass, where the leftover juice had gathered and was thicker. Again he supped. Again he flew away and returned – but quicker this time.

The wasp went through this ritual several times until, eventually, bloated with a false confidence, he ventured to the very bottom of the glass, where a rich pool of orange juice had gathered. He stayed longer this time, greedy for as much sucrose as he could drink in. However, when he'd had his fill and tried to fly away, he couldn't move. His feet and his wings were stuck in the juice. He was locked into the glass, destined to die in the very middle of his greedy indulgence.

I had my answer.

I tipped the glass up.

I let the wasp, my teacher, go free and I began the deconstruction of my harmful addiction.

## The mother starling

I was experiencing a cash-flow problem in my business.

Unable to make enough cash-money to meet my outgoing bills, I fell into the trap of believing that there simply were not enough business opportunities out there for me to make ends meet. Also, even though I'd prayed for the problem to be solved, I felt as though God had not answered my prayers, I felt that (perhaps) he had abandoned me. I was in my kitchen, looking out into the garden as I contemplated my situation. There were three starlings in the middle of the grass, a mother and two youngster starlings. The garden was literally full of bread.

I'd cut up half a loaf earlier that morning, and laid it out for the birds.

The mother, I observed, was picking up the pieces of bread and feeding her youngsters mouth-to-mouth, as parents are apt to do with their fledglings. Suddenly and unexpectedly the mother bird flew out of the garden and left the younger birds alone.

Presumably she did this to teach them: at some point they would have to feed themselves, if they were to survive in the world.

From my vantage point in the house I could see that the mother had not flown far. In fact she was on the roof of the house opposite, viewing her babies from above. The chicks didn't know this. As far as they were concerned, the mother had simply abandoned them, without any food.

Of course, the garden was absolutely littered with bread, there were chunks of fresh loaf all over the lawn; they were literally standing in the middle of a large supply of food. But, because they were not used to feeding themselves, the food was practically invisible to them.

They waited for the mother to return, to find the bread, to feed them.

And they waited.

She did not return.

Eventually, perhaps thinking that she might never return, one of the birds started looking for its own food; one piece of bread led to another piece of bread which in turn led to another. Suddenly the chicks were able to see what was there all the time: a garden full of bread.

I had my answer.

I went out and I found the work that was already there, that I'd just not been able to see because I was waiting for God to bring it to me.

God feeds the birds, as the popular idiom goes, but he does

not put the food in their nests for them.

## The Cyprus path

We were in Cyprus for a wedding, my son's.

To be honest, at the time, I didn't have much appetite for the wedding or for Cyprus. My son and his beautiful wife to be had just gone through (were still going through) a very challenging life-trauma, that had rocked us all. No need for detail. Enough to say that we were all emotionally raw. It was clearly evident that my son and his girl, despite declarations to the opposite, were both still suffering the devastating pain of their trauma. Watching them wear happy-masks, pretending that everything was fine, and that this exotic wedding would solve all their problems, and constitute the first day of their new life (when we all knew that it would not), was very painful.

I am embarrassed to admit that I absolutely did not want to attend this wedding in Cyprus.

I went anyway.

I love my son very much. I love his wife. The four horses and their entire apocalypse would not have kept me from shouldering at least some of their angst.

Just the anticipation of the trip made my wife Sharon physically ill before we left England. The subsequent fallout from my son's trauma had triggered opprobrium from people, folk who saw half a situation and added their own judgment to it.

The situation threw me and Sharon into a temporary dissonance: *why was this happening*, and more immediately, *where was it all leading?*

The epiphany happened on the first day of our trip to Cyprus, and it lasted for the next three.

When I awoke in the hotel room, Sharon was not there.

That's first.

She had woken early (I later found out) and gone for a run

along the beach to clear her head. It was very unlike her to disappear without at least a nudge or a note. When she returned to the room, an hour later, she was high and excited. She'd just run along the seafront, on a stone path and she was struggling to articulate just how beautiful this path was and how special the view was, and how later, after the wedding ceremony, we should go to the seafront so that she could share what she'd experienced with me.

*I don't know where the path leads,* she said with alacrity that she did not even recognise, *but it doesn't matter, it's just a beautiful path.*

And this was the whole answer.

We were in pain, we felt lost, we needed some direction, I had asked for direction in my prayers, some certainty and it was delivered to us by an old stone path on a Cyprus beach.

We didn't know where our own path led, but it didn't matter; it was still a beautiful path all the same.

Later, after the wedding ceremony and the party, I walked hand-in-hand along the path with Sharon at midnight. I could see beings bobbing in the sea, looking at us on our pathless-path and I could feel God in the air; magic was afoot. Sharon's excitement and her profound summation were still ringing in my ear: *I don't know if it leads anywhere, but it doesn't matter, it's just a lovely path.*

From that moment onwards all the pain I was feeling disappeared and a heavenly mist descended on the island for the duration of our stay. I was thrust into essential time. The food – as always happens with me in these expanded moments – was other-worldly. As I sat on the hill overlooking the sea, at the front of our hotel the next morning, everything in my eyeline had become animated and beautiful and full of colour and wonder. The people walking in and out of the sea looked like living-statues of Greek Gods. This was no holiday destination I'd ever witnessed before. It lasted until our final day. Perhaps it was our reward for holding our character and stepping-up when so many others lost their integrity and had turned away. As we drove to the airport I knew that the message of the Cyprus path would never leave me.

## Sad girl in the café

I walked into my usual café, close to my home in Coventry.

As I ordered my drink I noticed a young girl. She was sat with (who I presumed were) her mother and grandmother.

The girl was strikingly beautiful but desperately sad.

I could feel her ache; it was etched across her face.

I strongly intuited that she desperately needed to cry but that time and circumstance would absolutely not permit such an open display of emotion, certainly not at this moment, and definitely not in this public space.

I could feel that whatever her angst was, it would be greatly eased by the act of shedding her pain in tears. I couldn't stop looking at her. I felt such an overwhelming empathy that I wanted to walk over, I wanted to say hello, I wanted to touch her face gently and tell her that *all would be well*. No matter what had gone wrong in her life, whoever or whatever she had lost, it would be fine, and it would work out. I would tell her this. She would spontaneously cry, and at least some of her pain would ease.

The capacity to expand beyond our usual boundaries in times of trauma is one of the great human mysteries; it is certainly one of the divine gifts. Just when we are screaming at the very top end of what feels like our last emotional gear, suddenly we adapt, we evolve and we find a new dimension, a higher gear and the pain is transcended.

I knew of course it would be inappropriate for me to just walk over and introduce myself to this child, and tell her that all would be well.

I sat with my coffee and subtly watched her, her pain was

tangible, compassion rippled from my heart in waves.

I closed my eyes, and I meditated: *how can I help this girl?*

Suddenly, in my mind's eye, she walked across and sat opposite me.

I am aware now, writing these words, that in my meditation I invited her over. I invited her, she accepted and now, intellectually, she was sat opposite me. If not in person, certainly in spirit.

The room disappeared.

It was just me and this suffering girl.

The room contracted again; now I was no longer there in person, only the girl existed, sat cross from my observing eye.

I reached over. I touched her face as though she were my own child; she was probably a few years younger than my youngest daughter. I conveyed to her, without any need to know the nature of her pain – and in the words of Julian of Norwich – *all will be well, and all will be well and all manner of things will be well.*

The apparition of this girl in front of me burst out crying and the relief in her face was palpable. I was suddenly drawn out of my trance, I opened my eyes, and I looked across the room to where the girl was sitting with her family: she was openly sobbing. I closed my eyes. My spirit expanded and filled the room. When I opened my eyes again, the girl and her family had gone.

I realised in this moment that I didn't need to physically consummate my love and healing with words or even with my physical presence, I could do it all from the inside.

## Healing My Dad

My dad was a very old-fashioned man.

He was lovely and funny and warm, but he was old-fashioned; not a man taken to physical displays of affection. Like Hemingway's old man (in *The Old Man and the Sea*) he had his own ways, his love was spoken through his actions. The pathos in his eyes when he felt I might be worried about something, the silly jokes, the protective instinct he exuded when he was around me, all spoke overwhelmingly of love.

His devotion was obvious, it was so clear that hugs or worded affection were unnecessary.

When he was taken ill, my dad, when he was poorly and bedridden, I wanted to go to him, I wanted to put my arms around him and comfort him. I wanted to place the palm of my healing hand on his head so I could ease some of his suffering.

Physically, in the flesh this was never going to happen. It would not be tenable because my need to physically hold my dad was not commensurate with a gentleman of his generation. So, during that period I took to visiting him *out of my body*.

The mystics would call this bilocation.

I could be in my apartment in London and yet be with my dad, in his room (back in Coventry), at the same time. From a deep meditation, I would leave my body and take my heart, my essence to my dad. In this ethereal form, unhindered by the stiff protocols of his generation and the physical boundaries of his corporeal body, he allowed me to sit with him, he let me massage his back and put my palm on his head and his chest; he let me embrace him.

I did this exercise most days, especially when I was out of town.

One day my dad walked down the stairs in his house in Coventry, and said very happily to my mum, *"Our Geoffrey's just been in the room with me."*

My mum scoffed, *"Don't be silly, Ken, Geoffrey hasn't been here at all – he's in London."*

I was with my dad in Coventry while I sat in my room in London.

He saw me.

## Making Myself Small

I spoke with a man on the phone once, some years ago. He was a fan of my inaugural book *Watch My Back*, an anecdotal retelling of my adventures in the world of nightclub security. He'd been given my number by the local bookshop, and called hoping for a little advice on publishing.

During a conversation about the publishing world in general, he unexpectedly veered from the subject at hand and, as an unrelated aside, mentioned that he'd seen me from afar one day, in the city centre. He said he was very surprised (I sensed *disappointed*) at how small I was, considering the fact that I'd spent a decade working as a bouncer.

At the time, I was about 6 ft tall and weighed in at a rather large 16 stones. Not small by anyone's standards. My business partner Peter affectionately called me fatty. I was so big (he liked to joke) that wherever you sat in the room, you were sat next to me. I relayed my statistics to the man down the phone. I told him that I wasn't small, in fact I was pretty big, perhaps too big at the time. He didn't believe me. He was adamant that he'd seen me very recently and I was not big at all, in fact, *"you're quite small,"* he insisted, *"slight."*

I was momentarily confused, and then it dawned on me.

*"Where was I when you saw me?"* I asked.

*"You were talking to a shop assistant in Waterstone's bookshop."*

*"Ah,"* I said, suddenly understanding why I appeared small to him.

The shop assistants at Waterstone's were all lovely people, and very bookish. I was a large man with a large reputation in the city as a fighter. I knew that my size intimidated them, I'd felt it many times before when I'd spoken to staff at the shop, so I had taken to *shrinking* my size whenever I entered their atmosphere. I became smaller in order to make them feel more comfortable and less threatened. This man had seen me during a *small time*.

## Making myself bigger

When I first started to work as a bouncer in Coventry, I was tall and thin, probably weighing in at eleven stone. Sometimes, in the violent world of club security it helped if you were able to make yourself bigger, even if only temporarily.

One man I had a physical encounter with during this time (he initiated a confrontation with me, and was carried out of it) described me to his friends, post-fight, as *6 ft 5 and about 17 stones.*

He was a very violent man, a criminal trying to steal my door; he needed to be intimidated. To do this I first made myself small. I did this in order to drop his guard and bloat his confidence. Then, when he was primed and fat with arrogance, I rapidly expanded. I was eleven stone, but increased body to meet his eye at 17. This was something I learned to do unconsciously in the threatening world of 1980s nightlife. The sheer intensity of the job was the catalyst; it required that you develop this very subtle Siddha. I expanded and contracted so naturally and so often that I was hardly aware I was doing it.

One man, a filmmaker I'd met briefly at an industry screening, on hearing about my tough reputation in the world of martial arts, would not hear any of it: *I've met Geoff,* he insisted, *he's not a hard man, far from it; the lovely little fella I met was certainly no fighter.*

In front of him I'd made myself appear physically small and unthreatening.

Years later, when the same man came to train with me at one of my martial arts classes, he was introduced to my bigger and heavier self. I could see him looking at me confused, trying to figure out *where's the other fella gone; the little one?*

Making myself smaller and making myself bigger is a Siddha that I naturally developed on the doors of Coventry. I later perfected the art, when I entered the more sedate and benign and sensitive corners of society.

I shrink when I need to shrink.

I expand when I need to expand.

Morihei Ueshiba, the famed (but physically diminutive) founder of Aikido, was a man so steeped in the Budo tradition of his art that he'd learned to expand exponentially. When asked in an interview if he ever feared that, due to his martial reputation, people might challenge him to a fight, he laughed and said that he was unconcerned, *the moment they approached me,* he said, *they would realise that they were taking on the whole universe.*

In the early days, before I fully understood this natural magic, I would accidentally allow myself to be intimidated by a threatening situation, and shrink. I'd make myself very small when I should have expanded and made myself big. On other occasions, I lost control of my temper, and accidentally expanded, frightening everyone in the room; I expanded, when contraction would have served me better.

## Room of requirement

If you are a fan of the *Harry Potter* epistles, you will probably already be familiar with this concept. The premise is this: if your pilgrimage or mission is righteous, and you lack instruction, or means, or location to carry out or complete your journey, what you lack will be provided, it will appear as if by magic to accommodate your need.

In the fifth Potter outing, *The Order of the Phoenix*, Harry is compelled to teach his fellow school friends how to defend themselves against the dark arts, but they lack a room in which to practise, a secreted location somewhere inside the school, but away from the prying eyes of the schoolmasters. Professor Dumbledore – the school headmaster – assures Harry, with a nod and a wink, that *help will always be given in Hogwarts to those who need it.* Shortly thereafter, a mysterious doorway to a hidden room presents itself to them so that they can perfect their skills, in private.

Later, in the final episode of the Potter saga, when our hero's requirement has reached a critical nadir, the kindly headmaster amends his council and assures Harry that, *help will always be given in Hogwarts to those who **deserve** it.*

As I have probably said a few times in this book already, we are often shown, in exaggerated form, what we need to see in microcosm.

My own life has been so full of (examples of) requirements being met, in a mysterious manner, that it would take a whole book to record them. It was only usually after that fact that I realised their mysterious nature. Again, it would be easy to reduce my experiences to common coincidence, but that would be to misread the process, and if we do this, how are we ever going to learn its ways and repeat the method consciously?

It would also be to miss the obvious point: one minute you have a requirement, the next – no matter how coincidental it might appear – your requirement is met.

The word *requirement* is the key to this wonderful Siddha.

Requirement occurs when our definite and certain desire to evolve outgrows our means of meeting that desire. If what we require is righteous and it will benefit Nature; if we are certain beyond doubt that we want it *at whatever the cost*, our intention will act as a centripetal force, it will attract everything we need to bring our desired result about.

A few examples from my own life:

**Judo:** as a seasoned practitioner in the atemi arts (striking), I really wanted to learn the art of judo, to close the gaps in my close-range fighting. I was so certain and so excited about learning this art, that I manifested a class less than three miles from my house: it was run by Neil Adams, the greatest occidental judoka of his generation.

One minute the class did not exist in my consciousness, the next it did exist, a short drive from my house, and furnished with 20 international judo players, all of whom willingly schooled me in their art. Not only did they allow me to train in this Olympic level class full time, but they also let me train for free. I stayed with these incredible teachers for eighteen months, until I won a black belt and took my game to the level I required. After I left, the class disbanded. It is no longer there. It was as though this field of energy manifested just to meet my requirement, and then fell back into the ether again, once my purpose was served.

My desire was so profound that this elite room of requirement appeared just for me, and remained active only until my need was met.

**Theatre:** I have always loved the art of writing. After meeting the playwright Jim Cartwright, and reading some of his work, I was inspired. I desperately wanted to improve my art, and immerse myself into theatre, to learn its ways. I was so certain of this that I wrote a stage play when I was on holiday and sent it to the Royal Court Theatre in London, one of the most prestigious theatres in the world for new playwrights. Before very long, this incredible bastion of stage opened its doors to me, and I was invited into their young writers' group. In this revered space, I was exposed to some of the best influences in the world of theatre.

Before I met Jim, I didn't even know what the Royal Court was, I certainly didn't understand theatre; I had only ever been to London once.

My requirement created the room.

**Film:** ever since I was at school I always wanted to write films. I penned my first movie (and starred in it) when I was thirteen years old. Somewhere between leaving school and entering the workplace (and getting married very young) I lost contact with my dream. However, after I published my first book at the age of 32, the desire to make film retuned. I wanted to pen a script, but I lacked the savvy; I had no idea how I might enter the movie world. My burning desire, the need I sent out into the universe, created a requirement, and the requirement crafted a bespoke room to meet my need. I was introduced quite randomly to a film producer called Natasha Carlish, and the room of requirement opened. Through Natasha (and the work we did together) myriad other doors opened to meet my growing requirement: a local screen agency, that funded my first three films; BAFTA who opened their doors in Piccadilly, London to me, and gave me exposure to elite film talent from around the globe; I was introduced to actors, writers, directors, producers, musicians, designers etc. all of whom opened more doors, until I had access to almost every corner of the filmmaking world.

Again, my requirement, created the room.

When I look back on my blessed life thus far, I am able to see in retrospect what I was unable to comprehend as it occurred: many rooms of requirement appeared for me, exactly when my need met a point of certainty. The mystic Russel Williams said that when we open a new door, we should treat the handle as though it is an eggshell and turn it very gently. I must confess that I was too scared to even touch the handle on some of the doors that were presented to me, and many times I failed to enter the room at all, at the first time of offering. I was just too afraid in case I couldn't cope with the opportunity I was being gifted.

Looking back, I can see that my needs always found their means, but not until I made room, and never until I had developed the back and shoulders and legs to carry the weight of burden.

New knowledge is a heavy responsibility, be in no doubt.

We create the rooms by doing the work.

We must do the work.

You can have as much consciousness as you want, but you have to create the space for it first. When you do, whatever you need will make itself available to you; the books, the teachers, the rooms, the equipment, the money, the materials, the means of transport, supper – you will not go without, whilst you are going within.

My American friend, the pastor Bill McDonald, takes this

practice to the extreme. He travels the world with hardly a dollar in his pocket, to pass on his arcana and serve others. Wherever he goes, people feel compelled to serve him. He is fed and watered, offered free lodgings, he is picked up and dropped off, and he is gifted enough money to cover his sundries – the man is miraculous. I am so inspired by him. He travels the world on a wing and a prayer, his currency is faith, and his faith is never without reward.

## Breaking Machinery

Again, in the early days, when I was still fighting for sovereignty of my senses, I would often lose my temper at inappropriate moments, and the energy that I was still coming to terms with would spill. So much so that things around me – computers, machines, lights – would be affected, even broken. I have lost count of the amount of times media people came to film me and interview me, and their camera batteries mysteriously ran out of power, or the lights popped, or the sound failed, or the camera would not operate or they ran out of film at a crucial moment.

On one occasion, during a teaching session, one of my senior instructors, completely out of character, broke a precious martial arts etiquette, in front of a group of my students (he was disrespectful to me) and I lost my centre. I was so angry that the light above my head instantly popped and burst and the tea-urn that I was standing next to switched off and the element broke. The 'on' light disappeared and we couldn't get it to work again.

I think I was more upset about the loss of tea than I was of losing my cool in front of students.

## Invisibility

Invisibility is a siddha that can take on many forms.

It can vary from people not seeing who you really are – your identity, your abilities etc. – to literally not seeing you at all.

Mostly, people don't look at who you are because they are

too busy looking at who they *think* you are or who they imagine you are not, which makes *who you really are* invisible to them. When I worked in security, I would often use this *lack of seeing* to my advantage. If I felt it would work to my favour, perhaps I wanted to drop an opponent's mental guard, by luring him into complacency, I would *disappear* any physical prowess I was holding by making other elements of my person or personality expand, to cover them. For instance, even though I carried all the working scars of a fighter – cauliflower ears, broken nose, bulbous knuckles – all I had to do was soften my voice, drop my head, make myself a bit smaller, deliberately avoid eye contact, perhaps even allow a dribble of trepidation and a fear to bleed through my voice and my fighter aspect would become all but invisible.

This technique can be used to lessen the intimidation factor, which can be an accelerant in a confrontational situation, or it can be used as a flytrap to draw in a prey; it is easy to lure an opponent into a false sense of security by presenting yourself as weak or small or afraid.

In the self-defence world, lesson one was always to make yourself invisible as a victim by removing every element of vulnerability from your being. People are targeted by attackers because they display some or all the traits of a victim.

They are *visible* to any malefactor looking for an easy target.

If you consciously remove these traits, you become invisible to attackers.

For instance, it is impossible to be trolled on the World Wide Web if you have no presence on the World Wide Web.

I made myself invisible to a whole host of Internet shades simply by not having a presence there. If you want to wander around the virtual world, and observe without being observed, it is not difficult. It is easy enough to wander around the virtual world whilst being completely invisible.

In the external world and the internal world we make

ourselves invisible to attack by cleansing ourselves of any negative, matching frequencies.

If you do not emit any signs of fear, you can walk invisibly.

If you are completely centred in your being, if you are consistently established in your true I, you can come and go unnoticed, you can walk the streets and still remain unseen by the shades and the parasites that roam like lions looking for victims.

Al-Ghazali gives us a stark warning in his mystical instruction: *If you fall into vice, you will be noticed.*

Whether he means you will be noticed externally or internally doesn't matter; in metaphysical practice there is no discernible difference between out and in.

Your vulnerabilities are read like a neon sign by the criminally inclined.

Even children will be able to intimidate if you are situated in the vibration of fear.

If you are completely centred, whole opposing armies will not see you.

I have also been physically invisible on a few definite occasions.

Once, when I was in a deep trancelike state, my wife walked past me in our own home. I was sat in a chair, in our conservatory, and she passed me twice, without seeing me.

On another occasion – again, I was in a deep meditative state – a waitress in a hotel walked right past me with a drink I'd ordered but couldn't see me. She was so close to me that our feet nearly brushed. I remained invisible until I alerted her to my presence.

On another occasion still, at a comedy show, a heckling comedian made it his job to direct his act at me in the audience. In the second half of the show, I moved two seats back and I made myself completely invisible to him. When he returned to the stage he searched the room for me, intending to use me again as his comedy foil, he even asked one of my friends where I was. At one point, he looked directly at me but he couldn't see me.

Invisibility is easier if there is nothing inside you that wants to be seen, and that is a big job right here.

If the false ego – which of course always wants to be noticed – is subjugated, you can section off all internal noise, all stimulus, and sit in the silence and stillness of mind and you will disappear to most people in the room.

## Getting noticed

I was at the London Marathon with Sharon.

I'd arranged to meet her at the end of the race at Horse Guards Parade. What I really wanted to do was get into the private area, the runner's enclosure at the end of the race, to surprise her. As a spectator I was not permitted to do this. I noticed that the people policing the runner's enclosure this particular year were soldiers. I had sold many books to British military personnel all over the world, so I had a good following in the armed forces. I wondered if any of the soldiers guarding the runner's enclosure might have recognised me and, as a favour, let me in without a pass.

I stood by the entrance, hoping to be noticed, *trying* to get myself noticed, but within a few short moments I realised that there was no heart in myattempt,my egoic desire it was not in keeping with good spiritual practice. I abandoned my cause and found a quiet spot by a nearby tree. I leant my back against the trunk, shut my eyes and literally closed down all internal chatter, all internal noise. I slowed my breathing and separated myself from the tumult and the footfall all around me. Within the next 30 minutes, three separate soldiers noticed me, approached me, asked me for a photo or a handshake or an autograph, and thanked me for writing my books.

I was noticed, but I didn't ask them to get me into the enclosure.

In my early days of martial arts training, I was a keen aspirant and wanted to meet all my personal fight heroes. I felt that certain personalities in the MA world would be a good influence on my development, if only I could meet them.

In retrospect, I can see that I only desired the introduction because I thought I might imbibe some mystery from them, the secrets of Budo. Secretly, I was hoping that the proximity of these senior players might accelerate my learning without me having to do the work.

I talked constantly to my wife Sharon about who I would like to meet, and what I might say to them if I was lucky enough to be in their company. Sensing the misaligned nature of my desire, she gave me some of the best advice I have ever received: stop trying to meet your heroes. Do the work. Do the work, Geoff, and your heroes will want to meet you. This advice cut through all seven layers of my ego and reached my heart. Her advice has never left me. I got my head down, I did the work and within a few short years I was in the same room as my heroes, and yes, many of them did seek me out, they did want to meet me.

I follow the same advice in my work today, with writing, with theatre and film, and especially with my evolvement in the metaphysical arts: I do not try and meet my heroes, the gurus, the Rishi and the mystics. I do the work...

## Healing

I have witnessed many miraculous healings.

I have seen more healings than I can remember, not least my own, when I have been in the presence of grace.

I randomly bumped into an old friend recently, a man who had undergone a miraculous healing in one of my martial arts classes. One of his friends said to me, *you saved his life.*

I categorically did not save his life.

We do not heal people, although healing can be served through us.

His life was saved, no doubt, but it was not saved by me.

When I originally met this beautiful man, he was bent over, he was racked with pain and depressed. The doctors had given up on him, they told him that his disease was degenerate and he was destined for a wheelchair within a few short years. It was intuited to me immediately on meeting him, that if he chose it, he could be healed, and that I could lead him towards this healing. I told him this. He asked me how. I gave him the instruction to join one of my classes (it was a non-commercial private group that I ran), which he did, and over the next eighteen months, he was healed.

I directed him towards healing and I was witness to his miracle, but it was not me that healed him.

You are not the healer, but healing can happen around you if you are aligned; if you hold the divine sword, it can happen through you.

I was once healed of a painful back complaint, just by standing with a man who was on the carpet of proximity.

I was suffering with an old injury, and just by standing with my friend Sam who, on that particular day, at that particular moment, was so aligned that my pain vanished instantly, it could not exist in his presence. The week before I met him, he'd experienced a profound spiritual epiphany where he'd been in the presence of All. He was so affected by his clarity, he wanted to go out and tell the whole world about it, he wanted to save the planet.

On this particular day we were walking in London and he was trying to articulate what had happened to him. Suddenly he stopped walking, faced me and said, *let me look.* He wanted to look into my eyes. He wanted to see if I was truly aligned to the concepts I was teaching. He looked into my eyes. I felt a rush of fear rise in my stomach, which was interrupted by a quiet inner voice that said, *let him look, there is nothing hidden here.*

I relaxed; I let him look deep inside me.

A smile filled Sam's face: *"You really are there,"* he said.

My back pain disappeared and did not return.

I mentioned earlier about yaqeen (pronounced ya-keen). It is one of the 99 names of Allah, as mentioned in the Holy Quran.

Yaqeen translates as certainty.

When certainty is present, healing can and healing does occur. Not from you but through you. The atmosphere you bring dominates the space you occupy, it leaves no room for defilement.

The certainty I feel when I know that a healing is possible is difficult to articulate.

It is a definite knowing. An innate certainty that the person in front of me can be rebalanced. I am never sure how long this might take – one minute, one hour, a year, but neither is that important or even relevant, schedules are none of my business. I just know that healing is possible; time is not only irrelevant, when you touch the essential, time is non-existent.

I am aware also at these times that I'm a conduit for this healing – me, the divine ego, joined with the higher soul. At the same time I am also aware that my personality, Geoff Thompson, is not the healer. Whether or not healing can occur is intuited, all I have to do is follow the instruction that comes through me.

I am certain it is possible and this certainty needs no outside validation.

Neither can the healing be affected or blocked by any outside influence, unless I allow someone to disconnect my yaqeen.

Equally (and oppositely) I've been in front of people who are clearly very ill and I've known they could be healed, but it couldn't be done at that particular time through me.

In the New Testament even the prophet Jesus refused to attempt a healing if it was not ordained. On refusing to heal a woman who was begging for his help, Jesus told his confused disciples that *you do not throw pearls in front of swine.* This was not a personal insult aimed at a particular woman, it was simply

Jesus' way of saying that nothing can be done if the doing is not ordained by God.

Jesus did not do the healing, the healing was done through him. And even then, it only occurred when yaqeen was present and that can only be present when there is ordination.

My friend died recently of cancer.

I could sense even in the later stages of his disease that all hope was not lost. When I tried to speak with him about divinity, about connecting to his healing Source, he instantly and bluntly closed me down. Even in his sad and depressed and emotional state I could feel certainty, but only the certainty that I could do nothing for him.

I had a similar situation with a martial arts student who had placed himself into my world. He was a young man suffering from bladder cancer. He joined a class I was running, looking for balm; ultimately he was hoping for healing.

I thought he was an arrogant man.

Let me reiterate that, I don't want to sound judgmental or unkind. Let's say that this man *presented* himself to me as arrogant. Everything I suggested to him, as an aid or a technique to help him find a centre place, from where healing might occur, he dismissed, refused or simply shot down: *Oh, I read about that but… or, Yeah, I did look at that but…* even, *I heard about that before but…*

Everything I suggested was blocked and punctuated by the word **but**. This was followed by rhetoric as to why my suggestions would not work for him.

He was not open to anything I suggested; in fact, he actively opposed it to the point that he started to aggressively question everything I said. I am not in the business of intellectually grappling with people that come to me for help. Frankly it is too tiring. It also tells me that they are not open enough to receive help, they are not ready to surrender, and surrender is what each of us has to do if we are ever to be healed.

What I have learned and what I know is this: you can't help people if they don't want your help.

If they are wrestling with you, this is implicitly what they are saying.

I knew I couldn't help him.

I knew I was wasting my time and his.

I suggested he find someone else to work with, as I couldn't do anything for him.

He was shocked, he was emotional.

*"You can't kick me off the course,"* he said.

*"I'm not kicking you off the course,"* I replied. *"Anyway you hardly ever turn up, and when you do, you don't take the instruction. You are not humble enough to accept help."*

This shifted something in him. The confused expression on his face told me as much. He pondered on my words for a few seconds and then said, *"I'm not arrogant."*

I reminded him that I didn't say he was arrogant, only that he lacked the humility to accept help.

Suddenly, without any warning, he broke down and cried. He confessed to me that he was afraid of his cancer, he was scared of dying, but more than that, he was frightened of trusting me; in fact he couldn't trust anyone.

The certainty that I couldn't help him transformed instantly into an absolute certainty that I could. He had opened up. He had surrendered to grace. I told him to come to the next session and we could start work. The arrogant, sullen sceptic that had been in my class the session before was no more. When he turned up for the next class he bounded through the door, all smiles, a spring in every step and he lit up the room. From then on there was no block between us and in a very short time he rang me very emotionally to let me know that his cancer was healed. He was not only in remission, the doctors could find no evidence in his body of the disease.

In the same space (I called it *the Thursday group*), with the same certainty, I have personally witnessed a diagnosed schizophrenic living in fear, living off benefits, unable to work, become healed completely of his ills, get married, teach martial arts as a qualified coach, and return to full-time employment. It took a couple of years for him to fully surrender to the exposure of grace, but when he did, the healing occurred. Eventually this beautiful man found equilibrium and returned to his place as a contributing member of society. He became one of my best martial arts teachers and one of the kindest, gentlest men I have ever met.

Another man, who suffered from an *untreatable* muscle-wasting disease, healed and went on to become one of the top MMA teachers in the world. He was transformed from an ailing, skinny, pale youth, walking on crutches, to a handsome, fit, MA fighter on the world stage. People travel across the world to be in the company of this remarkable man.

Fifteen years after this healing, his dad still rings me every Christmas to thank me for bringing his son home.

Not me, I remind him, I just invited his son into the room.

The healing was enabled because this brave man placed himself on the carpet of proximity.

Many others have written me letters and emails to report that a talk I did, a letter I wrote, a phone call I made, an article I penned, a book I produced, a podcast I put out, a meeting I took, inspired them when they were suicidal and Grace brought them back from the brink.

When you are aligned, healing happens to you and to others around you.

It happens, even if they don't know you.

At its optimum, you can heal, inspire, direct, instruct people in a room just because you are there. Again, I must stipulate that it is not you that does the healing or inspiring; your certainty, your religion connects people to their own source and it all happens from there.

## Exorcism

It is a very loaded word I know.

It conjures up images of demonic creatures and satanic, horned beasts.

As I said earlier, if there are superhuman powers available to beings, they will be shown to us in their exaggerated form so that we can see in the magnification what often occurs in the subtle. The same applies with exorcism, the removal of dark or disturbed vibrations that might be trapped in our bodies or minds.

The word demon is a derivation of the word divide – to be divided – which also finds its root in the word divine – the divine *divided*.

Or, to be more specific – because the Divine in its true sense is indivisible – the divine energy distorted as it refracts through the prism of damaged human perception.

Eckhart Tolle calls these divides *pain-bodies*, and describes them as *semi-autonomous thought-forms*. Some of these thought-forms are inherited – our divine inheritance, gift or curse. Some of them we have been taught (this is known as *soft-inheritance*), others are thrust upon us by the prevailing winds of modern culture: the social mores, and of course some of them, as I mentioned earlier, the adverse forces, are airborne, always looking for an open door into the human psyche.

We are also possessed by the powerful machine of modern media, which sneaks division and duality and confusion into the masses while they are in a hypnogogic state – reading a newspaper, watching TV or poring over Facebook likes and Twitter feeds. Our perceptions are hijacked on a daily basis by powers – corporeal and otherwise – that stand to profit from our distraction or from our unconscious exchanges of energy.

If we are divided, it can be said that we have a devil in us, *the size of a dog*, as my lovely Irish mum might say. The lower soul, the divine ego, if it is not protected, will be invaded and possessed or semi-possessed by the strongest, most seductive most alluring or frightening impression in the room. If you have your nose in a tabloid newspaper for several hours a day or your eyes are locked on to the TV news morning, noon and night, or connected to any device that feeds you subjective often fake information, then of course you are inviting the adverse forces across your threshold, sitting them down at your dinner table and feeding them willingly on your own vital energies.

Like summer gnats, they assail us; they are parasitical bugs that feed off our energy if we engage them. That these invading influences are all around us is a given. That some of them are present in us is also evident, even though they have no right to be there, even though their origins are outside of us. But it is we who invite them in. It is we who create a covenant with them, and offer them free board and lodgings in our inner-world.

Then we complain about how divided the world out there is.

It is not the world we have to protect and clean.

It is ourselves we have to protect; it is us that need cleansing.

If you don't want division in the world, get division out of yourself.

How?

By doing nothing.

## The Clear View

Exorcising divided thoughts is one of the most powerful if unannounced and underrated Siddhas.

We learn to control the various vibrations in all their forms when we perfect this Siddha.

Doing nothing is how we prevent negative energies entering us, it is how we evict ungracious energies that already use our bodies and minds as a squat, and it is how we dissolve divides by our sheer silent presence, but, as I already said doing nothing takes a tremendous spirit.

To do *nothing* you have to be an adept, no less.

When they rise, when they march upon us to feed on our worries and our fears and our deepest desires, they always enter with a compelling story; a spill in our life is sold as a flood, a small flame of vicissitude is reported as a mighty inferno. We are convinced that what is close is far away or non-existent, and what is far away (or non-existent) is very real and very near. It takes great insight to see these pain-bodies for what they are; it demands strength to hold them back because they can be very convincing. They feel real.

Of course, there is only one thing that is real and that is Love.

Love is a constant. Like the Brahman of Hindu scripture, and the God of the Christian canon, or the Tao of Chinese mysticism or the Friend in Sufism, this all-pervading force is in us and around us at all times.

Even though we crucify ourselves daily with familiar laments, the same sorry song, the all-encompassing presence of God is ever near. When we sit in contemplation and find silence and stillness under our own Ficus Religiosa (the Bodhi Tree) and refuse to engage the complaint or arousal or assault that rises in us a *clear view* will eventually present itself. The righteous path that is usually obscured by these fears and worries will open up to us.

Doing nothing takes courage.

The Buddha sat under the Bodhi Tree for 49 days before enlightenment came.

When we are able to meet our fears at the neck dent, the doorway of our heart, and refuse them engagement, even though our bodies might be threatened with fear or seduced by lust or confronted by confusion, we exorcise our own demons.

If we refuse them our emotional engagement, they perish.

They know this of course, the adverse forces; they know that if we don't engage them, they will be dissolved, which is why their assault on us is both relentless and covert.

This is why our resolve needs to be equally tenacious.

We must rise every day, especially during periods of vulnerability, and meet these imposters at the doorway.

We must not insist on time-frames and there can be no let-up in our defence; and we must never indulge the wish to get rid of them quickly.

One friend said to me recently, in the heat of an emotional assault, *I can cope with this, Geoff, as long as I know it's not forever, as long as I know how long I've got to hold on for.*

As soon as he said this I knew he was lost.

We need the courage to penetrate deep into the heart of these feelings as they rise, as they lure and threaten. And not only be prepared to do so forever if necessary, but also be grateful for the opportunity. We have been chosen (at a deeper level I suspect that we actually chose) to bear these difficulties and we absolutely know that good will come from our endeavour. Space will be made for Grace, when we refuse or evict these malefactors.

The reason we must never actively try to get rid of our pain-bodies – even though we know that by refusing engagement they will be denied and removed – is because the very act of trying to get rid of something is in and of itself a form of emotional engagement. The pain-body loves it when you wrestle for your freedom. It will feed and sustain itself on the energy consumed in your struggle. If you feel the urge to escape or remove a pain-body, you already know that the lower ego has risen and identified with the divided thought-form. The ego runs from aversion, and it grasps for security and comfort.

The pain-body feeds off grasping, it dines out on our need for comfort.

The need to get rid of these vibrations is a fear-based, egocentric identification. It validates and nourishes and strengthens the pain-bodies that the soul would deny. Our job is to expose them, by disconnecting from the ego, engaging the observer self, and refusing engagement to anything that does not come from virtue, or love.

Pain-bodies only have the life we afford them through our engagement.

Objective observation is the panacea-technique, the devil-dissolving holy gaze that we employ when we sit and wait for enlightenment.

Silent observance is the weapon of no-weapon.

Our need to assure an end to conflict is an egoic attempt to negotiate with a non-corporeal energy. In trying to negotiate we engage from a fearful stance, and our communication affords them corporeality through us.

The very need for relief feeds the entity that challenges our peace.

In the Fourth Way, the mystic George Gurdjieff insists that we observe what rises in us, what approaches our borders whilst at the same time resisting the urge to try, or in any way to change it or remove it.

It seems like a paradox, I know, to deliberately *not try* and clear defilement, but at the same time, know that in *doing nothing*, it will be removed anyway.

The moment we put a time-frame on our endeavours, the second we wish the removal or the cessation of an uncomfortable element, our fear sustains the very thing we would see removed, because we have left our quiet space.

Doing nothing (as I said earlier) is **the** technique.

Doing nothing is the holy realm of the observer.

When we can do nothing, we know that the observer is in residence.

When we grasp or attempt to avert, we know that the ego is at the wheel.

It is a good rule of thumb to work from.

If we find that we are unable to immediately access silence as our weapon of choice, perhaps we have already been baited by the adverse forces, and they have broken through our borders, there are other effective methods of spiritual combat that can be equally miraculous.

## Paradoxical Intention (PA)

Viktor Frankl called this method of approach *Paradoxical Intention* (PA), and he forged his technique in the most severe crucible: the Nazi death camp, Auschwitz.

PA is a psychological technique. The premise is simple in concept: instead of panicking, and trying to get rid of an arousing stimulus (the pain-body) we instead ask for more of the thing we feel afraid of, we call for increase – in fear/pain/stress/worry etc. – and not decrease or cessation. This is a technique that you can use when you feel as though the rising or approaching energy threatens to overwhelm you, and take the mind-door by storm. Perhaps it has caught you off your guard, and your observer-self is temporarily disengaged. It is very effective when our will is tired, and the pain-body threatens to *stick around forever*, which it threatens often. Instead of engaging the fear that this might be true, we instead lean into it; we encourage it to enter, in greater proportions. We welcome the demon of fear, we invite it to *stay for as long as you like.*

It is said that the Buddhist saint Milarepa was once threatened by a hungry ghost that he found squatting in his cave one day when he came back from a walk. When the demon threatened to eat Milarepa alive, the saint threw himself immediately and directly into the jaws of the devil. On seeing that Milarepa was blatantly unafraid, the demon immediately vanished.

As I said earlier, and I have learned this from countless encounters: the very act of trying to get rid of fear, will increase its strength in direct proportion to your level of fear.

As pain-bodies feed off pain-bodies, so fear feeds off fear.

In the Gurdjieff method (the Fourth Way), specific exercises were designed and created (in manufactured environments) to draw out his student's defilements. But when the defilements presented, he instructed them to never deliberately try and remove them. Rather, they were encouraged to bring them out into the light, head, body and tail, and observe them without identification.

The reason he insisted that we don't try and get rid of (what he called) sub-personalities is because he discovered what I myself discovered: it is not us – the ego personality – that dissolves defilement; it is the observer, or consciousness.

The Siddha is not that we personally are able to exorcise demons; the miracle is that we are able to draw them out and bear them until they are dissolved by the light of consciousness.

Light dissolves shadow; this is the real Siddha.

What we expose to light, must itself become light.

We are sorely tempted, often compelled, to go to war with our shadows, and on some occasions, when we are cornered, as a last resort, we will find ourselves doing exactly that. But even as we win the battle, these vibrations are gathering their dispelled forces, and migrating into someone else or something else, ready to war all over again.

Ultimately, war only increases the strength of the enemy.

When Mother Teresa of Calcutta was asked to join an anti-war march, she refused the invitation. *When you arrange a peace march,* she said, *I will join you.*

There is a subtle distinction between the two, and it makes all the difference; one is wrestling with shadow, the other is creating light.

Catherine of Siena concurred; she encouraged her followers to place their *principal affection* in virtue rather than in penance or warring with sin.

In other words, we concentrate our consciousness on creating light, and not on fighting with the dark.

The enemy feeds off conflict – that's what it wants.

Drama feeds drama.

If we expose, but refuse to engage the shadow, it creates a

neutral space; the diseased energy has risen but has nowhere to dock. It makes itself mortally vulnerable when it leaves the safe mooring of its hiding place in the atmosphere, or within our bodies and minds. It relies entirely on our engagement for its reality.

Whether this is represented by a pain-body in us or as a troll on the World Wide Web or an adverse force roaming the atmospheres matters not; they meet the same fate if they find no engagement.

If it rises up and is not met, it will lose much of its strength in the effort; like a lion that expends tremendous amounts of essence chasing down an antelope that it doesn't manage to claim.

Anything that hunts but does not feed eventually perishes, nature teaches us this much.

We have to be both wise and wily with these shades.

They use guile and they employ disguise and artifice in their hunt for our engagement. They use our own ignorance and the fear this elicits to trip us up, to pin us down, to consume us and then make themselves stronger and fitter for the next encounter.

If we can arm ourselves with the kind of knowledge in this book and others like it, we will pack the only tool we need – a powerful observer – and the knowledge that what we do not engage will be consumed back into consciousness, and when it does, the nature of that defilement will be liberated.

I spent much of my early life reversing the hunt.

Instead of waiting around like a nervous antelope, I deliberately wrote down the fears I could openly recognise and practised hunting *them*, placing myself in situations that I knew would draw them out into the open so that the light of consciousness could consume them.

Once consumed, I was left with a vacuum that was immediately filled with a proportionate amount of consciousness.

I have found that, every time you are consumed by defilement, it grows and you weaken.

The reverse is also true.

Every time you refrain from engagement, the shadow is consumed and you grow in proportion and strength. You grow in wisdom. You grow in resolve. You grow in patience. You grow in belief. You grow in faith. You grow in consciousness.

Every good thing in you grows and is enhanced and expanded when you stop feeding vice and start courting virtue. The person that starts out on the journey of discovery and revelation will not be the same person that breaks through the winner's tape at the end. He (or she) will be completely transformed. The totality of your personality structure will be replaced. In its stead will be a new government; the diamond body, the jewelled structure of your true self.

The Buddhists call this the Tathagata (pronounced tuh-tah-guh-tah), *the one who has thus gone, the one who has thus come.* Instead of the schizophrenia of fluctuating, ever-changing multifaceted personalities all residing in the same body, we become a singularity, the one authentic Self that is associated with the Buddha-mind. This is a Self that is beyond coming and going, beyond the transitory phenomena of the manifest world. Christians call this the Holy Grail, the station that all humanity longs for. Muslims and Jews label it *the reality of the Holy Temple.* Tibetans call it *the wish-fulfilling gem.* It is, in more common terms, the totality of blessed individuality.

In theology it is known as the observer.

In the vernacular of this book I am calling it **the divine CEO**.

I am recognising it as the place, the location, the meeting point where the properties of the lower and the properties of the higher *communicate,* and we make our divine covenant with God. From this place we become the agents of God's command, or God's creativity. Here we become truly Self-sufficient because we identify only with our higher self or God. This is the place of prophecy and vision, the Pandora's Box of Siddhas and miracles.

If we reach this station, we can generate and manifest and actualise anything that the great heart of the universe desires. It is the ultimate body of bliss that generates blessings.

The young Geoff Thompson, that lovely but naïve inner-pioneer who started his search for truth by working as a nightclub bouncer, the young greenhorn on his first shift, was not the veteran who stood on the same doors some eight years later. And equally, that very well intentioned lesser-jihadist, courageous but ignorant, driven but ill-informed, is certainly not the peace-loving, God-serving soul that sits here today, at this computer, typing out the words that you are reading from the page.

These are vastly different beings.

The neophyte believed he had enemies in the world and he needed to defeat them with violence.

The stalwart, this authentic Self, knows that he has no enemies other than the enemies he harbours in his own heart.

I risked my life to acquire this knowledge.

I killed off and fought off many false beliefs and twisted perceptions and disparate personalities and adverse forces to reveal this truth.

The monsters, the devils, that approached me in those clubs and on my journey were manifest projections of what I had unconsciously invited into my heart.

That is what I was shown.

That is the summation of my learning.

My enemies were not in the world.

No they were not.

My enemies were in me, only projecting into the world.

Once I had placed a guard against the door of my heart, I no longer had enemies, in here, or out there; only energy forms looking to claim or be claimed.

I had to face down and absorb 99% of the lie in order to reveal this one nugget of truth.

It was worth every effort.

As I mentioned already, several times, if there are supernatural elements in the world, it is only by their exaggeration that we will see them in their reality. Once we recognise that the monsters and demons are merely projections from the bardo of our own minds, these three-dimensional monsters will become two-dimensional cartoons. And these two-dimensional cartoons will pop like inflated balloons under the scrutiny of an observing eye.

When we can see this, we become our very own exorcist.

As you oust the devils and demons of scripture, you reveal your true Self; your conscious net expands, and you automatically start to notice the shadow in others.

Your presence, your Light will draw out their defilements, and your observation of the same will leave them exposed and either running for their lives or dead in the air. You won't necessarily be aware that this is happening at first but trust me it will happen; you will notice your own expanded consciousness in the way your own expanded consciousness affects others. Some people will act oddly around you. They may appear agitated or uncomfortable, they might squirm in your presence; sometimes they even become aggressive or confrontational. Often their shadow will take them in the opposite direction and they'll become sycophantic and servile towards you.

Or they might just avoid your company all together.

Certainly, you will draw their criticism, although this will usually be from afar; the World Wide Web is an abode for many of these cowardly energies.

Others will simply be drawn to the goodness they feel in you. They will want to be close to you, but won't necessarily know why. They will want to hear you speak. They will feel the urge to physically touch you; many will be physically and romantically attracted to you.

This is all to be expected and taken in sober consideration.

You can see how easily this can be misused if you have not developed your inner control, if you are not constant in your covenant.

Don't let it go to your head. Just notice it as phenomena. And definitely don't let the ego dine out on the flattery. If you do the fish will die in the mouth.

It is not you they see, or want to hear, or urge to touch; it is divinity in you that attracts human-bees to the divine nectar.

Of those that do criticise and attack, don't take any of it personally, even if it seems to be very personal indeed.

Remember they are not themselves.

This does not mean they are not dangerous, many of them can be treacherous and you need to remain on your highest alert around these unstable energies. They should be guarded against, but none of it should be taken personally. If it feels personal to you, it means your lower ego has been baited and hooked and you are being reeled in. From a developmental perspective, this is all good; anyone that hooks you is your teacher, they will help you to evolve. They are showing you where you need to up your game and tighten your defences. They are the whetstones, and you can use them to sharpen and prove your consciousness.

Many of the critical types are selective-blind to their own shadow. To your face they'll absolutely deny that they have been critical of you. One man I cornered (in the street, in the flesh, no Internet pseudonym to hide behind) swore on the death of his own son that he had never attacked me, even though there was a trail of bile with his name on it all across the Internet. Another man, an old friend whose character had fallen, denied outright that he'd ever said anything about me, and even if he did *it was a long time ago*. He became mute when I quietly drew his attention to the fact that he was online only the day before saying the most unqualified and unkind things about me. Later that same day, when my name was placed on the Internet whipping-post for a further lashing, he posted: *let's take this discussion offline, there's a spy in the camp.*

He knew that I knew he was duplicitous, even as he posted he knew I was observing him, and yet was still unable to stop the demon of devise from possessing him, only hours after he'd denied all existence of deceit.

The reason you will draw attention is because you will be mask-less in a room full of masked people and this does not go unnoticed.

My daughter Lisa, who has the most beautiful nature, never gets involved in gossip or character-assassination in any of its forms. She doesn't have to work too hard at this, it is her way. One evening she, her boss at the office, and two other colleagues had to attend an after-work conference. My daughter was not drinking, so she offered to drive. A few minutes into the journey the boss started to slander a man in their office that she particularly disliked. Very quickly all of Lisa's passengers joined in the pillory and were devouring the man's character; it was relentless and unkind. It quickly became clear to everyone that Lisa was quiet; she was not joining in the attack. This greatly discomforted her boss.

*"So what do you think of him?"* she asked, trying to pressure Lisa into the fray.

Lisa said quietly, *"I really like him. He's very nice to me."*

The boss spent the rest of the very uncomfortable journey desperately trying to justify and defend her views, but of course was unable to. On arrival at their destination, the boss left the car completely deflated because *one* aligned person observed her behaviour, without engagement.

They quickly learned that Lisa was not the person to gossip in front of.

This is a small example of exposing demons.

Exorcism of these divided energies occurs when the person you are helping asks for their incongruence to be exposed.

I am not saying that being aligned is going to win you a bunch of friends, especially around people who like to defame others, but it will win you a clean heart.

I make a point of not telling people, unless they specifically ask me, if they are harbouring duality.

It is none of my business.

I have enough work to do still on myself without concerning myself with the shadows of others.

It is a full-time job trying to correct yourself, let alone anyone else.

It would also be folly on my behalf, trying to clear people of their shadows or their doubts or fears, if they haven't asked me for help or they are not aligned enough to accept help. For those I am called upon to assist, via my inner tutor, I do my utmost to expose what I see without any sense of judgment.

As a man that has committed every human error, I am not in a position to judge anyone. That leaves me ideally positioned to be an objective exorcist of shadows.

Within the small group of people I mentor, those who ask for my inner vision, I simply say what I see, perhaps qualify what I see if qualification is called for, and – if it is ordained – I may enter into a dissolving dialectic with them to help bring the defilement out into the open so that it can be disqualified and evicted.

Once the squatter is removed, nature will break it down into its constituent parts.

## Cleaning the Atmosphere

Once you are steady in your Self, your own conscious-presence, you will find that negativity will not sit easily around you.

This is a very gratifying Siddha.

Your atmosphere will be free to expand at will, and clean any area you inhabit.

I sat outside a café recently (by way of a small example). On the next table to me, two girls were destroying the character of an absent friend. Without engaging this in any way, without looking at them (my back was to them), I slowed my breathing, I stilled all my thoughts until they were completely silent, and I visualised waves of calm energy radiating all around me, like ripples of light.

It only took a moment or two before one of the girls grabbed her bag and her coffee and said to her friend, *"Shall we sit somewhere else?"*

She offered no reason, she just got up with her friend and they moved away.

There have also been times where it was me who has fallen out of alignment, brought a bad atmosphere to a place, and quickly found myself drinking burnt coffee, sitting next to a walking, talking defilement.

You really do take your atmosphere with you wherever you go.

On one such occasion, I was sat outside the same café in a dark mood (I had been pulled out of sync by a challenging personal situation). I looked to my right and there on the next table along sat a muttering, fidgeting, derangement of a man. He was two feet away from me, and he was snarling.

When this happens I know I have fallen out of religion.

As soon as I recognise my remiss, I work quickly to redress the balance and bring my world back into line.

You might think you have little or no effect on the atmosphere that surrounds you. My experience tells me that you *are* the atmosphere that surrounds you.

I take full responsibility for everything that occurs in my world.

Even if I can't detect the immediate reason for a dark-atmosphere, I always come back to myself for the original cause.

A young girl once ran into the back of my very posh car.

It was parked outside my in-laws' house. We were inside having tea when we heard the loud bang outside from the collision. The girl (it turned out) ran into the back of my parked car like it was invisible, she didn't even see it.

My first thought on hearing the collision was, *I am out of alignment. Where am I out of alignment?* When something as drastic as this happens in my own atmosphere, it tells me immediately that something in my inner life is awry. It alerts me to the fact that I must have already been given other more subtle signs, but for whatever reason, had not heeded them. This heavy shot across the bow was telling me loud and clear *you are not yourself.*

In theosophical circles this is knows as a spiritual **shock**; I will expand on this anomaly in the relevant chapter.

Enough to say that your atmosphere will draw out the defilements in others.

And, you will also be shown very clearly when you are out of alignment yourself.

This is a powerful, if exponential Siddha.

It comes into its own when people ask you to help them internally cleanse.

If you are not working with people directly, knowing the effect you will have on others is a welcome forewarning. You can adjust your atmosphere accordingly, tone it down as it were, or even switch it off if you find yourself unable to enjoy a coffee at your local Costa, for all the demons running around the place.

If someone has asked you for help, you can play your part in removing their pain-bodies.

This may very well be your dharma on this earth, or a part of it, but you must never lose sight of the fact that your job proper, first and foremost, is to evict your own shadows.

Self-cleansing is the very gist of the next chapter, the divine work.

## Chapter 9

# The Divine Work

The divine work may seem varied and specific, often it is *seemingly* random or confusingly disparate. Ultimately, the divine work always has a singular intent: work on the Self.

It is never going to get bigger than this.

In the Gita, Krishna, the Godhead, tells his fearful friend Arjuna Pandava, *lift the self by the Self, never let the self droop down, for the self is the Self's only enemy, the Self is the self's only friend.*

If I was to translate this so that it read a little more user-friendly, it would go something like this: *lift the lower ego, by the Soul, never let the ego droop down, the lower ego is the Soul's only enemy, the Soul is the ego's only friend.*

If I were to reduce it further still, to its very essence, I would say that, *the ego is the Soul's only enemy, the Soul is the ego's only friend.*

Working on the self, helping the divine ego to ascend, cleansing and preparing the vessel ready for the higher Soul to descend, so that integration can occur, this *is* the divine work.

Whether you are running a nine-figure charity, feeding the hungry at a homeless shelter or sweeping floors in a local factory, it's of little consequence if you are not working on yourself, *and* if you are not working from the Self.

An honour from the queen and letters after your name for service to the community is worthless tat if acclaim is your hidden purpose. It would be more powerful to quietly, anonymously pray for the person who abused you or slighted you or harmed your family.

Working on yourself is the divine work.

This might mean working on yourself whilst you head a global conglomerate, or it might mean working on yourself whilst stacking shelves in your local supermarket.

Either or either, it makes no difference, as long as you are working from Love.

If you are not working from Love, you are not working at all. You really are not working.

St. Paul says it more succinctly than most: *"If I could speak in all the tongues of the earth and of angels, but did not love others, I would only be a noisy gong or a clanging cymbal."*

He was saying that, no matter what you do, no matter how grand it might appear to the world of men, and no matter how richly society rewards you for it, if it does not come from love, it is as nothing.

And yet, the smallest, most insignificant offering, if it does come from love, will be enough to feed the Christ and the whole of His divine universe.

How do you know that you are working from love?

To start off with, if you are working from love, you will feel no need to announce your charity. You will not look for external validation or acknowledgement or reward. In fact you will actively avoid it. The need for recognition should be eschewed and public anonymity sought wherever possible.

The best charity is anonymous.

The need to share your charitable work with others, the desire for your goodness to be seen, is a sure sign that the ego has stolen recognition for something that the divine CEO has delivered.

In the Kabbalah, it warns us never to tell a living soul of the good deeds we do, not even implicitly. Guard your services like pearls, because the moment the ego makes announcements and steals credit, the thread of good-deeds is broken and your cache of aligned deeds annulled. The power gained is lost and those precious jewels scatter like worthless marbles.

All good works build up a cache of credit, owed-reciprocity, good karma that you will reap when the timing is right. But it can all be wiped out in an instant when we blab about our deeds to even a single soul. We have to decide early on: do we want the momentary bask of temporal reward, or do we desire the eternal glow for our gratis from the divine economy?

The Kabbalah also assures us, not to worry about our anonymity, what *we* keep secret someone will eventually discover and tell. Someone will find out about your divine work, they will inform others and the reward for your modesty will be multiplied.

When we hear about someone's tremendous kindness to others, but not from the benefactor themselves, they are automatically elevated in our esteem. But even then, when people do find out, still be modest. There is no room for personal pride; when you know that you are not the doer of your deeds, you are not the one who gifts: you are simply the delivery-driver.

Do the work, expect nothing.

A friend of the diarist Etty Hillesum said to her, *you always work with no expectation, and that is why you never leave empty-handed.*

Those who serve with no expectation are always rewarded.

Working this philosophy in the climate of corporate-earth is of course the greatest challenge.

To those of you reading these words who think my tender naïve and unworkable in a capitalist society, I dare say you just haven't tried hard enough yet.

The key, of course, is not just to make divine philosophy work from a remote location, a hut on a mountain in the middle of nowhere, or a cave hidden in the Amazon, separated from people. The challenge is to prove its efficacy on the razor's edge, in the very challenging, heavily peopled manifest world.

It is possible.

I have a powerful history of putting theory into practice in challenging environments.

In the martial arts, I didn't take anyone else's word for

anything. I put what I had learned in a safe sports hall to the test in hostile environments. I wanted to know that my technique would work against assailants who might kill me if it didn't.

I demand the same rigour and proof with metaphysical practice.

Companies, people and companies of people make it work.

They make it work because they put God at the very heart of all they do. And they cleanse themselves, their boardroom and their company – just as surely as the spiritual adept cleanses his body, mind and soul – of any defilement that prevents perfect function.

It is said that money is the root of all evil.

I have not found this to be true.

There can be divine money. There can be divine profit. There can be divine capitalism. The bibles are rich with examples of virtuous commerce. The Parable of the Talents (Matthew 25:14-30) is all about divine capital, passed from Father to sons, for investment in the 'marketplace' This karmic world of ours, too, is built on capitalist law; what is scientific reciprocity if not proof of the profit and loss of human action. Our body, by its very nature, is a capitalist state. The use or misuse of our seminal, essential energies in the body and through the body is all about investment and return. Even the essence (or spirit) gifted by our Source, when we agree a holy covenant, is a divine capital that we process through the bodily-infrastructure and invest into the universe.

It is intent that determines the nature of money or energy, not the money or energy itself.

Everything can be divine if Love – the frequency of love – is at the genesis of transaction.

If you are sat there now (yes, you!), reading this book, reflecting on your own life, your own business or work or company, perhaps already recognising some of your personal practices that are not in religion with Love, and the very idea of these changes seems intimidating and unlikely, take heart. If you can change one small aspect a day or a week or even a month in your business operations, before you know it you will have a divine workplace and the product, the service that comes out of it will be aligned.

Your company is an extension of you.

Of course it is. How could it be otherwise?

If there are hidden corruptions at work, they are the exaggerations of the hidden corruptions that exist in you.

You are the company.

The company is you.

A politician once tried to convince me that his depraved and dishonest personal life had nothing to do with his business in public life. There was no connection, he insisted. Who he was in private was completely separate to who he was at work. He believed that one did not affect the other; there was no relationship or communication between the two.

The very fact that he proffered this weak argument as a working belief should have automatically disqualified him from any sort of public office. It tells you immediately that he does not even have a grasp of basic causation.

Would a politician that betrays his wife and cheats his children treat us, the general anonymous public, any better? We, the folk in his constituency, are practically strangers to him. We don't share a mortgage with him; we do not have children together. If he can betray his best friend *his wife* and his own blood *his children*, what chance us?

Not much chance I would vouch.

If there is a leak anywhere, there is a leak everywhere.

Divine work cannot be delivered efficiently through a divided vessel, any more than clean water can be filtered through a soiled pipe.

Another man, a company CEO, rationalised that whilst his morals and ethics might waver a little in the cut-and-thrust of big business, he is the model citizen at home and around his friends and family (and he does a lot for charity). He spoke as though he becomes somehow immune from his business operations the moment he slides on his house slippers.

Our business life and our home cannot be separated, any more than our heart and lungs can be separated just because they are located in different parts of the body. They are both working in the same infrastructure; if one fails it will not be long before the other feels the effects, and fails too.

There is no big and small in the divine work, either.

If our actions are coming from love, the prime minister and the postman are equally potent. One is not more important than the other; one is not more powerful because he runs a country whilst the other runs a postal van.

The capacity to effect change in everything is equally present in both.

Love is qualitative. It knows no quantity, it recognises no boundary.

If I connect to the mains-electric in my small Coventry office, would it be any different to you connecting to the mains-electric in your penthouse office at Facebook headquarters, or in Buckingham Palace, or Westminster?

The world out there is temporal.

The temporal world only has the power to affect temporal things.

Nothing and no one can stop you (whoever you are) from connecting to the Unlimited, Unaffected, and Incorruptible source of Love. If you connect to Love, wherever you are, whoever you are, you share equal potential with anyone else walking this spinning planet. As a connected being, everything you do, from plastering your kitchen wall to painting the *Last Supper*, from leading a country, to parenting a child, is equally powerful.

Lord Krishna tells his servant that as little as a handful of rice, gifted with love, is enough to serve the Godhead, and the whole of his universe.

As to the specifics of divine work, each of us has a natural bias, an authentic talent, our very own specific story to live and to tell in our own unique way.

If we haven't discovered what this is yet, then our initial purpose is to find out and then have the courage and conviction to surrender to it, to follow it, despite the personal or familial or societal pressures to do otherwise.

We have to remove the veils of obscuration, through the processes laid out in this text. This cleansing will reveal the true Self, and the true Self will reveal the individual part we are each called to play in the divine plan. The task then is to orchestrate our lives in such a way that we can follow it.

At this time in our evolution, there is a worldwide trend of looking for fame or fortune or public applause outside of our natural bias. People seek acclaim for doing something or attempting to do something that is not in alignment with their true calling. They are humiliated on public television for vacuous applause, betting their souls against the house, and for what? A tin hat and a specious title? To wear the hollow-crown of celebrity?

We already know how this ends; we can bet against the house but the house always wins.

And every viewer who tunes into the televisual-colosseum of titillation and torture is as guilty of inflicting pain on *someone's daughter, someone's son,* as the current Caesar of modernity who gives the thumbs up or the thumbs down to contestants, some of whom are clearly mentally unwell.

A lot of people are looking for acclaim or celebrity, without doing anything to be acclaimed for or anything worthy of celebration.

Not necessarily because their talent is not impressive, rather because they are unconsciously presenting themselves as something opposite to their truth.

In motoring metaphor: it is no good trying to be a piston if your natural bias is towards being a wheel arch. What sense is there in trying to be a headlight when you are more naturally designed to be an indicator or a brake pad?

You meet schoolteachers who should really be artists.

You meet artists who are incongruent because their calling is to be a schoolteacher.

I worked with a wonderful woman once, an unlikely martial arts teacher, who taught self-defence classes to men, women and children. She presented herself as a martial arts pioneer. She was a good martial artist, but an adept she was not. It wasn't her calling. In reality her natural bias was towards art – she was born to paint. She never received the acclaim she craved in martial arts and she never will, because those who 'knew' knew that she was a woman in the wrong room.

Society – our early schooling and experience, or learned or inherited perceptions – and those adverse forces can and will lead us a thousand miles away from our true calling, if we let them. We are either herded towards mediocrity by negatively conditioned teaching, or we are seduced by bright-lights and shiny-keys, the false-signature of societal distraction.

Society can be guilty too of offering us a very black-and-white model of what success is and is not. From my own experience I can honestly say that the only true success is to live according to your nature, your unique intuitive bent.

When you do this you will automatically be working from Love.

When you truly love what you do, how can it be any other way?

If you are working from your own individual signature, it matters not in the jigsaw of life whether you are a hardly-noticed corner piece of light blue sky, or the central-eye of the canvas. No piece of the puzzle is any more or any less important than another, no matter how much this might seem to be the case. The only important thing is that you are fitted into the hole you were divinely cut for and not squeezed into an indent that clearly does not fit your shape.

It is much more common today, perhaps more so than ever before, to see people squeezed into the wrong hole in the wrong picture of the wrong life.

The natural bias reveals itself to those who want to see.

But even if you do know your purpose, the obstacles of conditioned life will still have to be removed before you can act on it.

I knew I was called to be a writer. It was my dream from a very early age, but it still took me many years of internal work before I could orchestrate my life to make the dream a reality.

The old conditioning, the fears, the doubts, the uncertainty have to be removed in order to make room for your unique voice.

I mentioned earlier that doing this is simple enough in principle but very challenging in process.

You will not make it happen without some form of invisible support.

Whether that inner help is inspired by a masterpiece in an art gallery, or a rock band at a festival, or through the stillness of meditation, or direct from the divine himself, is not important. What is important, in fact imperative, is that you **do** have inner help.

Locate your inner help.

Call on it for clarity.

Call on it for guidance and balm.

If the specific nature of your calling currently eludes you, ask.

Go into your inspired place, the church, the synagogue, through directed meditation, or spontaneous meditation in nature; go inside and ask.

This is what I did.

This is what I do.

If I get ever lost, if I lose my religion, this is my method of reconnection.

In the meantime, if you don't currently know your dharma, be present with where you are right now.

Be in the moment with the person you are with.

Be present with what you are doing in this exact instant.

Be patient with your current situation; that you have a situation at all in this glorious world is in itself the greatest gift.

Many disembodied souls would love to climb out of their oak sarcophagus, they would give every last penny for just one hour at the coffee shop you sit in right now; or on the train that is transporting you from here to there as you read these words, or in that bed with the gorgeous soul who shares it with you.

Once you fill your day with presence, with the simple and sincere gratitude for just being alive, all your works will be divine, have no doubt.

There is nothing more effective for removing the veils that hide your destiny than presence.

Once you locate and become aligned to your divine work, every exchange you make with your fellow beings will be an exchange of Love, an exchange of God, a divine exchange.

## Chapter 10

# The Divine Exchange

Most people spend their time trying to get on, trying to get ahead, trying to get out, or get in, or get laid, or get rich, or simply get by.

I spent most of my earlier life trying to get noticed.

I felt hollow and worthless inside.

I wanted skills.

I wanted success and money and knowledge and acclaim.

I craved accolades like a starving man at theking's table.

I wanted the big house, the fast car; I dreamed of the beautiful girl on my arm and the ear of friends in high places – all external things.

In my life so far, I have managed to experience all of the above but... none of it sated me. None of it filled the hole in me because I was a hungry ghost and ten entire worlds would not have satisfied my hunger.

I didn't know who I was.

Not knowing who I was, I either became what others were, or what others wanted me to be, or what they (or I) thought I should be. I modelled others; I copied, I mirrored, I wore masks, I donned a plethora of different disguises; I was the man with a thousand faces. I had a mask for every occasion, a fake-front that made me look like someone else *but not as good* because to be someone else is to be a fraud, a facsimile, a no-name-no-one. I did what other people did or what I thought other people approved of. I hunted for certificates and chased trophies and was quite happy to sneak under the fence and cheat the system in order to get acclaim, because it was the trophy that mattered to me, accolades mean you are someone... right?

I competed for the 10,000 things and I won, but they did not sate me.

None of the comforts I grasped at made me happy, because they were not me.

I needed to find me!

When I eventually did find myself, I didn't have to look far; he was there all the time, underneath the subterfuge, the clutter, just below those fancy masks.

I let the self-clutter go.

I can't tell you how liberating it was to jettison the ostentation, the labels I wore round my neck like a leper bell. I can't even begin to articulate how much easier I could breathe when I freed my lungs from the congestion of conceit and pretence.

When you *are* authentic, of course you automatically start to do authentic things. You find your natural bias (it comes as a package with the **real** you) and you start to do what you are meant to do. It is deliciously sating. You are filled. The hungry ghost of modern consumption dies and you no longer feel the need to be noticed as the personality Geoff Thompson or the individual John Smith or the birth-name Sarah Jones, because being authentic gets you noticed simply because you are unique; and in a world full of facsimiles, that is rare.

It's not the name on your passport that gets the attention; it is the light of originality that shines through you.

This is the process we have been following so far in this book: understanding eschatology; identifying the divine economy; transcending the fall; electing a sentinel ego; kicking out the shadow-squatters; cleansing etc. Once you find home, your original signature, you no longer crave or need external validation. The notice-me trophies of position, of acclaim or success are eschewed. In fact, the moment you arrive at your authentic self, you let go of anything superfluous. You don't need it. It is surplus to requirements. It dulls your original shine. It is stifling, all that glut, and so unnecessary, it's like wearing seven overcoats on a sunny day.

If there are two worlds, as we have suggested in this book, the manifest, temporal world, and the real world of eternity, then in the real world all you need in order to be noticed is your Self – capital S.

I read a beautiful story in a book called *Absence of Felicity* that I would like to paraphrase here. It illustrates my point perfectly. The book is about Helen Schucman, an American professor of medical psychology, who scribed a very famous book of spiritual revelation and instruction called *A Course in Miracles*. During the period when she acted as the medium for this book, she had lots of profound spiritual insights and visions. In one particular vision Helen found herself in what she referred to as *a new place*. She described her ethereal location as a beautiful, peaceful new world. In this place she met a very gentle man – someone that appeared in many of her subsequent visions, who she later identified as the prophet Jesus. Helen said this divine place was serene and calm, and without anxiety or fear. In the vision the man invited Helen to stay: *you can live here all the time if you'd like.*

Although the place was idyllic, Helen still felt perturbed: who was this man and what was the catch, what did he want from her?

*If I did decide to come here,* she insisted, *I'd have to bring all my things with me, my clothes, and my work.* The man assured Helen that all her personal items would be unnecessary, she would only need the clothes she was wearing, everything else would be provided for her. Helen felt a jolt of fear. *So you're telling me before we even start that there are limitations in this place, you are saying that I can't even bring my own wardrobe with me?*

The man smiled kindly. He assured her that she could bring anything she wanted to bring, she could bring everything if it made her feel better but, *once you get here, you'll realise you won't need any of it. As I said everything here is provided for you.* There was moment of impasse. Helen was confused.

*But... if I haven't got all my things,* she asked, *how will I be noticed?*

*Ah that's easy.* The man said. *Just be kind. Everyone will notice you if you are kind.*

**Just be kind.**

Just be kind – that is the sum of the total of every scripture of every bible I have ever read.

Just be kind.

Every bliss I ever felt, the ones that lasted, those that stayed with me, the moments that counted all came from either me being kind to other beings, other beings showing kindness to me, or simply witnessing the kindness of others in action; especially when the kindness was proffered at a time of pain or fear or vulnerability.

Kindness.

Treat others as you would have them treat you.

This one line is said to be the essence of the Torah, the Five Books of Moses, as delivered to him by Gabriel on the Mount of Sinai. And the Torah itself is believed to be the blueprint of the universe.

Be kind.

If you would be noticed, simply be kind.

Be noticed in the only place that matters. Not the dog-eat-dog world of fiscal and business scrimmage, where cold, hard, mutton deals are dressed up to look like lamb. I'm not talking about the hand that helps the sick and lame and then opens its palm for the coin of commerce or reward or acknowledgement. Certainly I am not talking about the heart that will not enter into any human interaction or transaction without the guarantee of return.

I am talking about an exchange of energy that is so pure and so spontaneous and so aligned and natural that the exchange itself is the only reward you will need, because it is saturated in bliss.

The business and the fiscal and material returns are not dirty or bad or wrong in any way. That is not what I'm suggesting. They are the usual compensations that come as a result of any exchange. It is only when we mistake the worldly reward for the goal *proper* that we fall from grace, and the connection of earth and heaven is broken.

At our current stage of human evolution, material exchange is the currency of the age. For the time being, this kind of conditioned barter is the way people do business. It would be naïve to ignore this, and while you are in the world – unless your home is a cave and you live off prana – some level of monetary exchange will remain necessary. There is no wisdom in hating money, it makes no sense to judge or hate capitalism or eschew the fiscal exchange. While you still need to put almond milk in your eco-friendly fridge, while you still need a fridge to put your almond milk in, in fact (as I said earlier) while you continue to walk around in that delightful body of yours, you are partaking in capitalism.

I don't care what your business is, or what line of work you find yourself in. Wherever you are you can still make divine-exchange your gold-standard. If you cut a £5 deal or turn a $5 billion profit, you can still put love at the heart of commerce; you can ensure that your intercourse includes its own *ethical and moral promises*, an elegance to the Hippocratic Oath, chief of which is *primum non nocere* – **to do no harm.**

If you have to lie, if you have to use subterfuge, coerce, bribe, exert pressure, omit facts, if you have to do anything that threatens your ethical and moral vow, you have already caused harm, not least to yourself.

This is not a slight at big business or an attack on capitalism (we are all capitalists).

The monk Thomas Merton was able to spend his life in study and contemplation at a beautiful monastery in the US *because* of the generosity of businessmen and women, some of whom, Merton said, were probably more holy than many of the monks who actually lived and studied in the monastery.

The Hindu mystic Sai Baba built a $100 million hospital in India from proceeds donated by the founder of a New York conglomerate.

The Brahma Kumaris – a wonderful worldwide female-led spiritual organisation – relies entirely on the fiscal donations of women and men who are not afraid to move their money in the direction of patronage, when intuition calls.

I have friends who hate money.

They hate money and they judge (read hate) people who deal in money.

In hating money, they eschew it.

But to hate money is to also hate God.

Money is one of the many shapes we sculpt with Divine effulgence.

Money is divine if money is used divinely, be in no doubt.

Either God is omnipotent or She is not.

If He is omnipotent and omniscient and omnipresent, He is present in every mote of dust and that includes the pound note or the dollar bill or the Chinese Yen.

If it is your calling, cash may be the medium that your dharma calls you to work with.

If your bias is away from the fiscal, you will be directed to limit your dealings with the world of money. Again, this is all to do with your connection to the divine CEO, and the individual communication you receive.

Spiritual discernment is the sword you will need to cut through the confusion of right and wrong in business, between knowing what is truly rational and rationalising what is clearly immoral.

I've met men running £100 million illegal drug operations, who use weak rationalisation to justify their business.

We all know companies that deliberately confuse, and mislead and fleece the masses.

They harm other human beings for profit.

They produce and sell goods and services that they know will harm, even kill their customers, but are still able to rationalise their dealings by contorting their ethics in order to justify their greed.

No matter. This is not for me to ponder over or judge, only to say that a deep dialectic is called for when we deal in any commodity, human or otherwise, that can garner greed.

If you are aligned in any way to the divine economy, you will not need me to tell you any of this.

Your conscience will already have told you, loud and clear.

Conscience is the first outcrop of consciousness.

Conscience is also the first thing to get buried when we start out on a dark path.

We can't let ourselves rationalise our deceits with comments like *there are a few grey areas in my company accounts, but... or that's just business, that's just how business works.*

As a savvy politician once advised, on achieving clarity with ethical behaviour, *If you wouldn't like to see what you have done written in tomorrow's newspaper, don't do it today.*

The purest exchange of divine energy is when there are no expectations, no agenda, and no defilements in the exchange.

It is an exchange without condition.

In business of course, as in life, there are many conditions attached to our exchanges; contracts that we're expected to honour – the promissory note, the fidelity of friendship or marriage, the contractual agreements of employment, even buying a loaf from the corner shop comes with the expectation that you will exchange an equal and agreed amount of coin for your daily bread.

The world of causation is an entire territory of karmic conditions that we break at our peril.

But, even amongst all of this, we can still work our deals, with the world, with the people and the institutions of the world, from a place of truth, from the stance of Love.

If the word love offends, or it isn't potent enough for you, operate – as I said somewhere else – from the philosophy of *primum non nocere* (to do no harm).

Or, if I can make it clearer still: don't lie to win the deal.

This is a difficult concept, of course, because even people who sell illegal drugs, and arms, and cigarettes, those that flog products and services in a way that they know *will* do harm, still rationalise their bad, saying that they are *not responsible* for the choices that their customers make, and that (this is a big rationalisation) if they didn't sell it (whatever their product is) someone else would.

Let's be clear; if you have to manipulate the truth in order to complete the exchange, you are doing harm.

You are starting a chain of causation that has its own autonomy, that contains its own inbuilt arc; it has a homing device that will always reunite the effect with its cause.

The discussion of ethics is a tome in itself, and we could go back and forth for millennia trying to discern what truth is. I won't do that, it would be patronising, because you already know what truth is, your conscience is screaming it at you. Why else would you be reading a book called *The Divine CEO*?

I will offer you the advice that was proffered to me, when I once took an ethical issue to a profoundly righteous business friend of mine (David Carr), looking for advice.

He said: **"I think you should do the right thing."**

He knew that I already knew what the right thing was.

I know that you know what the right thing is too.

We can dedicate ourselves to only choosing exchanges that are aligned and true.

If they are aligned and true, our covenant with the divine economy will be met. If the divine economy sanctions our exchange, we will see the optimum result in the world.

It is worth reiterating, too, that everything you give to others has to be processed through you first. This knowledge reminds us that every intercourse of energy, even sexual intercourse, needs to be pure. Sexual intercourse should be between you and your partner without a flood of foreign impressions, intercourse with no thought of another person or another image muddying the exchange. It is not a pure intercourse if, when I have sex with my wife, I am imagining having sex with someone else in my mind's eye, or if I am using pornographic imagery as an arousing stimulus.

Whoever said that *window shopping* (ogling men or women sexually, without physical consummation) is fine as long *as you don't go in and buy* obviously didn't know much about the sensitive nature of our impressionable minds.

All the bibles concur that, *if we have thought it, we have done it.*

Theologians recognise crime-by-thought as the first betrayal.

Psychologists will also tell you that the mind cannot discern between what is strongly imagined and what is actually done, so again, as far as our neurology is concerned, if we are thinking it, we are doing it.

When we are working with the divine economy, every exchange is equally important, none less so, none more so. Your interactions with those you consider to be of no importance or of no profit to you need to be as pure and aligned and considered as your interaction with the most influential person in your life.

I have friends who admire and look up to me.

They love me and they treat me with great respect.

They afford me the greatest reverence; there is nothing they wouldn't do for me, if asked.

Who is the most influential person in your life?

Do you treat everyone in your life with the same reverence as that favoured person?

Is your exchange with the least as pure and unconditional as your exchange with the best?

If not, then there is work to be done.

**The way you treat the least of you,** the Christ tells us, **is the way you treat me.**

This is not just some unworkable, unqualified ideology; it is a statement of fact.

Everything in the divine economy affects everything else.

The way you treat *the least* will affect you, physically, emotionally, psychologically, biologically, neurologically, physiologically, sociologically, metaphysically, consciously and divinely.

To harbour even a thought of ill-will towards another is a conceit; it is an act of ignorance that creates a cocktail of dangerous corrosives in your own being. Worse than this, it places obscuration between you and your Source. If you even consider someone to be less than you, let alone treat them as less, you know automatically and without doubt, know that you are *not yourself*; you have been hijacked by the false ego, and the fish dies in the mouth.

You will know this because the authentic self, the soul does not discriminate. It knows that everything has a divine signature; everyone is moulded from the same divine clay.

Everyone is you, and you are everyone.

What you do to others, you do to yourself.

This is why is makes perfect sense to be kind and to do no harm.

If you treat the *least of you* with compassion, compassion will permeate you.

If you treat *the least* with judgment, you automatically cast a dangerous spell of judgment on every conscious, sentient cell in your own body.

It might sound as though the divine exchange is asking everything of us.

Well, that's because it is. Of course it is.

But *everything* in this temporal realm is but a grain of sand by comparison to the vast beaches of abundance we receive in return.

Divine reciprocity is full of Beauty, it is the greatest Bounty.

It also asks everything because anything less than everything is not enough.

Complete and utter surrender to the divine economy is called for, if the doors to the kingdom are to open, otherwise it would be like knowing five numbers of a six-number combination lock. One number short is as impotent as six numbers short, because it still won't unlock the mechanism.

Holding a television plug close to the socket, even very close, will not connect me to the mains electricity.

There has to be complete, unconditional intercourse between the lower ego and Self, and between the Self and the divine.

The hardest thing, as I said, is making the divine exchange on the razor's edge, in the world of men, the field of human commerce.

And that is the work right there; this constitutes our daily practice.

The idea of this book is not to tell you that (in the words of Jesus) *you must sell everything and follow me*; rather it is to suggest that you create a personal paradigm shift, take your exchanges to a completely different dimension, get rid of the mundane methods of exchange and follow consciousness.

You must sell your old egoic ways and follow conscience.

This new standard may take you completely away from the life you lead now, or it might lead you deeper into the same life, but with the new broom of awareness.

I have no idea which way you should go or where you will end up.

I'm not privy to your unique role in the divine plan.

But you... you can know and you can make those alterations and you can make sure that, if nothing else, you are living a life where you are kind in all your dealings, at the very least you can live a life where you are doing no harm.

Once you are established in this station – and this shift can happen in an instant – every opportunity to exchange energy (money, goods, service, emotional) will be an opportunity to make the exchange at the level of divine joy. You will be walking around with a smile on your face because you'll recognise that everything is divine, everything is conscious. You will see that you are already intercoursing with the 10,000 things, only now that you know it, you will be able to start doing it more consciously.

Then it will feel as though everyone you interact with is presenting themselves as they truly are: naked, without artifice, mask-less, and they'll all be available to make an exchange of energy that will be optimum for all involved.

There will be no more contrivances.

All networking will be divine networking.

You will be placed in front of the right people at the right time and in the right manner to make the right exchange.

The hierarchy of man will be redundant.

The most powerful person in a room will not be the one with the most expensive car or the most powerful contact-book; these things in and of themselves have no value in the divine economy. The most connected person in the room will be the one you have been ordained to meet, sanctioned to serve, and instructed to engage.

You will start to recognise the *soul* behind every mask.

You will see hidden-authenticity behind even the most hideous exterior.

Everything in the temporal world will present to you as a coded message from above. A code that you will be equipped to break.

The divine exchange, service at the level of Love, is what we are here to do.

Like the bees of the field collecting nectar for their queen, when we serve others divinely en route, every other living thing in our universe will be pollinated as the exponential effect of our gathering.

If this sounds complicated, it is, and it is not.

All the holy texts will tell you the same thing: the truth is simple, it is undeniable, and it is right in front of you.

If, at this moment in time, you are struggling to see truth, don't worry, there are teachers who can help. Some of them will come to you in human form, and some will present themselves in an incorporeal manner. These divine guides are waiting in the wings, they have been recruited particularly for those seeking knowledge, and they have been assembled specifically for you.

# Chapter 11

# Divine Teachers

There is disagreement in theological circles as to whether or not the student of metaphysics needs a guru, or whether it is possible to turn directly to the source and connect with the genesis of all teachers.

It is a squabble that presumes much, not least that every man is not his own organic 'vaticanus ager' with its own papacy and its own congregation.

*Every man is his own church,* Father Martin Luther assures us.

To say that we need a corporeal guru to reach our potential is also to miss the obvious (perhaps not so obvious): when we begin the journey to our own personal Omega Point, our movement is *noticed*, and in being noticed, every conscious molecule in the cosmos is ordained to us as teachers. We become a pupil of the whole universe when we fully surrender ourselves to instruction. Every atom will bend itself to our service. Every element will fall at our feet and offer the divine triptych of instruction, nourishment and service.

You might think that this is a metaphor, a grand announcement that God is everywhere and will bring all Its servants to your aid when you open the human tabernacle to learning.

It is not a metaphor.

I am being literal.

*Where are they then, these teachers, these servants?*

I was asked this question by a sceptic once, a naysayer.

*Where are these servants, in this world of pain and lament, where are they?*

## Servants

Let's look at those who serve us first.

Where are they exactly?

They are everywhere. Of course.

And, if you've not yet developed the art of observation, they are nowhere to be seen.

Your body is your first servant.

Let's start with that shall we; your body is the most amazing servant to the soul.

It is made up of trillions of individual cells, each conscious, each and every one throwing themselves into the fire of your consumption.

I've seen these cells.

In a divine vision, I witnessed them.

They are conscious of you, their king, they know you.

They are conscious of you and your world, even if you are not conscious of them and their sacrifice.

Our ability to see and hear and smell and touch and sense is miraculous in itself, these are gifts beyond fathom. The body's capacity to shape-shift at your command is also a miracle. It hasn't been forged by the furnace of millennia just so that you can watch cats doing crazy things on the World Wide Web. It was not designed, this fleshy spaceship, for slouching on the settee, drinking beer and angrily throwing your slippers at the goggle-box every time the latest reality star doesn't meet with your approval.

What a waste!

Millions of your ancestors have banked their experiential learning in you, all you have to do is bypass the social conditioning and you can access it.

Your body is your first servant.

But, of course, if you haven't yet taken control of it – the physical infrastructure, the mind, the ego, the senses – someone or something else will, and they will use this breathing miracle to run roughshod over you; like the biblical cities of Sodom and Gomorrah, they will consume you in the fire and brimstone of subsequent vice.

You can see the evidence of this without having to leave your own home.

I don't see the human body as a collection of skin and bone, and muscle and sinew and organs. I see it as a universe in its own right; occupied by community, trillions of conscious cells all looking to serve and be led in a purposeful direction.

But, led by whom?

That is the question.

Our cells are led and instructed by perception.

The problem with perception, as I mentioned already, is that it is heavily conditioned and largely subjective, and as a consequence very often harmful, to others and to ourselves.

The aligned adepts bypass subjective perceptions. They are led consciously by the divine CEO, which is directly sourced by the motherboard itself, the original perception, or God.

The CEO takes instruction from only one place: the Source, the divine economy.

The hierarchical chain of command (known as the five bodies) looks like this:

*The divine body (the CEO or soul).*
*The egoic body.*
*The mind body.*
*The physical body.*
*The sensual or emotional body.*

All five bodies when aligned to each other communicate and pass uninterrupted instruction along the chain of command.

Each body or force in the hierarchy is subordinate to the force directly above it. This is the only way the divine command can properly function.

If there is a break in the command structure at any point, alignment is interrupted, the hierarchy breaks down and the communication is unsuccessful.

The **Original Instruction** is communicated from the divine economy (or consciousness) to the divine CEO, from the divine CEO to the sentinel ego, from the sentinel ego to the mind, and from the mind to the muscles and senses.

This is the communication of all the properties.

A successful command will send trillions of cells to work, and they make the ultimate sacrifice to carry out their part of the divine plan.

There are uncountable servants in your body alone, and either you command them or someone else does.

To enforce these commands in the volitional world takes a lot of energy. To accommodate this you are fuelled directly by the life force itself, the breath (prana, the vital force, animation). The supply of fuel is uninterrupted for the whole duration of your span on earth.

Breath feeds every cell in your body.

Breath is your servant.

Every time you spark a thought, lift a finger, move a leg, devise a plan, command and lead others or build an empire, trillions of cells sacrifice themselves in order to make this happen.

It is good to understand this.

It is unintelligent to deny the life-enabling potency of these gifts.

We appreciate them quickly enough when circumstance takes them from us. Anyone who has experienced even a few seconds without breath will be aware that life in this body cannot exist for very long without it.

The water you drink, the food you eat, are your devoted servants.

I've seen these food-elements in their divine form; water is not water, food is not food – water and food are communities of beings servicing you so that you can fuel this body in order to serve the divine.

After eating a meal, my dad would always insist that I uniformly align my knife and fork on the empty dinner plate.

*Respect the tools,* he would say.

It never made any sense to me back them, but this was a man who, when he was close to death, could not bear to see a dripping tap, it upset him if people flushed the toilet cistern unnecessarily. Perhaps in his dying he was better able to see the living universe, perhaps he was able to see what I have been gifted to see in my waking state: that everything is alive, everything is aware and we should respect it as such and not waste a single thing.

We are gifted with servants every minute of every day, and the harder and longer we labour, the more energy-servants we attract.

When I breathe in, the poet Rilke is literally in my breath, he is in my lungs, he is infused into every cell in my body.

The same with Shakespeare and Milton and Dante and Hafiz and Blake.

I have walked down the very street where William Blake lived in Soho, London. I have breathed his genius in and out of my mouth, my lungs have expanded and contracted with the molecules of the poet William Blake.

Shakespeare is swimming around my veins, as we speak.

He is serving me right now; he is in the air as I write.

Every poet and every playwright and every scientist and all of my ancestors that went before me, each and every one of them reside in me, they are conscious, willing me to follow the one instruction given to me in the book of Ecclesiastes, *Follow the commandments of the Lord thy God.*

In secular vernacular: *follow your divine intuition.*

## Teachers

And what of the teachers?

Where are all these teachers?

I hear endless complaints about the lack of gurus.

The people who complain do so out of unknowing.

The teachers are there, and they are there in abundance.

The teachers are there all right, but where are the students willing to take hard instruction?

The teachers are waiting for you *the student*.

They will come to you, your teachers.

Your Sufi will arrive, in blood, in bile, in water, in food, in breath and in person as soon as you create room for them.

They will form themselves these masters, the guru and the Rishi alike, into any teaching-device and learning-aid and directional schematic you favour.

When I hold the diaries of Etty Hillesum in my hand, as I did just two minutes ago, it is not merely the pages and print of a bound testament that I hold close to my heart, it is Etty herself, mysteriously manifesting in my world, somewhere out of time and space, presenting herself as my personal mentor, a teacher of the word.

Etty was a powerful being who tested and proved her truth in the darkest dungeons of the human history.

Etty is with me now in my home.

She is an honoured houseguest, my divine guide while I write this book.

I go to Etty every morning at 6am.

I speak to her, or should I say she speaks to me and she teaches me her best song. She is my teacher.

She reminds me very clearly that the book I am writing, the book you are holding in your hand, must be full of purpose; it must be brimming with truth.

This writing is important, otherwise why would I be delivered such a saint to guide me through the pages?

The hand that holds the pen writes the history.

The 12 divine cantos of the Srimad Bhagavatam are on the

shelf to my right.

They were delivered to me as teachers preserved and living in print, some years ago when I made space for them in my human-house, after a long painful atonement. The 35,000 words of instruction, the Vedas, were first put into writing by Srila Vyasadeva, said to be the literary incarnation of God, and now they have been assigned to me, these gurus, they have been sent to fill the vacuum left by the recently evicted pain-bodies. The teachers came into my home, they sat with me through every instruction and they are still with me now as I scribe these words.

Whilst reading the Tenth Canto of the Bhagavatam, which recounts the birth of Krishna, I was in the presence of the Godhead himself.

This beautiful being schooled me about the birth of consciousness. He taught me how the emergence of awareness threatens the prevailing rule of the ego-king. He instructed me through parable, and metaphor and historical retelling about how demons (divided-thoughts/adverse forces) are sent to corrupt and kill consciousness while it is in its infancy. He showed me how each of those vibrations could be neutralised, and how consciousness expands as a consequence of submitting to these shadows. He explained how eventually, after building my battle-strategies, I would grow strong enough to wrestle and defeat the Satan himself (the false ego).

And when I do, I'll reclaim my throne and full consciousness will return.

On the lower bookshelf to my right I have the Zohar: all 23 volumes.

Every teacher and every lesson from the tablets given to Moses all those thousands of years ago are waiting to serve me as oracle, as didactic word.

These teachers of divine lore arrived on my doorstep as a gift. They landed on my mat the very day I made room for them.

I could go on.

I have a house that is a living library.

Gandhi lives with me. Al-Ghazali sits nearby. Rumi is by my side always. Milarepa is a friend. The Buddha helps me to digest the problems of the world. The I-Ching is my go-to oracle of Confucian wisdom. Musashi is my master of the immediate inner way. St. Francis walked with me for six solid weeks – I was schooled by him personally. Jung taught me to let go of the limitations of psychology and take a leap into the metaphysical. The Holy Prophet assured me that Abba favoured those who strive. The Guru Granth Sahib bid me to stay connected to my warrior self. Swedenborg showed me that there are realities within realities, and that the blueprint to these other worlds is coded into the exegesis of the Torah. Christ-resurrected proves my potential and provides me with a living bridge to the Logos.

I always knew that these teachers were with me and in me and around me, and that schooling is always available. If the teacher is corporeal or if she is in spirit or in a book of words, what difference? They are there, they are real, and I am educated.

But the space needs to be made before a teacher can approach.

If the space is not made in you, it will be like trying to put new wine into old caskets.

## First we do and then we hear

This is one of the great secrets of esoteric practice.

New knowledge is impotent if it is not required; in fact it is unlikely to appear unless a need is created.

Necessity is the mother of all invention, as they say.

Create the need for knowledge, by outgrowing your old knowing, and you will receive it. New knowledge comes quickly when we make room; the space we prepare is filled with the perfect teachers for our needs.

The teachers and the books, the 5,000-year-old Vedic texts, the 100-year-old writings of Gurdjieff and Ouspensky are teachings that are part of the mysterious eschatology. They exist already, in me. It is all in me. It is all in you, waiting to be revealed, ready to be unveiled and brought into the light of conscious knowing.

They say that when a student is ready the teacher will appear. This is hackneyed but true.

What few people ask, however, is this: *how does the student get himself ready?*

He gets himself ready by doing the work.

Books are a waste of time and so are the teachers if we have not created the room to receive them.

In my early days, I rushed into a lot of esoteric teachings, I arrived before I was ready, I approached before I had made the room, everything they taught and everything I read made absolutely no sense to me. Some of the teaching sounded so ridiculous to me that I felt insulted. Later, when I *had* made room, when I'd readied myself, the very same teaching, read again, heard again, was profound.

*Stop trying to find great teachers. When you do the work the teachers will find you.*

When I did the work, when I exhausted the work, teachers appeared in all their many forms and gave me a tip here and a note there and a place to go next.

Great teachers are often closer than you think.

A gentleman came to me for advice. He was an old friend (I'll call him S), looking for guidance and a little balm. He was a fine metaphysical teacher, working on the world stage with some worthy adepts. He only ever came to me when he was really troubled. On this particular occasion the trouble in question was his brother, who was causing him a lot of emotional pain. The brother was angry; he was homophobic and profoundly hated S's sexual leanings. He also took every opportunity to ridicule his spiritual beliefs.

A prophet is not without honour, except in his own town, except in his own home.

S told me how, despite the abuse he'd received, he'd forgiven his brother, in fact he prayed for him every night.

This is what people think they should say about those who test them because, well... that's what you do when you're spiritual, right? That's what you say.

S had not forgiven his brother.

If you are still hurt and wounded and offended by your assailer, you automatically know that you have not forgiven them. Not yet.

You may be praying for them, but the words are not aligned; they are not reaching Grace, compassion is absent.

I know this because once you forgive proper, anger and hurt and dissonance – which S was still feeling in spades – disappear.

They can't exist in the light of forgiveness.

If you forgive, compassion, love is all that remains.

On this particular day, in this specific café in Coventry, I was not S's best teacher.

His brother was his best teacher.

Whether either of them knew this consciously or not, his brother was teaching S exactly where his spiritual armour was compromised.

He was also implicitly giving him a masterclass in forgiveness.

If you can forgive your own blood when they betray you, how much easier will it be to forgive a friend, or an acquaintance or a complete stranger who insults you on a message board, on the World Wide Web?

His brother was a spiritual enigma that, once solved, would open S up to a level of consciousness he'd never before experienced.

The feelings his brother was evoking in him were his entry-point.

*Identify the children,* Lao Tzu tells us, *trace the children back to their mother: find the mother, find the cure.*

*Your brother is your teacher,* I told S. *He is a divine gift. Send him a thank you note and a cheque for his services. You will not find a better teacher.*

At the very least use your perceived enemy as a whetstone to sharpen your forgiveness on. Use him to sharpen your consciousness.

On this particular occasion my friend was not quite ready to see his brother as his teacher, or even a whetstone. S was a spiritual adept. He was accomplished. He shared a platform with the elites of the metaphysical pantheon, people travelled the world to sit before him: how could his uncouth, unschooled, angry, homophobic brother in any way be his teacher? How could he learn from someone so base?

What I have learned and what I know is this: the Divine will deliver his schooling through any vessel, especially corrupted beings, those that get a rise out of us, those who draw out our defilements. And there can be no better way to highlight a personal blemish than to place yourself before someone you judge as being below you.

No one is below you.

There is no one who is incapable of teaching you.

Anyone that draws a vice from you is your teacher, he is showing you with precision exactly where you need to work.

Another man I mentored was a beautiful Sufi, highly versed in the Holy Quran and steeped in the teachings of the Prophet.

He too came to me with problems that would be better solved and cheaper bought if he'd looked to the woman sharing his bed, rather than reaching out to me via Skype. He was a sensitive but driven soul, who spoke several times during our sessions about *taking a sabbatical* back in India, the country of his birth, working there for a year, and tracing his roots. He spoke, too, of *seeking out a great teacher.* His last one, an esteemed Sufi mystic, was *good with scripture and quotes, but he did not offer me any modalities.* And his wife... all he wanted to do was get away from her, but in a subtle, dishonest way. Telling his wife that he was taking a sabbatical in India, *or following the work,* or *exploring family roots*, was easier than saying, *I need to get away from you.*

A spiritual sabbatical sounds much nicer than a trial separation.

I was able to point out three things that would help him if he could hear me.

Number 1: I was not his best teacher.

Number 2: he was not really looking for modalities.

Number 3: his wife was the best teacher he would ever get.

She drew shadows out of him that would make Gurdjieff jealous.

I asked him if he had faith in the Allah.

He insisted that he absolutely did.

I asked him if he believed that Allah worked through everyone.

He was sure this was true.

And, if Allah was to come and stay with you, I asked, as your houseguest, how many ways would you bend yourself to take his instruction and serve him? Would you run away from God and hide in a distant country?

He was adamant that *he would not.*

Would you accuse him of not offering you modalities?

He shook his head; by now I think he was getting a fix on where I was going.

I gently pointed out that he was several stone overweight. His guru was not giving him esoteric modalities because he had not yet even mastered the exoteric controls. He couldn't manage his own body and mind; his senses were kicking sand in his face every time he picked up a cake. When you master the mundane, I promised him, you will be noticed, and the magical will present itself at your door.

As for his wife, as far as I could see, she was the Prophet in his own bedroom and he should treat her as such. Certainly he should embrace the fear she evoked in him, root it out *head, body and tail,* and give it back to Nature.

If you want modalities, I suggested, take your clothes off and look in the mirror.

What the reflection reveals is your starting point.

How are we to resist the temptations of Al-Shaytan if we still can't say no to a second dessert?

His wife was the very best teacher.

She drew out everything he needed to work on.

He would automatically know when he'd mastered these three modalities, because he would no longer run away from his wife and call it a sabbatical.

When he can feel a direct and uninterrupted love for his wife, he will be impervious to anything she says or does, and then he really will have honoured the Holy Prophet in his own home.

Again, unfortunately, on the occasion my instruction (the modality) was an ask too far. My friend took his sabbatical and searched for the mystery in all the places he knew he would not find it.

This was the case with me too, as I was learning.

This is the case with most of us.

St. Francis walked 100 miles to Rome in bare feet in the hope of hearing a divine instruction at St. Peter's tomb that might be more palatable than the one given to him directly by the Christ in a crumbing church outside his home town, Assisi.

These days, I will take my teaching from anywhere and from anyone if it is qualified, because I know it all comes from the same Source.

I mentioned earlier that I was once taught about the dangers of excess by a garden wasp. Well, I also took some sage advice from an oak tree.

In folklore, the oak is said to be the doorway to other dimensions.

I entered one of those dimensions through an oak in Coventry. I asked it a question, and I heard a replay. I heard a voice that led me directly to a book that specifically and profoundly answered my question.

An ant on the same tree taught me about believing in invisible things.

*Just because the oak I walk on is too big for me to see,* he told me, *does not mean that the oak I walk on does not exist.*

Similarly, just because the ant on the oak lacks the optical capacity to see me standing by the tree, observing him, doesn't mean I am not there, or that I don't exist. It was suggested too, that, just because people can't immediately see mysterious anomalies, incorporeal beings or hidden dimensions does not mean they have no existence.

I watched a mallard as it paddled down a stream in the country park near my home.

He was fast approaching a post-storm waterfall, a veritable Niagara to this small creature. *How will you deal with the oncoming turmoil,* I asked him in my mind. As though hearing my inquiry, the mallard flew out of the water, just before the fall, and landed several feet past it where the stream was calm.

A heron in the same park taught me – amongst other things – about patience, about how to wait.

I saw him perched statue-like in the water, hunting for his dinner. I asked him, *what can you teach me?*

*Hang around,* he said, *and I will show you what I know.*

So I hung around and I took his class.

The heron was so static in the water, so very still that one or two people, also walking past, commented that the heron was not real, that he must be a fake plastic bird, or perhaps a statue inserted in the water by the park rangers as a decoration. I must admit, for the first ten minutes of watching him (he never moved even a feather) I wondered if they might be right.

*Hang around,* the heron said to me, *see for yourself.*

Whilst the other curious folk lost their patience and went back to their lives, I stayed. I leaned on the fence by the water, and I made myself as still and as silent as the heron. I watched. I observed whilst all the time resisting the temptation to wander away, impatiently. Eventually, after a very long time, I saw the heron move its head very slightly, it shifted its stance just enough so that its eyes alighted a little closer to the water.

So you are real, I thought.

He stayed motionless in this posture for the next 30 minutes without a single movement. Then, suddenly and without warning, **bang!** He stabbed his long sharp beak into the water and retracted it just as quickly; there was a wriggling fish in its mouth.

I stayed and watched for an hour and witnessed him catch five fish.

The only reason I was able to observe this master at work, whilst so many others were not, was because I made like a heron, I became a heron and I waited.

I was patience in action.

The heron was able catch so many fish because he too waited. He'd mastered the art of stillness.

His hunting tool was patience.

But that was not the masterclass the heron taught me, though in and of itself it was a worthy lesson.

What he taught me was more valuable than both of these virtues.

The heron was so still in the water, that the fish didn't see him, they didn't even know he was there, that is how he was able to catch them.

*You thought I was going to teach you about patience and stillness,* he said to me, *but all along I was teaching you how to be invisible whilst in plain sight.*

The heron taught me how to be invisible.

Instruction is all around us, if we are awake to learning.

If everything has consciousness, then I can communicate with everything through my mind, just as easily as I can talk to my mum over the telephone or my friend on Skype, or my wife over breakfast.

This means that everything can instruct me, the teachers are everywhere.

The teaching, of course, is not the main thing; it is doing something with what you are taught, and completing the instruction that matters. Once you complete the first instruction, you create a vacuum for the next instruction.

There is always a next instruction.

We are often guilty of searching for a new instruction before we have even carried out the first.

I have been witness to this truth many times with the people I instruct.

Those who excel and attract elevated and escalating instruction are always those that go to work immediately on the communication they have received. When they have completed this instruction, the universe is compelled to offer a next.

I had a wonderful student called Iain, a world renowned martial arts teacher. If I said to him on the Saturday, *you need to learn judo to improve your game,* by the Monday he would already be having his first lesson with the best judo teacher available to him.

I have never seen a man excel as quickly as Iain.

His growth was accelerated because he took the instruction, he did the work. He put in the labour, and he drew the finest tutors to him, gurus who wanted to give him everything they had.

This could only happen because he made room for advanced instruction.

Another man I mentored, who seemed on the surface equally keen, did not take the first instruction.

When he came back to me for a second I told him that I had nothing else to offer him.

How can there be a second instruction, when the first still

remains unfinished?

I have never dropped a student so quickly.

Where I felt compelled to offer more to the one who worked, I felt equally compelled to push away the one that did not.

In the Parable of the Talents (Matthew 25:14-30), we are informed that, *those who have are given more, those that have not, even what they do have will be taken away from them.*

You grow what you sow.

You lose what you do not use.

You don't need to find a teacher.

Do the work.

The teacher will find you.

Also, once you understand the conscious nature of all things, you will recognise teachers everywhere. Your enemy will be a divine teacher, more so than your best friend. The grimace on his face, the creases in his hands will offer you a direct portal to God. And when they are no longer our enemy, they will disappear from our lives, because they will have taught us everything they can.

When we forgive our enemies, when we evict the anger and the pain and the dissonance they feed on, they lose all power over us. Whilst we hold even a morsel of negative emotion towards them, they will remain our enemies, and thus our very best teachers.

A teacher is anyone who shows you where your defilements are.

A teacher is also anyone that points out your strengths.

Teachers don't have to wear an orange robe or don a dog collar to do that.

Sometimes the teacher will arrive in the form of discomforting internal jolt – disproportionate fear, or exaggerated trepidation, or perhaps the desperate need for spiritual balm.

The Hikam reminds us that: *removing sickness from the heart requires shock treatment, which is based on great fear of disaster as well as great yearning for guidance and salvation. Without these jolts and shake-ups, the heart may remain enveloped and dead.*

In esoteric practice this jolt is known as the divine shock.

# Chapter 12

# The Divine Shock

As well as introducing the divine shock at the end of the last chapter, I have hinted at it throughout the book, so hopefully the concept is already familiar.

The first time I felt a divine shock I didn't really know what it was, only that it was overwhelming in its intensity, as though I was being given a warning that I must not ignore, *could not* ignore. Later – after experiencing many more shocks – I learned more about them, not least that the intensity of my jolt was in direct proportion to the degree of my astray. To be more succinct: I had drifted (spiritually speaking) into dangerous territory, and the shock pulled me back into safe-alignment. It was as though my spiritual heart had fallen into an irregular rhythm, or it was not beating at all, and the divine defibrillator was used to reset or restart it.

## Spiritual Pride

There are many ways we can lose our religion, or become adrift from our spiritual ideal, some of which we will explore here, but the most deadly error of all is spiritual pride, or arrogance.

Spiritual pride is a dangerous vice.

It is dangerous because it opens the door to every other roaming lion.

It is wise to remember that even if you are spiritually awake, you will still be in a constant state of vulnerability. By this I don't meant that you will be constantly anxious, rather, you will be like a car driver who wears a seatbelt to protect against the possibility of a crash. It is very easy (and it happens a lot) to experience the supernatural nature of spiritual ascent, become seduced by it, and fall into arrogance and pride.

*The gifts* can make you feel special, aloof, or even elite. When you suddenly become aware that you understand more than the people around you, arrogance can quickly set in.

Arrogance is the birth of pride.

The fastest way to hell is on the hand-basket of pride.

This is especially so if you, your words or your presence, your books or any of your spiritual outputs, start to draw a crowd. When you inspire people, or they experience alignment or healing through you, it is easy to fall into the trap of believing that you – the small you – are working the Siddhas *from* you, rather than the Siddhas working *through* you.

If you fall into spiritual pride, it means you have broken your holy covenant. It signals that the lower ego has taken over the vessel, it has usurped the throne, and is taking credit for the work of the higher soul.

As you know, the moment this happens **the fish dies in the mouth**.

This means you have cut the umbilical cord of grace.

Worse than this, if arrogance and pride are present, it means you are unaware of the disconnect and this is what makes it dangerous, this is why you need a holy-jolt to realign you.

## Why dangerous?

I know I've made mention of *danger* in the spiritual process more than once, and hopefully I have qualified this already, specifically in the chapter on the divine covenant. I am not trying to be alarmist, I'm just relaying what I have personally experienced.

To reiterate, and in order to comprehensively qualify the spiritual shock, this is the reason why it is dangerous for the developing or even established adept to break religion, once connection has been established; the human vessel – especially once it has forged a bridge to divine essence – is the greatest prize for any malignant energy-form, human or otherwise, pervading the atmosphere. When you become the bank-of-God, you will attract robbers and thieves in all their guises, and they will make every effort to penetrate your security, in order to steal your wares. Spiritual pride knocks out your personal alarm system, and allows malefactors open access to your vaults. Not only will they enter *through* the open door of spiritual pride, they will also feed directly *from* the leaking energy of pride – arrogance is supper for the legions.

Pride comes before the fall, as they say, and the spiritual fall can land us on the unforgiving rocks of every vice.

As I have said in other places, the higher soul is susceptible once housed in the body. We are its guard. Its only protection is our sustained connection with the divine economy.

It is our absolute duty, therefore, to keep the soul sheltered, just as urgently as it is for a parent to protect their newborn child, or a monarchy to protect its King or Queen or Prince.

As you rise higher up the spiritual echelons, you become more vulnerable; you are a rich target, hence the necessity of a divine alarm system, the spiritual shock.

St. Paul was so spiritually aligned that he was highly susceptible to the weakness of arrogance and pride. It is very easy to start believing people when they flatter you on your ability to demonstrate spiritual arcana and miracles. It was said that Paul had two demons by his side at all times to assure he did not stray from the path. Spiritual essence at the level of the apostle is highly potent and allowing it to leak or spill or be stolen into enemy hands would lead to the greatest corruption.

Whatever standards great men set, the rest of the world will follow.

If great men fall, the masses fall with them.

The divine shock is there for our benefit.

The *shock* is also there for the benefit of those around us.

As your divine centre becomes more perfected, people will be drawn towards it; for succour, for healing, for instruction and sometimes just for curiosity.

There is another reason people find the energy of an adept so compelling; he is on the carpet of proximity, he looks into the face of God, he is close to the Source. People innately know that the one who looks into the face of the one who looks into the face of God, also looks into the face of God. When people present themselves in your proximity, in your care, it is not you they are looking for (even if they think it is), they are looking for the Divine through you.

Jalal ad-Din Rumi noted in one of his poems that many people were drawn to him because of his powerful spiritual presence (they still are now, 700 years after his death), and he wondered if they realised that it was not him that they were attracted to, it was God in him that they sought.

It is very common for adepts to forget this; it is *the divine* people are attracted to and not them.

It is even more common for gurus to encourage – or certainly to not discourage – this kind of worship.

This is a recipe for disaster.

This is how cults start.

The New Testament reminds us that those who lead, follow. The spiritual hierarchy is inverted: those at the top of the pyramid follow Christ (or consciousness) and, then, serve all those on the preceding steps.

If we are divinely elevated, it is only so that we may serve our Source, and through us our Source may serve everyone else.

This is as true in the microcosm of the body as it is in the macrocosm of the world.

Presidents and Prime Ministers are elected to lead and serve the rest of the populace.

The divine or sentinel ego is elected to lead and serve the rest of the body (body/mind/senses).

The hierarchy fractures if the leader of the free world or the leader of the body is usurped by a false ego.

This is why Gurdjieff, a great spiritual adept, violently repelled his students if they started to worship him as an individual, if they fell into the false belief that he – the messenger – was the message itself. He booted them away very quickly if their allegiance strayed from the Source towards him.

It is also common, if you fall even a little to the left or the right of centre, to consciously or unconsciously take advantage of the people placed in your care.

Once you are aligned to your divine CEO, and you become an agent of God's creativity, you must remind yourself constantly that what people see and feel and sense comes through you not from you. Any praise, any flattery, needs to be referred without err to its rightful owner, God.

The divine CEO is in residence. It is a figurehead. It is in direct contact with the Source. Like any worldly dignitary, it needs to be protected. The queen in Buckingham Palace, the prime minister in Downing Street, the president in his White House; they do not move without protection.

Our first line of protection is the body-armour of **self-awareness** that we have built up; **the divine sword** of discernment: the long-bow of ordainment placed in our hands by the Brahman (or creator); the quiver filled with an infinite supply of **truth-arrows** that we can use to disqualify the rhetoric of any defilement; the powerful **observer-eye** and our **sound-guards** that stand sentinel at the doorway of the heart; **silence** – our ability to connect to complete stillness, which kills all known germs dead.

If our personal lines of protection are breached we will receive a **divine shock**.

This jolt is our ordained back-up system. It is an alarm that goes off when all of our usual defences fail.

When I stood on nightclub doors, we developed a not dissimilar system of security: the awareness and discernment to know our enemy on sight and the power of voiced-sound to take command of our space and dissolve threat. The local judiciary was our overseeing presence. The law protected us from those who strayed too far outside the law. It also protected our customers from us if we forgot our purpose and hurt those we were elected to guard.

These worldly sentries were real, and they were immediate. Those who were alert to the hierarchical constabulary were better protected because of it. And of those who forgot: some paid with injury, others lost their liberty or their mind, and too many paid the ultimate price – their folly cost them their lives.

Inside the club, at all the usual hot-spots – the bar, the dance floor, the café – we had alarm buttons installed. If there was a heated argument or a fight broke out amongst the customers, a staff member would raise the alarm, a corresponding buzzer would sound in the foyer to alert the door staff, who would rush in, control the situation and bring the club back to order.

In the spiritual body it is very similar.

Our awareness patrols the body and mind at all times looking for signs of possible breach. If our religion slackens and we fail to catch the inner-affray early, our alarm rings in the form of a shock or jolt, and we are immediately made aware of the remiss.

It is hard to describe a spiritual shock, only to say that you will know it when you feel it because it will be unlike anything you have experienced before. Also, it will happen close enough in proximity to your remiss, that you will be able to directly connect to it.

For me, the jolt usually manifests in a very strong feeling of fear and dread, or a deep prolonged sense of anxiety. It is almost unbearable. It is so potent that it calls you immediately inwards, back to your source, to seek clarity and relief.

As an example: I was running a masterclass for martial arts teachers from all around the country. People would spend four hours with me, once a month, for six to twelve months. During this time I would guide their martial development and spiritual growth. One of my students, a skilled martial artist (I'll call him L), had taken to our very direct method of practice and, over a period of time, altered his whole life to make our way the centre of his teaching. This necessitated him leaving old and established associations. It meant losing friends who were too afraid to join him. It also created enemies from old friends, some of whom actively and aggressively opposed his decision. His change of direction also incurred financial worries; if he moved from his old association, where he was comfortably established, to ours, there was a real possibility that he would lose existing students.

L was a brave teacher. He made courageous decisions to find a better path. But the paradigm shift affected his health for a short time, particularly his back, which had recently become the cause of debilitating pain. On one of the sessions, L mentioned to me that his back was playing up. I flippantly passed his pain off as *just psychosomatic*. I said that it was little more than the psychological effect of all the changes he'd recently made. His back complaint (I insisted) was nothing more than a bodily resistance, a physical reaction to change.

I was right. What I was saying was true. But in my very clever knowing, I had forgotten a crucial detail: L was in pain. In my *forgetting*, I had ignored the human element. I had completely overlooked how utterly terrifying it can feel when we make radical changes in our measured and controlled and safe lives.

My omniscience was full of pride, it was bloated and without compassion.

*It's just psychosomatic,* I told him again, with all the hubris of a clumsy neophyte, *it's psychological: you can get rid of that with your mind.*

I can still feel the smug grin on my face now. I can see the look of dejection on L's face. If I'd delivered the same lines with knowing and with compassion and balance, his back pain may well have disappeared then and there, on the spot. Love would have drawn his fear out into the light and popped it like a boil.

As it was, my conceit only added dissonance to his pain and perhaps a sense of anger. I had basically told him, *it's all in your mind, pull yourself together.*

In the mind or not, psychosomatic pain is as real as any pain you will ever feel, perhaps even more so because mind-based pain does not respond well to physical medicines.

The next day, I was going away on holiday for two weeks on a Mediterranean cruise.

The day we boarded the ship, *my* back went.

There was no specific reason for it, I didn't fall, or bend awkwardly, or twist my spine in some freak athletic-moment; it just went.

You will not be surprised to hear that my *unbearable pain* located itself in exactly the same place that my student L's had.

My back was killing me. Even just standing sent paroxysms of pain-waves through my whole body. I tried to sit in it, I tried to stretch it out, I lay down and rested, I even tried to meditate it away. It would not shift.

A sage voice in my conscience reminded me of my words to L, *it's just psychosomatic. You can get rid of this with your mind.*

I knew by the fact that my pain was causeless, that it was disproportionate and that I could find no physical relief, that this was a **spiritual shock**, and it was alerting me to my fall, my pride.

I was shown L in my mind's eye. I felt his pain in my body.

I immediately saw the link.

If I could have jumped off that ship, there and then I'd have driven straight over to L's house, and offered a sincere and unreserved apology for my folly.

That (unfortunately) was not an option, so my humbling would have to wait.

Knowing the cause of my pain did not immediately remove it.

Let me be very clear about this; I could not remove it.

I took painkillers and I meditated but it did not leave me until I fully acknowledged my error and accepted my lot.

I spoke to my inner tutor: *I see where I went wrong,* I said, *please forgive me. I accept this pain; leave the pain with me so that I don't forget again. I accept it.*

The pain gradually grew over the next few days into something that I can only describe as *beautiful agony.* When it wracked my body, I felt an unbearable love permeating through me. The pain was divine.

Before the cruise ended, my back pain eventually dissipated, and stopped hurting. On the next class, I pulled L to one side. I profusely apologised for my thoughtless disregard. I sat with him and told him that I admired him, I lauded his decisions, they were rare and strong and brave. I promised him that his back would, in time, cease its complaint.

This is an example of a spiritual shock in all of its manifestation.

We should never forget how painful change can be for people.

Never – it is the greatest sin.

I have written before about this next example of spiritual shock. I have written it up in great detail in my book *Notes from a Factory Toilet,* so I won't relive the whole debacle again, word-for-painful-word in these pages, only in brief.

I had a long running covenant with sexual pornography.

Some might argue that my *unhealthy association* was the result of historical sexual abuse. As a boy I was groomed and assaulted by an adult teacher. So I concur. I am testament to the fact that damage to the young psyche can detrimentally affect and determine the behaviour of the damaged child, in his adult years.

Those who suffer sexual assault as children are often left with an unnatural proclivity toward extreme behaviours as an adult, specifically sexual behaviour.

In a form of twisted symbiosis, the psychological-schema – a sort of scar left on the child's psyche inflicted by the causal abuse – feeds, over time and space, on his behaviour when he acts out as an adult.

Abuse that is left untreated leaves a parasitical, semi-autonomous thought-form on the psyche that feeds off extreme behaviour.

In biblical parlance this would be called possession or semi-possession.

In my case, the extreme behaviours in question were self-harm, as child and adult, a ten-year period of displaced violence as an adult, and an addiction to sexual pornography.

When we are abused, it leaves us conflicted and divided.

If abuse is possession, then forgiveness is exorcism; forgiveness evicts the parasite of abuse from the mind.

But – and I speak only for myself here – you can only blame your current behaviour on past abuse for so long before it starts to get boring. You can only blame the past for a limited period before the past becomes the reasoning for every wrong you commit. At some point you have to take responsibility for the actions you take today, no matter how tempting it is to deny responsibility, and blame it on what happened to you yesterday, or last week or last year.

What happened to me when I was eleven was completely out of my control.

The actions I take today, as an adult, are not. They are completely within my dominion.

As a grown man, having studied the psychology of abuse, I knew that sexual pornography fed my original defilement. It kept it alive.

I also knew that porn opened the heart-door to a whole raft of new defilement, each a little worse than the last, until your body and mind become a cesspit that attracts the beast and fowl of those adverse forces.

I knew this and yet I still kept allowing myself to be drawn into sexual pornography. I'd had lots of warnings about this too, lots of small divine shocks in the guise of guilt and conscience and regret, but I was not heeding them, I was not reading the signs.

I was accessing porn less and less these days, but I was still allowing it to happen intermittently and occasionally, and that made it dangerous.

In spiritual practice, a leak anywhere is a leak everywhere.

Either we kill our addictions dead, or they will remain a threat.

Even a cinder of addiction can ignite into a raging inferno if we do not douse the very last spark.

Though I was actively working on it, I had not completely killed the covenant I held with pornography.

On the last occasion that I accessed sexual porn, I was brought to my knees with fear, with terror, with pain and stark regret and a deep need for personal salvation.

I have never felt so much naked fear.

To put the experience into context, I had just finished a six-week exorcism. A play (*Fragile*) I'd written had just been performed at the Belgrade Theatre, in my home city of Coventry. The drama was a comprehensive cleansing of the abuse I'd been submitted to as a child and the damage it had wreaked upon me in the following 30 years. The play was a deep-cleansing; I washed out every sordid detail of that personal debacle and the effort left me temporarily empty and defenceless.

I accessed the porn on my phone, two days after the play ended.

My soul was bare and exposed; it was as raw to the touch as a nerve ending. Any defilement acting upon it, even the smallest, would burn it like fire. Through this one unfortunate situation I was shown the absolute sensitivity of the soul when it is present in the body, and the disproportionate amount of torture we heap upon it and, by proxy, ourselves when we enter the den of vice.

The need to protect it against defilement was made

frighteningly clear.

I accessed porn on my phone in a moment of tired folly. Almost as soon as I did so, I caught myself, I disconnected from the site, and put my phone away, angry that I had fallen *again*.

The phone immediately beeped in my pocket. I had a message. My provider was alerting me to the fact that I was being charged for accessing the site.

I was probably on the site for five seconds before I disconnected. I didn't see anything, not even a single image. But I was still going to be charged, it would be on my next bill which meant...

My wife would read it. She would read it and she would know where I'd been.

A bomb exploded in me.

A literal bomb.

I have never felt fear like it.

It was like I'd opened the doors of hell itself, and every demon was entering me at the same time.

The terror was outrageously disproportionate to anything I'd ever felt before.

More context: my porn issue was not a secret. My wife knew all about it. I had written publicly about my struggle with sexual imagery. My wife understood the problem and its heritage and was helping me to overcome it.

And yet, still the terror reigned.

Over the next hour I was an absolute emotional wreck.

I was crying. I was distraught. Nothing in the world could ease me. I turned inwards and asked for divine mercy: it came in the form of a stark warning.

Firstly, I was shown the extent of my astray; it was laid out in front of me like a post-life review.

Secondly, I was made to witness the dire effect of my sin.

I was shown a visceral and brutal vision of the soul, and what we do to the soul when we expose it to the daggers of depravity.

The vision so startled me, it was so disturbing that it left me emotional and dissonant and afraid for weeks afterwards; in fact it has never left me.

In the horrific vision I saw a portrayal of myself raping a naked baby.

I watched in horror like an omniscient bystander as I raped the child, and then afterwards, tried to hide the evidence of my abuse.

I was beside myself with fear and horror and confusion. *What does this mean?* I asked in my mind. *I would never hurt a soul, not least an innocent child?*

My taste in porn – as damaging to myself as it was – had never strayed beyond the usual heterosexual orgy of adult men and women.

I was told in no uncertain terms that every time I willingly succumbed to a lust – for porn, for violence, for greed – I willingly and directly invited in the adverse forces, and they inflicted this level of torture on the divine-guest now resident in me.

The naked baby in the vision, I was told, represented my soul.

I was left in absolutely no doubt that the equation was as simple and as literal as the vision I as shown.

No rationalisation, no excuse, no Freudian defence mechanism could now hide me from my own actions.

I was also being shown that the higher-soul had fully integrated itself in me. It had committed to this body, and in committing, it was like a child under my protection. I had flippantly ignored previous warnings, and this was why the spiritual shock I received was so jarring.

The soul is in you.

It is your absolute duty is to protect it by any and every means.

At this level of communication, there is no tolerance for astray.

You can no longer succumb to even a second of temptation.

You do not protect a soul by willingly and blatantly placing it in a torture chamber whilst you masturbate over profane imagery.

I vowed that day never to expose myself to vice, ever again.

This was the worst divine shock I have ever experienced.

The ripples of it did not stop for a whole month.

It was so stark. I was left in no doubt that the prince inside me was divine and that every cell in my body must be called on to protect it, they must be conscripted and trained in the art of protection. Any defilement that rose up in me or approached from the outside must be dashed mercilessly against the rocks at the very onset of its approach.

I didn't see this shock as malicious in any way.

It was not inflicted by some external judge, dashing out a severe punishment; I saw it more as the natural alarm system that comes in-built with the delivery of the divine cargo.

When we feel its keen sting, we may be tempted to judge it as the savage lash of a holy arbitrator, but once we have settled with and become accustomed to our divine houseguest, we realise that the jolt is a gift, one of the many mysterious Siddhas that accompany expansion of consciousness. Like a rare and expensive car that comes with a state-of-the-art alarm system, or the advanced security that surrounds a piece of art or a palace. We just need to recognise its signature and learn to heed its warning.

Once the holy houseguest is in situ, we are also gifted sensual, visual, auditory and olfactory antennae that probe out into the atmosphere to alert us to the sense, the sight, the smell or the sound of threat. Again, in the early days, I didn't notice these signs as spiritual siddhas, but as time went on I learned to read them as clearly as a warning sign on a hazardous road.

Your sharply attuned *spider-senses* will feel the alert of danger in the small nuances of people's gait or in their tone or in the small micro-movements on their face. We will also start to smell danger; the putrid stink of defilement in others is unmistakable.

I did a small motivational event in Coventry for some martial arts students, one of whom presented very nice on the surface, but gave off the most unholy smell. When she asked for a selfie with me, I could smell her defilement, it was palpable. And when I looked at the photo she'd taken on her phone, I noticed fog on the image, it was all around her.

Noticing these signs, I immediately placed a stronger protective awareness around me, and after the event, I politely avoided contact with her.

This is in no way a judgment of the woman; it's an objective assessment of her inner-being, which alerts me to potential danger further down the line. Her smell and the fog were code, they rang out like a leper-bell, and once deciphered, they spoke to me just as clearly as a virus alert on a computer.

On other occasions I might notice the subtle impatience in a person's voice, or the self-pity in their vernacular or even the hardly discernible intonations of hidden aggression. If left unchecked, these defilements can bloat very quickly into full-on arrogance, even violence. Depending on the situation I either call people out on their incongruence, or I will effect a very still and quiet gait; this creates a vacuum that quickly checks or dissolves their imbalance.

All of these muted signals give you an instantaneous read-out of a person's state and intent. In clocking and checking them as soon as they rise, you announce to the potential offender that their shadow has been noticed. When it is noticed, it is brought into the light. And what we expose to light must itself become light.

There is another danger here too, a trap that I fell into many times before recognising it. Wily shadows (often adverse forces working through people) will often probe your atmosphere with loss-leaders, small tester-attacks to test your guard: an ambiguous comment, hardly concealed sarcasm, a veiled judgment or threat, or an uncomfortable line or phrase in a conversation, in an email or text that displays hints of dissent. It may be (it usually is) hidden in the mix of other completely reasonable, even highly complementary rhetoric, but your senses will alert you to it. It's important that you don't ignore these anomalies because you feel afraid. Often we don't act on the signs, for fear of causing offence or embarrassment, or perhaps for fear that in consciously noticing the incongruence we might exasperate a situation that we'd prefer to avoid. More often still, we ignore the initiating indiscretion, because we fear a full-on confrontation. If you let the small things go, the small things will get bigger; they will quickly be followed by greater indiscretions, each braver and each bolder and each bigger and more offensive than the last, until you feel the defilement trying to take you over.

In the middle of a telephone conversation some time ago, a producer I was working with fleetingly mentioned that the financiers of our film might, at some point, want to take my script and write over me, put their own spin on the narrative, as it were. I felt a shock race through my body; it said to me, *don't let this go.*

In the film world it is implicit that you never write over an auteur. It is very poor etiquette. She dropped the announcement subtly into a longer conversation about the film in general adding that *of course, that would only be as a last resort – none of us really want that to happen,* before speeding on to other matters.

I stopped the conversation immediately, and drew her attention back to the error.

If I'd not caught this and stopped it in its tracks, I would eventually have lost the script. No doubt. I stopped her and said, *"What you just said there. About the producers writing over me. Just so as you know, that won't be happening. No one will be writing over me. That is not in my contract. That is a deal breaker."*

She stopped talking.

*"A deal breaker?"*

"*Yes, a deal breaker,*" I repeated.

She moved on and it was never mentioned again.

This might seem peripheral to the point, but it is connected; if you let small things go for fear of (whatever it is you fear) those small things will take root, and before you know it, they will become big things, and you will be overrun.

Not actively and consciously stopping defilement at the doorway of the heart is as good as inviting it in.

None of these defilements have any power over you whatsoever, unless you invite them across the threshold. Whether we do that actively or passively makes little difference. Once they are in, they are in, then you will have a real battle to get them back out again, because they take root quicker than a garden weed.

Of course it also follows that if you invite one defilement in, you invite all defilements in.

Like will attract like.

Often the divine shock will alert you very unexpectedly, like a bolt of fear in the pit of your belly. An incongruent line in an otherwise completely reasonable email might be the harbinger of bad things to come. When you read it, you feel a jolt that says *take notice of this.*

I was working with a famous actress on a film. We had talked at length about collaboration and agreed on a script idea. We had also agreed on directors and producers. I had an investor who was prepared to invest £15k for me to write a first draft. Everything was agreed until... the actress sent me an ambiguous text the day I was due to start writing proper, the day I was meant to get paid: *can't wait to get started, excited to be working with you; oh, by the way, I might want to direct this film myself.*

I felt the divine shock. Everything inside me did not want to be alerted, I did not want to see the glaring incongruence in her text.

The whole deal, the money, the producer, the script, *everything* was based (and agreed) upon us working with a specific director. The director had happily joined the team. He was on board. He'd already started doing prep-work. Every shadow inside me was saying, *ignore her text, deal with the director issue later,* but I knew that if I didn't heed this early-alert, later my integrity, and with it my holy alignment, would be compromised, and for what, £15k and a film with a Hollywood A-lister. Certain industry people told me that I should just let the director go, he would understand, *everyone* would understand. It might be standard in film to break vows like plates at a Greek wedding – which tells you a lot about the film industry in general – but it was not standard for me. What use every film in Hollywood, and all the money that comes with it, if you have lost your soul?

I rang the actress. She didn't pick up. I sent a text: *we need to talk about the director issue.* She arranged to contact me the next morning, but never made the call. I spoke with the producer, and reminded him that the film had been promised to the director, and that I couldn't take the money, or start the writing until it was confirmed that he would be directing the movie, and not the actress.

There was no such confirmation.

The film disappeared, the money stayed in the pocket of our lovely investor, and my spiritual integrity was not only maintained, it was strengthened by the testing.

It can be very tempting to ignore a spiritual shock that tells you what you need to hear, but not necessarily what you want to hear, and it is imperative that you don't ignore it.

The shock might be so great that all you want to do is turn away from it, run away.

This is the enemy in full, rude assault; it always tempts you to do the wrong thing because doing the wrong thing is easier, more convenient, and – in the short term – more comfortable or profitable than doing the right thing.

Sometimes the opposite happens; when you are on the right

track, and you are heading in a divine direction, the adverse forces will try every trick in the book to divert you, to make you change course, and force you to turn back. They will fill you with trepidation and fear and depression and urge you to take immediate action to make a call, send an email and cancel, cancel, cancel.

Discerning between right and wrong message (between right and wrong action) is a practised skill. If it is not clear whether you are hearing the voice of the divine, or being tricked by the whispering of the adverse forces, do nothing. Resist all temptations to make hasty decisions. Do not send that email, or make that call. Take some time out. Sit very still. Access complete silence. Ask for higher guidance and it will come. The enemy cannot exist in complete silence. When you quiet the alarm, when you strip away the noise and tumult the right answer will reveal itself soon enough, because it will be all that is left.

Etty Hillesum reminds us that there are two forces unleashed on the world, one of loving kindness and the other hatred and fear. We must take the field against hatred by actively courting love.

Like Gandalf, facing down his Balrog, *Durin's Bane* (in *The Lord of the Rings*), we should bellow at these devils, rising from the fiery pits of hell to claim us, *you shall not pass.*

Once we learn to recognise the holy signature of the divine shock, like a child touching a hot stove, we will be more aware the next time.

The shock is only ever administered for your good, and only then if you have fallen out of alignment.

The severity of the shock is wholly determined by the extent of your astray: a nudged elbow or a tingle of adrenalin if your drift is slight; a full-on dump of terror, if you suffer a complete fall from grace.

If you don't fall out of alignment, you won't be shocked any more than an electrician will be shocked if he sticks tightly to his safety protocols.

The shocks are real.

They will be felt in you; they will be felt all around you. The divine power has use of every being and every element in the universe and will work through any medium, even inanimate objects, if you are in need of religion.

I will tell of one such incident where inanimate objects were employed to shock me when I had unconsciously fallen out of alignment.

I was going to a film screening in London. The film in question, *The Pyramid Texts*, is a discourse on fear and loss and regret (it is not a comedy). The story arc is driven by an old boxer (portrayed beautifully by James Cosmo), who speaks his lament into cine-camera set up on a tripod set up in a boxing ring. The subtext of the story, however, is about the human body as a living sarcophagus, through which the sins of our ancestors can be atoned and purged and their spirits released into the afterlife.

The film is important in its message.

The film is full of divinity so, of course, like any divine poultice, it will draw out the defilements of anyone close to it, mine included. I allowed myself to forget this and in forgetting I placed myself in danger. My awareness of the film's nature should have been forewarning enough, but I was tired, I was vulnerable, the process of bringing the movie together had stretched me, and I forgot to tighten my helmet straps.

To get to the cinema in the East End, I had to take the Tube.

As I was waiting for my train, a beautiful woman standing on the platform next to me caught my attention. I found myself scanning her physicality with my eyes. It was so subtle at first that I hardly noticed.

No harm, I told myself, looking at an attractive girl on a subway platform.

She's pretty. I rationalised, what's wrong with looking at a pretty girl?

I felt a strange tinge of conscience rise to my defence, a small warning: *you open the door to one vice; you open the door to all vices.*

The demon of error in this situation was not simply looking at a beautiful girl. I appreciate all forms of beauty, male, female, animate, inanimate, corporeal and incorporeal. This was not about admiration of beauty; what I very subtly sensed rising in me was the beginning of covetousness.

What was rising in me was not my self, hence the ring of conscience in my mind.

The Tube arrived, the girl climbed on before me. The carriage was packed with rush-hour-sardines. The girl struggled for a space. I got on behind her and when she was pushed back by the swell of commuters, I gently placed my hand on the small of her back to steady her. When she turned and smiled at me, an instant attraction lit up in my mind. I found my ego-eyes flirting with hers and **Bang!** The closed train door opened suddenly without warning and for no apparent reason, then slammed shut again banging hard against my shoulder as it did so.

The violent contact jarred me; I was shocked out of my flirtatious reverie and back into alignment.

I immediately saw the sign. I got the message, and realigned.

But not well enough it would seem.

At the cinema I fell again; post screening, another beautiful woman, an actress, caught my gaze.

You might be thinking that a little light flirtation is harmless fun, nothing really to be concerned about, but I have witnessed catastrophe entering through the portal of flirtation; I have seen worlds ended, and people maimed and killed when flirtation manifested a jealous boyfriend or an insecure wife, and a little eye contact became a bloody debacle where not everyone got to walk away.

It is not about the beginning of things. The beginning of things usually always presents as harmless. It is where those beginnings might end that is of concern.

In the divine covenant you are always aware that you can be lured out of alignment by what might seem at first like an innocent distraction, but it can lead you into deep waters very quickly if you do not *thrash your little ones against the rocks*.

If a flirtation leads into a confrontation which results in a fight, I could quite easily be yanked from my divine path and thrust into a prison cell or a hospital bed or worse. One error at this level of play can mean end-game.

The beautiful actress stood close to me at the bar. I am a loyal man. I love my wife. I do not cheat. I do not deceive. It would be a betrayal of everything I hold dear if I did, and yet... and yet, a voice in my head, one that would never have gained entry had I been better prepared, whispered, *she's beautiful, tell her she is beautiful. Tell her.*

It is an embarrassing tale to retell, knowing that my wife will read this confession when she types it out for me. It is embarrassing, not just because I felt an urge to tell someone they are beautiful, I am an artist, beauty is the world I see all around me, it is where I live, I am always telling someone – man, woman, child – that they are beautiful. What is embarrassing is that the voice compelling me to say it was not my voice, it was the voice of (what the Muslim Esoterics call) *a whisperer*, a defilement, the intent in the compliment did not come from an aligned place, it came from the wrong place.

I am embarrassed because I got caught out by such a rookie move.

I leaned forwards to tell the girl how beautiful she was: **CRASH!**

Several glasses exploded on the bar next to us for no reason at all.

There were spears of shattered glass everywhere.

The glasses were not touched. They had not fallen. They just spontaneously exploded.

I was thrust back into alignment in a jarring millisecond; I was *shocked* before anything even more sinister could happen.

I was inspired by this tangible display of spiritual shock.

I knew instantaneously where the sign had come from.

I knew I was heavily protected.

I was also chagrined. I should not be falling into such amateur traps.

Every shock I have received, over time – and there have been many – has helped me to recognise the unique modus operandi of the ethereal jolt, and has encouraged me to *get in line and stay in line*.

Knowing that we are being observed, and that our covenant is contained within its own protective, electrical field (that will shock those who venture out), should encourage us to be fastidious with our alignment. Once consistent religion is achieved, the *clear view* becomes our spiritual vantage point. Like the great Taoists of lore, we learn to read the flow of nature, and connect to its creative rhythm.

This protects us from experiencing the divine shock.

It is from this aligned stance that we learn to consciously work with the power of causation *in the positive*, and set up divine pipelines: natural and perpetual channels for charitable delivery.

## Chapter 13

# The Divine Pipeline

What excited me about the discovery of the divine economy – the reciprocal universe – and what awed me in equal measure was the fact that the universe is not arbitrary; there is no whim-or-whimsy about it. Every effect has its originating cause and every cause produces an equal and opposite effect. Also, every effect becomes a new cause in itself, which will create more effects and causes, ad infinitum.

This is exciting because, once we understand the basic mechanics of karma, we can use our knowing to great advantage: for nature, for ourselves and for everyone else. No more danger of naïvely planting the seed of nightshade, then looking on in dazed astonishment when it doesn't flower and fruit into a grapevine. And no more concern about whether or not the good seed planted will bring a harvest of loving kindness, it will. It must. It's law. I am certain of this.

Certainty about nature and its dependable laws enables us to stop blundering through life, chased by the consequences of our own forgotten actions, wondering why the world is so cruel to us, so random and unkind.

Instead, we become conscious beings, like the pioneering nurseryman Johnny Appleseed, who planted apple trees throughout the United States, knowing that the seeds would flower and fruit, and provide perpetual food banks to future Americans.

Of course, as I touched on earlier, we can't totally avoid the (seemingly) random occurrences caused by the karma of our ancestors, and the human race at large. But we can clear our own karmic account in the internal-cleanse, and we can assure that every present and every future action we take – knowing as we do that each action is a seed planted in the soil of causation – will be considered and responsible and kind.

The moment I fully understood divine reciprocity, I immediately dissolved any defiling energy I was harbouring so that these pain-bodies could not create harmful causes in me and in the world, against my will.

I actively started to take every opportunity, in my body, in my mind, in the world, to think good, to say good, to do good and to be good, knowing with earned certainty that the immediate return for my deed would be the bliss-reward I received for processing the love before I passed it on to others.

This is not an expectation. There is no gamble involved here. There is no bartering with Law; this is simply stating an objective fact.

That your divine pigeons will come home to roost is not in doubt. How they will return and when, and in what form, is the great mystery.

But, they will return, and they will return in equal measure (plus profit).

It is exciting to know that I can build my future and the future of all sentient beings, brick-by-brick, with the actions I take now, in this moment, today.

This understanding really encouraged me to self-clean and to keep cleaning so that no new defilements could enter, and no old defilements could stay and rise up in me to usurp sovereignty. It inspired me too, to *forgive my brother* and keep forgiving my brother, *seventy times seven times* (the number that symbolises boundlessness – Matthew 18:22) because to harbour hate or fear or dissonance is to house a hungry ghost.

It instructed me to expand my knowing exponentially and wash out my foggy eyes and sharpen my uncertain speech and cleanse my inner ear so that I could intuit instruction more accurately and, subsequently, scatter my conscious intentions in the fertile world.

I made this my raison d'être.

Eventually, luscious fruits were returning to me from places I was not even aware I'd sown seeds. There are opportunities every second or every minute of every hour of every day to partake in this wonderful reciprocity and fill your life with wonder. I sit here daily, knowing that the phone might ring, or that an email might land, or a letter might reach my postbox or someone might turn up on my doorstep, delivering the beautiful effect of a cause-seed I sowed and forgot long ago.

I have lost count of the number of gifts I have received, so many that sometimes it feels as though presents are falling out of the sky.

As well as taking the conscious, spontaneous opportunities to serve, I also set up divine pipelines so that, even while I am asleep, the karma of my actions can still be at work.

The **divine pipeline** is built on the premise that we can make an automatic process out of some of the work that is often restricting and unnecessarily manual.

The pipeline analogy is inspired by a famous parable about a small village and a well. The villagers in question had one water supply, situated a mile away from their homes. To meet their daily needs, every individual homeowner had to visit the well with their bucket twice a day, every day of their lives.

This took up a lot of time, and cost a lot of effort.

One of the younger villagers, tired of the daily yomp, made a radical proposal: he would lay a pipeline directly from the well to the village. Laying a mile of piping in the ground would mean a lot of hard work initially, and it might take some time before it was completed, but he would only have to build the pipeline once, and the water would be delivered automatically to every home in the village for the rest of their lives.

Hopefully the metaphor is clear enough: righteous pipelines, set up in accord with heaven and earth, take a great deal of work, but once they are established they will act as autonomous seed-spreaders, working for you, for your fellow man and for Nature long after you have left this mortal realm.

Remember this: the best (some would argue the only) real charity is anonymous.

No one should know what you do by way of service. Or if they do know, it should not be because you told them.

The quickest way kill charity is to announce it, or brag about it.

Philanthropic-pipelines should be (as) anonymous (as possible) to avoid the ego being corrupted by the temptation of taking credit for the work of the higher soul.

## The Human Pipeline

The first pipeline you set up of course is the human pipeline.

You are the connection between heaven to earth, from the infinite well of effulgence, to the mortal realm of man. This whole book has been about taking the time out to lay a pipeline from this physical body, to the divine economy. If there is a list of important jobs to do on this worldly sojourn, this is the first, this is the most important. Without this groundwork, nothing else will be effective. Like the concrete foundation of a building, the human pipeline has to be laid, before we can build any infrastructure on it. Once we have the pipeline in situ, we become a direct link to the source, the inlet and the outlet of divine essence.

As I mentioned earlier, once we create a covenant with the holy economy, we will be instructed about where to go and what to produce in the world of men. This will always be about service in one form or another.

I'll offer just a small selection of the divine pipelines I have constructed over the years. I will detail some that I have seen others successfully construct. I will also include pipelines that I simply noticed as I went about my daily business.

## Pray for Others

When you recognise the power of karma, you understand that causation is the secret to perpetual motion. Once you release an aligned prayer into the atmosphere, it will generate a perpetual movement of charity that will not stop, unless it is acted on by a greater force.

Prayer that is aligned to love and heartfelt is the perfect pipeline.

As soon as the prayer leaves your heart, it will break out into the ether, and start to work. It will be received in all densities, human or otherwise. Like any action, the cause will create an effect that will itself become a cause, which will create its own effect ad infinitum.

It is important that your prayer is from the heart. You have to feel it. You need to connect to the person you are praying for – even and especially if that person has been unkind to you – and wish for them what you would wish for yourself. If everything is connected – science and religion concur that it is – your internal prayer will have no less effect than an external action.

Prayer is particularly effective when we direct it towards our (supposed) enemies. These are probably the most difficult people to serve. They have hurt us, which makes them uncomfortable to look at, let alone pray for. I have found that when we think kindly about difficult people, we help them, but we also help ourselves, because our charity strengthens the bridge between us and our source. If we allow any barrier to stand between us and even one person, the same barrier will stand between us and the divine.

It is equally powerful to pray for souls who are no longer in a physical body. Those who are dead to the manifest world are in the most need of our help, especially when it comes to spiritual atonement. Without a physical body to act as a divine washing machine, they can't cleanse their worldly mistakes. They lack the fleshy infrastructure to process the residue of sin. But we can help by bringing them into our consciousness, and petitioning the divine on their behalf, through prayer.

No need to announce your charity. Don't tell anyone else what you are doing. The prayer needs to stay between you and God. No one else need know. If you blab, you break the alignment, and you become just another fat ego, dining out on the approval and applause of others.

## The Book Pipeline

If I invest a portion of my time in writing a book, getting the book into print and releasing it into the world, instead of having to manually and personally travel the world to tell my story to people, one by one, I can speak to thousands, perhaps hundreds of thousands or millions, all at once. The published book will also be registered with the British Library, which means that if someone is searching for my teaching in a thousand years' time, they will be able to find me in the archives

## The Podcast

If I make a podcast, proffering my truth on the World Wide Web, my recorded-facsimile can be delivering water-from-the-well to millions whilst I am fast asleep in my bed and for a long time after I have left this body.

Every person who hears my podcast will hopefully be affected by it.

That effect will become its own cause.

If people are inspired to change a habit, or kill an addiction, or perhaps tell a friend about the podcast (book etc.), the effect of my words becomes the catalyst for action. That action constitutes a brand new cause that will itself create its own perpetual ripple of cause and effect.

A book is the same. The written word will cause an effect, the effect becomes a cause, and the cause ripples out in a million unfathomable and incalculable ways.

A depressed, suicidal man might read a line from my motivational book *Warrior* today, tomorrow, or 50 years after I'm dead. Perhaps the line offers the depressive hope, and hope turns into positive action, an inspired volition. The man decides that he really wants to live, he finds purpose through the words in a book (or podcast) and he sees a reason to appreciate the beauty and the splendour and the evolutionary potential of this mysterious life. His new-found aspiration is attractive, people are drawn to him because of it, and women are attracted to this *leader*: he falls in love and they have children.

The one single cause – the book, the podcast, the kind act – has literally saved a life and subsequently created new lives that will go on to cause their own effects. All of this will hopefully aid the elevation of the individual, and ultimately the evolution of the species.

I have lost count of the number of letters I have personally received that have said exactly this, or something equally affecting.

An aligned book is a pipeline.

A righteous podcast is too, or an article in a magazine or newspaper.

It is worth every effort to place your word into the world, and affect those that are looking for a divine intercession. It is worthy of every effort.

I wonder if Rilke had any notion that the letters he wrote and the poems he scribed would carry Etty Hillesum through the darkest hour in modern world history, a conflict that didn't even begin until some 20 years after his death.

I wonder, too, if the Sufi mystic Rumi could possibly have known that his words would carry my own soul through a long dark night, some 700 years after his exit from the world.

And St. Francis: did he understand, I wonder, that his courage and conviction in the face of debilitating fear would become healing and instruction for millions of people – myself included

– nearly a millennium after his passing.

It is worth all your effort to work very hard now to leave your testament for posterity. I can assure you that your completed truth will enter the noosphere (the Akashic library) and act as a reference for all of humankind.

Once a divine pipeline is constructed it will work for you, it will work for the world and it will serve Nature, long after you have gone.

Here are some other ideas for divine pipelines that might inspire an idea of your own; remember, even if your small act of kindness is simply planting a seed, it will still create a pipeline, because seeds flower, flowers fruit, fruits are consumed, and the species evolves as a direct result.

Make sure that the pipeline or seed-planting comes from a place of love. If there is any desire for credit or thanks or acknowledgement, it will land on stony ground.

## Start a charity.

If you have the wherewithal, start a charity. Make it as anonymous as possible.

My late friend David set up a pipeline in the guise of a charity that was so anonymous even his family didn't know about it until after he'd died.

## Plant a tree.

I found out recently that an old friend of mine liked to steal out in the middle of the night and plant trees all over the countryside where he lived. He planted thousands of trees over time. He did this anonymously, knowing that trees give oxygen, they feed people.

Even if you just plant a tree in your own garden, it is a start.

Make it your intention to feed people in any way you can.

An evolving species is a hungry species: they need to be fed.

### Drop a book.

If you have a book that has really inspired you, next time you go out, why not anonymously leave it on a bus, or in a café, or on a park bench, for a random stranger to pick up and read. And then sit in wonder, imagining the unfathomable effects your gift might have on the soul that picks it up, and where the book might go after that person has read it, and the next person etc.

You could even leave a note in the book: **a gift – please pass it on after you have read**.

I have a friend who has (I discovered by pure accident) left thousands of books in random places over the years. He said the excitement of how his gifts might have affected people he would probably never meet was worth all the effort and expense.

If you practise book-leaving, don't be seen. Be discreet. Anonymity is the golden rule with all charity.

### Glove a hand.

I had a friend who carried a dozen pairs of woollen gloves in his holdall (again, I found this out accidentally, not directly from him) all through the winter. When he was out and about, he'd offer a pair to any rough-sleeper he thought might appreciate them.

Don't hang around afterwards. Don't look for acknowledgement.

### Pay for a meal.

Perhaps you are in a restaurant or a café and you notice someone who you intuit could use a free meal. On the way out of the establishment, when you pay your bill, pay theirs too. Ask the waiter to tell you what they owe, and add it to your own bill. Ask them not to let the people know until you have left the restaurant, you don't want to be seen; you can't afford the risk of being thanked for your generosity, when it was supposed to be anonymous.

It might not seem like much, but it can have a tremendous forwarding effect. I remember reading about a man in a café who had hit hard times and was broke. A stranger, seeing that he was struggling to pay for his meal, paid it for him. He was so emotionally affected by this single act of spontaneous charity, that he later became a successful business philanthropist, and paid it forward to thousands of people.

What can you do?

Where is your inner-guide leading you?

How can you set up your own private pipeline, where can you plant a seed, one that will serve anonymously, something that the ego can't steal profit from?

What can you do or begin to do right now, this moment, that might act as a pipeline or seed for continuous service in the heavens and on earth?

Something to ponder on.

Something to begin.

A secret to keep.

Keeping secrets is an important part of the divine economy.

The power is leaked when the secret is shared.

## Chapter 14

# The Divine Secret

We are not a secret society but we do keep secrets.

We do not hold back our gifts.

But we do hold on to them until the right moment.

We *do not give what is holy to the dogs; nor cast our pearl before swine, lest they trample them under their feet, and turn and tear you in pieces* (Matthew 7:6).

A prophet would rather take all his gifts to the grave than share them where it has not been ordained.

We hide nothing in the shadows, but we do hide things in plain sight.

It is there, our secret, but it is so still and so quiet and so unannounced that it is invisible in a world that displays its wealth in hollow crowns.

Like the quiet heron in nature, we hunt by stealth. We stay secret by staying quiet.

As a veteran bouncer, with 10,000 hours of experience under my belt, I manned my station at a bar that paid me handsomely to protect their door. I was wearing my favourite, baggy green cardigan, my quiet bulk hidden beneath wool. The artifice of a balding pate and a soft voice and a kind nature deemed me all but invisible to anyone looking for a threat or searching out a victim.

My heart sat better in my breast than it did on my sleeve.

A stranger approached me with a keen eye, and an inquiring manner: *you don't look like a fighter,* he said, *and this is a bar that only hires fighters and pays them four times the hourly rate of a day worker. You must be a martial artist or a boxer or just a maniac. If they are hiring you here and paying you, and you don't look like a fighter, that tells me that you must be one hell of a fighter.*

I was only spotted like this once in nearly a decade of quiet subterfuge and that was by a young student who had observed the terrain, calculated the odds and come to a steady conclusion. Antoine de Saint-Exupéry reminds us that *what is essential is invisible to the eye. One sees clearly only with the heart.*

Why do we need to be secret about the invisible world?

We don't have to be secret.

But we don't share what we know until we are directed to do so by our CEO.

The need to share where we have not been guided, the urge to display our gifts for applause or approval is a sure sign that we are not ready yet, certainly we are not ripe. To offer arcana where it has not been directed or asked for, is akin to throwing seed on stony ground: it will not take. This means that our expenditure has been invested foolishly, it has been wasted. And I can tell you, from painful experience, that if you offer your holy things to those unable or unwilling to take them, they *will* be trampled under their feet, and the dogs of dissent will turn and tear you into pieces for trying to cross their threshold without explicit permission.

The heron does not bound loudly through the lake, heavy of foot, announcing its arrival; it does not preen and posture to display its impressive wingspan or pout to show off its powerful beak, or brag about its perfected hunting technique. Any announcement to impress would scare away the fish.

And let us be in no doubt, he is only there for the fish.

He has whittled the art of the hunt down to its rawest essentials, not an ounce of essence is wasted, all is preserved just for the fishing. He knows too that the energy preserved by avoiding unnecessary action will be needed after the hunt to take his large body into flight.

If you fail to preserve your energy because you feel the need to be noticed, you are still more *lower ego* than you are higher soul, which means there is still a lot of work to do.

No judgment or slight intended.

When I first came to my gifts, I felt the excitement and the uncontrollable urge to tell everything; I wanted to share my findings with everyone, even if it had not been requested, even when it was not aligned.

This is a dangerous and immature waste of energy.

If you follow the divine dictate, you will only give what each is able to receive.

One hour if one hour is ordained; a day if a day can be received, none at all if you are guided to close the outlet of your essence to a soul who is not ready.

You will know when to give and how much to give and who to give it to and in what quantity and manner. And once the giving is done, you learn to close the door and move on. You do not return to share even one drop more if it has not been sanctioned.

It is common in the honeymoon period of awakening to try to give everything to everyone.

You learn quickly, often to your own cost, the folly of this.

The energy you are given to deliver will naturally reciprocate if it is served at the right time to the right person and in the correct measure. You will give and he or she will receive in a divine intercourse. Both will leave the exchange sated and delivered. If, however, you throw your pearl before swine, the essence, like seeds thrown on to barren ground, will die in the air as it leaves your hand, or be snaffled by creatures as it lays on the unreceptive ground, and the receptacle (you) will be left empty, and the person you have tried to serve, defiled.

A strong word I know, but to attempt a divine exchange with an unwilling recipient is the greatest abuse to you, to him and to the Source for whom you are an agent.

This of course means withholding what you know and hiding what you have from those that are not on your delivery list.

You are a metaphorical and metaphysical postman. Each

letter or parcel of essence contained in your sack is private and personal. It is not meant to be shared with anyone but the specific person on the address label. The name for each recipient is written in code, so that only you can read it. What you have, where and to whom it is being delivered is no one's business but yours.

You are the postman.

Don't deliver your letters and parcels to the wrong people.

And don't take the credit for what you deliver.

You are not the giver of the gift, only the deliveryman.

What you deliver must remain between you and the recipient, and not shared with anyone else.

To talk about what we do and how we do it and its innate power and our ordainment into the covenant is to invest copious amounts of talent where it can bring no return. When we feel the urge to share what we know for the glory of applause or acclaim, we must recognise that we have fallen asleep and the ego has usurped the throne.

The need to tell secrets does not come from a divine place; it comes from a lower region, the circle of the ego.

Why do we have to keep our secrets?

It is not I that has to keep secrets, not the royal I.

It is the lower ego that we have to be wary of.

The lower ego is easily seduced, and will take credit for everything if the higher awareness does not keep it in check.

The moment the ego takes credit, Religio is broken, and the fish dies in the mouth.

In the early days of my own ascension, I shared where sharing was not called for. Sometimes I missed the memo completely and did not share at all. Or I shared a little where a lot was asked for, or gave a lot where only a little was needed and sometimes I shared everything where nothing was ordained.

In my defence I was still learning. I hadn't yet sharpened or even established my divine sword, so more often than not I was swinging blind in the dark with a blunt weapon.

I learned my lesson the hard way.

I was vampired once at a book signing and it left me so empty I thought I might expire.

I was ordained to do a talk at the bookshop and take questions afterwards for an hour; three and a half hours later I was still taking questions. I was still talking and sharing.

Unknowingly I was haemorrhaging energy to a legion of vampires cleverly disguised as customers.

They siphoned nearly every last drop of life force with the simplest trick in the book: flattery. I had an answer to every question they asked, and their glowing appreciation flattered me into sharing more. I held the floor; nothing was beyond my knowing. What I failed to discern was that these people were not looking for answers, they were hunting for an energy-feed, and I was their prey.

My wife had foreseen this happening.

She'd tried to warn me of the danger but I couldn't hear her.

On this day, I gave everything to anyone who asked, ordained or not, and I kept giving until I had nothing left. From this one encounter I learned painfully about the dangers of giving where giving is not earned or called for, and I never did it again.

And when I say that I never did it again, what I really mean is I *could* never do it again.

After the event, I felt like I was dying.

The energy that I'd spent, because it was not aligned, was not reciprocated and I was literally bled dry. I was as empty as a husk. I was so ill that, after leaving the bookshop, I had to lie on the carpet outside a restaurant toilet. Then later, I lay long and still on a bed in my hotel.

Something in me broke that day.

It took me months to recuperate and fully recover my energy.

Those who take our essence without reciprocation, who trick their way across our threshold, are known in esoteric circles as

**vampires.**

I have met many of them. I have walked with more than a few.

How do you know if they are vampires?

I walked with one man for two years. We met once a month. He came to me for instruction. One day he happened to say to someone close to me, *yeah I always go and see Geoff when I need a top-up.* It was then that I realised he had taken none of my instruction, he had not moved his position in two years, all he took from me was my energy.

I stopped walking with him.

If you are alert to the higher self, you will spot vampires from a hundred yards, because your intuition will mark them out as dangerous, and best avoided.

Vampires take but never give.

They ask for advice, but never follow it.

Their position never changes; from one year to the next they do not shift.

If you have an exchange with someone, and you feel depleted afterwards, it is usually because you have been vampired, or you are working from ego, and not Source.

If the energy exchange is aligned, you will come away with more energy than you entered with.

Vampires are necessary to your development as a metaphysical postman. They will show you where you are loose, where you have leaks, where your game needs to be tightened, and how to develop pragmatic defences against invading energies.

**Keep your secrets.**

Share your secrets only when it has been ordained.

Guard your essence: only give it where the intercourse has been divinely arranged. Then you will never be vampired, you will never run out of essence, you will always be protected.

We are not a secret society but we do keep secrets.

Not because we have anything to hide, but simply because we

know that sharing what has not been ordained is an abomination.

We do not release energy-beings, only to see them consumed by beast and fowl. Like the talents of the parable, our gifts must not be buried in the ground of ego, or cast before dogs of narcissism; rather they must be wisely invested in the receptacles that have made room.

Why am I sharing my secrets in this book (you might ask), shouldn't I be practising what I preach, shouldn't I keep my gifts hidden?

We are not sharing all our secrets, only some, and of those, only to you the reader, you who have already expended energy in order to get here; you who have made room for what we share.

We only share here what has been ordained to share here.

And, of course, there are secrets within secrets.

For those seeking entertainment or mystery, *that's* all you'll find in these pages, and for those looking for spiritual arcana, how many layers deep will you go?

For the ones who do *the work*, you won't have to look far for secrets, you will find God in every page and in every paragraph and in every comma and in every letter and in every word and in every space in-between; there is nowhere He is not. Every syllable contains the whole of God to those with eyes to see.

And whole volumes of words will read empty to those who are not yet awake.

# Chapter 15

# Divine Visitors

You will be visited.

Be in no doubt about that, you will be visited, you already are visited, you always have been.

Only now that you know it, you will start to consciously notice the visits.

Not always as they occur – although you may sense a *strangeness*, in a look, in a word, in a touch – often it is only after the fact, perhaps moments, even days later that you realise you have had a visitor.

I sense that this delay in recognition is deliberate. It's for our benefit. It allows the fragile human brain a little wriggle-room, a space to rationalise the experience if it is too much for the conditioned mind to process. It allows us (if we choose) to put our vision down to imagination or a coincidence or some other rationalisation in order to protect the self-system's organised model of reality.

I was on the radio once, talking to a very talented but sardonic host: *so you believe in angels then?*

He asked the question, as though I was an eight-year-old child, talking about the existence of Father Christmas.

The Murshid Samuel Lewis picked up on this dichotomy, especially around traditional religion: *if you say you believe in angels you are in, but if you say you have experienced angels you are out.*

Equally, with spirituality, people are happy to accept you if you say you believe in God, but they become very suspicious if you say you have actual experience of God.

*Yes of course,* I replied to the radio host, *I have had experience of angels.*

I looked him in the eye with the certainty of a man who knows enough to be comfortable with the divine mysteries. But his sardonic smirk told me that he was not convinced.

He reminded me of a snail on a busy country path, who ridicules his friend (a fellow snail) for believing in unseen things, realities that exist somewhere beyond their small snail-world and their narrow snail-path: *if there was anything else out there,* I hear him scoff, *I would know about it, I would see it.*

I imagine him spouting his cynical rhetoric, as the feet of myriad giants, beings too big for him to conceive, carefully negotiate their way around him, lest they crush him underfoot.

Even if, like the cynical snail, you think this notion absurd and highly unlikely, you will still be divinely visited.

Sometimes a solid message will be delivered by these visitors, other times you may just receive confirmation of a situation or a warning that you must not miss. Oftentimes, the visit will simply be the divine doffing its hat at you, just to acknowledge your progress.

I also sense a degree of fun in the visits, as though the spirit is teasing us with its mystery.

People like Rumi and Boehme, Swedenborg, Gurdjieff and Yogananda and many other adepts – too many to mention here – enjoyed direct and undeniable divine experience without the need for subterfuge or rationale. They had expanded their awareness enough so that the idea of something extra-dimensional appearing and disappearing before their eyes did not send them into a dissonance or a psychosis.

The experiences, the visits, at least in my own case, have steadily increased in their directness and intensity according to my ability to cope with them.

Eventually you come to recognise that all encounters, even with supposedly standard human beings, contain the greatest mystery, because you detect spirit in them all. If the observer-self or the soul is who you really are – and I have experienced my consciousness out of the body in the waking state, so I know it is – and it is simply wearing the human body as a complex spacesuit, then we are all (if not angelic) beings from another dimension, experiencing the manifest world as a school of learning, a dimension of perfection. We are all aliens, scoffing at, ridiculing or flat-out denying the existence of other aliens. It is exciting when you start to recognise spirit in others, because (as I said) you realise that you are having alien encounters every day. Beings are wandering in and out of your atmosphere all the time. Once you see this you start to treat every meeting as significant, and every encounter as an opportunity to receive a message, exchange energy, and interact with non-human beings. Whilst we are still afraid (or don't recognise the mystery) of worldly things, we are unlikely to be exposed to the so-called other-worldly.

There is no room in this higher economy for the comfort of certainty or intellectual understanding that the lower ego craves. Some of it is, and will remain (for now), beyond fathom, so seeking the balm of cognitive concordance or the crutch of peer review to confirm the mysteries will not help.

The higher soul (the observer self) is not perturbed by the supernatural, any more than you are confused by the everyday world around you. This is its realm, and the extrasensory experiences that many people might struggle with mentally are absolutely workaday to the soul. Therefore, if there is dissonance it means you have fallen out of Religio, the ego has been engaged, and is trying to bring understanding and control to something that is beyond its pay grade.

The mysteries are beyond our rational understanding. We can know them directly, but that doesn't mean we are able to articulate them to others. We have to become comfortable with this contradiction. In the divine economy, there is too much to know and to know this is to know enough.

The only certainty will be that you had the experience.

The need to understand this intellectually is what can drive people to dissonance. When you can accept that you may never fully fathom divine knowledge with the human mind, you will be more prepared to experience it.

Those that joke about mystery, those who ridicule and attack it are I suspect those who are most afraid of it. The use of ridicule, the need to attack what is not understood, is egoic by its very nature. It shows you the level someone is operating at if they feel the need to employ Freudian defence mechanisms, to cope with experiences beyond their fathom.

My rule of thumb is this: if in doubt, suspend judgment, and keep an open mind.

Although, just saying you have an open mind is not the same as actually having an open mind.

I listened to an esteemed scientist on *Desert Island Discs* recently; he was being interviewed by the delightful Kirsty Young. He was a very beautiful man, he was gentle and learned, and a leader in his field. He started the interview very strongly I thought. He talked earnestly about how imperative it was for scientists to keep an open mind. He said that in his field, the adept scoffed at the very notion of scientific certainty, in fact, he and every other scientist worth their salt vigorously eschewed it. Everything is an interim in science, a stepping-stone that offered secure footing to the next truth, and so on. He was on the ball this impressive man until the very end of the program, where as an accidental aside, he commented on *the ridiculous idea of a God*, and suggested that an all-knowing presence in the universe was comfort-candy for juvenile minds.

I am paraphrasing here, but his message was clear: science is the only messiah.

Kirsty Young interrupted him. She is the consummate professional. Her job on *Discs* is not to debate with people, only to help them to tell their story. But this, she couldn't resist...

*You sound very certain that there is not a God,* she suggested, *but, at the onset of our interview, you said you had a healthy disregard for certainty?*

For the first time in the interview this giant of science stumbled and erred and he mortally wounded his credibility as an open-mind by saying that *some things are just obvious though.*

And, like kindness itself, Kirsty let this big fish wriggle off the hook and the moment passed.

I made mention already about some of the mysteries I've experienced, moments of clarity, serendipity, synchronicity, communication through dreams, books and teachers appearing when I need them most, money manifesting when money has been a requirement.

Twice now I have manifested £10k out of thin air. The first time it happened was some years ago. Our business was rapidly expanding, it was an exciting time, but worry was high on the agenda because cash-flow was very tight. Sharon said flippantly, *"We only need £10k – that would be enough to balance us."* The very next day I had a random call from my publisher informing me that they had missed a series of Amazon payments for my book-sales.

*"How much do you owe me?"* I asked.

*"£10k,"* he said.

These are all visitations in their own right, they are all mysteries that you could quite easily put down to coincidence, but as they happen, when they happen, you are aware they are not. One day you are in need of £10k, the next day £10k appears, out of the blue. You can easily join the dots and say, *yes but it was owed you, that money was coming to you anyway,* but this would be disingenuous. This would be to miss the point.

One day the money is not there. The next day it is.

As I said already, in eschatology, everything is available, it is already in situ. We just have to reveal it. When a desire or need or message is manifested, it will come in the form that you can manage. If you need your gift to come with a lineage, a history, that is exactly how it will arrive. If you have a stable and controlled nervous system, and a tolerance for the mysteries, and are able to mentally cope with miracles, they will arrive naked, with no lineage, and no discernible cause.

I'll relay a small selection of my visitations as they happened and what I felt at the time.

## Out of Body

I'd been out of my body before; more than once, but usually by accident rather than design. On one occasion, I literally fell out of my body in the night. The essence that I now recognise as my true Self separated from the physical body that I know as the personality Geoff Thompson. I looked at my corporeal body lying on the bed, I touched my body and my hand went right through it. I looked at my wife lying asleep next to my body and I panicked. I called out for my guardian Michael; suddenly I was jerked awake and was back in my body again.

This has happened to me several times over the years, and on each occasion, the separation with my body frightened me. To rationalise what had happened, and ease my dissonant mind, I put it down to some kind of sleep paralysis and didn't think about it again.

Later, as I developed my inner life, as I steadied the energies and became less afraid of uncertain phenomena, I was *taken*, or released, out of my body, consciously while I was wide awake. It was at a time when I was still wrangling with my life purpose, I didn't know exactly what it was and I oscillated between different paths: did God want me to write, did he want me to teach, or did he require me to become a recluse and spend my time in study and contemplation?

This particular night, I woke with a start; I didn't feel right. I felt a movement of energy in my body that was uncomfortable and foreign, as though I was about to be ill. I lay on my back to rebalance myself; a jolt of adrenalin hit my stomach. I am used to adrenalin. I calmed it with diaphragmatic breathing. I was wide awake, the kind of alert-awake you experience when you think that someone might have broken into your home and you are all ears, listening for the evidence that it might be true. I lay on my back, staring at a 2am ceiling, stark silence was my golden companion. Whatever was happening to me I accepted; full acceptance. If I was going to die this night – this was one of the thoughts going around my mind – I accepted that too. I felt a light go on in my lower stomach. I saw it as a circle of light in my mind's eye, but felt it more than I saw. It was strange to *feel* a visual cue. This was followed by another three lights. They made a noise too, in my inner-being. It sounded like subtle locks opening all along the front of my body – lower stomach, solar plexus, chest and throat. It felt as though I was secured in the body by these locks (secured rather than imprisoned) as though my true Self was strapped electronically into a fast ride at the funfair, *secured* for my own safety rather than incarcerated against my will. The locks were there to hold me in, to stop me falling accidentally out of my body-vehicle.

The armour of my physical body was opened up.

I felt an ecstatic buzz as each lock opened.

I felt my consciousness, what I recognised as the authentic I, float upwards and out of my body. There was no fear at all, only a strange curiosity. I was not curious because of what was happening to me, only that it was happening in this particular manner, as though leaving the body was completely normal, a nightly ritual, but usually it was not consciously witnessed.

I was being shown in my awake, conscious state what happens unconsciously every night when I go to sleep. I was aware that I was being given experiential certainty, yaqeen, of life outside the body. There could be no doubt that I was separate from my physical body. There is no denying that I was still conscious when it happened.

After the separation, there was no more confusion; I didn't

feel as though I was dying. Once I had left my body that thought never entered my mind again. I just knew that I was being allowed out of my body, whilst awake, so that I could be witness to existence beyond the physical body. And also so that I could categorically identify my true Self, my essential being. This had already been identified in my everyday life; my esoteric practice had identified who I was through negation, but this absolutely confirmed it.

The I that left my body, the consciousness that floated into another density was the quiet I, the *still* Self, the observer that I connected to in my meditation, in my moments of clarity, and every time I worked from a place of certainty and love.

This was confirmation. It helped me to recognise my core so that I could immediately reconnect to it whenever egoic life took over and I lost alignment.

I was out of my body. I floated up. I could see Sharon below me on the bed, asleep. I left the world as I knew it. I floated up through clouds, and found myself in a crowded place, a gathering of sorts. It was an outside, in what I presumed was a town square; an audience was standing before a speaker, a bearded Indian man who was orating from an elevated platform. They were listening intently to him. He was speaking to them, but I was aware that the hearing was for me: *we are doing the work of the many,* he said with the absolute certainty of a master adept, *they will criticise you. Do the work anyway. They will attack you. Do the work anyway. They will hate you. Love them anyway.*

Once I'd heard the message, my clarion call, once his message was clear, I floated back into my body and fell asleep.

The next morning, I climbed out of bed, I walked to the bathroom, and the same message repeated itself in my mind, like a sub-vocal recording: *we are doing the work of the many. They will criticise you, do the work anyway...*

Where some people doubt or deny life beyond the body, I am in no doubt about what I experienced: an ethereal consciousness, and dimensions beyond the physical.

I have been out of my body whilst awake. I have my proof.

I also have my job; this book of course is a part of what I have been called to do.

## The Sound Bath Experiences

I was struggling with some trapped energy. It had come to a halt on its journey from unconsciousness to conscious awareness, and created a roadblock in my midriff. Often, in the process of individuation, certain stubborn pain-bodies, for whatever reason, become lodged in particular areas of the body. Over the years, I have experienced this phenomenon several times; stalled energy has jammed itself in just about every area of my body – groin, bladder, rectum, spine, neck, throat, mouth, tongue and head, to name but a few.

This mobile energy-form has an element of autonomy and intelligence. It moves around your body quite freely. It will read your physical and mental vulnerabilities, alight itself on your sensitive sweet spot, and either just sit there throbbing or tingling uncomfortably, or it will imitate the symptoms of (just about any) disease, in its bid to win your emotional engagement. It particularly selects a disease or injury that your conditioning has taught you to fear. On this particular occasion, the energy parked itself around my abdomen and I was unable to shift it on my own.

On personal recommendation, I decided to visit the friend of a friend (Helen Braithwaite) who was earning a powerful reputation as a shamanic sound healer. I told her about the block, and I asked if she could help me free it up. She agreed and conducted (what is known as) a **sound bath** for me.

I have already talked about the power of sound as a healing force in the body, using your voice-instrument to locate and dissolve defilements. The sound bath works on the same principle but employs an impressive array of exotic instruments (gongs, rattles etc.), as well as the human voice, to penetrate the block and free up its movement. The healing session and the sound-instruments used are wholly determined by the nature of your complaint. Helen will intuitively and intimately choose certain sound-vibrations to meet specific needs.

I've now had many sessions with Helen, and I have to tell you that she has delivered me some of the most profound spiritual (and physical) experiences I have ever had. I have seen strange and beautiful and exotic creatures appear vividly in my mind's eye. I have seen flirty, giggly fairies fluttering around my head. Incredibly powerful, fiercely protective guardian angels have appeared before me, and stood sentry during my sessions. Christ rose out of my body on one occasion; he lifted himself out of my torso, and looked at me beatifically. I have also witnessed previous lives during sound baths. On two occasions I watched my own death, in a past life, like an omniscient observer. Another time I found myself standing on a mountain path somewhere in India, and Ramana Maharshi walked past me, on the path below; he simply looked up at me as he walked past with his entourage and smiled lovingly and knowingly. He was animated by light, and substantially more real than any reality I have ever viewed with my physical eyes.

The most profound experience happened on the very first session, when I went to Helen about the block of energy in my stomach. I had never had a sound bath before, so I didn't really know what to expect. Helen is a consummate professional, she told me as much as she could about what I might expect, but she also told me that the bath was individually experiential; everyone that took her session experienced it in their own unique way.

I lay down on a consultation couch and put an eye mask on to block out the light. I closed my eyes and waited. Helen started to play the sound-instruments. At times (when she felt called) she even sang. I can remember a strong egoic resistance rising in me almost immediately, a scared voice saying, *this is a bit weird.*

It was trying to convince me that the very idea of a sound bath was silly and that *nothing is happening*, and *nothing will happen*. I was patently aware of the ego-nature; if the ego was making a lot of noise, it was because I was in divine proximity and it was causing it to squirm. I quieted the voice. I clicked into the observer-self, and immersed my conscious attention into the very heart of the sounds as they entered my body. Just when it felt as though I was not going to experience anything at all, I felt a physical movement in my lower spine. It was as real as if someone had placed their hand firmly on the small of my back, and moved it up my spine, only this was on the inside and not on the outside. It was not painful in any way, but it was substantial, and it moved up my body with its own autonomy. The energy had a healing signature. It was not malign in anyway. It was in me, but I knew that it was not of me. As the energy moved up my body I had to physically adjust my position on the couch, and arch my back to allow it a thoroughfare. I could feel that it was heading towards the energy that was stuck in my abdomen. As it reached the block, it sat behind it and slowly, gently pushed it up towards my chest. As the movement reached my breast area, several very large, translucent, almost formless beings appeared around and over me. Although they were largely featureless, their presence was as clear as it was certain. Mine was like a patient's point of view, looking up from an operating table, as doctors hover over and do their work. As soon as the energy reached my chest area, my sternum gaped open, and one of the beings reached deep inside me with both arms and very gently, very lovingly lifted a child out of my body.

He was a boy of about eleven or twelve years.

It didn't feel as though the boy was dead, but he was definitely unconscious. I innately knew that these beings would take the boy and care for him. They exuded so much compassion; I can't even begin to measure it.

The beings took the boy away in their arms, and disappeared

from my view.

It was only after the session, when I told Helen about my experience, that the full emotion hit me. As soon as I mentioned the boy that was taken from my body, I broke down in sobbing tears.

I was sexually abused when I was twelve years old, the same age as this boy. I intuited that the night I was assaulted – most of which is completely lost from my memory – something innocent in me either died, or was shocked into some sort of suspended state. These beings were recovering – or helping me to recover and repair – the psychological schema that was left as a result of the assault. I suspect that this trapped child, this energy-form inside me, was like a breached baby, unable to pass through the womb entrance in conventional birth; the spirit beings were conducting some kind of spiritual caesarean section.

## Seeing Mrs Tweedie

I am an avid reader.

My teachers visit me on the page. I open a book and they rise from the ink, these sages. I always consider every new book in my home to be a new teacher and I honour it as such.

Usually.

Sometimes, in my rush to learn, in my hurry to know, I forget this important precedent and I do not show the respect due to my visiting rishi.

Mrs Irina Tweedie was a Russian-British Sufi who lived in the manifest world between 1907 and 1999.

I spent several wonderful weeks under her literary tuition at my home in Coventry.

Mrs Tweedie was an old-fashioned, strict, no-nonsense teacher of the Naqsh Naqshbandiyya-Mujaddidya order. I had been intuited to read and study her work, *Daughter of Fire*, which documented the diaries of her spiritual training under the Sufi Master Radha Mohan Lal, in Kanpur, India.

Her teacher had requested that she keep a detailed diary of her training, predicting that one day it would become a published book, and it would benefit people from around the world.

Here I was, decades after her death, taking instruction from those very diaries.

Mrs Tweedie, like her own teacher, was known to be kind but direct, firm and, where necessary, disciplinary.

Her book is a tome: 822 solid pages detailing every aspect of her five-year training regime in India. Everything is in there, all the difficulties, the sordid confessions, the hopes, the fears, even the doubts and the self-pity and her continual perception that her master was being unkind to her.

I am embarrassed to say that, because of my impatience, I did not respect Mrs Tweedie in my home.

Something rose in me that was intimidated by the prospect of an 800-page read. Something hurried and disrespectful presented itself in me. I wanted to rush through the book. I desired its secrets but did not want to work for them; I was not prepared to make room by making-work. I didn't want to sit with my teacher and let her present the learning to me in her own time.

In short I was rushing the book.

I felt the alarm in my body as I rushed: the prickly impatience, the need to urinate frequently because I couldn't get through the book quickly enough, the urge to put the book down and sack it as a bad job, or somehow cheat, and skip through the pages to find *the good bits*.

This is no way to treat a teacher in your home.

The signs were there. I was not listening.

On this particular day, I was in town with Sharon. We were at a café queuing for a cup of tea. There was an old lady being served in front of us. I hardly noticed her, only that she was a little slow in ordering her beverage and I was in a hurry to get past her to enjoy my tea. When my impatience finally failed me, and in the gentlest way possible, I squeezed past her to get to the cutlery which was situated just behind her.

As I edged past her, something strange happened.

This old anonymous lady was suddenly standing directly in front of me with a stern look on her face. She looked familiar, as though I knew her but couldn't identify from where. She grabbed my arm, *you are rushing me*, she said. I felt the room disappear for a moment. I felt a disproportionate emotion wash over me.

*I'm so sorry,* I said, *please forgive me, I had no intention of rushing you.*

*You could have bloody hurt me,* she said. And on seeing the genuine dismay on my face, she kissed me on the lips, giggled and disappeared into the restaurant.

When she said, *you are rushing me,* I knew it was Mrs Tweedie. I knew that she had visited to warn me, *do not rush my teaching.*

As soon as I got home, I picked up her book. The image on the cover of Mrs Tweedie in her later years bore an uncanny resemblance to the lady in the café. I went on to the Internet to access more images. It was definitely her. I smiled, delighted, honoured that such an esteemed Sufi would take the time to see me in a Coventry café, even if it was to give me a telling off for rushing her.

Every time I picked her book up after that, I thanked her profusely before starting my read, I thanked her after I'd finished reading and I savoured every word on every page and I took on every teaching my Sufi had to offer. And, after I'd finished the book, I gave it to my eldest daughter to read, but I warned her, *do not be rushing Mrs Tweedie.*

## The Disappearing Man

Sometimes I have been visited for a specific purpose, a message, as was the case with Mrs Tweedie, other times I am aware, perhaps only afterwards, that the visit had no specific meaning other than to say *we are here, we are letting you know we are near.* I am also aware that the visitations were a deliberate and gradual exposure, desensitising and preparing me for the direct and unadulterated visitations I would receive later in my spiritual development.

I was sat in a café, writing, much as I am now; filling the papyrus with my current knowing. It's nice. It is a delightful pleasure to be able to take your work – your pen, your pad, your world – to a public place with a perfect coffee and let the world around you disappear into the page.

I'd been writing for a couple of hours and I needed to use the bathroom. In this particular café there were two toilets side by side at the back of the room, each with its own door. As I approached the toilet, two people entered the cubicles before me, one through the right door, and one through the left door next to it. I watched the men enter and close their respective doors and I thought no more of it, other than, *I'll have to wait until they have finished.*

The man in the right cubicle put the lock on as soon as he entered, you could hear it click into place and you could see the red engaged-sign register on the outside of the lock.

The man in the left-hand cubicle, however, did not engage his lock. There was no click of the mechanism, there was no red engaged-sign, the indicator stayed decisively white: **vacant.** I found this a little curious and after a moment or two, when he still hadn't engaged his lock, my curiosity grew. When it became clear that he was not going to lock his door, I decided to try and open it, to make sure that the man was all right, just to be sure that he hadn't collapsed or something. I very gently, carefully eased the door open.

The cubicle was empty.

There was only one door in and out. The cubicle was sealed, but there was no one there.

I had watched a man enter the cubicle but no one left; *we are just letting you know we are here.*

I smiled and quietly thanked them for my gift.

## The Amazonians

Visitations tend to happen when I'm inspired. Often they occur when I am scared, or when I am on the carpet of proximity. It is said that siddhas, miracles, divine visitations are rarely contrived at will; they mostly occur as *happy accidents*. There is a lovely old esoteric saying: *we don't know exactly when happy accidents will happen or how to make them happen, but we do know how to create the conditions that make us more accident prone.*

I met with a close friend from out of town. She was a spiritual adept of some note (I will call her B), a brilliant and beautiful woman, who had been divinely introduced to me some years before. On this particular day she had come to me for guidance. A personal problem had cornered her and she'd been instructed during meditation to visit me for help.

I arranged to meet her at a local café. The problem B came to me with is not important in the context of this book, only that I had spotted the problem *and* its solution some years before, and knew that at some point, in the future, when she was ready, she would come to me and I would pass on what I was shown.

That moment was now.

B's specific problem was personal and private. It would not be in the true spirit of this book to share it. But I will tell you the solution I offered her, because it is general, and won't betray any confidences.

This is what I told her: *whatever it is that pursues you, or confronts you or pins you to the ground is ordained.*

Everything is ordained.

It all comes from God.

No matter how dark it might appear, it all comes from the One Source and it can avail us; but only if we stop running from it. Only if we stand before it, and face it down. People have the false notion that there is evil in the world and we must fight it, not knowing that what we fight, we feed; not understanding that what we resist will persist; a march against war with angry banners feeds the very war they would see crushed.

If we are to march at all, let us march for peace, let us work to remove hate by smothering it with love.

I said to my wife Sharon one day, after coming in from the garden: *there are too many weeds in the garden.*

*Not too many weeds,* she noted sagely, *not enough flowers.*

B was being chased by the same fear that chases many people away from their dharma. The manifestation of her fear was making a shape that fitted perfectly into the wound that she was carrying. Her wound was a belief, the perception that there are dark forces in the world that God, Love, cannot protect us from.

This is a trick, a lie; the *roaming lion* often employs it to trap the uninformed.

Our fear, the daemon of scripture, is God's master burglar, arrived at our walls to test for fractures. B's fear was multiplied by the false belief that it was possible for something, anything, to exist outside of the divine jurisdiction. How much quicker would we meet every vicissitude if we understood that gratitude and love would dissolve even the darkest shade?

When the Christian monk, Francis, was assailed by demons, he vanished them by accepting their assault as a divine gift, and thanked God for the great honour He'd bestowed upon him.

B had expanded in consciousness since I last saw her, almost beyond recognition. Her circle of divine influence had swelled exponentially. I knew this the moment I walked into the café and saw her at the back of the room, bathed in light.

In Islamic theology, this spiritual glow is known as Nur (pronounced Noor, and considered to be one of the 99 names of Allah) and she was basted in it.

After saying hello, hugging and getting our drinks, we retired to one of the seats outside the café, and we talked. She asked me what I knew she'd come to ask, and I gave the answer that had preceded the question.

The meeting was divine, it was alive with spirit, we absolutely disappeared the room. This phenomenon occurs when you are completely present with someone, when you are so intent on serving that all agenda, all expectation disappears and the world of 10,000 things vanishes.

This level of spiritual intercourse is what I call **pure function**. It manifests when you discipline your heart and mind to be perfectly present with the recipient of your engagement. The room literally does fall away.

I was no longer there either; there was only consciousness.

This ability is one of the many happy accidents of siddha; one of the miracles that occur when you let go of the world.

We'd been speaking for over an hour, enveloped in our own divine bubble when we became aware suddenly that we had company. The world that had disappeared returned. We were outside the café and there, standing over us, were two beautiful Amazonian black women. They were tall and ethereal and glowing, much like my friend had glowed when I entered the café. They knew me, they addressed me by name, they marvelled like foreign visitors at *how great it is around here* (we were outside a café in a shopping precinct). The taller one of the two ladies introduced the other woman as her sister, who she was showing around. She too had a look of awed wonder at how amazing the place was, and again, reiterated that they were *just looking around*. And, as is always the way with visitation, they were familiar to me, so very familiar but I was never able to quite work out how I knew them or where I knew them from. I was filled with a strange adoration and fascination for them both. They hugged me, and then – even though they didn't know her – they hugged B. But not the usual polite hug you offer the friend of a friend; this was a connected embrace, the kind you give someone you love.

Then, as suddenly as they had arrived, they disappeared again. I don't even remember them leaving, or which way they walked, or if they walked at all; only that they were there and then they were not there. I have never seen this pair again since. It took me a week before it dawned on me that, once again, I had been visited. The meeting with my friend had been divinely ordained. The two of us together, locked in spiritual discourse, created the exact frequency needed to attract consciousness: this opened the door for these two beautiful beings to present themselves – if only for a short time.

## The Warning

Now and again the visitations are not otherworldly beings appearing to you in aligned moments. Sometimes, they present as positive *or* negative energies working through other people. Many times – more than I can recall – I have experienced a presence moving in someone very familiar to me.

One friend, a jovial, joke-a-minute, older man, completely morphed into someone different one day when I was sharing a moment with him. I happened to casually mention that I was experiencing the movement of Kundalini in my body and that I anticipated a full Kundalini anytime soon. I said it with such flippancy that he suddenly stopped speaking and, in a voice that I did not recognise as his, said, *you should be very careful with your desire to experience Kundalini, Geoffrey.*

It was little short of an outright bollocking.

And he called me Geoffrey. He had never called me Geoffrey before, and he never has since. The only people who ever called me Geoffrey were my brother Ray – who is unfortunately no longer with us – and my dad, who is also deceased. And they only called me by my full name if I was in trouble. My friend's warning was so stern and so unexpected that it jarred me into silence. He went on to tell me that my flippancy regarding any divine initiation – specifically Kundalini, which he'd experienced many years before – can be very dangerous if you desire it too much and then rush or hurry its onset. His voice changed, his face took on a wizened hue, and he looked and felt like a different person. And then, as suddenly as this new person had arrived, he disappeared again and my jovial friend was back, chuckling away as though nothing had been said, as though nothing had happened.

On another occasion a friend I'd been talking to about spiritual matters suddenly went quiet, as though something I'd said had insulted her ego and drew out defilement. It was the strangest phenomena. I watched as her face made the shape of something hard, something unkind. Then she said to me in a derogatory tone, *when I look at you, I do not see an evolved man, I see a man struggling, I see a man in pain. I do not see an adept.*

Stunned by this *stranger*, I sat back in my chair. I studied her face; I didn't even recognise the old friend in front of me. Then I understood it. This was a visitation but of an altogether darker kind.

I knew who I was, I was awake, even back then when this happened. And I knew what was going on with the person in front of me; she was not herself.

*You are threatened by my certainty,* I said with a delivered intent, *that's why you're attacking me.*

She became very quiet. I watched her face flush red, and the hardness fall away from her beautiful face like a veil, and I witnessed the girl I'd know for a long time return.

*I'm so sorry,* she said, with an awareness that was uncanny, *I'm so sorry, that was not me.*

I attended the birthday celebration of a friend. It was held at a working men's club in my home city of Coventry. I am teetotal, so – without any deliberate intention on my part – I must have stood out amongst the ale and the spirits of this old-school drinking establishment. Another very old friend, J, someone I admired but hadn't seen in a while, was also in attendance. After his third thirsty pint and some casual banter, he suddenly – and it was shockingly sudden – morphed into someone I did not recognise. My soft drink clearly stood in direct opposition to his hard liquor and his hard living, and he felt the need to let me know about it.

Again, I blame my own naivety. This was 15 years ago. I was still developing at the time; I'd not yet identified that spiritual attacks could be around every next corner. They could be perpetrated through any weak host, even friends and family, *especially* friends and family. It is often around those we love that we give our vigilance a night off and leave our heart open to attack.

J, as much as I loved him, and as much as his muscle-bulk said otherwise, was a weak man. He had long since lost sight of his own ethical borders, and his covenant with the carnal and the profane was widely known.

Several of us were drinking and laughing and sharing old stories about the good times when I noticed J had fallen into a sullen quietness. I should have learned from my days dealing with violent people in heady nightclubs that people often became monosyllabic before initiating an attack.

Out of nowhere and without rhyme or reason, he suddenly found his voice and spat out, *why the fuck you drinking orange juice?*

The man in front of me was no longer the same man I'd hugged just an hour earlier when I entered the bar.

There was a snarling stranger, working through my friend J, and he was looking for a little contact.

*You know I haven't drunk for twenty years,* I said, smiling, touching his arm to placate him, trying to anchor the fact that being teetotal was a life choice for me, and not a judgment call on him.

*You think you're fucking better than us. You think that you're going to live forever; you'll be dead in the ground long before any of us.*

By now he was gurning his words. I can't stipulate enough that this was not J's usual character; certainly he had never been like this with me before, not in all the 20 years I'd known him.

He punctuated his opening assault with, *this is a party, why the fuck aren't you drinking?*

As soon as I realised that this was a dark visitation, coming through a weak friend, I aligned myself. I squared up to him and brought a level of truth to my words that landed on this troll like the dawning light.

*I'll tell you why I don't drink, and I'll tell you why I look after myself,* I said, *it's because I am not a sheep like you.*

Whatever it was that had temporarily possessed J collapsed. It literally fell out of him. He instantly became my soft-faced old friend again. For the rest of the evening he was tripping over himself with apologetic rhetoric and a daisy-chain of superlatives announcing me as the man he had always admired most and wished he could have been like.

Just this one incident gave me fair warning that visitations can happen at any time and the dark kind should always be anticipated in these types of environment, because hard-talk can quickly spill into hard violence if you are not absolutely on your guard.

I have come to recognise, as I have mentioned, that I have divine cargo in the hold that is best kept secret – no grand announcements, and it should be honoured and protected at all times.

Why should this be such a surprise to me?

As a nightclub bouncer I was the target of attack every night: attacks of violence, attacks of seduction and temptation, people queued up to assail me. In that place at that time all I was guarding was the licence of the nightclub, the security of the building and the customers (who often needed protecting only from themselves).

Here, now, at this time in my development, I am protecting the living spirit that resides in me; the dove, the soul, the naked self, and he is defenceless without my guard. When I elect a royal guard, it is not other people or myself or even the divine spark

I am serving, it is God. I am defending an apostle of the Source who calls on me to assist Him in the outcrops of his earth. In the arc of my life, He is the narrative. In relationships, He is my only love. In business, He is the only customer I need to serve.

In protecting my cargo, the light that shines through me, I am serving God directly.

Of course, negative elements hiding in the dark are going to attack anyone who enters their atmosphere with a lighted match or a torch, of course they are. To anticipate this as a given is to afford yourself the first and best protection of awareness.

When you stand on club doors, you know that you will be the target of attack. That's why so few people do the job. That's why the pay and the perks of that seductive employ were so rich.

## Invite to the palace

I have also been invited into rarefied atmospheres. Places that are full of light.

In these enlightened rooms, the angelic visitations were very real but unannounced. They were definite, but they were discreet; they were present but indirect. I was also patently aware during these experiences that my invite was divine and I was being covertly observed. The sense of it was so palpable that it couldn't be denied.

One such occasion was when I was invited to visit Buckingham Palace.

The honour was not directly mine. I was invited as the guest of a friend, Jason, who was being honoured by Prince Philip for his work with The City & Guilds. The Prince was their benefactor and patron, and Jason asked me along as his guest.

I say that the honour was not mine, but of course, the honour was all mine. If you are invited into the room, you are invited into the room. No matter how or why the RSVP finds its way into your mailbox, the fact remains that it does. I was patently aware of this. I was also aware that whilst I had not been personally invited by the palace itself, I *was* being sent a divine invite through the ether.

I am conscious of the fact that I have already written about this story elsewhere, with a broader insight into what I saw and what I learned there, so I will limit my retelling to the parameters of this chapter on divine visitors.

You could say that this story falls into the realms of divine visit, rather that the divine visitor, but I'd like to tell you what I read there, what I was witness to, what I felt in the air; truths that could not have been more specific if they'd been announced by the town crier. I have not written specifically about this aspect of my visitation anywhere before because it has taken me this long to process it. Also it has required gestation for me to be able to articulate what occurred with the clarity it deserves.

I didn't want to go to the palace.

I suppose I should start with that.

I am not one for grand occasions and I find formality stifling. I am not keen on fuss and neither does ostentation call me. It doesn't offend me either, but a cup of tea in a quiet café with my wife or my kids is my idea of the palatial.

I am not a royalist. I am not anti-royalist. I don't see anyone as having more than me or less than me. No one is better or worse, and my view on social class is that it is a self-perpetuating lie; it is a small idea that I disqualified long ago as a perception of limitation that de facto sustains the very limitation it struggles to end.

If I have the earth below my feet and the sky above my head, what more could I want?

Human nature is a level playing field. We all have the same potential. Discrimination and hierarchy can only exist at the level of personality.

I am therefore the equal of every citizen.

And yet... I *was* nervous about the invite to the palace.

Why had this invite landed in my life, out of the blue?

And why now, why was it happening at this moment in time?

I realised in hindsight that the invite landed because I was doing the work.

I was eager to learn and grow. I was keen to be exposed to a wider perspective.

I liked the idea that the gates to Buckingham Palace are closed and locked and heavily guarded by an elite Guard.

The gates are closed!

You could not break through them, not with an army of trained men.

And yet, they open wide and without resistance when an invite is proffered. The guards, seeing the gold emboss on the invite, with your name emblazoned across it, allow you unopposed thoroughfare.

I was invited. I didn't want to go, but I did go. I went because I realised that the summons had a divine signature, and I wanted to see what that meant.

When I arrived at the palace with Jason and his wife, we were taken with the other invited guests through a grand entrance into the great halls, and I mixed for a short time with royalty.

To merely call them royal without qualification is to do them the greatest disservice. I was mixing with the beings who were royal, not because of lineage or position or entitlement, rather, in my eyes, they were royal because they had dedicated their entire lives, certainly in the case of Prince Philip and the Queen, to the selfless service of other people.

This was the first thing I was shown.

Prince Philip was 90 years old at the time of my invite. He had been serving The City & Guilds for 50 years, operating in 80 countries.

The next thing I was shown was that the idea of *us and them* was not valid, not in this place. It is a popular and inflammatory concept, bandied about by the hysterical, but in this room on this day I could see that it was a fallacy. It did not exist in this building.

The people I met there were dedicated. Their raison d'être was service; they'd surrendered their lives to help every soul who asked. And they encouraged everyone in the room to elevate themselves and become captains of industry, and to do so by serving selflessly in their own communities.

The awards given out by the Prince were all in honour of service. And this was no gentle incentive; I could feel the divine energy in the room positively compelling people to leave their conditioning behind and excel.

The next thing I was shown, gently but definitely and without any sense of judgment, was that I was not doing enough. I had done enough, no doubt, to bring me into the frequency of these dedicated servants, but I was doing less than I should, certainly less than I could.

I was serving people, but I was not serving God.

This is a very important distinction.

To serve people is a limiting concept. To serve God, however, who serves other people through you, transforms the finite into the infinite.

I was not doing enough and the service I was providing was only in areas where I felt comfortable. I was now being asked to do more, specifically in the areas I feared to go. I already knew where these were (I'd been quietly avoiding them for some time) and I was being given the experiential example of how this should be done, in the guise of Prince Philip and the Queen. That they had dedicated their lives to this service was laudable enough, but what made them worthy of every admiration was that they served under extreme duress. The fact that the royal family need an army of guards around them for protection at all times told me that what they were doing was of the utmost importance. It assured me too that, as my own service expanded, my visible and invisible protection would be increased in relation to the threat.

These were living, breathing examples of people *doing the work of the many*, as I'd been shown in my out-of-body vision. People criticise the royals, but they do the work anyway. People attack them, still they do the work. Some people hate the royal family, but they love them anyway, and they still do the work, even and especially for those who choose to assail them.

One of the biggest lessons I was given on my day in the kingdom was that these people were doing the most divine service in plain sight, and yet their service was still invisible; it was still anonymous. The critics are so busy looking at what they perceive them to be doing wrong, that they can no longer see what they are doing right.

Obviously, they are also criticised for their luxury and wealth; the palace, the jewels, and the money.

But (I asked myself), what is a palace?

On closer inspection, I could see that it is a large hub; it is the central headquarters of a family who use their base to serve 80 countries and millions of people.

What about all the money? The wealth.

Cash money is just one of the many means of exchange. It is an energy shape that our developing species use to ensure guarantee of return, because we have lost our confidence in natural, reciprocal exchange. In a territory that still deals in the symbols of exchange, money is a necessary tool of service.

And, if you are going to serve 80 countries, like any big business, you will need working capital, just as the religious institutions need money to build their churches and print their bibles.

And the precious jewels?

To the enlightened eye, a grain of sand is equal to any gold crown or diamond tiara. The whole world becomes a jewel to the adept. It is only perception that values one element over another. When people expand into the awareness of this truth and enter the city where yellow-metal and sparkly-stones are no longer recognised as the coin of exchange, there will be bags of gold and chests of jewels abandoned at the gates.

Above all, what I noticed here was that – as I walked around and as I spoke and conversed and shook hands with the other souls in attendance – I was being watched. I was noticed.

A sense of recruitment – as in **I** was being recruited – was implicit too. It was in the air. It was as though I'd been formally invited into a new room, and by attending I was being given a chance to *try-before-you-buy* (so to speak).

Do you want to join us at this new level?

In my sub-vocalisation, I recognised this calling and said *yes*.

I accepted the invite.

I wanted to be recruited into higher service. I was intimidated but excited. A whole new realm was about to unfold before me. Not a realm that I specifically understood at the time and not one that I was able to immediately share with anyone.

How can you share what you cannot yet articulate?

And, of course, some things are secret.

They are secret and they need to remain secret, not because we are a secret society, rather because society hasnot yet developed the metaphorical legs to carry the weight of secrets.

# Conclusion

I was embraced once on a busy Tube. I was embraced from the back, by a stranger.

A laugh just rose in my stomach as I wrote this: *a stranger?* The implication is that I should not be so coy.

*It was no stranger,* my heart tells me lightly, *and you know it.*

It was not a stranger that embraced me.

To mix metaphors, I was standing with the other sardines, packed like a smarty in a full-tube, thinking how blessed I was; not just because I was living in London particularly, but blessed to be living in general. Most days I would sit on the Tube in a state of mild ecstasy, looking at the myriad faces and bodies around me. In turn I would tell each of them in my mind, I love you. I love you. I love you...

Her arms did not enfold me – I felt it was a feminine energy – but her body wrapped me so close and so warm I felt completely and utterly contained by it.

The feeling, this connection, was so divine that I knew it must be from the angelic realm. The love transmitted to me was simply an affirmation that they were close by, that they were near, always. I didn't turn around when I felt the embrace. I was not even tempted to consummate the embrace with any kind of confirmation of identity. Consummation, even with the eyes, would have reduced the embrace to some passing external phenomena. In all of my angel encounters, I have had the same feeling; no need for confirmation or consummation, any doubt, any need for identification or confirmation would break the contact and the divine would quickly fall into the banal.

Angels sometimes appear to me in an autonomous and unique shape that is pleasant, and other times they act through the body of an open stranger who seems as surprised by their momentary charity towards me as I am.

Either way, I'm grateful.

Oh, and I meant to say earlier, but forgot, when I mentioned the odour of a dark visitation, the putrid stench of decay and the cloud-cover and dark atmosphere; with the aligned visitor, there is always a subtle halo or glow of light around them (Noor), and often a smell too, but a pleasing, arresting and intoxicating aroma; incense is as close as I can get to it in worldly description, although any human articulation of it falls short.

The hug on the Tube was beyond any human touch I have ever felt in all my six decades. I felt it too in Edinburgh, when a beautiful, very slight girl, glowing as I remember her, hugged me so tightly after watching my play *Fragile* that I think if someone had not interrupted us, we might still be in that embrace now. She held me so tight that there was no discernible gap between her body and mine.

Regarding my play, she said, *"I didn't know we were allowed to be this honest."* She said it as though to underline and substantiate the urgent need for naked truth in works of art.

*"What's the point of writing if we can't be honest?"* I said. *"Who would it serve?"*

And another time, in Edinburgh, another divine film, *Romans*, a story (a fictionalised version of my own story) so rich with divine capital that I was afraid to sit with an audience, in its glare. Afterwards a young man and woman, two beautiful messengers, caught me before I was whisked away to an official function by the organisers. The young man made sure I knew the film's divine purpose, *my* divine purpose.

*"Your film will act as an intercession,"* he said.

*"This film,"* he continued, *"will meet people at a vulnerable juncture in their lives and it will take them in a healing direction."*

I felt like I wanted to talk with them all night, but before I could get any kind of clean lock on them, I was diverted away and left trying to piece together the fragments of our conversation.

**Intercession:** what a beautiful word, what a biblical notion.

**The act of intervening on behalf of another.**

**The action of saying a prayer on behalf of another.**

Intercession can come in many distinct forms: prayer; alongside adoration, confession, and thanksgiving.

Could there ever be a more noble reason to be in the world?

Could there ever be a better vehicle to lift you above the territory of the world?

The word intercession (borrowed from a long-forgotten biblical lexicon) inspired me to reflect afterwards that this brief liaison was another welcome visitation.

It underlined that intercession, above all else, was my dharma in this lifetime.

But who is it that is interceding?

Not me, not this failing personality Geoff Thompson that's for sure, although he plays his part, this beautiful, brave servant.

The divine CEO is the holy intercessor, the holy dove who must, as Paul tells us in his epistles, take *vessels* through whom He can intercede.

I thought back to the many intercessions I myself had experienced and the amount of teachers in all of their forms that had left a prayer for me, in a book, in a film, in a conversation, in a play or a work of art. Munoz, with his backlit sculptures, projected angels just for me at a time when I most needed to see angels.

What these two young people from beyond were gifting me, in that Edinburgh cinema, was my life's purpose in a single word: **intercession**.

Christ is the consciousness of the church, a church that, as St. Francis was rightly shown, was in great need of repair. God asked Francis to *repair my church*. Francis initially took the instruction to be literal. He thought he was being asked to rebuild the crumbling walls of a small chapel in Assisi where Christ had appeared to him in a vision. Later, Francis expanded his understanding and believed that God was asking him to repair the whole institution of the Catholic Church, which was also falling down. But, I have found that every man is his own church, and the divine CEO will not enter this fleshy tabernacle, he cannot use it as his divine vessel to leave the prayer of intercession for others if his church is not fit for holy habitation.

Our own body is the only church in need of repair.

The divine message is muscular.

I will ask everything of you.

It is not the whimsical, work-shy wish-fulfilment of new age spirituality.

*For wide is the gate and broad is the road that leads to destruction, and many enter through it,* Matthew warns us, in the New Testament.

The question of consciousness is the hard question. The way to consciousness is through the narrow gate. And the narrow gate is the road that leads to life and only a few will find it.

The question we are each left with is this: which of the two gates will we choose to enter?

I pray this book acts as a small intercession, and that it inspires you to enter through the narrow gate, and do the work of God.

When you do the work of God, you do the work of the many.

Geoff Thompson
Coventry, England, 2019

# Bibliography

Title: The Hikam
Author: Ibn 'Ata' Allah
Publisher: Zahra Trust UK
ISBN: 1-919897-07-0

Title: Man's Search For Meaning
Author: Viktor E. Frankl
Publisher: Beacon Press
ISBN: 0807 014 29x

Title: The Holy Bible: King James Version
Author: Collins Staff
Publisher: Collins
ISBN. 978 0007 259762

Title: The Bhagavad-Gita – As It Is
Author: AC Bhaktivedanta Swami Prabhupada
Publisher: Bhaktivedanta Book Trust
ISBN: 0-89213-250-7

Title: The Srimad Bhagavatam – As It Is
Author: AC Bhaktivedanta Swami Prabhupada
Publisher: Bhaktivedanta Book Trust
ISBN: 978-0892132645

Title: Mahabharata
Author: Krishna Dharma
Publisher: Torchlight Publishing US
ISBN: 978-18870891173

Title: An Interrupted Life: The Diaries and Letters of Etty

Hillesum
Authors: Etty Hillesum and Eva Hoffman
Publisher: Persephone Books Ltd
ISBN: 978-0953478057

Title: Daughter of Fire
Author: Irina Tweedie
Publisher: The Golden Sufi Centre
ISBN: 978-0963457455

Title: A Course in Miracles
Author: Helen Schucman
Publisher: A Course in Miracles Society
ISBN: 978-0976420057

Title: The Physicians of the Heart
Authors: Wali Ali Meyer, Bilal Hyde, Shabda Kahn, Faisal Muqaddam
Publisher: Sufi Ruhaniat International
ISBN: 978-1936940004

Title: The Old Man and the Sea
Author: Ernest Hemingway
Publisher: Arrow
ISBN: 978-0099908401

Title: Stress Buster
Author: Geoff Thompson
Publisher: Geoff Thompson Ltd
ISBN: 978-184024-5093

Title: Watch My Back
Author: Geoff Thompson
Publisher: Geoff Thompson Ltd

ISBN: 978-1-84024-716-9

Title: Warrior
Author: Geoff Thompson
Publisher: Geoff Thompson Ltd
ISBN: 978-0-9569215-1-2

Title: Fear the Friend of Exceptional People
Author: Geoff Thompson
Publisher: Geoff Thompson Ltd
ISBN: 978-0-95692-155-0

Title: Fragile (a stage play)
Author: Geoff Thompson
Publisher: Geoff Thompson Ltd
ISBN: 978-0-956921543

# SPIRITUALITY

O is a symbol of the world, of oneness and unity; this eye represents knowledge and insight. We publish titles on general spirituality and living a spiritual life. We aim to inform and help you on your own journey in this life.
If you have enjoyed this book, why not tell other readers by posting a review on your preferred book site?
Recent bestsellers from O-Books are:

### Heart of Tantric Sex
Diana Richardson
Revealing Eastern secrets of deep love and intimacy to Western couples.
Paperback: 978-1-90381-637-0 ebook: 978-1-84694-637-0

### Crystal Prescriptions
The A-Z guide to over 1,200 symptoms and their healing crystals
Judy Hall
The first in the popular series of eight books, this handy little guide is packed as tight as a pill-bottle with crystal remedies for ailments.
Paperback: 978-1-90504-740-6 ebook: 978-1-84694-629-5

## Take Me To Truth
Undoing the Ego
Nouk Sanchez, Tomas Vieira
The best-selling step-by-step book on shedding the Ego, using the
teachings of *A Course In Miracles*.
Paperback: 978-1-84694-050-7 ebook: 978-1-84694-654-7


## The 7 Myths about Love...Actually!
The Journey from your HEAD to the HEART of your SOUL
Mike George
Smashes all the myths about LOVE.
Paperback: 978-1-84694-288-4 ebook: 978-1-84694-682-0


## The Holy Spirit's Interpretation of the New Testament
A Course in Understanding and Acceptance
Regina Dawn Akers
Following on from the strength of *A Course In Miracles*, NTI
teaches us how to experience the love and oneness of God.
Paperback: 978-1-84694-085-9 ebook: 978-1-78099-083-5


## The Message of A Course In Miracles
A translation of the Text in plain language
Elizabeth A. Cronkhite
A translation of *A Course in Miracles* into plain, everyday
language for anyone seeking inner peace. The companion
volume, *Practicing A Course In Miracles*, offers practical lessons
and mentoring.
Paperback: 978-1-84694-319-5 ebook: 978-1-84694-642-4

## Thinker's Guide to God
Peter Vardy
An introduction to key issues in the philosophy of religion.
Paperback: 978-1-90381-622-6

## Your Simple Path
Find Happiness in every step
Ian Tucker
A guide to helping us reconnect with what is really important in
our lives.
Paperback: 978-1-78279-349-6 ebook: 978-1-78279-348-9

## 365 Days of Wisdom
Daily Messages To Inspire You Through The Year
Dadi Janki
Daily messages which cool the mind, warm the heart and guide
you along your journey.
Paperback: 978-1-84694-863-3 ebook: 978-1-84694-864-0

## Body of Wisdom
Women's Spiritual Power and How it Serves
Hilary Hart
Bringing together the dreams and experiences of women across
the world with today's most visionary spiritual teachers.
Paperback: 978-1-78099-696-7 ebook: 978-1-78099-695-0

## Dying to Be Free
From Enforced Secrecy to Near Death to True Transformation
Hannah Robinson
After an unexpected accident and near-death experience, Hannah
Robinson found herself radically transforming her life, while a
remarkable new insight altered her relationship with her father, a
practising Catholic priest.
Paperback: 978-1-78535-254-6 ebook: 978-1-78535-255-3